"I warmly recommend this well-documented book to all friends of Israel in Europe (and others!) for effectively combating the surge of anti-Semitism and anti-Israelism on their continent."

—MEP Bastiaan Belder, Committee for Foreign Affairs/vice-chair of Israel delegation, European Parliament

"Delegitimizing Israel is a critical objective for its most determined enemies. Gerstenfeld explains what the dangers are and what to do about them in this important book."

—John Bolton, former U.S. ambassador to the United Nations

"Manfred Gerstenfeld not only carefully documents the plethora of current expressions of hatred of Jews and Israel, its instigators and promoters; by connecting the bits and pieces, he confronts the reader with a chillingly accurate picture. It is a book not just to read but to act upon."

—Daniel Herman, minister of culture, Czech Republic

"This is a must-read book that unravels the complex process of the delegitimization and demonization of the Jews and Israel. It lucidly exposes the perpetrators and suggests how to combat them successfully. I recommend it to anyone who cares about effectively presenting Israel's case."

—Steve Linde, editor in chief, *The Jerusalem Post*

"I hold to this inescapable historical truth: it will never be time to forget Israel. There will never be a time when we can abandon the cause of justice for the Jewish people: the right to be. Peace in the Middle East, to which we all aspire, will only be possible when all, and I mean everyone, effectively recognize and respect the right to the existence of the state of Israel. Stop denying it and cease to assault it. This book is about this central question."

—José Ribeiro e Castro, former MEP, former chairman of the Foreign Affairs Committee and current vice-chairman of the European Affairs Committee of the Portuguese parliament

"As the shadow of Adolf Hitler falls across Europe once more, Manfred Gerstenfeld has written a scholarly, hard-hitting, and inspiring book about how to deal with this terrifying situation."
—Dr. Andrew Roberts, British historian and author

"This book offers a much-needed antidote to the many palliating voices on rising anti-Semitism in the world."
—Prof. Uri Rosenthal, former minister of foreign affairs, the Netherlands

"Many people, quite many, think that anti-Semitism merely existed in some countries in Europe during the 1930s and 1940s. That is one of the biggest lies in world history. Anti-Semitism often exists just around the corner where we find ourselves today. This book is a profound eye-opener."
—Alf Svensson, former minister of development, Sweden

"A compelling book; a vast canvas on misinformation and false propaganda; an effective antidote to the poison of anti-Semitism and double standards against Israel. It should be read carefully by policymakers in the Arab world as well as in Western countries, especially in Europe."
—Giulio Terzi di Sant'Agata, former minister of foreign affairs, Italy

Manfred Gerstenfeld

The War of a Million Cuts

The Struggle Against the Delegitimization of Israel and the Jews, and the Growth of New Anti-Semitism

JCPA | RVP PRESS

This book is dedicated
to the memory of Leon Poliakov,
pioneer of anti-Semitism studies.

Jerusalem Center for Public Affairs
Beit Milken
13 Tel Hai St.
Jerusalem, 92107
Israel

RVP Publishers Inc.
41 East 11th Street, 11th Floor
New York, NY 10003

Library of Congress Control Number: 2015939592

ISBN 978 1 61861 341 7

www.jcpa.org
www.rvppress.com

"Man is not clever enough for this life.
He never catches on to all the lies and cheats."
—Bertold Brecht, *The Threepenny Opera*

Table of Contents

Acknowledgments

I WOULD LIKE TO EXPRESS my gratitude to the Jerusalem Center for Public Affairs for initiating and publishing this book. I appreciate in particular the support received from Dore Gold and Chaya Herskovic, respectively president and director-general of the JCPA. Many thanks are also due to Ahuva Volk, who was responsible for the production of this book.

Jamie Berk has contributed greatly with her research to many of the topics discussed here, and so has Liane Nibley. Many thanks are due to Leah Horton for patiently typing the various editions; toward the end of the project Ruthy Waknine completed her work. Many thanks are also due to David Hornik for the copyediting.

Foreword

by José María Aznar
Former President of the Government of Spain

ISRAEL IS A LITTLE NATION with a great people. Unfortunately it has been under constant attack since its birth back in 1948. It was first assailed by armies of its Arab neighbors as in the 1940s, 1960s, and 1970s; struck later by hideous suicide bombers as in the 1990s and 2000s; inundated finally by a rain of rockets and terrorist drivers as today.

But make no mistake. What was and is at stake is not this or that policy of the government of Israel. Jerusalem itself seems instead to be the real problem; the very existence of Israel is what is under threat. There may not be military forces trying to invade the country, but other less visible and differently structured forces at play still seek the annihilation of the state of Israel. This delegitimization of Israel has many expressions but one goal: to make it impossible for Israel to exist as we know it, as the democratic and prosperous state of the Jewish people.

For years people of good faith genuinely believed that the narrative against Israel could be countered with better public relations. Despite all efforts in that front, the delegitimization campaigns have increased in number and extended in their reach. This book by Dr. Manfred Gerstenfeld shows clearly how much and how. The truth is that Israel today is still at war. Apparently a different war, for it is of an ideological nature, but it can indeed become as lethal as traditional wars. This book is a good analysis of the arguments and means used by those who want to suppress Israel through its delegitimization. As such it is an excellent contribution to better understanding the indirect attacks against Israel.

The problem for many in the West is that they fail to see that undermining Israel makes us more vulnerable as well. Israel is a mature democracy and the provider of many technical innovations. In today's struggle when the forces against modernity are presenting a real challenge to our system and way of life, from the Islamic State to a nuclear Iran, Israel happens to be a centerpiece of Western civilization. That is why it is under constant assault, and why we should do everything in our power to allow Israel to remain strong, free, and prosperous. This book is an excellent contribution to doing just that.

Introduction

THIS BOOK SHOULD HAVE BEEN written many years ago based on the wide knowledge already available at the time. For decades now, Israel has been the target of an all-out propaganda war by its multiple enemies. This major battle has greatly intensified in the twenty-first century. All experts have agreed by now that a new anti-Semitism has arisen, particularly in Europe, which expresses itself as anti-Israelism.

When did the current phase of incitement gain momentum? The 2001 UN World Conference against Racism in Durban, South Africa became both a turning point and a symbol of the massive incitement against Israel. It revealed internationally in a major way the global resurgence of classic anti-Semitism and its new mutation, anti-Israelism. A huge number of nongovernmental organizations (NGOs) met there in an adjacent forum that turned into an Israel-hate event.

The declaration of the NGO Forum said about the Palestinians and Israel:

> Recognizing further that the Palestinian people are one such people currently enduring a colonialist, discriminatory military occupation that violates their fundamental human right of self-determination including the illegal transfer of Israeli citizens into the occupied territories and establishment of a permanent illegal Israeli infrastructure; and other racist methods amounting to Israel's

> brand of apartheid and other racist crimes against humanity. Recognizing therefore that the Palestinian people have the clear right under international law to resist such occupation by any means provided under international law until they achieve their fundamental human right to self-determination and end the Israeli racist system including its own brand of apartheid.
>
> Recognizing further that a basic "root cause" of Israel's ongoing and systematic human rights violations, including its grave breaches of the fourth Geneva convention 1949 (i.e. war crimes), acts of genocide and practices of ethnic cleansing is a racist system, which is Israel's brand of apartheid. One aspect of this Israeli racist system has been a continued refusal to allow the Palestinian refugees to exercise their right as guaranteed by international law to return to their homes of origin. Related to the right of return, the Palestinian refugees also have a clear right under international law to receive restitution of their properties and full compensation. Furthermore, international law provides that those Palestinian refugees choosing not to return are entitled to receive full compensation for all their losses. Israel's refusal to grant Palestinian refugees their right of return and other gross human rights and humanitarian law violations has destabilized the entire region and has impacted on world peace and security.[1]

This extreme anti-Israeli statement also illustrated another contemporary phenomenon: the massive racism and anti-Semitism in what is often called the "antiracism camp." This hatred is supported by many political and "humanitarian" NGOs. The latter anti-Semites usually operate behind a seemingly benign mask.

Many others incite against Israel, often referring to dubious interpretations of a poorly consolidated discipline, international law. These are only some illustrations of the newest type of anti-Semitism, anti-Israelism.

I should not have felt compelled to write a book like this. It is the responsibility of Israel's government to defend its citizens from all types of attacks. That should be true for the propaganda war—also called "political war"—as well. However, despite the great intensity of this major battle against Israel in the current century, no comprehensive and systematic approach has yet been undertaken by the Israeli government to fight it.

A System of Total Misinformation

The many ongoing global and local attacks on Israel often combine into a system of total misinformation, as if controlled by an invisible hand. This complex propaganda war against Israel frequently targets the Jewish people as well. The battle has many different characteristics. It also contains numerous hate elements that appeared commonly in the past concerning Jews, such as calls for genocide. This is the case mainly but not exclusively in parts of the Muslim world.

Many new aspects of this war are made possible by developments such as globalization. In recent decades, technological improvements in advanced communications have also accelerated the spread of anti-Semitism worldwide in all its permutations, including anti-Israelism. The internet has added a new, rapid means of transmitting prejudice, hate, and incitement.[2]

This new avenue of attack, called "cyberhate," plays a major role in the global war against Israel and the Jews.[3] Nazism used mass media effectively to demonize the Jews. The internet plays a similar role but is much faster. Modern media, such as television and the internet, disseminate anti-Semitic writings and cartoons with great speed, adding to the globalization of Jew-hatred. This gives the phenomenon an intensity and immediacy it did not have when the Nazis began spreading their propaganda.

In its September 2006 report, the British All-Party Parliamentary Inquiry into Anti-Semitism recognized the impact of today's communication technologies: "Anti-Semitism can now [be] disseminated faster and further than ever before. Egyptian and Syrian state television broadcast anti-Jewish propaganda to millions of homes, including in the UK, and far right and radical Islamist organizations are using the internet as a key component in their campaigns of hatred."[4]

There are many others who incite against Israel. These include a number of Western institutions and politicians, many media, the United Nations and associated organizations, a variety of academics, some church leaders, manifold Muslim groupings and individuals in Western societies, many on the extreme left and the extreme right, numerous Social Democrats and Laborites, various trade unions as well as numerous high school teachers. A variety of racists in the antiracist camp such as certain political and pseudo-humanitarian NGOs have already been mentioned. These and many other factors together produce a new system of propaganda warfare.

The anti-Israeli propaganda war meshes with other types of combat against Israel, and these together create a global conflagration of a new kind. The most extreme players against Israel in the various types of propaganda combat are several Muslim and Arab states, organizations, and individuals, the Palestinians and their allies. This war is enduring, but not necessarily continuous in all of its components. It manifests itself in many fragmented ways.

Components of the War

The major component of the conflict between Israel and its enemies is military and violent in nature. It is manifested in wars, military incidents, suicide attacks and other terrorist assaults. Since Israel's withdrawal from Gaza in 2005, rocket attacks and other terrorist activities emanating from there are frequent and important elements of this warfare. The fight against it is conducted by Israel's army and intelligence services.

Another facet of this huge battle against Israel is the cyberwar. Israeli Prime Minister Benjamin Netanyahu said in 2012 that many daily attempts are made to infiltrate Israel's computerized systems, largely by Iranian cyberwarfare teams. To combat this, Israel established a National Cyber Directorate in 2011.[5] Netanyahu also stated, "We are building a digital Iron Dome," indicating that Israel intends to make its system against cyberattacks as effective as the one it employs against rocket strikes.[6]

The Total Propaganda War

The total propaganda war consists of direct attacks including lies, evil accusations, false arguments, calls for anti-Israeli action, and committing discriminatory acts against Israel. It also employs many other means to indirectly defame the Jews and Israel, or to distort their image. This includes the neglect or belittling of major criminal acts by their enemies. Gradually, after World War II,

Holocaust denial became an example of this phenomenon.

In recent years, the accompanying effects of the propaganda war include ignoring frequently extreme anti-Semitic expressions against Israel in many Western quarters. The European Union is a source of major examples. These include the West's disregard for explicit calls for genocide, even when they appear in official Muslim and Arab media such as state-owned television channels or newspapers.

Another aspect of the propaganda war comprises false arguments such as double standards, false moral equivalence, sentimental appeals, scapegoating, and other fallacies. These are frequently used by European and other democratic governments, media, as well as racist human rights organizations.

The Main Inciters

The main sources of hatred of Israel and the Jews can be found in Arab and several Muslim countries. Comparisons between Israelis and Nazis are commonplace in the Arab world. This "Holocaust inversion" is also frequently found in Arab cartoons.[7] In Arab societies it often coexists with Holocaust denial.

Although Europe ranks second in anti-Israeli hate promotion, it is far behind the Muslim world. Many Europeans—in fact a very large minority of them—believe that Israel behaves toward the Palestinians as the Nazis behaved toward the Jews. Another version of this extreme defamation is that Israel conducts a war of extermination against the Palestinians.[8] This book will devote much attention to Europe, though not only for this reason. It is also necessary because of some other disparate factors: Europe's lengthy history of anti-Semitism, which has become part of its culture; the complexity of its societies; and biased political actions taken against Israel by the European Union and individual countries.

The massive nonselective Muslim immigration into Europe over the past decades has greatly increased anti-Semitism and anti-Israelism there. Individuals and segments from this community have fostered an intensification of anti-Jewish and anti-Israeli hate-mongering in many European countries.[9]

A 2013 study by the European Agency for Fundamental Rights (FRA) on discrimination and hate crimes against Jews in the European Union confirms this point. It found that 76 percent of Jews across ten European countries report that anti-Semitism has increased in their country over the past five years. Furthermore, 40 percent of survey respondents who experienced anti-Semitic violence were attacked by someone with a Muslim-extremist outlook. This is a high percentage in view of the number of Muslims in these countries. In numerous categories of physical and verbal anti-Semitic harassment, the highest number of perpetrators came from those with a Muslim background.[10]

The Hatred of Jews and Israel

Systematic hate-mongering against Jews goes back close to two millennia. Theological anti-Semitism originating from the Catholic Church and several other Christian currents permeated Europe and has far from disappeared totally. The core motif of anti-Semitism is that the Jews—and nowadays also Israel—are absolute evil. It manifests itself in writings, declarations, and in many other ways. Christian anti-Semitism created an infrastructure of Jew-hatred in Europe. On the thus established diabolical image of the Jews, the Nazis built further. This culminated in the Holocaust genocide in the previous century.

Since 2000, hatred of Jews and Israel has progressed increasingly in Western societies. It is partly based on the remaining infrastructure in place, albeit latently, for many decades after World War II.[11] In a globalizing world, similar incidents appear in a variety of places, almost simultaneously. The Holocaust only temporarily suppressed anti-Semitism in Western societies. Today, it is still often not politically correct to publicly declare oneself an anti-Semite in those societies. Yet a substitute target has been found in Israel for the anti-Semites to direct their hatred at.

The major contemporary anti-Semitic hate themes have recurred in various forms over more than two thousand years. They mainly derive from the one core motif of the Jews—and nowadays also the state of Israel—as absolute evil. This central theme and its offshoots recur in several ways, some of which nowadays are not explicit.

Anti-Israelism

After World War II, the new version of anti-Semitism targeting Israel gradually evolved. It has intensified radically in this century. Hate-mongering and discrimination against Israel are its major components. This incitement is often called "the new anti-Semitism," "anti-Zionism," or "anti-Israelism."

This has led to a major development that can best be described as demonizing or delegitimizing Israel. At the same time, classic forms of anti-Semitism have become much stronger since 2000. These types of incitement often appear together. One also finds anti-Israelism among people who do not discriminate against Jews. The reverse form of anti-Semitism, which focuses on Jews while supporting Israel, also exists but is rarer.

Anti-Semitic propaganda reached a new postwar peak in September 2001 at the abovementioned UN World Conference against Racism in Durban. The main defamers of the Jews and Israel there were Arab governments, supported by many Muslim countries and a considerable number of NGOs, including Western ones. As noted, the NGO Forum in Durban was a major illustration of the widespread anti-Semitism in the so-called antiracist camp.

The anti-Semitic character of anti-Israelism can be proven through the analysis of opinion survey findings, cartoons, statistics about incidents, and semantics. During the Second Lebanon War in 2006, much further proof emerged that anti-Semitism and anti-Israelism go hand in hand. This became even clearer during Israel's subsequent military campaigns against Hamas in Gaza.

Studies and Anecdotes

The major presence of classic anti-Semitism and the eruption of anti-Israelism are supported by many studies. The extent of the demonization of Jews and Israel is so massive that it indeed amounts to nothing less than a total global propaganda war.

In many Arab and Muslim countries, anti-Semitism represents the feelings of society at large. In a 2010 Pew Research Center survey of attitudes toward other religious groups in the Muslim world, of the nine countries surveyed, only one, Nigeria, had less than 50 percent of respondents viewing Jews unfavorably. Israel's neighbors Lebanon, Jordan, Syria, and Egypt had "unfavorability" ratings of Jews of 95-97 percent.[12]

In 2011, a Pew Global Attitude Project survey again illustrated that respondents in many Muslim countries overwhelmingly viewed Jews unfavorably. In Pakistan, Jordan, and Egypt, only 2 percent of respondents viewed Jews favorably. In Lebanon, Jews received 3 percent favorability ratings, and in the Palestinian territories, 4 percent.[13]

Pew undertook a separate study in Turkey in 2014. The survey asked those polled about seven countries, the European Union, and NATO, and whether these were seen as "favorable" or "unfavorable." It turned out that all were seen negatively. Saudi Arabia was viewed the most favorably, with 26 percent regarding it favorably and 53 percent unfavorably. Seventy-five percent saw Iran unfavorably, 14 percent favorably. Israel closed the list with 86 percent of respondents viewing it unfavorably and 2 percent viewing it favorably.[14]

Statistics show that the number of people in Europe who hold extremely evil beliefs about Israel is so major that such attitudes have significantly permeated mainstream society.[15] They no longer come exclusively from Muslim, extreme-right, and extreme-left fringes.

The magnitude of current anti-Semitism can be further substantiated by a huge number of vignettes and anecdotes. Those mentioned in this book are mere samples of the widespread hate-mongering. Hatred coming out of large parts of the Muslim world is similar and sometimes even more severe than what was propagated by Nazi Germany.

Twentieth-century Europe was a continent in which a war criminal or a mass murderer had a better chance of survival than a Jewish child. The reason was twofold: the murderous character of the Holocaust, and the subsequent leniency of European democratic societies toward many criminals who had murdered Jews.[16] One might add that nowadays, if all contemporary hard-core anti-Semites of various kinds in Western Europe were to die quickly, their number would far exceed that of the victims of World War II.

The massive anecdotal material about European anti-Semitism and, in particular, anti-Israeli incitement in recent years indicates that the borderlines of anti-Semitic malice in contemporary Europe are crumbling even further.

Postmodern Anti-Semitism

As circumstances changed over the centuries, the main anti-Semitic motifs were dressed up in different ways, often according to the local situation. As time passes, the main subthemes also fragment and mutate. Sometimes major new ones are added. Holocaust denial, inversion, and other distortions of the Shoah are examples of this from the previous century.

Understanding the nature and mechanisms of the contemporary demonization processes requires familiarity with a number of key characteristics of contemporary Western society. The latter is often called "postmodern." Nowadays anti-Semitic mutations and fragmentations occur frequently. This is what makes contemporary anti-Semitism so difficult to analyze and such a many-sided, complicated challenge.

Prewar anti-Semitism was transparent. Anti-Semites did not hide their hateful feelings toward Jews and were often proud of them. This was also true for those Christians who infused European society with anti-Semitic thought—theological and other—and activity for many centuries. Anti-Semitism became even more transparent and explicit with the rise of Nazism in Germany, Austria, and other countries. Ultimately it also became exterminatory. Six million Jews were murdered in a crime-ridden Europe.

The War of a Million Cuts

Postmodern anti-Semitism is far from monolithic, however. It is often opaque because perpetrators frequently phrase their anti-Israelism indirectly. It is not only multi-sourced and fragmented but also, in large measure, diffuse and discontinuous. There is no one government, organization, or person that stands out as the prime propagator of anti-Israeli and anti-Jewish hate.

There is no one, large attack on Jews and particularly on Israel from a single identifiable source; instead there is an almost unlimited number of usually small ones. These are sometimes coordinated by groups of perpetrators, yet also often not. For Israel's main Arab and Muslim enemies, these attacks should lead to Israel's disappearance; many of them say so explicitly. There are also many non-Arab enemies of Israel who support them, for various reasons. This global propaganda war against Israel and the Jews might be called the "War of a Million Cuts."

For a few years now, the Simon Wiesenthal Center (SWC) has published its annual ranking of the world's top ten anti-Semitic/anti-Israeli slurs. For 2012, the variety in the names illustrates the global character of the hatred. The SWC put Egypt's Muslim Brotherhood in first place, followed by the Iranian regime. Next in line were Brazilian cartoonist Carlos Latuff, Europe's anti-Semitic football fans, Ukraine's Svoboda Party, Golden Dawn in Greece, and Jobbik in Hungary. These were followed by the Norwegian Muslim convert Trond Ali Linstad, German journalist Jakob Augstein, and U.S. Nation of Islam leader Louis Farrakhan.[17]

In 2013, the SWC ranked Ayatollah Ali Khamenei first on its list of the ten people responsible for top anti-Semitic/anti-Israeli slurs. In second place was Turkish Prime Minister Recep Tayyip Erdogan; he was followed by UN Special Rapporteur Richard Falk. In fourth place came the BDS (boycott, divestment, and sanctions) movement. In that context the SWC specifically mentioned the American Studies Association, musician Roger Waters, and the United Church of Canada.

Next came the Hungarian Jobbik Party. In sixth place came a number of people who believed Hitler was a hero. These included Lebanese singer Najwa Karam, and Dutch Muslim teens who made statements on Dutch TV including, "What Hitler did to the Jews is fine with me" and "Hitler should have killed all the Jews." Also included were two students from Turkey who gave the Sieg Heil salute at the entrance of Auschwitz, Muslim Brotherhood spiritual leader Yusuf al-Qaradawi, Iraqi cleric Qays bin Khalil al-Kalbi, and Saudi cleric, lawyer, and poet Muhammad al-Farraj.

In the next place came several cartoonists, among them the Frenchman Zeon and the Norwegian Thomas Drefvelin. The Pine Bush School District in New York State came eighth. Next were authors Alice Walker and Max Blumenthal. Qualifying for the tenth place were various sports events with anti-Semitic manifestations. The Croatian national soccer player Josip Simunic was listed for leading the chanting of pro-Nazi slogans.[18]

The top ten anti-Semitic slurs have now become an annual feature. The most recent one from 2014 includes events from Belgium, Jordan, France, Germany, Turkey, Sweden, Hungary, the United States, and the United Kingdom.[19]

In January 2014, Israeli Strategic Affairs Minister Yuval Steinitz said, "There is no doubt that Abu Mazen [Palestinian Authority President Mahmoud Abbas] is now worthy of the title of the Number One anti-Semitic leader in the world." He added, "The incitement is present in Palestinian schoolbooks, on state-sponsored television and on websites, including Abbas's official site." In saying that Abbas was inciting "as it once occurred in the most dismal times in Europe," Steinitz clearly alluded to Nazi Germany during World War II.[20]

When in 2014 the mass murders and beheadings in Iraq and Syria by the extremist Muslim organization Islamic State (ISIS) gained wide publicity, some observers started to label ISIS the embodiment of absolute evil. This was accompanied by two phenomena. Some whitewashers of Islam claimed that ISIS was not Islamic. In a speech about the movement, President Barack Obama said it was "not 'Islamic'" and added, "No religion condones the killing of innocents."[21] This sentiment was shared by British Prime Minister David Cameron, who stated, "They boast of their brutality. They claim to do this in the name of Islam. That is nonsense. Islam is a religion of peace. They are not Muslims, they are monsters."[22] After the murders of seventeen people primarily in Paris at the *Charlie Hebdo* offices and a kosher supermarket in January 2015, French President François Hollande said, "Those who committed these terrorist acts, those terrorists, those fanatics, have nothing to do with the Muslim religion."[23]

One might remark that, whereas Plato spoke about the philosopher-king, Obama, Cameron, and Hollande seem to introduce a new concept, that of the political leader-theologian. This is the more remarkable as they refer to the theology of a religion they do not belong to.

American terror expert Andrew C. McCarthy points out, however, that:

> Nevertheless, the perception that the Islamic State is something new and different and aberrational compared with the Islamic-supremacist threat we've been living with for three decades is wrong, perhaps dangerously so. Decapitation is not a new jihadist terror method, and it is far from unique to the Islamic State. Indeed . . . it has recently been used by Islamic-supremacist elements of the U.S.-backed Free Syrian Army against the Islamic State.[24]

The other phenomenon is the comparing of Israel to ISIS. According to Member of Knesset Haneen Zoabi of the Arab Balad Party, "They [ISIS] kill one person at a time with a knife and the IDF at the press of a button [kills] dozens of Palestinians." Zoabi added that an Israeli pilot "is no less a terrorist than a person who takes a knife and commits a beheading." Zoabi did not mention the huge number of killings by the Islamic State other than by beheading.[25]

If ISIS, or for that matter Al-Qaeda's Syrian offshoot were indeed aberrant Muslims radically opposed to a peaceful tradition, one would find almost total rejection of their aims in a relatively moderate Muslim country such as Jordan. A September 2014 study by the Center for Strategic Studies at the University of Jordan, however, found that not more than 62 percent of Jordanians polled considered ISIS a terrorist organization, while only 31 percent considered the Syrian-based Al-Qaeda affiliate Jabhat al-Nusra a terrorist organization.[26]

Deceptive Pretensions

Contemporary anti-Semites often have deceptive pretensions about their beliefs. Many of those who commit anti-Semitic acts in the Western world deny that they are anti-Semites. They may even claim this in articles in which they make anti-Semitic remarks about Israel. Some anti-Israelis may even express their "love" for the Jewish people at length, while at the same time they exhibit anti-Semitic attitudes toward the Jewish state. Some Jews even come forward to defend these anti-Semites by declaring that they are "true friends of Israel."

This author's book, *Behind the Humanitarian Mask: The Nordic Countries, Israel and the Jews*, exposes many Scandinavians who promote false ethical claims about themselves.[27] One example occurred in 1992 when then-Norwegian Labour Party Prime Minister Gro Harlem Brundtland stated in her New Year's speech, "It is typically Norwegian to be good."[28] The anti-Israeli hate-mongering of the Labour Party-dominated government of Prime Minister Jens Stoltenberg—defeated in the 2013 parliamentary elections—illustrated even more how absurd this statement really is.[29]

A 2013 book by journalist Eirik Veum has shown that in wartime prisoner camps in Norway, the cruelty of some local guards even shocked SS members.[30] After some time, all Norwegians had to be replaced by Germans.[31]

The Key Elements of Delegitimization

The focus of this book is on the process of delegitimization of Israel. Its main topics are its mechanisms, originators, and modes of transmission. It is thus not a description or overview of contemporary anti-Semitism, though examples of anti-Semitism are often mentioned.

A number of steps have to be taken to clarify this delegitimization process. First one has to describe its main elements. That involves assessing how the characteristics of anti-Israelism are similar to those of the classic forms of anti-Semitism—the religious and nationalist-ethnic ones. It also requires a discussion of definitions of contemporary anti-Semitism.

In other words, the first step in understanding the methodology of the total propaganda war against the Jews and Israel is to identify the weapons and ammunition that are used. In the war's extreme form, these can be reduced to the use of a single core motif: the Jews and Israel are the paradigm of all evil. Or, to phrase it differently: the Jews and Israel are not only evil in what they do, but in their very existence. This characterizes all three types of extreme anti-Semitism.

This step requires analyzing the multitude of false statements, deceptive arguments, and acts of hate directed at Jews and Israel. In other words, an inventory must be taken of the main hate messages and deeds. Because many messages come in masked form, it is crucial to understand how ancient hate motifs have mutated over the centuries.[32]

For instance, the classic blood libel accused Jews of killing Christians to use their blood for religious purposes, such as baking matzo. Current versions include the claim that Israel entered the Gaza Strip in the Cast Lead campaign (December 2008-January 2009) with the aim of killing Palestinian women and children, or that Jews kill Palestinians to harvest their organs. It is also imperative to identify major incitement instruments including double standards, false moral equivalence, sentimental appeals, and scapegoating.

That must be followed by an analysis of the next key element of the demonization process: perpetrator groups. How can those who concoct and transmit the messages of hatred be categorized? That, in turn, leads to the next major element of the delegitimization process that needs to be assessed, namely, methods of conveying the hate messages to the public.

This has to be followed by an analysis of the impact, so far, of anti-Semitism and anti-Israelism on Jews in the Diaspora—perhaps one should instead use again the term exile—particularly in Europe, and on Israelis worldwide. It is also necessary to note some organizations that fight back against the propaganda war.

Finally, this book offers recommendations on how to improve the professional combat of Israel and its allies in the propaganda war.

Multifaceted Anti-Semitism and Anti-Israelism

The amount of data on recent manifestations of anti-Israelism and anti-Semitism is huge. One cannot even cover all of the polls, let alone a significant part of the massive anecdotal information. In the analysis that follows, such vignettes serve mainly as illustrations. This author's 2013 book, *Demonizing Israel and the Jews*, contains fifty-seven interviews with experts on various aspects of the propaganda war.[33] It shows how multifaceted anti-Israelism and anti-Semitism are. One can easily add many other important subjects to the ones discussed there. Since the book's publication, this author has published another fifty interviews on additional aspects of hate-mongering against Israel and Jews.

Much has been written about the fact that many in the world hold an extremely negative view of Israel, or hate it. Publications on this topic were often based mainly on anecdotal evidence, or data on a single country. The appalling findings from various polls of European attitudes toward Israel often received little attention in the media.

Israel's Precarious History

Israel has developed remarkably in its short history. Most remarkable of all is the survival of its democratic character under siege. Its vulnerability, however, remains great. Israel is confronted with existential threats that few countries face. Its security systems are frequently challenged by its enemies in grave, unprecedented ways. In one major area, however, there is little breakdown of authority: the Israel Defense Forces have a hierarchical structure and a conscription army, and this has been a unifying factor for the nation.

Israel's future has always been precarious. Nahum Goldmann, who was a longstanding leader of the World Jewish Congress, told in his biography how Israel's first prime minister, David Ben-Gurion, said to him shortly before his seventieth birthday in 1955:

> When you, Nahum, ask me whether I will live in a Jewish state and be buried in it, I rather believe that. How long can I live? Ten or twelve years—until then, there will certainly be a Jewish state. If you ask me whether my son Amos . . . will have the opportunity to die in a Jewish state and be buried there, I would say, at best, 50%.[34]

The late Amos Ben-Gurion, who died in 2008, was indeed buried in Israel.

Former Prime Minister Yitzhak Rabin told Israeli Ambassador Yehuda Avner, who was a close staff member, why he was in favor of the Oslo Agreements. He said that without some kind of peace, there was no way to guarantee Israel's continued existence. Rabin also pointed out that Israel was the only country whose existence was still publicly debated.[35]

Current Prime Minister Benjamin Netanyahu also expressed concern about the country's survival, saying, "Iran is developing nuclear weapons and poses the greatest threat to our existence since the War of Independence. Iran's terror wings surround us from the north and south."[36]

Yet the propaganda war endangers Israel's existence as well. Even though its effects are slower than a possible Iranian nuclear strike, they can be disastrous in the long run. The huge number of Israel's enemies compared to its population highlights the need to fight the propaganda war far more efficiently. The problem is enhanced by the fact that demonizing people is far easier than fighting demonization.

It is impossible to cover all major aspects of such a multifaceted process as the delegitimization of Israel. In the coming pages, examples will be given from many countries and sources. These illustrate the global character of contemporary classic anti-Semitism and anti-Israelism.[37] The accumulation of these vignettes may suggest that the danger is acute. That is not necessarily so, but it indicates a possible future deterioration, gradual or rapid, of the reality of both Israel and Diaspora Jews.

CHAPTER ONE

How Anti-Semitism and Anti-Israelism Overlap and Intertwine

WHEN DISCUSSING ANTI-SEMITISM, ONE FIRST has to define what characterizes it. An often-used and classic definition has been: "hostility toward or discrimination against Jews as a religious, ethnic, or social group."[1]

This definition was suitable for the two classic forms of anti-Semitism, the religious and nationalist-ethnic varieties. However, it does not fit the newer postmodern form of the same hatred, anti-Israelism. Several authors have realized this in particular since the beginning of the twenty-first century, as anti-Semitism has erupted in Europe with an intensity not seen since the end of World War II. These authors have tried to redefine anti-Semitism to include the anti-Israeli category.

Cotler's Early Approach

Since the beginning of the past decade, many have inquired into what "new anti-Semitism" embodies. One pioneer analyst has been Irwin Cotler, a former Canadian justice minister.[2] He observed, "Traditional anti-Semitism denied Jews the right to live as equal members of society, but the new anti-Jewishness denies the right of the Jewish people to live as an equal member of the family of nations."[3]

Cotler described the new, Israeli-oriented anti-Semitism in several ways.

One is that it denies the Jewish people the right to self-determination, delegitimizing Israel as a state and attributing the entire world's misfortune to it. It ascribes a mix of evil qualities to the country; Cotler called this cultural anti-Semitism. It also involves calls for restrictions on countries trading with Israel, or economic anti-Semitism.

As it is sometimes difficult to pinpoint the boundary between criticism of Israel and anti-Semitism, Cotler proposed some guidelines. He said that critics of Israel become anti-Semites when:

- They publicly call for the destruction of Israel and the Jewish people. This is the case with the covenants of Palestinian terrorist groups (the PLO and Hamas) and some militant Islamic legal rulings (*fatwas*), as well as the Iranian threat to annihilate Israel ("genocidal anti-Semitism").
- They deny the Jewish people's right to self-determination, delegitimize Israel as a state, and attribute to Israel all of the world's evil ("political anti-Semitism").
- They Nazify Israel ("ideological anti-Semitism").
- Israel is characterized as the perfidious enemy of Islam ("theological anti-Semitism").
- Israel is attributed a mix of evil qualities by salon intellectuals and Western elites ("cultural anti-Semitism").
- They call for restrictions on those trading with Israel ("economic anti-Semitism").
- They deny the Holocaust.
- They support racist terrorism against Israel.
- They single out Israel for discriminatory treatment in the international arena through denial of equality before the law.[4]

Cotler thus drew attention to several of the points later included in the working definition of anti-Semitism of the European Monitoring Centre on Racism and Xenophobia (EUMC). This body later changed its name to European Agency for Fundamental Rights (FRA). Examples are Cotler's mention of: calling for the destruction of Israel and the Jewish people, "Nazifying" Israel, and discriminatory treatment of Israel by denying it equality before the law.[5] Former Swedish Deputy Prime Minister Per Ahlmark pointed out:

Anti-Zionism today has become very similar to anti-Semitism.

Anti-Zionists accept the right of other peoples to national feelings and a defensible state. But they reject the right of the Jewish people to have its national consciousness expressed in the state of Israel and to make that state secure. Thus, they are not judging Israel with the values used to judge other countries. Such discrimination against Jews is called anti-Semitism.[6]

Sharansky's 3Ds

Natan Sharansky, until his resignation in May 2005 as Israeli cabinet minister responsible for the Diaspora, initiated a concise working definition of "new anti-Semitism." He developed the "3D test"—demonization, double standards, and delegitimization—to separate legitimate criticism of Israel from anti-Semitism.[7]

Sharansky wrote:

> The first "D" is the test of demonization. When the Jewish state is being demonized; when Israel's actions are blown out of all sensible proportion; when comparisons are made between Israelis and Nazis and between Palestinian refugee camps and Auschwitz—this is anti-Semitism, not legitimate criticism of Israel.
>
> The second "D" is the test of double standards. When criticism of Israel is applied selectively; when Israel is singled out by the United Nations for human rights abuses while the behavior of known and major abusers, such as China, Iran, Cuba, and Syria, is ignored; when Israel's Magen David Adom, alone among the world's ambulance services, is denied admission to the International Red Cross—this is anti-Semitism.
>
> The third "D" is the test of delegitimization. When Israel's fundamental right to exist is denied—alone among all peoples in the world—this too is anti-Semitism.[8]

FRA Working Definition of Anti-Semitism

As verbal attacks on Israel intensified, there was an increasing need for an updated and well-accepted definition of anti-Semitism and anti-Israelism that could expose the racist and anti-Zionist permutations of it. In its 2004 report on anti-Semitism, the abovementioned European Monitoring Centre on Racism and Xenophobia (EUMC) noted the lack of a common definition and requested one from a small group of Jewish NGOs. The resulting definition was gradually accepted in many circles, and is now known as the FRA working definition of anti-Semitism.

The document that contains the working definition mentions various contemporary examples of anti-Semitism. One of these is: "Accusing the Jews as a people, or Israel as a state, of inventing or exaggerating the Holocaust."[9]

The FRA text has been increasingly accepted. For example, delegates to the May 2005 Cordoba Conference of the Organization for Security and Cooperation in Europe (OSCE) constantly referred to this definition. In another example, the *Report of the British All-Party Parliamentary Inquiry into Anti-Semitism* recommended that "the EUMC Working Definition of anti-Semitism—since then the FRA definition—is adopted and promoted by the Government and law enforcement agencies."[10]

The FRA document also states that "criticism of Israel similar to that leveled against any other country cannot be regarded as anti-Semitic." It lists examples of how anti-Semitism can manifest itself regarding Israel:

> Anti-Semitism is a certain perception of Jews, which may be expressed as hatred toward Jews. Rhetorical and physical manifestations of anti-Semitism are directed toward Jewish or non-Jewish individuals and/or their property, toward Jewish community institutions and religious facilities.
>
> In addition, such manifestations could also target the state of Israel, conceived as a Jewish collectivity. Anti-Semitism frequently charges Jews with conspiring to harm humanity, and it is often used to blame Jews for "why things go wrong." It is expressed in speech, writing, visual forms and action, and employs sinister stereotypes and negative character traits.
>
> Contemporary examples of anti-Semitism in public life, the media, schools,

the workplace, and in the religious sphere could, taking into account the overall context, include, but are not limited to:

- Calling for, aiding, or justifying the killing or harming of Jews in the name of a radical ideology or an extremist view of religion.
- Making mendacious, dehumanizing, demonizing, or stereotypical allegations about Jews as such or the power of Jews as collective—such as, especially but not exclusively, the myth about a world Jewish conspiracy or of Jews controlling the media, economy, government or other societal institutions.
- Accusing Jews as a people of being responsible for real or imagined wrongdoing committed by a single Jewish person or group, or even for acts committed by non-Jews.
- Denying the fact, scope, mechanisms (e.g. gas chambers) or intentionality of the genocide of the Jewish people at the hands of National Socialist Germany and its supporters and accomplices during World War II (the Holocaust).
- Accusing the Jews as a people, or Israel as a state, of inventing or exaggerating the Holocaust.
- Accusing Jewish citizens of being more loyal to Israel, or to the alleged priorities of Jews worldwide, than to the interests of their own nations.[11]

The document also gives many examples of the ways in which anti-Semitism may manifest itself regarding Israel, including:

- Denying the Jewish people their right to self-determination, e.g., by claiming that the existence of a State of Israel is a racist endeavor.
- Applying double standards by requiring of it a behavior not expected or demanded of any other democratic nation.
- Using the symbols and images associated with classic anti-Semitism (e.g., claims of Jews killing Jesus or blood libel) to characterize Israel.
- Drawing comparisons of contemporary Israeli policy to that of the Nazis.
- Holding Jews collectively responsible for actions of the state of Israel.[12]

In 2013, the FRA removed this definition from its website rather suddenly.[13] This may well have been because when applying this definition, it becomes evident that the European Union from time to time commits anti-Semitic acts.

Though it has no official working definition of anti-Semitism, the U.S. State Department has published an anti-Semitism fact sheet, with much of the FRA document copied verbatim. Some items in this fact sheet that partly differ from those found in the FRA definition are:

- Using the symbols and images associated with classic anti-Semitism to characterize Israel or Israelis.
- Drawing comparisons of contemporary Israeli policy to that of the Nazis, blaming Israel for all inter-religious or political tensions.

Also included in this definition are double standards for Israel, including those of "Multilateral organizations focusing on Israel only for peace or human rights investigations."[14]

The Three Main Categories of Anti-Semitism

The history of anti-Semitism starts in Egypt, several centuries before the birth of Christianity. The first pogrom took place in Alexandria in 38 CE.[15] For many centuries, anti-Semitism as a major force manifested itself as religious anti-Semitism.

Pieter van der Horst, a Dutch expert on early Christianity and Judaism, says:

> Christian anti-Semitism began much later than Jesus' life. In the Gospels of Matthew, Mark, and Luke, which are the historically more reliable ones, Jesus views himself as a messenger of God to the Jews and as a member of the Jewish people. He wanted to prepare them for what he saw as the approaching end of time and God's imminent kingdom. Jesus was not planning to initiate a new religion. The writer of a later book, the Gospel of John, has Jesus make anti-Semitic remarks. That book, however, is much less historical.[16]

The beginning of violent European anti-Semitism is often traced to the Crusades at the end of the eleventh century. Others claim it commenced in 1010 with organized mass murders of Jews in France, followed by massacres in areas that are now part of Germany.[17] Anti-Semitism also led to the expulsion of Jews from many European countries during the Middle Ages.

The Core Motif Mutates

As the perception of absolute evil has mutated over the centuries, the attire of this recurring core motif has changed as well. In classic Christian anti-Semitism, the key accusation is that the Jews have killed God's alleged son and therefore their descendants are eternally responsible for this crime. It follows that those who are abysmally wicked enough to be God-killers must be the embodiment of Satan on earth. Once society internalizes this demonization, the way to virulent attitudes and extreme anti-Jewish violence is wide open.

The demonization of the Jews often had far-reaching consequences. It led some Christians to the conclusion that if certain people, that is, the Jews, were the representatives of Satan, the world would be better off without them and they should be killed. Those who thought so proposed an escape option to the Jews: conversion to Christianity. During the Crusades this stark choice was offered in numerous locales; many Jews who refused to convert were murdered.

For almost a thousand years, versions of religious anti-Semitism have been accompanied by other manifestations of Jew-hatred in political, economic, academic, and cultural spheres. During the nineteenth century, a second major type of anti-Semitism emerged, namely, nationalistic-ethnic anti-Semitism. It found its genocidal expression in the Holocaust.

After World War II, anti-Semitism broadened into a third major category, that of anti-Israelism. This form of anti-Semitism is characterized by similar hate motifs to those of religious and nationalistic-ethnic anti-Semitism. Its multiple manifestations also include extensive genocidal incitement against Israel and the Jews, predominantly in the Muslim world.

As aforementioned, this variant of Jew-hatred is now often referred to as "new anti-Semitism." Its Western perpetrators often call themselves anti-Zionists. They aim to isolate Israel and portray it—in the words of Berlin Technical University's Center for Research on Anti-Semitism—"as a state that is fundamentally negatively distinct from all others, which therefore has no right to exist."[18]

The Three Categories of Anti-Semitism Overlap

There are many common elements between the three main permutations of anti-Semitism: religious anti-Semitism, or anti-Judaism; nationalist-ethnic (racist) anti-Semitism; and anti-Israelism (anti-Zionism). The current delegitimization of Israel overlaps and is intertwined with classic anti-Semitism. Verbal or physical attacks are often against both Jews and Israelis. This merging of targets is one major proof, among many, of the substantial overlaps between anti-Israelism and anti-Semitism.

One phenomenon, then, cannot be analyzed without the other. Both classic anti-Semitism and anti-Israelism have become global in nature. Any inquiry into the delegitimization of Israel and how to confront it requires a broad understanding of the characteristics and developments in contemporary global anti-Semitism, as well as its past.

Although the most extreme current demonization of Israel and the Jews comes out of parts of the Arab and Muslim world, similar motifs and semantics are also expressed in extreme left- and right-wing Western circles. This also pertains, though at lower intensity, to segments of the Western mainstream.

A particularly effective way to demonstrate all this is by analyzing anti-Semitic cartoons. Like all caricatures, these rely on familiar and immediately grasped stereotypes. Cartoonists in mass media must employ these broad typecasts as they are easily recognizable by most viewers. In contemporary society, in which knowledge is extremely superficial, caricatures remain a successful tool for concisely conveying opinions including hate messages. This is particularly true for countries with a high percentage of illiteracy, such as in the Arab world.

European cartoons also flaunt many parallels between Jews and Nazis, the Star of David and the swastika, the security fence and the Warsaw Ghetto wall. One finds anti-Semitic cartoons in leading mainstream papers remote from fascism or the extreme left. These include the London *Independent,* the Italian *La Stampa*, the Spanish *El País*, and many others. Even if these instances are incidental, it still indicates that many moral borders have been breached in a continent where, seventy years ago, the overwhelming majority of the Jews were murdered by Germans and Austrians with the assistance of many other Europeans.

Absolute Evil Mutates

Anti-Semitism's classic core theme that Jews embody absolute evil has been propagated intensely for many centuries. This extreme lie and its principal submotifs have remained largely the same over the ages. Their representation, however, has evolved according to the prevailing worldview at a given time.

The perception of what constitutes absolute evil has changed over the centuries. In Christian anti-Semitism, the most evil act imaginable was deicide—that the Jews had killed Jesus whom many Christians believed to be God's son.

When Christianity dominated public opinion, the Jew was often portrayed as the killer of God, the anti-Christ, and also as Satan. Joshua Trachtenberg summarized how medieval Christendom saw the Jew as "sorcerer, murderer, cannibal, poisoner, blasphemer."[19] The main Christian demonizers of the Jews, however, such as the Church Father John Chrysostom, already dated from the fourth century.[20]

The Jew is also denounced as the "quintessential other," as perceived at that moment. In periods of strong nationalism, Jews are characterized as radically alien elements. When the societal emphasis is on race, Jews are depicted as an extremely inferior one.

Nationalistic-Ethnic Anti-Semitism

Once societies turned more secular, the false accusation of killing God's alleged son no longer meant much to many Europeans. In the second major category of anti-Semitism, nationalistic-ethnic anti-Semitism, the theme of the Jews as a paradigm of absolute evil reappeared in a new guise. The criminal worldview of the Nazis reinvented the core motif that the Jews are the carriers of all evil. For the Nazis, who were largely neo-pagans, the Christian accusation of the Jews of the murder of God's alleged son was irrelevant; they perceived absolute evil differently—for instance, as having a subhuman character. The Jews thus had to be branded, among other things, as bacteria or vermin, implying that they had to be exterminated.

In an environment where nationalism increasingly became a primary societal value, the Jews were also accused of being cosmopolitans without any national loyalties, and thus evil people acting against the interests of the nationalities of their compatriots. This also led to the accusation that Jews conspire to control the world. The main supporting "document" for this conspiracy theory was *The Protocols of the Elders of Zion*, a Czarist forgery that has been reprinted in large numbers.[21]

The Nazis further detailed the accusations that the Jews are the source of all evil. They also saw Bolshevism as evil; hence the Jews had to be branded, among other things, as communists.

Anti-Israelism

In contemporary Western society, absolute evil is often seen as the crimes of the Germans and their allies during World War II, with the Holocaust and committing genocide as its paradigm. After the Holocaust, for a certain period anti-Semitism became politically incorrect in the public domain. Many Europeans also started to become aware that if there was absolute evil in the world, it was represented by substantial parts of Europe rather than the Jews. For many others, however, this was too painful to admit. It created the psychological necessity to again attach evil to the Jews, this time mainly to Israel, the Jewish state.

The presentation of Israelis as Nazis goes back to high-ranking Englishmen in the 1940s during the time of the British Mandate for Palestine. Historian Robert Wistrich says, "An example is Sir John Glubb Pasha, who was commander of the Arab Jordanian Legion fighting against Israel in 1948. He was an upper-class conservative Englishman and a lifelong Arabophile, with a special love for desert Arabs. He was also a convinced anti-Semite."

Wistrich adds:

> Glubb was not alone. One can find in British documents similar statements from high-ranking officials in the Palestine administration . . . One figure high up in the Palestine administration was Sir Edward Grigg, later Lord Altrincham. He referred to what he called the National Socialist

> character of what became the Israeli Labor Party (Mapai) and of the Hagana (the core of the Israeli army). He saw in the Zionist youth movements a copy of the Hitler Youth.[22]

This comparison of Israel with the Nazis developed strongly in the communist world. Simon Wiesenthal, in an article in 1968, found in particular that East Germany's news service was far more anti-Israeli than that of other communist countries.

> Wiesenthal noticed that the words used in the DDR's press and propaganda deviated from the commentary of other socialist countries. Some utterances even corresponded literally with remarks in former National Socialist newspapers and journals. Very soon it became evident that the anti-Israeli articles in the East German press had been written by the same persons who, during the Third Reich, had published articles about the "Jewish peril."
>
> On 14 July 1967, for example, a cartoon appeared in the *Berliner Zeitung*, depicting a flying Moshe Dayan, with his hands stretched out toward Gaza and Jerusalem. Next to him stood Adolf Hitler in an advanced state of decomposition. He encouraged Dayan with the words: "Carry on, colleague Dayan!"[23]

The conspiracy motif also recurs in more recent times. This is, for instance, the case in Arab television programs, a mode of communication far more effective and encompassing than books or written media. The fraudulent *Protocols of the Elders of Zion* is widely reprinted in the Arab world. It has also been published in recent years in several Western countries, Norway being one of the examples.[24] The truth about contemporary conspiracy is different: now that Nazism and communism have failed, the jihadi current of Islam, however fragmented, is the only major movement actively conspiring to rule the world.

The conspiracy motif also appears in multiple forms and in many other circles. This was mentioned in the *Report of the British All-Party Parliamentary Inquiry into Anti-Semitism*, which noted: "We were told that Jewish conspiracy theories have been applied to many contemporary issues."[25]

Common Characteristics of Anti-Semitism and Anti-Israelism

The three permutations of anti-Semitism have a number of major common characteristics. There is an ongoing, powerful promotion of a discourse of Jew-hatred. Verbal or physical attacks occur against both Jews and Israelis. Jews and nowadays also Israel are judged by standards that are applied to them but not to others.

Contemporary anti-Semites use a number of major hate motifs, several of which have been repeated in various forms for more than two thousand years. As noted, one of these is that the Jews—which now also includes Israel—embody absolute evil and are behind all disasters. Nowadays this motif recurs in many forms, some of which are not explicit yet implied—as in the notion that the Israeli-Palestinian conflict is the greatest danger facing the world.

A variant of this was promoted by U.S. Secretary of State John Kerry when he tied the rise of ISIS to the lack of progress in Israeli-Palestinian negotiations. He did so at a State Department dinner for Muslim guests in October 2014. Kerry is not anti-Semitic in his personal outlook and has been a friend of Israel. Nevertheless, he was using a motif that many anti-Semitic spokesmen have previously promoted.

One of the common characteristics of the three main permutations of anti-Semitism is an ongoing and vigorous promotion of hatred. This demonization has developed major subthemes over the years, which recur in various guises and gradually permeate society's narrative. With time, accusations become increasingly complex and more difficult to unravel. The Jews' enemies continue to build further on this infrastructure when the circumstances are suitable, when they wish to attack a specific person or group, or when they seek out a scapegoat in any given situation.

The core motif of the Jews and Israel as extreme evil manifests itself in many other ways. The Jews (and Israel) are again accused of responsibility for a large number of disasters. Historically, the Jews were blamed for various plagues such as the Black Death in the fourteenth century. Germans invented the "stab in the back" (*Dolchstoss*) legend, which held the Jews responsible for Germany's defeat in World War I and was subsequently used by the National Socialists in their murderous anti-Semitic campaigns.

On a local level, when Christian children who had disappeared were found dead, Jews were sometimes accused of having murdered them, often out of religious motives. This was the classic anti-Semitic version of the blood libel. Nowadays the blood-libel accusation reemerges with respect to Israel in different mutations.

After a huge mining disaster in Turkey in May 2014, the progovernment Turkish daily *Yeni Akit* criticized on its front page the owner of the Soma Coal Mine Company for having a Jewish son-in-law. The paper claimed this was the reason why "foreign" media outlets were attacking Turkish Prime Minister Recep Tayyip Erdogan for the tragedy. The headline was followed by a later-deleted tweet by Burhun Kuzu, a senior parliamentarian from Erdogan's AKP party. He wrote that the "Foreign Jewish lobby pounced on Erdogan because of the Soma disaster. But the mine owner's son-in-law is Jewish."[26]

Today, strong ideological currents promote universalism; at the same time, the state of Israel is demonized as nationalist, racist, and colonialist. Meanwhile the mainstream view of absolute evil as committing genocide or behaving like the Nazis has become a very widespread perception of Israel in Western Europe.

Anti-Semitic Cartoons

Once again cartoons can illustrate this point. The Palestinian Authority does not only promote anti-Israelism but also anti-Semitism of the most extreme kind, conveying that Jews are absolute evil. One example is a late-1999 cartoon from *Al-Hayat al-Jadida*, the Palestinian Authority's official daily. It depicts an old Arab man in a *djellaba*, symbolizing the twentieth century, taking leave of a young Arab man symbolizing the twenty-first century. In between them stands a small Jew with a Star of David on his chest, above whom an arrow points to him saying, "the illness of the century."[27]

The Jew depicted as the devil is yet another incarnation of absolute evil. In a Syrian paper, the Zionist devil is presented as a hairy creature with a tail. He has a black kippa (skullcap) on his head and a black beard, which are Jewish stereotypes and not Israeli ones. On his forehead is a Star of David, in his hand a pole with a seven-branched candelabrum.[28] This is one more example of the blending of anti-Jewish and anti-Israeli themes.

In 2006, the Iranian daily *Hamshahri*, owned by the Tehran municipality, launched a Holocaust-cartoon competition. Among those exhibited were several cartoons with the message that Israel is perpetrating a Holocaust against the Palestinians. Abdolhossein Amirizadeh of Iran shows a Jew as a horned devil with vampire fingers reading from a book on which "Holocaust" is written. Next to him is a staff in the form of a seven-branched candelabrum topped by a Star of David.[29]

The Moroccan cartoonist Naji Benaji went further by suggesting that Israel behaved even worse toward the Palestinians than the Germans treated the Jews during World War II. He was awarded a special prize for his drawing of two bottles. One, on which "Holocaust" is written, contains a few skulls; the second carries the Palestinian flag and is filled with skulls.[30]

Belgian political scientist Joël Kotek writes:

> Long before [Ariel] Sharon came to power [as prime minister], the theme of the Israeli as a Nazi appeared in Arab cartoons everywhere. According to them, all Zionists from [Ehud] Barak to Sharon, by way of [Shimon] Peres, drew their inspiration from Nazi methods. The paradox is glaringly obvious when one remembers, first, the Arab sympathies for the Nazi cause during the Second World War and then the support—seldom denounced—given by several Arab intellectuals to denial theory. According to this perspective, "The Zionist crimes appear far worse than 'exaggerated' Nazi crimes."[31]

The medieval perception of the Jew as devil has also reappeared in Norwegian caricatures.[32] The Jewish Satan was represented in a 2003 caricature by Oddmund Mikkelsen in the Norwegian local daily *Hamar Arbeidersblad*, which is close to the Labour Party. It showed then-Prime Minister Sharon with horns.[33]

Over the years the leading Spanish daily *El País* has regularly published anti-Semitic cartoons. Several of these referred to the Holocaust. For instance, it printed a cartoon by Romeu where two people talk to each other. One says, "Sharon's wall is identical to the wall of the Warsaw Ghetto." The other answers, "They are not comparable. Sharon's wall is much more effective." In another cartoon that appeared in *El País* the muse of history, Clio, places a Hitler mustache on Sharon's face.[34]

Anti-Semitic Submotifs Recur

Over the past millennium, the notion that the Jews, who were maligned as having murdered God, were the paradigm of absolute evil and thus capable of all imaginable misdeeds developed into many anti-Semitic submotifs. These, in turn, like the "absolute evil" core motif, recur over the centuries and are also cloaked according to the predominant narrative of the period. Seemingly, there is a large variety of disparate contemporary submotifs of the core hate motif. Yet analysis shows that the major variants are few in number. The main submotifs of the two anti-Semitisms and anti-Israelism are identical, though they may be dressed up somewhat differently.

Deconstructing cartoons enables easy identification of the recurrent submotifs of anti-Semitism. The array of anti-Semitic cartoons from the Arab world is so large that it offers the best starting point. Subsequently, one can also see how contemporary demonization of Israel and the Jews has seeped into caricatures published in mainstream European newspapers.

Several authors have carried out research on anti-Semitic Arab cartoons. Particularly important here is the work of Kotek, an expert analyst of cartoons. His analysis illustrates that Arab cartoons use the same anti-Semitic stereotypes against Israelis and Jews.[35]

Major Anti-Semitic Submotifs

From the perspective of contemporary anti-Semites, the transforming of ancient hate themes into contemporary versions has clear advantages. It is often the case that a proven motif that has succeeded in the past will work in the present if it is somewhat updated.

This mutation of ancient anti-Semitic themes can be seen, for instance, in the promotion of conspiracy theories. As noted, these accusations found their culmination in the Czarist forgery, *The Protocols of the Elders of Zion*.

Boston University historian Richard Landes says:

> In this new century, we see a revival of conspiracy theories. Muslim societies

are most prominent in the production, circulation and belief in them. The best known conspiracy theory is probably that Americans themselves, or the Mossad, carried out the 9/11 terror attacks and not the jihadist Al-Qaeda perpetrators. This belief permeates the elites throughout the Muslim world.

Landes observes:

> Conspiracy theories coming out of the Muslim world are accompanied by another surprising phenomenon. In the past, conspiracists blamed a malevolent other—the Jews, the lepers, the witches, the communists. Now we find Western believers in conspiracy theories which target themselves—for instance on 9/11—in which they *confirm* the paranoid accusations of their enemies. *Postmodern* conspiracy theory's siren song runs: "'We' are to blame, 'our' enemy is innocent."[36]

The supposedly pivotal role of American neoconservatives—a codeword for Jews—in launching the First Iraq War is another recurrent theme. One of the more astute responses was given by Malcolm Hoenlein, executive vice-chairman of the Conference of Presidents of Major American Jewish Organizations. He told how once, replying to listeners' questions on an African American radio station, he was asked about the Jews being behind the Iraq War. He answered in detail, but others kept repeating the question. "I see that the secretary of state is Colin Powell and the national security adviser is Condoleezza Rice," he remarked. "It seems to me that it is more of a black conspiracy." Thereafter the questions stopped.[37]

More Conspiracy Theories

A few examples from a short period at the beginning of 2006 further illustrate the widespread use of conspiracy theories by leaders in the Muslim world. In one case, Iranian President Mahmoud Ahmadinejad said the Jews were behind the Danish cartoons satirizing Mohammed, and declared, "They [who insult the founder of Islam] are hostages of the Zionists. And the people of the U.S. and Europe should pay a heavy price for becoming hostages of Zionism."[38]

In February 2006, the Syrian state-controlled paper *Al-Tawhra* asserted that Israel was responsible for the expanding bird flu phenomenon. It said Israel had spread the virus in the Far East to distract the world while aiming to attack the Arabs.[39]

Later that month, Iran's religious leader Ayatollah Ali Khamenei claimed that Zionists and foreign forces were behind the bombing of the gold-domed Shiite mosque in Samarra, Iraq, on February 22. His words were echoed by Ahmadinejad, who said that "these heinous acts are committed by a group of Zionists and occupiers that have failed. They have failed in the face of Islam's logic and justice."[40]

Germany

A book by German journalist Thomas Jaecker analyzed some examples of twenty-first-century anti-Semitic conspiracy theories in German left-wing, right-wing, and mainstream media.[41] Jaecker focused on three topics: September 11, the battle in the Palestinian refugee camp of Jenin in April 2002, and the First Iraq War.

Jaecker pointed out that, scientifically speaking, the term "conspiracy theory" is misplaced and "conspiracy ideology" or "conspiracy myth" is much more accurate. The basic approach, he explained, is to ascribe complex processes to simple origins. These "theories" display common patterns in that a supposedly powerful group of conspirators is unmasked by a small number of people who resist them. The invented story is then believed by many who do not check the alleged facts.

In Germany since the Holocaust, anti-Semitism has centered partly on the claim that the Jews have managed to extort large sums from the Germans in the form of reparation payments. This is portrayed as an instance of the lust for revenge, attributed to the Old Testament. The next step is to claim that Jews are an international group of conspirators, and that they seek to cast a dark influence over Germany by keeping the Auschwitz theme alive in the media. This, in turn, prevents Germany from becoming a normal state. Some of these motifs have been used by prominent Germans such as Rudolf Augstein, the late publisher of the weekly *Der Spiegel*, and the novelist Martin Walser.[42]

Jaecker also mentioned the bestselling German author Jan van Helsing, who promoted anti-Semitic conspiracy theories. His books sold "hundreds of thousands" of copies in the mid-1990s before they were banned. Van Helsing claimed, for example, that certain German politicians were Jews, without this being known. One of his "examples" was Helmut Kohl, whose true name was, according to him, Henoch Kohn.[43]

Extreme Lust for Power

The false accusation of the Jews' extreme lust for power is one of the major anti-Semitic submotifs. Another submotif is a derivative of it: the Jews have a lust for money and through it, corrupt the world. Today this expresses itself, among other things, as: "Jews control the United States" and "Jewish money controls the world." A third anti-Semitic submotif is that Jews thirst for blood and infanticide. It had precursors in the pre-Christian world but developed mainly in Christian anti-Semitism. The "blood libel" has been used against Jews for many centuries. Today it translates, for instance, into false claims that Israel aims to kill Palestinian children, or that Jews kill Palestinians so as to harvest their organs for reuse.

Another related submotif is that the Jews are poisoners. It has been around since the early fourteenth century when the false charge that Jews were poisoning wells was propagated in parts of Germany and France. One finds the poisoning theme nowadays in several European cartoons.

Yet another submotif is that Jews are subhuman. This was a central theme in Germany under the Nazis, with Jews depicted as vermin or bacteria. It appeared frequently in cartoons that showed Jews as animals. Nowadays this zoomorphism is a staple of Arab anti-Semitic cartoons.[44]

A Current Version of the Conversion Theme

Trying to convert others was, and is, a major characteristic of Christianity. Jews who converted were mostly protected from anti-Semitism and discrimination. This motif has its own current secular mutation: some Jews or Israelis can escape condemnation by their friends provided they publicly oppose Israeli policies. This sometimes also happens in selective academic and similar boycott campaigns against Israel where those Israelis who are willing to denounce their government may be excluded from a boycott.[45] In other cases, Israelis who are suffering from the boycott publicly state that they dissent from their government's policy.

Another variant is that Westerners call on Jews to disassociate themselves from Israel's policies. An example occurred in March 2006 when the editor of a British dance magazine, *Dance Europe*, said she would only publish an article on Israeli choreographer Sally Ann Freeland if Freeland condemned the occupation. She refused and the article was dropped.[46] Economic boycott campaigns against Israel, however, usually leave no room for exceptions.

Behavior of Anti-Israelis

Anti-Zionism and anti-Semitism overlap. Behavior and statements by anti-Israelis about Jews provide additional proof of this point. In 2003, Richard Ingrams wrote in the British weekly *Observer*: "I have developed a habit when confronted by a letter to the editor in support of the Israeli government to look at the signature to see if the writer has a Jewish name; if so, I tend not to read it." He also asserted that those who side with Israeli policy should say whether they are Jewish so as to make this transparent. The British Press Complaints Commission considered Ingrams's position legitimate.[47]

In the same year, Patrick Klugman, then president of the French Union of Jewish Students (UEJF), observed:

> On some university campuses like Nanterre, Villetaneuse and Jussieu, the climate has become very difficult for Jews. In the name of the Palestinian cause, they are castigated as if they were Israeli soldiers! We hear "death to the Jews" during demonstrations which are supposed to defend the Palestinian cause. Last April [2002], our office was the target of a Molotov cocktail. As a condition for condemning this attack, the lecturers demanded that the UEJF declare a principled position against Israel![48]

In the Netherlands, thousands of fans of the Feijenoord soccer team often sang "Gas the Jews" from the stands when it played against the Ajax team of Amsterdam.[49] The same chants occur elsewhere as well in Dutch soccer games. In recent years, the more frequently heard version has a Middle Eastern element: "Hamas, Hamas, Jews to the gas!" Although Ajax is not a Jewish team, it has a group of fervent non-Jewish supporters who, mostly as a reaction to the racist attacks, call themselves "Jews." The word Jew in this context does not refer to actual Jews but is used as the name of a clique. Somewhat similar anti-Semitic chants are also sung on other European soccer fields—for instance, in the UK by opponents of Tottenham Hotspur, a London team with many Jewish supporters.[50]

Two Dutch authors relate another example of how anti-Israelism and anti-Semitism intermingle:

> On 13 April 2002, a pro-Palestinian demonstration on the Dam [Amsterdam's main square] became violent. American and Israeli flags were burned. Placards with texts like "Sharon is Hitler" and "the lie of the six million" dominated the streets. In front of Hotel Krasnapolsky, a man with a kippa was beaten up. The police allowed all of this to happen.[51]

Extreme anti-Semitic and anti-Israeli signs—frequently carried by Muslims—are often seen in marches by antiglobalists and antiwar demonstrators. In many cases these are tolerated by the organizers.

In January 2014, a mass rally in Paris took place. This "Day of Anger" was not related to any specific Jewish topic. Part of the protest was against French President François Hollande's economic plans. However, various groups of participants started to shout anti-Semitic slogans. They included, "Jews, France doesn't belong to you" and (the Holocaust denier) "Faurisson is right," as well as "the Holocaust was a hoax."

French journalist and public intellectual Michel Gurfinkiel wrote that it was shocking that nobody had acted to remove the anti-Semitic protesters. Not even the police had done anything, even though the shouts were in violation of the French hate-speech laws. Gurfinkiel questioned whether French democracy was capable of holding anti-Semitism in check.[52]

The Interrelationship between Anti-Semites and Anti-Israelis

French human rights expert Christophe Ruffin, in a 2004 report he prepared for the country's interior minister, explicitly linked anti-Semitism to the prevalent anti-Israeli mood: "It is not conceivable today to fight actively in France against anti-Semitism in its new forms without going all-out to try and balance anew the public's view of the situation in the Middle East."[53]

The 2004 GMF survey in Germany interviewed 2,656 representatively selected German-speaking people in the country. Thirty-two percent of them agreed, or largely agreed, with the statement: "Because of Israel's policies I have increasing antipathy toward Jews." Forty-four percent agreed that: "Given Israel's policies, I can well understand that people have something against Jews."[54] The same question is asked periodically in polls and the results usually show a correlation.

The study's authors wrote that criticism of Israel is to a certain extent a cover for anti-Semitic attitudes. In their quest to locate the borderlines between anti-Semitism and criticism of Israel, they concluded:

> Criticism of Israel is anti-Semitic when it denies Israel's right of existence and of self-defense. When it draws historical comparisons between Israel's policy toward the Palestinians and the persecution of the Jews in the Third Reich, when it judges Israel's policy with a double standard, when it transfers anti-Semitic stereotypes onto the state of Israel or transfers this criticism to Jews in general and makes Jews generally responsible for events in the Near East.[55]

The 2006 Lebanon War

The Second Lebanon War in 2006 brought much further proof that anti-Semitism and anti-Israelism go hand in hand. During the war, at a demonstration "attended by many Moroccan youngsters in Amsterdam one could see signs like: 'Jews, the army of the Prophet Mohammed is marching.'"[56]

After that war, the European Jewish Congress published a document titled *Anti-Semitic Incidents and Discourse in Europe during the Israel-Hezbollah*

War.[57] A few examples from it highlight the overlap between anti-Semitism and anti-Israelism:

- Gerald Grosz was then head of the right-wing Alliance for the Future of Austria Party (BZÖ) in the Austrian state of Styria; the national party was then led by Jörg Haider. Grosz demanded that the Jewish communities of Vienna and Graz "publicly issue a condemnation of the 'cruel and cowardly murder.'"[58]
- Dan Kantor, executive secretary of the Central Council of Jewish Communities in Finland, noted that: "Marginal extreme-left groups, often in co-operation with Islamic groups in a so-called 'Peace Movement' held weekly small marches, where signs were observed equating the Star of David with Nazi symbols. Such groups make little distinction between Israel and local Finnish Jews, Kantor stated, adding that this is 'nothing new.'"[59]
- In France, the Representative Council of French Jewry (CRIF)—the umbrella body of French Jewish organizations—reported that: "Demonstrations in support of Lebanon took place in different cities throughout France, with anti-Semitic placards visible reading 'Death to the Jews—Death to Israel,' and stars of David emblazoned with swastikas."
- A leaflet sent to a synagogue said: "Wake up France, and join us in refusing that 'Jewry' massacres the Palestinians in their own homeland . . . In France, your duty as well is to combat the Jew. The enemy is the Jew, and they need to be chased from the media, finance, institutions."[60]
- In Germany, over three hundred letters were received by the Jewish umbrella body Zentralrat der Juden in Deutschland "directly attacking both the organization and German Jews for both blindly supporting Israel and spending state money to support a 'fascist state' in the Middle East." Stephan Kramer, then the Zentralrat executive director, referred to the quantity of letters received as "mind-boggling." Furthermore, reports on harassment of Jewish students by Muslim and non-Muslim schoolmates were received by the Berlin Jewish community.[61]
- In the Netherlands in July 2006, Socialist Party chairman Jan Marijnissen "compared Islamic terrorism in the Middle East to the actions of the Dutch resistance against the Nazi German occupiers in World War Two." After major criticism, Marijnissen eventually apologized. He still claimed that the Islamist terrorist groups exist "because of Israel's occupation of Palestine, the American presence in the Middle East and the West's support to undemocratic regimes."[62]

- In Spain, an article

    that appeared in [the leading daily] *El Mundo* entitled *Cauchemar Estival*, made a link between Nazi Germany and Israel, accusing Israel of using the same arguments made by the Nazi leaders to justify "its aggression." The article continues, "Now the victims of this period (the 1930s) have become the executioners . . . The victims of today are systematically taken hostage, reduced to live in ghettos, and closed in by a horrible wall."[63]

Part-Time Anti-Semites

To better understand contemporary Western classic anti-Semitism and its latest major mutation anti-Israelism, two new concepts must be introduced. The first one is *part-time anti-Semites*. These are people who commit anti-Semitic acts intermittently and may even on other occasions make positive gestures toward Jews and Israel.

Norway's prime minister during World War II, Vidqun Quisling, was a "fulltime anti-Semite," twenty-four hours a day, seven days a week. Several contemporary left-of-center Norwegian political leaders commit or condone anti-Semitic acts, including applying double standards to Israel. Yet they may show solidarity with the Jewish community on other occasions, or even speak at Holocaust memorial meetings. It may well be that for some of them, this is an attempt to show that they are not anti-Semites.[64] This, however, does not whitewash their anti-Semitic acts, which may contribute not only to the demonization of Israel but also to the harassment of the country's Jews.

In recent years, one of the major inciters against Israel in the Norwegian Labour Party-dominated government—defeated in the 2013 elections—has been former Foreign Minister Jonas Gahr Støre. Yet this politician also occasionally visited Oslo's synagogue. It happened, for instance, in January 2009 after the major anti-Semitic riots in the Norwegian capital.[65]

An iconic example of a part-time anti-Semite was Austrian Jewish Prime Minister Bruno Kreisky. This Socialist politician said about the Jews, "If they are a people, they are an ugly people."[66] Wistrich described Kreisky as the quintessential left-wing, self-hating Jew. Kreisky claimed that he suffered no anti-Semitism in his youth, which seems highly improbable in view of the widespread anti-Semitic hatred in Austria during the pre-World War II period.

Wistrich also writes that Kreisky was "the one Jew who could grant gentile Austrians full exculpation from a latent sense of guilt over their prominent role in the Holocaust." Kreisky did this in several ways. He ruthlessly attacked Simon Wiesenthal, branding him "a dangerous reactionary." Kreisky was a pioneer in the slandering of Israel as a "semifascist" and "apartheid" state. He also called Israel "undemocratic," "clerical," and "militarist."[67]

Humanitarian Racists

A second concept required for accurately analyzing the current situation in Europe is *humanitarian racism*. This type of racism is rarely recognized. It can be defined as attributing reduced responsibility to people of certain ethnic or national groups for their criminal behavior and intentions, even if these are of major dimensions. Humanitarian racists judge delinquency and crime differently according to the color and socioeconomic status of those who engage in them. For example, white people are held to higher standards of responsibility than people of color.[68]

Israel is frequently blamed for whatever measures it takes to defend its citizens. Palestinian responsibility for suicide bombings, rocket attacks, promoting genocide, glorifying murderers of Israeli civilians, and massive incitement, including that similar to Nazi-type hatred, is often downplayed if not ignored altogether. Similarly, many of those who fight Islamophobia in the Western world remain silent about widespread anti-Semitism in Muslim communities.

The Total War of the 1930s and 1940s

The total war against the Jews of the 1930s and first half of the 1940s was essentially a genocidal crusade against the Jews by their enemies—Germany, Austria, and their allies. It was modern, centrally directed, and continuous.

The main murderous propaganda against the Jews originated with the leader of the National Socialist German Workers Party (NSDAP) and later German chancellor, Adolf Hitler. The major anti-Jewish measures and attacks were initiated by him, or resulted from the policies he proclaimed publicly. They exceeded the discrimination existing elsewhere.

The discriminatory policies were promoted and enacted through the bureaucratic systems of the German state and the NSDAP. From Germany, ideas and instructions flowed to sister parties, affiliates, as well as unorganized sympathizers and collaborators abroad. Once World War II started, many of these people, as well as others, would assist the Nazi occupiers in encouraging and implementing anti-Jewish measures and sometimes even in murdering Jews.

There was other anti-Semitic propaganda as well. Some of its perpetrators collaborated with the Germans, others worked alone. One prominent Arab ally of the Nazis was Haj Amin al-Husseini, the Mufti of Jerusalem, whom many considered the main leader of the Palestinian Arabs. "Openly and knowing about Auschwitz, he had advocated the Shoah. 'Germany,' he declared in 1943, has 'decided to find a final solution to the Jewish menace, which will end this misfortune in the world.'"[69]

In the first half of the twentieth century, the teachings of the Catholic Church, several other churches, and many diverse institutions continued to play a substantial role in propagating international anti-Semitism. On a national basis, governments in the Soviet Union, Poland, some Balkan countries, and others also participated in the hate propagation. There were also important anti-Semitic organizations in many countries that were not linked to the National Socialists; France was a prime example. However severe the anti-Semitism of many others, it usually paled next to that of the murderous system Hitler controlled.

One might compare the anti-Semitism of the 1930s with noxious factories. From their large chimneys, poison and pollution constantly spread over a wide area. Contemporary anti-Semitism, however, comes from many sources, like the pollution from a huge number of car exhausts. That also explains why the propaganda war today has the character of "a million cuts."

Promoters of the contemporary total propaganda war against Israel have many precursors in Christian anti-Semitism over the centuries. Examples were medieval monks who went from town to town spreading hatred of the Jews, which often led to their murder. The Crusades and their mass murder of Jewish communities had many elements of a propaganda hate campaign. In the fourteenth century, many European Jewish communities were massacred after false accusations of poisoning water sources were spread.

The twentieth-century Germans, with their ideology of political anti-Semitism and National Socialism, turned the mass murder of the Jews into an international industrial operation. Its major elements included registration, systematic discrimination, transportation to—extermination or other—camps, forced labor, and murder.

The Postmodern Propaganda War

The current total propaganda war against Israel in the twenty-first century is of a different overall nature than its predecessors, partly because of its fragmented character. It has both major similarities and differences with the widespread hate campaign against the Jews that led in the previous century to the Holocaust.

One main similarity is that both hate campaigns encompassed a large number of perpetrators and accomplices. Another is the considerable role that governments play. In the first half of the previous century, this mainly involved Germany and other extreme nationalist countries. Today it includes politicians, officials, and state-owned media of many Arab and Muslim states, including those with which Israel is at peace. The main difference between today's total war and that of the previous century lies in the dispersed character of the hostilities.

The *Report of the British All-Party Parliamentary Inquiry into Anti-Semitism* also observed:

> Anti-Zionist discourse can be polluted with anti-Semitic themes in different ways and with different levels of intent. It can be used deliberately as a way to mask or articulate prejudice against Jews. It is difficult to counter because one must first identify and explain the anti-Semitism behind the language and imagery. For instance, a far right party may use the terms of "Zionist" and "Zionism" instead of "Jews" and "Jewish."[70]

The Three Stages

Another important aspect of the total propaganda and discrimination war is the development of its various stages. The war of the 1930s and thereafter had three partly overlapping phases. The first consisted of systematic and extreme defamation of the Jews. The second aimed at gradually excluding them from society. The third centered on their annihilation.

The total war against Israel in the twenty-first century already contains elements of all three phases. We are now primarily in the first stage, that of extreme defamation. The assault is mainly aimed at Israel; Jews are a lesser but still significant target of contemporary anti-Semites.

Several elements of the second stage have emerged mainly in recent years. These include various attempts to exclude Israel or Israelis from international forums. Another aspect involves boycott initiatives of various kinds. Some initiatives aim at Israeli universities and academics; others, in part instigated by certain liberal Protestant churches, are directed at certain suppliers of Israel. Yet others act against Israeli companies, mainly but not only from the West Bank. Still others try to persuade artists not to perform in Israel. A further approach is to promote divestment of shares of Israeli companies. The most extreme boycott Israel entirely.[71]

Elements of the third stage are (yet?) largely verbal in nature. However, they also manifest themselves in some murderous attacks on Israeli civilians as well as Jews abroad. There are many, mainly in Arab and Muslim countries and environments, who aim for the physical destruction of Israel.

For example, in June 2002, Iran held the International Conference on Imam Khomeini and Support for Palestine, in which the country's Supreme Leader Ayatollah Ali Khamenei participated. "The Iranian organizer of the conference, Ali Akbar Mohtashemi-Pur, declared, 'Israel is a cancerous tumor in the heart of the Muslim world which should be removed,' and lauded the attacks carried out by Palestinian suicide bombers."[72]

Many politicians and religious leaders in the Arab world support homicide bombings by radical Muslims against civilians. As for Palestinian suicide bombings, one of their best-known senior religious supporters is Egyptian-born Sheikh Yusuf al-Qaradawi, who currently heads the Sunni Studies Department at Qatar University.

Al-Qaradawi appears frequently on the Arabic satellite TV channel Al Jazeera, reaching a wide audience. Among other things, he criticized the Imam of Mecca: "It is unfortunate to hear that the grand imam has said it was not permissible to kill civilians in any country or state, even in Israel."[73]

One finds explicit support for murder among some Westerners as well. Others express their profoundly anti-Semitic mindsets by stating their desire that the Jewish state disappear.

One example is Ted Honderich, a Canadian-born philosophy professor (emeritus) at University College in London. He has publicly stated that the Palestinians have a moral right to blow up the Jews. He even encouraged them to do so by saying, "To claim a moral right on behalf of the Palestinians to their terrorism is to say that they are right to engage in it, that it is permissible if not obligatory."[74] Honderich has repeated this position frequently, including at the University of Leipzig in Germany.[75]

Gianni Vattimo, a leading Italian philosopher, said in a radio interview during the 2014 Protective Edge campaign that there should be international brigades as in the Spanish Civil War to fight Israel. He called the Israeli government "fascist" and claimed it was destroying an entire people. He also said that a genocide was taking place. He called the Hamas rockets "toy rockets" and said he wanted to organize an international financing campaign so that true weapons could be purchased for the Palestinians. He added that Europe should give the Palestinians arms free of charge.[76] He also said in the interview, "I would like to shoot those Zionist bastards."[77]

Numerical Data

Various numerical data offer evidence of how much the hatred of Israel and Jews has increased. At least 150 million citizens of sixteen years and older in the European Union embrace a demonic view of Israel. Proof of this comes from a study published in 2011 by the University of Bielefeld. It was carried out on behalf of the German Social Democratic Friedrich Ebert Foundation.[78]

The study was undertaken in seven European countries. Researchers polled one thousand people per country over the age of sixteen in fall 2008. One of the questions asked was whether they agreed with the assertion that Israel is carrying out a war of extermination against the Palestinians. The lowest percentages of those who agreed were in Italy and the Netherlands, with 38 percent and 39 percent respectively. Other percentages were: Hungary 41 percent, United Kingdom 42 percent, Germany 48 percent, and Portugal 49 percent. In Poland the figure was 63 percent.

In the first years of this century the University of Bielefeld undertook a similar study, this one relating to Germany only. More than 2,500 people there were asked whether they agreed with the statement: "What the state of Israel does today to the Palestinians is in principle no different from what the Nazis did to the Jews in the Third Reich." Fifty-one percent answered in the affirmative.[79]

Sixty-one percent concurred with the statement: "I am fed up with hearing over and over about the German crimes against Jews." Sixty-eight percent agreed that: "Israel undertakes a war of destruction against the Palestinians."

The study concluded that criticism of Israel is to a certain extent a cover for anti-Semitic attitudes and opinions. In their earlier-mentioned definition of anti-Semitism, the study group of the University of Bielefeld had stated that it was anti-Semitic to compare "Israel's policy toward the Palestinians and the persecution of the Jews in the Third Reich."[80]

According to this definition, the majority of Germans polled hold extreme anti-Semitic views. Thirty-five percent fully agreed and 33 percent were inclined to agree that Israel is working to destroy the Palestinians. Twenty-seven percent fully agreed and 24 percent were inclined to agree that Israel's conduct toward the Palestinians is essentially the same as the Nazis' toward the Jews. Only 19 percent totally disagreed and 30 percent were inclined to disagree.[81] The findings of this survey, published in 2004, reinforced findings of earlier surveys on German anti-Semitism that several authors have analyzed.[82]

More Studies

A study published in Switzerland by *gfs.bern* in 2007 found that 50 percent of the Swiss population see Israel as "the Goliath in the extermination war of the Palestinians."[83]

In 2012, in a study carried out by the Center for Studies of the Holocaust and Religious Minorities in Norway, a sample group of people were asked, "Is what Israel does to the Palestinians identical to what the Nazis did to the Jews?" Thirty-eight percent of Norwegians interviewed gave an affirmative answer.[84]

In September 2014, the Friedrich Ebert Foundation and Bielefeld University carried out another study in Germany. One of the questions was again whether people agreed with the statement: "Israel conducts a war of extermination against the Palestinians." Forty percent of Germans agreed; the comparative figure for 2004 was 68 percent. The question was asked also in another way: "What the state of Israel does today to the Palestinians is in principle no different from what the Nazis did to the Jews during the Third Reich." In 2014, 27 percent answered affirmatively, compared to 51 percent in 2004.[85]

Some may be surprised that researchers ventured to ask questions about Israel as committing genocide or as a Nazi state. Yet the answer to this question is simple. The researchers had probably realized that this extreme anti-Semitic belief about Israel is widespread in their social environment.

As additional studies are published over the years, asking similar questions, the percentages of respondents may greatly vary. That does not, however, change the main finding: a huge number of Europeans have a diabolical view of Israel.

A Very Negative Picture of Israel

In 2003, a Eurobarometer study asked whether a number of countries were a threat to world peace. It turned out that 59 percent of Europeans believed Israel posed such a threat. No other country on the list was considered a similar threat by such a high percentage. Iran and North Korea tied for second place at 53 percent. At the bottom of the list was the European Union, which only 8 percent of Europeans saw as a danger to world peace.

Among the then fifteen EU countries, the highest percentage viewing Israel as a threat to world peace was found among the Dutch at 74 percent. Next in line were the Austrians with 69 percent.[86]

In 2013, the BBC published a poll asking twenty-six thousand people from twenty-five countries around the world whether they viewed a list of sixteen countries and the European Union as having a "mainly positive" or "mainly negative" influence in the world.

> Germany topped the list with 59 percent of respondents viewing it positively, followed by Canada (55%), the U.K. (55%) and Japan (51%). Only North Korea, Pakistan, and Iran had lower positive scores than Israel. Twenty-one percent of respondents viewed Israel's influence as mainly positive, while 52% saw the Jewish State's influence as mainly negative. Israel's "positivity" ranking was identical to the score it received in the 2012 BBC poll.
>
> Just 15% of respondents considered Iran's influence as mainly positive, while 59% said the Islamic Republic's influence was mainly negative. France finished fifth as a positive influence (49%), followed by the E.U. (49%), Brazil (46%), U.S. (45%), China (42%), South Korea (36%), South Africa (35%), India (34%) and Russia (30%).[87]

All these data together indicate how profound the demonization of Israel has become. Blaming contemporary anti-Semitism in Europe primarily on Muslim immigrants and their descendants is an easy and convenient yet partly false explanation. If Muslims formed the dominant percentage of people who had answered the questions about Israel negatively, such high figures for extreme views of Israel would not have been possible. Yet there is no doubt, and the few studies available show it as well, that the major nonselective immigration from Muslim countries into Europe has brought with it a higher percentage of anti-Semites and also more extreme ones compared to the autochthonous population.[88]

Italian and Other Polls

An Italian poll conducted by Paolo Merulla in fall 2003 found that only 43 percent of Italians are sympathetic toward Israel. Seventeen percent said it would be better if Israel did not exist. Twenty percent thought Jews were not real Italians; 10 percent thought Jews were lying when they said that Nazism murdered millions of Jews.[89] This study is yet another indicator of a connection between anti-Semitism and anti-Israelism.

Even more telling was a major survey conducted in 2003 among approximately 2,200 Italian youngsters aged fourteen to eighteen. Broadly speaking, one-third of them considered that Jews hold the reins of financial power. Twenty to twenty-five percent considered, among the negative traits of Jews, that they "feel themselves superior to everyone else," "are too attached to money," and "can never be completely trusted." About 20 percent felt that Jews exaggerate when speaking about the Holocaust and close to 20 percent thought Jews should "return to Israel." That similarity proves again that hardcore anti-Semitism and anti-Israelism are linked.[90]

Yet another poll carried out in nine EU countries around that time for the Italian daily *Corriere della Sera* found substantial anti-Semitic trends. In all countries, anti-Semitic sentiment paralleled anti-Israeli sentiment.[91] A poll conducted around the same time in the United Kingdom found that almost 20 percent of the British consider that a Jewish prime minister would be less acceptable than a non-Jewish one.[92] This was particularly relevant as Michael Howard, the Conservative Party's leader at the time, was Jewish.

A 2014 Pew study found that 47 percent of Greeks viewed Jews unfavorably. This was followed by 26 percent of Poles, 24 percent of Italians, and 18 percent of Spaniards. In France, the UK, and Germany, 10 percent or fewer of respondents viewed Jews unfavorably.[93]

Across Europe, anti-Semitism and anti-Israelism have been on the rise. In some countries anti-Semitism has increased, with 50-60 percent of people polled stating they have an unfavorable view of Jews. Many of those polled had never met a Jew before. Results of the poll for *Corriere della Sera* also showed that 35 percent of Spaniards aged eighteen to forty-four could not place the Holocaust chronologically, and two-thirds of European respondents did not know how many Jews were killed by the Nazis.[94]

A 2011 study that partially focused on Italian anti-Semitism was commissioned at the initiative of Fiamma Nirenstein. She was then an Italian parliamentarian and chairperson of the Sub-Committee of Inquiry into Anti-Semitism. The study found several disturbing aspects of how Italians perceive Jews. Forty-four percent of those polled were found to "harbour some prejudice or have a hostile attitude toward Jews." One in three Italians find Jews to be "not very nice."

One in four Italians agree that Jews are "not fully Italian." Additionally,

> About 10 per cent have a more traditional anti-Jewish prejudice, religious in nature; 11 per cent accept a "modern," more xenophobic, prejudice; 12 per cent have a "contingent" prejudice often linked to their opinion of Israel. Then there are a further 12 per cent, driven by pure anti-Jewish sentiment: these are the interviewees who declare their agreement with all the anti-Jewish statements in the questionnaire.

This study also found that 26 percent of Italians believe that Jews are more loyal to Israel than to the country of their birth, 26 percent think that "Jews have changed from being a race of victims to a race of aggressors," 21.6 percent consider that "Jews are doing to the Palestinians what the Nazis did to Jews," and 15.1 percent agree that "Basically Jews have always lived at the expense of others."

Furthermore, 25.3 percent believe that "Jews control the mass media in many countries," 31.7 percent agree that "Jews run the world's banks for their own benefit," 27.1 percent agree that "Jews always manage to wield disproportionate political power," 30.3 percent feel that "Jews talk too much about their own tragedies and ignore other people's," and 26.7 percent agree that "when it comes down to it, the Jews always hold the purse strings." Lastly, 24.5 percent consider that "Jews exploit the Nazi extermination to justify Israel's policies."

Other Italians polled did view Jews favorably. Some 27.1 percent think that "Jews have made a great contribution to different areas of Italian society," 26.8 percent agree that "modern science would not be what it is today without the contribution of Jews," 23.3 percent agree that "Despite the conflict Jews are sensitive to the suffering of the Palestinian people," and 22.6 percent agree that "Western culture owes a debt of gratitude to Jewish culture for many fundamental ideas."[95]

In 2015, a YouGov poll was commissioned by the Campaign Against Anti-Semitism in the United Kingdom. The poll found that:

> one in four (25%) Britons believed that Jews chase money more than other British people . . .

> One in six (17%) felt Jews thought they were better than other people and had too much power in the media, while one in 10 people (11%) claimed Jews were not as honest in business as other people . . . One in five believed their loyalty to Israel made British Jews less loyal to the UK, while one in 10 people (10%) said they would be unhappy if a relative married a Jew.[96]

Negative views about people are politically far more dangerous than positive views are beneficial. Although several polls indicate that many people in Europe hold positive views about Jews, these have less impact than those of the anti-Semitic hate-mongers.

The 2013 FRA Study

Statistics also show that a substantial number of Jews in Europe have encountered anti-Semitism. A 2013 study by the FRA proved this. Of those who had undergone anti-Semitic incidents with recognizable perpetrators, 27 percent blamed Muslims, 22 percent blamed people with left-wing views, and 19 percent blamed extreme rightists.[97]

The statistics regarding Muslim incitement were even higher for those who had experienced extreme anti-Semitic violence. Most respondents perceived 40 percent of perpetrators of extreme physical violence as someone with a "Muslim extremist view," 25 percent as being teenagers, 20 percent as "someone else" or "other," 14 percent as someone with a "left-wing political view," 10 percent as "someone with a right-wing political view," and 9 percent respectively "a colleague or supervisor at work" and a "neighbor."[98] Those who made negative statements about Jews were found to be 53 percent left-wing, 51 percent Muslim extremist, 39 percent right-wing, and 19 percent Christian extremist.[99]

Researchers at Yale University analyzed an Anti-Defamation League (ADL) opinion survey of five hundred citizens in each of ten European countries. They found that anti-Israeli sentiment "consistently predicts the probability that an individual is anti-Semitic, with the likelihood of measured anti-Semitism increasing with the extent of anti-Israel sentiment observed."[100]

As aforementioned, already in 2004 in a report for the French interior minister, Christophe Ruffin explicitly linked anti-Semitism to the anti-Israeli mood prevailing in that country.[101]

In a 2006 report titled "Campus Anti-Semitism," the U.S. Commission on Civil Rights found among other things that "Anti-Israeli or anti-Zionist propaganda has been disseminated on many campuses that include traditional anti-Semitic elements, including age-old anti-Jewish stereotypes and defamation." A second finding was that "anti-Semitic bigotry is no less morally deplorable when camouflaged as anti-Israelism or anti-Zionism." The report also stated: "substantial evidence suggests that many university departments of Middle East studies provide one-sided, highly polemical academic presentations and some may repress legitimate debate concerning Israel."[102]

Classic Anti-Semitism

Many Europeans continue to hold classic anti-Semitic stereotypes.[103] Several opinion surveys show that tens of millions of Europeans are hard-core, classic anti-Semites. A 2002 poll conducted on behalf of the ADL in Austria, Switzerland, Spain, Italy, and the Netherlands found that one out of five respondents "harbor strong anti-Semitic views."[104]

A 2012 ADL survey in ten European countries asked people whether they agreed with a number of statements.[105] In six out of ten countries, the majority of those interviewed agreed that it is probably true that "Jews are more loyal to Israel" than to their own country. The highest percentage was in Spain with 72 percent, followed by Poland and Italy with 61 percent, Norway with 58 percent, Hungary with 55 percent, and Germany with 52 percent. The lowest percentage was in France with 45 percent, the Netherlands and Austria were at 47 percent, and the United Kingdom was at 48 percent. This data indicates that large percentages of Europeans continue to question the loyalty of their Jewish compatriots.

A 2005 ADL poll in Europe asked whether the Jews were responsible for the death of Jesus. Nineteen percent of Belgians, 21 percent of Danes, and 19 percent of the Swiss people polled answered affirmatively.[106] The 2012 ADL poll in Europe asked the same question. It was found that among those polled

18 percent of Austrians, 14 percent of Germans, 38 percent of Hungarians, 15 percent of Italians, 16 percent of Dutch, 19 percent of Norwegians, 46 percent of Poles, 21 percent of Spaniards, and 18 percent in the United Kingdom believed this fallacy.[107] In a 2011 ADL poll in Argentina, 22 percent also believed the Jews killed Jesus.[108] Agreeing with this statement is a stereotypical example of anti-Semitism.

The 2012 ADL survey also asked the respondents whether their opinion of Jews was influenced by Israel's actions. Thirty-nine percent of those interviewed in Norway said yes. They were followed by 37 percent in Austria, 34 percent in Germany, 29 percent in Spain, 27 percent each in Poland and Hungary, 26 percent in Italy, and 25 percent in the Netherlands. The two countries with the lowest figures were France with 12 percent and the United Kingdom with 23 percent.

Those who responded that their opinion of Jews was influenced by Israel were asked a follow-up question: whether Israel's actions made their opinion of Jews better or worse. Sixty-five percent said they made it worse. The highest percentages were among respondents in the Netherlands at 85 percent, Hungary at 80 percent, and Norway at 78 percent. That figure may indicate that close to 30 percent of all Norwegians hold a more negative opinion of Jews because of their negative view of Israel.[109]

In a 2011 poll in Argentina carried out by the ADL, the Delegation of Argentine Jewish Associations, and the Gino Germani Research Institute, 26 percent of respondents strongly believed that "Jews are more loyal to Israel than to this country." Twenty-six percent partially agreed, for a total of 52 percent of Argentine respondents agreeing that Jews are more loyal to Israel.[110] The ADL also performed the same survey in the United States in 2013. Here, 30 percent of respondents believed that "Jews are more loyal to Israel than to their own country."[111]

The 2014 ADL Global Survey

In May 2014, the ADL released a global survey of anti-Semitism, the largest such report ever. It covered more than a hundred countries, and its results indicate that there are seventy anti-Semites for every Jew.[112] Thus, if the world's billion-plus adult anti-Semites were living in a single country, it would be the third largest after China and India. This is even an understatement, since, as children would be included, that country would probably be the largest on earth.

One of this survey's important contributions was new, key information about massive anti-Semitism in the Palestinian territories and the greater Muslim world. This added much to what was known earlier from several Pew Research surveys about hate-mongering there.

The ten territories with the highest index scores were, in order: the West Bank and Gaza, Iraq, Yemen, Algeria, Libya, Tunisia, Kuwait, Bahrain, Jordan, and Morocco. In all of these 80 percent or more of respondents demonstrated anti-Semitic views. The next six countries also came from the Arab world.[113]

The study as presented, however, also raised question marks about anti-Semitism in various countries, regions, and religions. One of the key issues concerns its definition of anti-Semites. ADL pollsters asked eleven questions about anti-Semitic stereotypes; they then defined those who agreed with six of them as anti-Semites.

These questions included the four included in the 2012 study. The other seven were: "Jews don't care what happens to anyone but their own kind," "Jews have too much control over global affairs," "Jews have too much control over the United States government," "Jews think they are better than other people," "Jews have too much control over the global media," "Jews are responsible for most of the world's wars," and "people hate Jews because of the way Jews behave."

However, questions asked did not include: "Do you believe that Jews are apes and pigs?" This question is very relevant in Muslim environments. The Nazis claimed that Jews were subhuman. Anyone who believes that Jews are animals has a similar extreme anti-Semitic mindset regardless of how he or she answers those eleven questions.

The same goes for another unasked question, which is mainly relevant in Christian environments: "Are Jews responsible for Jesus' death?" That belief laid the infrastructure of the "satanic Jew"—or the Jew as absolute evil—which in turn led to discrimination, pogroms, and expulsions in a number of Christian lands. According to the ADL study, 9 percent of Americans are anti-Semitic.

However, an ADL study in 2013 found that 26 percent of Americans believe that Jews killed Jesus.[114]

No questions were asked about anti-Semitic attitudes regarding Israel. Only one question derives an indirect indication of the extent of hatred of Israel from the "positive" answers to the survey question: "Jews are more loyal to Israel than to the countries they live in." With 41 percent answering "probably true," this is the most believed of all stereotypes in the 2014 ADL study.

The exclusion of questions about anti-Israelism led to a mistakenly positive view of European countries. The ADL Global Index ranked Sweden as the third least anti-Semitic country among the 102 analyzed—with 4 percent of the population anti-Semitic—after Laos and the Philippines. The 2013 FRA study, however, found that among the eight EU countries surveyed, 60 percent of Swedish Jews see anti-Semitism as a big or fairly big problem. Thirty-seven percent of Swedish Jews said anti-Semitism had increased greatly over the past five years, while 43 percent responded that it had increased a little. Twenty-two percent had personal experiences of verbal insults or harassment and/or physical anti-Semitic attacks over the past twelve months.

Sixty percent of Swedish Jews never or rarely wear anything in public that makes them identifiable as Jews. This was the highest percentage for any country in the FRA study. Malmö, the third largest city in Sweden, is often considered "Europe's capital of anti-Semitism." This gives a very different picture than Sweden's "benign" ranking on the ADL index.

The fourth least anti-Semitic country according to the ADL index is the Netherlands. The 2011 survey by the University of Bielefeld asked people in seven EU countries whether they agreed with the—extremely anti-Semitic—statement that Israel "is conducting a war of extermination against the Palestinians."[115] Forty-three percent of all those surveyed answered in the affirmative; in the Netherlands the figure was close to 39 percent. The ADL study implies that there are fewer than seven hundred thousand adult anti-Semites in the Netherlands. The Bielefeld study indicates that there are about five million!

Perception and Reality

It is revealing to compare the number of people killed over the past years 2007-2012 in all of the conflicts Israel was involved in with those of other recent wars and violent conflicts. In Israel's largest military campaigns from 2007 to 2012, Operations Cast Lead and Pillar of Defense in Gaza, altogether 2,500 casualties were recorded. Outside of these larger conflicts, most violence has involved Palestinian attacks and targeted actions by the Israel Defense Forces.[116, 117]

These death totals were far below those of the civil wars in Syria and Iraq and the wars in Afghanistan and Iraq. In the latter two, several European countries were involved. The global impact of these violent conflicts goes far beyond political issues. They have, for instance, entailed a huge expenditure for the United States, which has greatly added to worldwide concern about the stability of the dollar. If confidence in the dollar declines further due to this instability, it is likely to cause even more problems worldwide.

In 2007, Gunnar Heinsohn and Daniel Pipes ranked world conflicts since 1950 with more than ten thousand casualties. There were sixty-seven of them, and the Arab-Israeli conflict came in forty-ninth place.[118] Some of these other conflicts totaled tens of times more deaths than the Arab-Israeli one. Yet the fallacy that the Israeli-Palestinian conflict is the greatest threat to world peace is repeated on a regular basis.

The notion that Israel is a major threat to world peace was promoted by one of the leading Jewish anti-Israeli inciters, Noam Chomsky. In 2012, he called the United States and Israel the greatest threats to world peace. He wrote that Israel is a greater threat than Iran because "Israel refuses to sign the Non-Proliferation Treaty and allow inspections, as Iran has done. Israel continues to defy the overwhelming international call for a nuclear-weapons-free zone in the region." Chomsky added a major lie about the number of people killed by Israel:

> Like its patron, Israel resorts to violence at will. It persists in illegal settlement in occupied territory, some annexed, all in brazen defiance of international law and the U.N. Security Council. It has repeatedly carried out brutal attacks against Lebanon and the imprisoned people of Gaza, killing tens of thousands without credible pretext . . . Iran too has carried out aggression—but during

> the past several hundred years, only under the U.S.-backed regime of the shah, when it conquered Arab islands in the Persian Gulf.[119]

In fall 2013, Iranian Foreign Minister Mohammad Javad Zarif told the BBC that sectarian tension between Shiite and Sunni Muslims is probably the most serious threat to world security.[120] One hardly if ever hears this from Western experts who should have stated it long ago.

The aforementioned studies illustrate that demonic worldviews about Israel are widespread in mainstream Europe. That these studies are virtually ignored by political and civil leaders is yet another indicator of Europe's decaying norms and values.

Extreme Slander

The accusation that Israel is exterminating the Palestinians constitutes extreme slander. During the two years from the end of 1941 to the end of 1943 in the extermination camps of Treblinka, Belzec, and Sobibor alone, two million people—mainly Jews—were murdered by the Germans. Technology, including that of murder, has greatly "advanced" since then. If the genocidal accusations against Israel were true, the last of the Palestinian adults and children would have been killed long ago.

In reality, the number of Palestinians has continued to *increase* greatly over the past decades. Palestinian children are born in Israeli hospitals and sick ones are treated by Israeli doctors.

Not only Palestinians but also a number of Syrian war victims are treated in Israeli hospitals. By April 2014, that number exceeded a thousand. With Syrian hospitals lacking proper equipment to take care of the war's most severely injured, both rebel forces and Bashar al-Assad supporters have been treated by Israeli doctors at hospitals in northern Israel. This occurs even though Israel and Syria are in a state of war and have no diplomatic relations.[121]

The aforementioned data not only illustrate the widespread overlap between contemporary anti-Semitism and anti-Israelism. They also offer compelling proof of the demonization of Israel in a sizable part of the European mainstream. This, in turn, is an indicator of a reemerging and widespread criminal European mindset, for which the infrastructure has been laid by many opinion makers over the decades.

CHAPTER TWO

Postwar Europe, Anti-Semitism, and Anti-Israelism

The history of European anti-Semitism goes back many centuries. Its impact, however, differed from country to country. Although its anti-Israeli mutations are particularly widespread, the hatred and incitement are so fragmented that also major aspects of European classic anti-Semitism must be analyzed in more detail. This is especially so given the huge criminal acts and attitudes toward its Jewish citizens on the continent in the past.

The overall relationship between Europe and Israel also needs to be assessed in this context. The interaction can be characterized as complex, tense, and historically loaded. Their respective political outlooks are also increasingly diverging. At the same time, relations in areas such as trade, science, culture, and sports have continued to grow over the decades and have only been somewhat affected by political discordance.

It is frequently claimed that assessing European-Israeli relations requires establishing an average level of the interactions in the various fields. To consider this a balanced approach, however, is mistaken. European political actions can continue to cause Israel such major harm that they may increasingly dominate all other aspects of the relationship in the long run.

The European Union (EU) consists of twenty-eight states with a population of over five hundred million people covering a territory of well over four million square kilometers. Israel's population is eight million. It is a small country surrounded by enemies, even if some of these are at peace with it. Israel covers a territory much smaller than one-hundredth of the EU's size. Twenty-four of the EU member states have a larger territory than Israel. Hence, Europe and Israel are not comparable entities. Given this imbalance in power, populations, and geographic size, an analysis must focus primarily on the much larger European side.

Post-Holocaust Discrimination

European anti-Semitism did not disappear after the Holocaust. In the immediate postwar period, reestablished democratic societies such as Norway, the Netherlands, and others discriminated against Jews in various ways and in many domains.[1] Often Jews returning home found that they were not welcome.

Dutch political scientist Isaac Lipschits said, "Post-war discrimination against the Jews in the Netherlands manifested itself in many ways. Authorities belittled the Jews and neglected their interests. Public feeling was that the Jewish community no longer represented anything."[2]

Norwegian historian Bjarte Bruland, who played a key role in the country's restitution investigations of the mid-1990s, said that among the survivors of the small prewar Norwegian Jewish community, there were many "stateless Jews who had fled to Sweden, some of whom had lived in Norway for as long as 50 years, prior to the war. The Norwegian government initially refused to allow them to return to the country, a position which only later changed."[3]

Postwar legislation and its implementation in many countries frequently favored those who possessed the Jews' stolen property while, at the same time, liberated countries embellished their war history. The Netherlands is one of many examples. The Anne Frank story has largely overshadowed many aspects of negative treatment of Jews in the Netherlands.

Johannes Houwink ten Cate, a Dutch Holocaust and genocide expert, notes that the Belgian historian Pieter Lagrou wrote about the Dutch postwar national memory that it was

> "harsh" toward those who had suffered more than others. "The Jewish survivors of the genocide in particular suffered from a lack of recognition . . ., from a lack

of support," both in material terms and in terms of "their need for integration."[4] Thus, the few Jewish survivors—75% of Dutch Jewry was deported to Eastern Europe in order to be murdered—"struck a bad deal," according to the impartial Lagrou: "no solidarity for them, no consolation."[5]

Houwink ten Cate adds:

> It took a long time until Holocaust awareness developed in Western Europe. Academics studying this subject found that much went terribly wrong in these societies during the initial post-war decades. This manifested itself in several ways. One was that prominent European politicians promoted self-images of heroic resistance against the Nazis. Another was that these politicians were unwilling to help Jewish survivors financially.
>
> They shifted responsibility for the persecution and extermination of the Jews as much as possible onto the Germans. This meant ignoring the huge assistance that the Germans received from many members of the occupied nations in their expropriations and deportations of the Jews.

He furthermore remarks:

> In France in 1987, eminent historian Henry Rousso coined the neologism "Résistancialisme" to describe the Gaullist effort to lump together Resistance, nation and state, but this effort was not as dominant as its Dutch counterpart. Nevertheless, for 35 years, French historians ignored the co-responsibility of the Vichy government for persecution of the Jews. It was not until 1981 that American historian Robert O. Paxton and his Canadian colleague Michael R. Marrus, fully described this co-responsibility.[6]
>
> The situation was not fundamentally different in West Germany. It first became a habit of the authorities in various states of the Soviet bloc and later of the German left to correctly proclaim that the track record of the German Federal Republic in bringing Holocaust perpetrators to justice was poor.[7]
>
> It was as poor as the actual performance of the French, Belgian and Dutch states in bringing their bureaucrats who had aided the Germans, to trial. These civil servants went unpunished as a group.[8]

Latency and Reemergence of Anti-Semitism

During the decades after World War II, European anti-Semitism became increasingly latent. In the twenty-first century, however, it has become clear that many Europeans hold anti-Semitic opinions of both the new and the classic kind. This widespread resurgence of anti-Semitism, despite the "lessons of the Holocaust" and the proclaimed policy of "never again," suggests it is an integral part of European culture and its value systems. Much of Europe's history provides extensive proof of that point. This should not imply that all or most Europeans are anti-Semites, though many are concerning either Jews or Israel.

French sociologist Shmuel Trigano was one of the first to analyze the outbreak of anti-Israelism in the new century. He focused on the greatly increased violence against Jews in France since 2000. Years later he said:

> The situation of the Jews in France was aggravated as various media expressed opinions claiming that the violence and hate was quite understandable in view of events in the Middle East and Israel's policies. This implied that the destiny of French Jews was determined by Israeli policies and French criticism of them.
>
> During the first months of attacks, French Jewry requested help, but no one listened. This led many French Jews to realize that their place and citizenship in the country was now questionable. They understood that the authorities were willing to sacrifice the Jewish community to maintain social peace. This attitude was reinforced by the French pro-Arab policy in the Iraq War.
>
> Jewish citizens could not understand that violent acts were being committed against them in the name of developments 3,000 kilometers away. Today, there are those who still remember the words of Hubert Védrine, former Socialist minister of foreign affairs, which have been repeated in different variations by several politicians: "One does not necessarily have to be shocked that young Frenchmen of immigrant origin have compassion for the Palestinians and are very agitated because of what is happening to them."[9]

French philosopher, political scientist, and historian Pierre-André Taguieff was also among the first in the new century to discuss in detail that by the end of 2001, anti-Semitism had reached levels unprecedented in post-Nazi periods in both the Arab world and Europe. His insight was enhanced by living in France where, among West European countries, the anti-Semitic attacks were particularly violent.[10]

Taguieff also exposed the widespread fallacy that Islamophobia was a larger problem than anti-Semitism at the time. The risk for Jews of being attacked in France was and probably remains many tens of times greater than for Muslims.

Of the Jewish communities surveyed in eight countries by the 2013 FRA study, French Jews experienced the most anti-Semitism in public space. Seventy-one percent of French Jews surveyed experienced anti-Semitism in the media, 84 percent encountered "Expressions of hostility toward Jews in the street or other public places," 79 percent had seen anti-Semitic graffiti in France, and 78 percent had seen vandalism of Jewish buildings and institutions. These figures were the highest for the eight countries surveyed.[11] Furthermore, 73 percent of French respondents felt that the Arab-Israeli conflict affected their feelings of safety "a great deal."[12]

Lastly, of all the eight EU countries, French Jews worried the most about physical and verbal anti-Semitic attacks. Seventy percent of French Jews worried about becoming the victim of a physical attack, and 60 percent worried about becoming the victim of a verbal attack. Additionally, 76 percent worried that a family member or person close to him or her would become a victim of a physical attack, and 71 percent worried that someone close to them would become a victim of a verbal attack.[13]

In May 2014, Roger Cukierman, president of CRIF, gave a lecture at the French consulate in New York. He pointed to three major challenges facing French Jewry: "an increasingly radicalized Muslim immigrant population that scapegoats Jews, the growing popularity of the far-right National Front Party headed by Marine Le Pen and widespread anti-Israel sentiment among French leftists." He added that in France, 40 percent of violent hate crimes target Jews. Cukierman remarked, "It's not so pleasant living there as Jews at present." He also noted that Qatar is in a position to influence France's economy and, while this has not yet happened, it is a further threat.[14]

Some of the many attacks get more attention than others. In December 2014 a Jewish couple was attacked in Créteil, a Parisian suburb in which the Jewish population constitutes more than 20 percent of the one hundred thousand residents. Three people assaulted the couple in their home, raping the woman and stealing their belongings. The perpetrators assumed that because the victims were Jewish, they were rich. The names of the three suspects indicate that they are, in great probability, Muslims. Many condemnations followed, including from President François Hollande and Prime Minister Manuel Valls.[15]

One has to distinguish between actual incidents and fears. Both have an impact on Jews, as their proliferation leads to further fears. This leads in turn, among other things, to many Jews partially or entirely concealing their identity.

European Anti-Semitism: Alive, Active, and Virulent

In 2002, then-UK Chief Rabbi Jonathan Sacks summed up the situation:

> Let me state the point as simply as I can: anti-Semitism is alive, active and virulent in the year 2002, after more than half a century of Holocaust education, interfaith dialogue, United Nations declarations, dozens of museums and memorials, hundreds of films, thousands of courses, and tens of thousands of books dedicated to exposing its evils; after the Stockholm Conference, after the creation of a National Holocaust Memorial Day, after 2,000 religious leaders came together in the United Nations in August 2000 to commit themselves to fight hatred and engender mutual respect. . . . What more could have been done? What more could and can we do to fight anti-Semitism?[16]

Two years later, Sacks's ideas had evolved. He asserted that when civilizations clash, Jews die. In his view, within certain European circles, revenge is being taken against the Jews because "nobody will ever forgive the Jews for the Holocaust." Sacks drew attention to the manipulation of words like genocide and ethnic cleansing by Israel's adversaries. He added that what should have been learned from the Holocaust is: "one, that bad things are preceded by demonization—and right now Israelis are being demonized—and, two, the early warning sign in culture is when words lose their meaning."[17]

The oft-repeated assertion that postwar outbursts of European anti-Semitism parallel developments in the Middle East conflict is no longer true. It appears in waves, which may, but do not necessarily, correspond to developments in the Arab-Israeli conflict—with each wave being higher than the previous one.[18] In the Arab world, anti-Jewish incitement raged in parallel with the Oslo process. During the 2013-2014 "peace process" the same occurred. In France anti-Semitic incidents increased greatly after Mohammed Merah murdered a Jewish teacher and three children in 2012.[19]

The use of double standards against Israel is a common practice in Europe. For instance, European Commission guidelines bar the organization from funding Israeli entities in the disputed territories where Israel has ruled since the 1967 war. Yet there are many similar situations where the European Union does provide funding, such as in parts of Cyprus occupied by Turkey.[20]

One typical case of European anti-Israeli incitement occurred after these guidelines were issued, when a group of former senior European personalities sent a letter to then-EU foreign policy chief Catherine Ashton. Calling themselves, with a certain arrogance, "European Eminent Persons," they urged the European Commission to fully support the guidelines. Members of the group include former NATO Secretary-General Javier Solana, former Austrian Foreign Minister Benita Ferrero-Waldner, and former French Foreign Minister Hubert Védrine. Yet nothing is known about actions of the group concerning the many threats to Europe stemming from parts of the Muslim world.[21]

The Jew as Victim

The Holocaust also led to a gradual modification of the widespread negative image of the Jews in Europe. In part, this slowly mutated into the symbol of the ultimate victim.[22] Hence for several decades a taboo on public anti-Semitism emerged in many, though not all, European democracies. This taboo was particularly strong in Germany; there, too, it has been fading in recent years.[23] Anti-Semitism, however, remained present in all European countries in its latent form.

Beginning mainly during the Six Day War—when the magnitude of the Israeli victory shattered the image of the Jew as a victim—and intensifying after the 1982 Lebanon War, a third category of anti-Semitism developed in Europe from a small base and targeted Israel as a Jewish collective.

In the Muslim world it had been present in extreme forms since Israel's establishment, combined with classic anti-Semitism. Since anti-Israelism does not encounter the resistance of the previous two types, which many consider politically incorrect, it has grown rapidly in recent years. Taguieff also understood early several key aspects of the methods used by the defamers of Israel and the Jews. He exposed the process by which the crimes of the allegedly deprived, to whom the Palestinians claim to belong, are condoned. Taguieff also described the role of the media in justifying violence and portraying criminals as victims.

He pointed out that the next step in the distortion process is to declare the criminals—dressed up as victims—not responsible for their acts, because they are molded by their socioeconomic conditions. This is an updated version of Marxist determinism. A further step is that the Islamist version of Islam becomes the religion of the poor and the victims. Another facet is to declare that Muslims or Arabs behave as they do because they are supposedly humiliated or persecuted.[24] What Taguieff said here fits in well with the earlier-mentioned "humanitarian racism."

The new myth of the "intrinsically good Palestinian" is often linked to extreme anti-Zionism aimed at destroying Israel. The Palestinians have become the standard-bearers of democracy's enemies. This goes hand in hand with the criminalization of Israel and the West.

Taguieff also observed that blind pacifism places the aggressor and his victim at the same level of morality and turns legitimate self-defense into a criminal transgression. Abstract utopianism and "blind angelism" still tend to favor the multinational model, even though multinational states have led to partially ethnically-cleansed states, as became particularly evident in Yugoslavia.[25]

Anti-Israelism

The late-twentieth and early-twenty-first-century explosion of anti-Israelism, a hate phenomenon that existed for decades at much lower levels, caught the Jewish world and Israel by surprise. Some authors, however, had already described much earlier several aspects of the anti-Zionist mutation of anti-Semitism.

In 1979, in the original French version of his book *The Anti-Zionist Com-*

plex, Jacques Givet wrote: "The anti-Zionist becomes an overt anti-Semite as soon as he goes beyond criticism of the policies of the Jerusalem government (a favorite activity of Israelis themselves) and challenges the very existence of the State of Israel."[26]

In France—where new mutations of anti-Semitism are often pioneered—the overlap of anti-Semitism and anti-Israelism occurred at an early stage. It was partly linked to the large number of communist intellectuals. This emerged, for instance, during the "doctors' plot" in 1953. Doctors—most of them Jewish—in the Soviet Union were accused of having caused the deaths of leading political figures by incorrect diagnosis and treatment. This was accompanied by a campaign against "cosmopolitanism" and Zionism.

French communist intellectuals organized a major solidarity meeting in Paris. Several speakers explained that it was normal to suspect doctors of poisoning people, as Mengele had done in Auschwitz. A Jewish physician publicly stated, adducing German behavior during World War II, that one could not rule out that Jews or Zionists had decided to poison Soviet personalities.[27] It was yet another mutation of the ancient anti-Semitic accusation that Jews are poisoners.

David Zohar, a retired Israeli diplomat who in the early 1980s was stationed at the Israeli embassy in Oslo, told how he had been invited to speak on Israel's military strategy at the General Headquarters of the Norwegian army. During question time, one of the generals asked why the Jews had "crucified our Lord." The Israeli diplomat asked the questioner what that had to do with the topic of his talk. The general replied that he had taken this opportunity to ask the question because the diplomat was the first Jew he had ever met and presumably could give an answer, since his ancestors were probably responsible. The diplomat then suggested that he call up the Italian ambassador, as he was likely to be a descendant of the Romans who had pronounced the verdict.[28]

Complex Societies

The European Union is a prime example of a large, complex system without proper checks and balances. It is in urgent need of drastic revision rather than further uncontrolled integration.

Had the disadvantages of increasing complexity been understood a few decades ago, European communities would not have allowed the nonselective mass immigration of non-Westerners with radically different cultural backgrounds, the more so as xenophobia is ubiquitous in Europe. To make matters worse, significant percentages of these immigrants are adherents to antidemocratic ideologies, racists, anti-Semites, and proselytizers. Angela Merkel, Nicolas Sarkozy, David Cameron, and several others have declared—far too late, however—that multiculturalism is a failure.[29]

In such a complex and opaque situation it is not difficult to apply double standards and other fallacies to Israel. In 2006, British author Frederic Forsyth wondered how European politicians could dare to call the Israeli response to the Hizbullah attacks disproportionate when their own countries had behaved far more fiercely in the Yugoslav Wars:

> Why did the accusers not mention Serbia? . . . In 1999 five NATO air forces—US, British, French, Italian and German—began to plaster Yugoslavia, effectively the tiny and defenceless province of Serbia. We were not at war with the Serbs, we had no reason to hate them, they had not attacked us and no Serbian rockets were falling on us.[30]

European Politicians Promote Double Standards

Such double standards against Israel are common among many European politicians.[31] To make matters worse, some of them promote the use of double standards against Israel. In December 2014, Danish Ambassador to Israel Jesper Vahr said at the Jerusalem Post Diplomatic Conference in Jerusalem, "Europe should apply a double standard to Israel when judging its actions compared to other Middle Eastern nations . . . Israel should insist that we discriminate, that we apply double standards, this is because you are one of us."[32]

There is much wrong with what Vahr said, which cannot be discussed in detail here. Cynics might say that for more than a millennium the Jews were discriminated against because "They were not one of us," and now they should be discriminated against because they are "one of us." The remark about double standards is, in any case, a recycling of colonial attitudes toward the other Middle Eastern nations where Westerners separated people into two categories, the superior white classes and the lower nonwhite classes.

Vahr is not the only one to propound the distorted concept that Europe should apply double standards against Israel. In a lecture at Tel Aviv University in December 2013, Dutch Foreign Minister Frans Timmermans said, "In the relation between Israel and Europe, double standards are used. Why? Because Europeans consider Israel to be a European country. Israel is judged in the same way as other European countries judge themselves and other European countries."[33]

Germany

In the context of developments in Europe, Germany requires special analysis. The way its citizens perceive the country's history in the previous century, and particularly in the World War II period, is a factor influencing its attitude toward Israel and the Jews. This leads to a certain dualism that many authors have analyzed.

German society and many members of its cultural elite display an extremely complex relationship with Israel and the Jews. Nazism was widespread in German society for more than a decade. The crimes Germany initiated and committed were so extreme and massive that it is unthinkable that, with Germany's defeat in 1945, this worldview completely disappeared from German society and is totally absent from Germany today.

Many former Nazis never spoke to their children about the crimes they had committed. They did not necessarily remain totally silent about their Nazi ideas, however. This past, which has had so much impact on Germany's history, must inevitably play some role in current attitudes and beliefs of many Germans.

Today Germany speaks with multiple voices. There has been an increasing trend of seeking to cleanse the country's past by accusing others of wrongdoing. One strong message is that of false moral equivalence between Germany's World War II crimes and the behavior of others, then and now.

Members of the country's elite have developed various formulas to whitewash Germany's dark history. A major one is that while the Germans were indeed Nazis, how important is this fact if so many others conducted themselves comparably in the past, or are behaving similarly now? If so many others are guilty of such criminality, why single out the Germans?[34] This is manifested, for instance, in the evil mindset of half the German population who falsely believe that Israel commits genocide against the Palestinians, or behaves toward them like the Nazis did toward the Jews.[35]

The most effective approach in trying to sanitize Germany's immense past crimes is to accuse Israel of acting similarly. Israeli psychologist Nathan Durst remarked:

> If the guilty person is bad, the Jewish victim becomes good. The moment it can be shown the latter is bad too, the "other"—that is, the European—is relieved of his guilt feelings. To claim that Israelis behave like Nazis reduces the sin of the grandparents. Then the children of the victims can no longer be the accusers. This equalizes everybody.[36]

Jeffrey Gedmin, who at the time was director of the Aspen Institute in Berlin, said in 2005:

> Perhaps the most crucial element in Europe's increasingly hostile attitude toward Israel is the continent's history. Each time a European editor, intellectual, or politician points out that Palestinians are victims and Israelis are belligerent aggressors, these Europeans unburden themselves of their past. In their discriminatory attitude toward Israel, the pathological-psychological elements dominate the ideological one. On top of that, there is much plain anti-Semitism among Europeans, as my experience as a non-Jew proves.[37]

German historian Susanne Urban says:

> Germany erected many memorials and museums at former concentration camps, as well as for the murdered Jews. The extent of the attention given to Holocaust education in schools and other educational institutions is outstanding. At the same time, one also observes an increasing self-perception of

> Germans as victims—because of the Allied bombings, the flight and expulsion from Eastern Europe and so on. Furthermore, prejudices such as "the Jews still make money off the Holocaust; they use the Holocaust against Germany and Europe for their own benefit," continue to float around.[38]

She adds:

> Anti-Zionism as one variety of anti-Semitism often manifests itself as "criticism of Israeli politics, strategies and actions." It is found in all spheres of German society, be it Leftist or Rightist, Muslim or Christian. Anti-Zionism and secondary anti-Semitism often overlap for instance by making comparisons between Nazis and Israeli politics or between Holocaust victims and the Palestinians. This is also used to deny contemporary responsibility for Germany's history or commemoration of the victims. Anti-Zionist attitudes do not differ if one is ideologically on the left, right, or a liberal.[39]

False "Political Correctness"

German journalist Daniel Killy remarks:

> The silent tyranny of political correctness often leads to internal censorship when writing about Israel. This is combined with the German neurosis of being "just." With regard to Israel, this means that one must be critical of it. Otherwise one might be considered pro-Israel because of German history. In addition, a widespread leftist anti-Zionism prevails among public broadcasters and other media. This "anti-Zionism" is a synonym for Germany's glossy and "trendy" anti-Semitism.

The clandestine code of politically correct conduct begins far from the Israeli-Palestinian conflict. In Germany Jews are usually called "Jewish co-citizens" (*Jüdische Mitbürger*). This expression of "co-citizen" is used only to describe people who don't really belong to society. One also hears "Turkish co-citizens." No one ever speaks about "Lutheran co-citizens."[40]

Journalist Benjamin Weinthal has pointed out that various anti-Israeli inciters are bestowed with high honors by senior German bodies. He observes:

> There is growing indifference in the Federal Republic toward Jew hatred and attacks on Israel. One of the many indicators of this is the awarding of prizes throughout the last decade by German organizations and politicians to Israel bashers, among them Jews. Some recipients have made statements which are within the definition of run-of-the-mill anti-Semitism.[41]

One of those is a former Israeli, Felicia Langer, who compared Israeli military detention centers with concentration camps. German President Horst Köhler presented her with the Federal Cross of Merit for her civil and humanitarian work. Weinthal remarks, "Her promoting the equivalence of Israel with Nazi Germany helps alleviate German guilt over the Holocaust. Market demand for her 'services' is significant."[42]

In 2012 the Adorno Award was given to Judith Butler, a Jewish anti-Israeli professor of rhetoric at the University of California at Berkeley. She has claimed that Hamas and Hizbullah are progressive left-wing organizations. Furthermore, former German President Roman Herzog presented Lutheran Palestinian Reverend Mitri Raheb with the German Media Prize in 2012. Raheb is one of the authors of the Kairos Document, which calls for a boycott of Israel.[43]

Then-Christian Democrat Mayor Petra Roth of Frankfurt invited German-born French Jewish intellectual Alfred Grosser to deliver the 2010 Kristallnacht speech in the St. Paul's Church. There, Grosser drew parallels between the conduct of the Nazis and Israel.[44]

Funding Anti-Israelism

Of a somewhat similar nature is the fact that Germany's political parties fund anti-Israeli NGOs and organizations in the disputed territories through their foundations. Professor Gerald Steinberg of Israel's Bar-Ilan University, who heads NGO Monitor, says a detailed report by his organization shows that "while German political foundations claim a mandate for promoting democracy, peace and human rights, a significant portion of their activities related to Israel are immoral."[45]

Germany's relationship with Israel and the Jews will remain fraught with problems for a long time to come. Its basic elements are relatively simple. A huge, widely supported criminal movement such as Nazism leaves residues in a society for many generations. Major crimes also induce feelings of guilt. Contemporary Germans are not guilty of what their ancestors did. Nor are they responsible for it, because one can only be held responsible for one's own deeds. Yet contemporary Germans must see to it that their country's history is not falsified, and they must oppose its frequent whitewashing.

At the same time, there are also many positive German attitudes toward Jews and Israel, including a desire to expose the crimes of that period. Some German researchers attempt to uncover more and more of the crimes that were committed. A number of major businesses have given historians a free hand to document what took place within their firms during the war.

France

France is another country that requires special attention. One reason is that the wave of anti-Semitism that erupted there from autumn 2000 onward was more intense than elsewhere in Europe. The Socialist government then in office attempted to deny or minimize the anti-Semitic nature of severe verbal and physical attacks on Jews, even though anti-Semitism continued on a large scale.

After the electoral defeat of the Socialist government, attitudes changed. In June 2002, Nicolas Sarkozy, the then right-wing interior minister, called for an all-out struggle against anti-Semitism. President Jacques Chirac, however, maintained his stance of denial that anti-Semitism existed in France, until in November 2003 a Jewish institution of the Chabad movement was burned in Gagny. By the time Chirac finally admitted the truth, attacks on Jews had already been taking place for three years. From then on, French anti-Semitism was acknowledged publicly by most French authorities.

Murders of Jews by Muslims in France

A second reason for paying attention to France is that several brutal murders of Jews by Muslims, motivated by anti-Semitism, have taken place there. As aforementioned, on March 19, 2012 Mohammed Merah, a Frenchman of Algerian origin, killed a teacher and three children in front of the Jewish school in Toulouse, Otzar Hatorah. Earlier that month he had murdered three French soldiers. A few days after the murders at the school, Merah was killed in a shootout with French police.[46] Later his brother Abdelghani published a book in which he recounted that their parents had educated them to be fanatic anti-Semites. His sister Souad and brother Abdelkader are also extreme anti-Semites.[47]

Merah's murders created a bandwagon effect of attacks on French Jews. In 2012 France saw an increase of 58 percent in anti-Semitic incidents compared to the previous year, according to a report of the Jewish defense organization Service de Protection de la Communauté Juive (SPCJ.) It stated: "2012 has been a year of unprecedented violence against Jews in France."[48]

Another reason France occupies a special place is that the 2013 FRA study shows that, as aforementioned, the percentage of French Jews who fear undergoing anti-Semitic incidents is higher than in any other nation surveyed.[49] The same study found that 88 percent of French Jews thought anti-Semitism had increased in the country over the past five years. Fifty-one percent of French Jews "frequently" or "all the time" avoid wearing things that might help people identify them as Jews in public.

The anti-Semitism in France sharply accelerated in 2014 with a huge increase in incidents, some of them of an extreme character. In the summer months there were massive attacks on synagogues, of which the one on the La Roquette synagogue in Paris was the most severe, and on Jewish shops.[50] This was followed in January 2015 by the murder of four Jews in a kosher supermarket in Paris.[51]

On the day of these killings, a Friday, the authorities closed the Great Synagogue of Paris. Its last closure by the authorities on a Friday night occurred during the German occupation, and many noticed the symbolism.[52] The only vaguely similar precedent of synagogues closing on the Sabbath due to threats is a canceled synagogue service in 2010 at the small Conservative synagogue of the Dutch town of Weesp. In this case the decision was taken by the community leaders after they received a threat.[53] In 2006, on one occasion, the Jewish community of Malmö, Sweden moved the service from the synagogue to a secret location.[54]

Scandinavia

The Scandinavian countries, in particular Sweden and Norway, also merit special attention. A broad range of cases of anti-Semitism and anti-Israelism show how these countries are falsely regarded as "model democratic societies." This is partly due to the fact that they did not have colonies. In 2009 during Operation Cast Lead in Gaza, the largest anti-Semitic riots in Norway's history took place in Oslo. A Christian who walked to a pro-Israeli demonstration with an Israeli flag was beaten and severely injured. Projectiles that could have killed people were thrown at pro-Israeli demonstrators. All or almost all of the perpetrators were Muslims. Eirik Eiglad has described this in detail in his book *The Anti-Jewish Riots in Oslo*.[55]

Norway's Labour Party was in office from 2005 until 2013 and usually ignored foreign criticism of anti-Semitism and the widespread, extreme anti-Israelism in the country. It was assisted in this by the leading media, which usually do not report on such criticism. This stonewalling became impossible, however, when a three-member OSCE delegation visited Norway in summer 2012.

After their visit, the delegation published a report criticizing Norway for intolerant attitudes toward both Jews and Muslims. The authors stated that the police did not monitor hate crimes or fight them in any measurable way. The report also recommended increased security for the Norwegian Jewish community. The OSCE delegation further commented on the Norwegian government's attitude toward the Israeli-Palestinian conflict, warning that a "strong anti-Israeli attitude can develop into anti-Semitism."

The delegation urged the foreign minister to encourage a discourse that would promote a less biased view of the conflict and would not lead to demonizing the Israeli state. It also remarked that the continued ban on kosher slaughter was seen as having negative implications for Norway's reputation of tolerance and inclusion.[56] The OSCE report and its multifaceted criticism of Norway received some attention in the Norwegian press.[57, 58]

In any history of postwar European anti-Semitism, Norway will have a substantial place because of extreme writings, incidents, and hate cartoons. In a societal environment where civil society and most media are deeply immersed in what at best may be called moral relativism—if not racist bias—the most extreme anti-Semitic views, disguised as anti-Israelism, can also be voiced in the mainstream. One example of this occurred when the major daily *Aftenposten* published an article by the internationally known author Jostein Gaarder during the Second Lebanon War in 2006.

Gaarder wrote: "Israel is history. We do not recognize the state of Israel. There is no way back. The state of Israel has raped the recognition of the world and does not get peace before it lays down its weapons. The state of Israel in its present form is history."[59] Gaarder also attacked the Jews in general.

Mona Levin, a Norwegian cultural journalist, was one of the most high-profile critics of Gaarder's article: "This is the worst piece I have read since *Mein Kampf*... He proceeds from talking about Israel in one paragraph to attacking the Jewish people in the next paragraph."[60]

Yet another Norwegian scandal, among several that attracted international attention, occurred toward the end of 2008. The comedian Otto Jespersen said in a program on TV2, the country's largest commercial station: "I would like to take the opportunity to remember all the billions of fleas and lice that lost their lives in German gas chambers, without having done anything wrong other than settling on persons of Jewish background."[61]

Two years earlier the same comedian had burned pages from the Old Testament on live television. Although there was criticism, the television company did not see this as a reason to terminate his employment. Jespersen then also explained that he would not burn the Koran, as he wanted to live longer than a week.[62]

During the 2014 Protective Edge campaign there was much anti-Israeli incitement in Norway. The Norwegian physician Erik Fosse, who was in Gaza during the campaign, claimed that: "The people are cheering when rockets hit Tel Aviv . . . the people around here are sitting around the television cheering, and I think that's because they have no longer anything to lose, they are going to be killed slowly by starvation, or quickly by the [air] strikes. So that's their choice."[63] Yet starvation has not been a problem in Gaza, and aid flowed into it at a greater pace during the operation.[64]

Sweden

Sweden's third largest city, Malmö, is often mentioned as the capital of European anti-Semitism. The perpetrators of the many anti-Semitic acts there are mostly Muslims. Hannah Rosenthal, U.S. government special envoy for combating anti-Semitism, visited the town in 2012. She spoke out about anti-Semitic statements made by Social Democrat Mayor Ilmar Reepalu. Rosenthal also remarked that under this mayor Malmö was a "prime example" of "new anti-Semitism," as anti-Israeli sentiment serves as a guise for Jew-hatred.[65] A record number of complaints about hate crimes in the city in 2010 and 2011 did not lead to any convictions.[66]

It is not surprising that the 2013 FRA study found that 51 percent of Swedish Jews considered hostility to Jews in the streets and public spaces to be a fairly large or very large problem. Thirty-four percent of Swedish Jews always avoid wearing, carrying, or displaying things that might help identify them as Jews in public places; another 26 percent avoid this frequently. These are the highest figures for any country covered by the study. Twenty-two percent feel that they are constantly being accused or blamed for what Israel does; 27 percent said that this occurs frequently. Twenty-five percent say that anti-Semitism is a major problem.[67]

Denmark

Because of the many problems for Jews and the Israel-hatred in Norway and Sweden, little public attention is given to Denmark. This may well be mistaken. An indication of that occurred when in early 2014 Denmark's largest bank, Danske Bank, broke off its relations with Israel's Bank Hapoalim.[68]

In 2012, Israel's ambassador to Denmark, Arthur Avnon, was quoted telling the French news agency AFP: "We advise Israelis who come to Denmark and want to go to the synagogue, to wait to don their skullcaps until they enter the building and not to wear them in the street, irrespective of whether the areas they are visiting are seen as being safe." He also advised visitors not to speak Hebrew loudly or wear visible jewelry with Stars of David.[69] The main assaults against Jews are perpetrated by Arabs. The Jewish community has complained in vain about the authorities' inaction.[70]

Finn Schwarz, president of Mosaisk Troessamfund, the Danish Jewish community, said in a 2013 interview that the organized community had lost 25 percent of its registered members over the past fifteen years and was down to 1,899 members. He said this was partly due to anti-Semitism.[71]

In early 2014, Denmark outlawed ritual slaughter. At the same time, the country continues to allow sex with animals. Bestiality is promoted by the owners of animal brothels.

A poll in Denmark in autumn 2014 found that 74 percent of its citizens believe that male circumcision should be banned. Only 10 percent of those polled believed that the decision should be left to parents. Hans Christian Schmidt, a former health minister and current parliamentarian, claimed that circumcision contravenes the United Nations Convention on the Rights of the Child.[72] An overwhelming majority of the circumcisions carried out in Denmark are done by Muslims.

In the book *Behind the Humanitarian Mask: The Nordic Countries, Israel and the Jews*, this author provides a much more detailed analysis of the anti-Israelism and anti-Semitism in Europe's Nordic countries.[73] A new book claims that Danish Nazis actively participated in the murder of 1,400 Jews at a prison camp in the Belarus town of Bobruisk during World War II. This greatly damages the wartime image of Denmark.[74]

Toward a New Criminal Europe?

The European Union's attitude toward anti-Semitism is double-edged. With its discriminatory anti-Israeli declarations, the EU plays the role of arsonist, fanning the flames of anti-Semitism. It also serves as fireman by trying, at the same time, to quench the flames of classic religious and ethnic anti-Semitism.

Besides change, political dynamics often create confusion. For many years, a key Israeli claim against Europe has concerned the latter's frequent political double standards toward Israel. This accusation is based on comparisons between how Europe judges itself, how it acts toward Israel's enemies, and how it regards third parties.

The statistics from various polls about widespread European criminal beliefs about Israel, and about the lack of security that European Jews feel, are indicators of a developing ideologically criminal Europe. All in all, these data remove the mask from the new "humanitarian" postwar Europe.

A French non-Jewish philosopher took these negative judgments of Europe a step further. Jean-Claude Milner titled one of his books *The Criminal Inclinations of Democratic Europe.* In an interview, he referred to anti-Semitism —other than Muslim—in Europe:

> I think there is a homegrown anti-Semitism in Europe that doesn't find its roots in the past, but from the future . . . Today we see an anti-Semitism that doesn't originate from old people, but from youth, and thus is not likely to disappear but instead will become stronger . . . This is a real problem. We are dealing with a modern anti-Semitism.[75]

If 150 million adult EU citizens out of 400 million have unjustified opinions about Israel that are evil in the extreme, it means that they have a criminal mindset. The EU should investigate how they arrived at these beliefs. Who has encouraged them? Which media, politicians, leading civil-society figures, and so on are responsible? The next question, then, is what is the EU going to do about it? This becomes a Pandora's box that Europe does not want to open. Somewhat surprisingly, Israeli officialdom does not want to challenge the EU on this issue, an attitude that harms Israel's interests.

Politicians Seeing Israelis as Nazis

The anti-Semitic motif of seeing Israelis as Nazis has appeared in the European mainstream for decades already. Leading European politicians such as the late Swedish Socialist Prime Minister Olof Palme[76] and the late Greek Socialist Prime Minister Andreas Papandreou have accused Israel of using Nazi practices.[77]

Rather similar remarks have been made by other politicians. Franco Cavalli, then parliamentary leader of the Swiss Social Democrats, said at a meeting in 2002 where Israeli flags were burned that Israel "very purposefully massacres an entire people" and undertakes "the systematic extermination of the Palestinians."[78]

Political scientist Efraim Karsh noted that in 2001 in an interview to the news magazine *Suomen Kuvalehti*, the Socialist foreign minister of Finland Erkki Tuomioja denounced Israel's attempts to protect its citizens from the terror war launched by Arafat's Palestinian Authority in September 2000. Tuomioja, who is currently again Finland's foreign minister, compared Israeli defensive measures to the Nazi persecution of European Jewry: "It is quite shocking that some implement the same kind of policy toward the Palestinians which they themselves were victims of in the 1930s."[79]

In March 2002, Greek Socialist parliamentary speaker Apostolos Kaklamanis referred to the Israeli "genocide" of the Palestinians, after which government spokesman Christos Protopapas said he had expressed the sentiments of the parliament and the Greek people.[80]

The political elite's anti-Semitic views on Israel also filter down to lower levels. Indications of this anti-Israeli attitude are widespread in Europe. In 2004, on the municipal information board in Oleiros, a small town in northern Spain, a bright red illuminated sign stated: "Let's stop the animal, Sharon the assassin, stop the neo-Nazis." When the Israeli ambassador called the mayor of Oleiros, Angel Garcia Seoane, to discuss this incident, the mayor told him that he fully stood behind the message. The municipality was also selling T-shirts with anti-Sharon slogans on its website.[81]

This happened in a country where in March of the same year, Muslim supporters of an international Islamist organization murdered almost two hundred people in Madrid and wounded many more.[82] Why did the mayor decide to devote this billboard to Sharon? Why not to Bin Laden or another Islamist terror leader who had laid the ideological infrastructure for the murder and wounding of so many Spaniards?

There are other political aspects as well. In July 2004, Egyptian Muslim cleric Yusuf al-Qaradawi, who lives in Qatar, visited London. There he praised Palestinian suicide bombings, and was given a cordial welcome by the then Labour mayor of London, Ken Livingstone, who appeared jointly with him. Before his arrival, the Board of Deputies of British Jews gave the police a dossier containing the texts of interviews with the cleric. The British authorities decided that there was "insufficient evidence" of a criminal offense to prevent his visit to the UK.[83]

Cartoonists: Israelis as Nazis

From time to time hate cartoons appear in mainstream European papers. Several of these cartoons from Norway well expose the overlap between anti-Semitism and anti-Israelism. In 2002 the Norwegian German-born cartoonist Finn Graff published a cartoon of Ariel Sharon as a Nazi in *Dagbladet*, Norway's third largest daily.[84]

In one of his later cartoons, Graff portrayed then-Israeli Prime Minister Ehud Olmert as the Nazi camp commander from the movie *Schindler's List.* The cartoon was published by *Dagbladet* in 2006.[85] In 2011, the same cartoonist drew a cartoon about the prisoner swap for captured Israeli soldier Gilad Shalit. The illustration hints at Palestinian prisoners being released into another "prison"—Gaza—with the inscription from Buchenwald: *Jedem das Seine* (To each what he deserves).[86]

In 2007, King Harald V of Norway awarded the country's highest honor, the Medal of Knight in the Order of St. Olav, to Graff for his work.[87] Haakon Lie, retired secretary-general of the Norwegian Labour Party, wrote in his autobiography: "The Labour Party conducted serious attacks against Israel; it used caricatures of Finn Graff, which evoked in detail the anti-Semitic illustrations of *Der Stürmer* in Hitler's days and of *The Crocodile* in Moscow."[88]

CHAPTER THREE

The Mutation of Ancient Hate Motifs

A KEY CHARACTERISTIC OF DEMONIZATION is that when both very positive and extremely negative remarks are made about people, the negative ones usually stick more, even if they are far less numerous. Frequent repetition of the negative remarks enhances the demonization.

The first major, long-lasting demonization campaign against the Jews, the Christian one, helps clarify the demonization process throughout the centuries. Van der Horst explains:

> The New Testament contains some anti-Semitic passages. One finds them only in the latest documents. The main example is in the Gospel of John. It was written after the split between Christians and Jews had occurred. The anti-Jewish sentiment permeates the whole book, and it contains the most anti-Semitic verse in the New Testament.
>
> John has Jesus distance himself completely from the Jewish people. He lets him speak about the Jews, their laws and festivals, as if he himself is no longer one of them. Worst of all, in a dispute between Jesus and the Jewish leaders, John has him say: "You have the devil as your father."[1]

In later Christian literature, that expression is picked up.

> This short but fatal remark has had lethal consequences over two millennia. It cost tens of thousands of Jewish lives in later history, especially in the Middle Ages. This verse was taken by Christian Jew-haters as a license to murder Jews. These murderers believed: "If Jesus said that Jews have the devil as their father, we should eradicate them as best as we can."[2]

A Multifaceted Process

The current far-reaching demonization of Israel and widespread anti-Semitism result from a complex, multifaceted process. There is no large, well-coordinated attack on Israel or Jews from a single identifiable source, but a huge number of relatively small ones. These are sometimes coordinated by perpetrators, yet also often not. It is, another words, a "method of a million cuts."

The demonization processes of Israel and the Jews have a number of common ancient motifs, which have been transformed over the centuries. Better understanding the current hate-mongering requires analyzing the main verbal themes throughout the centuries and how they have mutated in our times. After that, the focus should shift to the various categories of demonization.

Jews and Israel Seek to Dominate the World

The core motif of demonization, namely, that the Jews are absolute evil, has already been analyzed. Below we will detail some of the most common submotifs of this central theme and their contemporary mutations.

One major anti-Semitic motif is that Jews "lust for power." The most extreme accusation that the Jews seek to dominate the world is contained in *The Protocols of the Elders of Zion*. Current versions of this theme are "The American Jewish lobby controls the United States" and "Jewish money dominates the world." In other contexts, however, Jews are regarded as mean and miserly.

Malcolm Hoenlein notes that European media are obsessed with "Jewish power":

> In every interview with the BBC and other European and Japanese media, the main question inevitably boils down to the influence of "the Jewish lobby." They do not understand and, therefore, ascribe negative connotations to what is consistent with American democracy, which offers minorities a say if they choose to get involved.[3]

In its 2010 list of top anti-Semitic slurs, the Simon Wiesenthal Center put former UPI senior White House correspondent Helen Thomas in first place. She said in 2010, "Jews should get out of Palestine. They should go home to Poland, Germany, America and everywhere else . . ."[4]

Fiamma Nirenstein, as noted earlier, chaired a parliamentary Sub-Committee of Inquiry on anti-Semitism of the Italian parliament. She wrote: "There has also been ample evidence of growing intolerance about our Sub-Committee of Inquiry, which is accused of being the long arm of the Jewish hold on Italy and its Parliament."[5]

The fallacy of Jewish "lust for power" recurs in Arab television programs, a method of communication far more effective and encompassing than the written book. In addition, *The Protocols of the Elders of Zion* is widely reprinted in the Arab world. It has also been published in many Western countries in recent years, Norway being one example,[6] France another.[7]

As mentioned earlier, cartoons often offer rapid insight into widespread stereotypes. An Algerian American caricaturist, Bendib, "designed a monkey with a Star of David on its breast sitting on top of the globe on which small figures of the Pope and an Arab are drawn. The monkey [i.e., Israel] says: 'Jerusalem: from New York City to Kuala Lumpur, undivided eternal capital of Israel; everything else is negotiable.'"[8]

In 2003, the Greek extreme leftist Mikis Theodorakis, a well-known composer, said at a press conference that the Jews are at the root of the world's evil. Two government ministers were present and remained silent. Only after strong Israeli criticism did the Greek government distance itself from Theodorakis' statement. Greek government spokesman Christos Protopapas added, "Apart from our disagreement for this position, Theodorakis always remains high in our esteem for the work he has offered and for his great contribution to our culture and our country."[9]

Radical Islam's Lust for Power

The truth about contemporary conspiracies aiming to "dominate the world" is different: since the failure of Nazism and communism, the major contemporary forces seeking global rule come from parts of the Muslim world. Jihads and its various supporters are by far the main ideological movement actively conspiring to control the world. This aim has been stated by many jihad leaders.

While much attention is given to the "Jewish lobby," there is little interest in the Arab lobby in the United States. Mitchell Bard, author of *The Arab Lobby*,[10] says:

> The Saudis have almost unlimited financial resources, which they use to reward former officials in hopes of influencing those still in office. As Prince Bandar, a former Saudi Ambassador to the United States, once said, if the Saudis get a reputation for taking care of their friends when they leave office, you'd be surprised how much better friends you have who are just coming into office.
>
> The former government officials can guide the Saudis on how to manipulate U.S. policy makers. They can use the contacts they have developed during their government career to gain Saudi access to decision makers. As the media often call on them to comment on Middle East affairs as non-partisan experts, they also act as Saudi propagandists.[11]

Foreign governments, including Arab ones, also try to influence the American thinktanks by making donations. In September 2014, *The New York Times* published an analysis on how various countries finance American thinktanks. One example was that Qatar had made a $14.8 million, four-year donation to the Brookings Institution to help fund an affiliate of the institute in Qatar, and a study on the relations between the United States and the Islamic world. The paper said some scholars had said that it was implicitly understood that the institution that received the donation should not criticize the donor.

The Times quoted Saleem Ali, who had been a visiting scholar at the Brookings Doha Center in Qatar. He said he had been told during his job interview that he could not take critical positions on Qatar. He remarked, "If a member of Congress is using the Brookings reports, they should be aware—they are not getting the full story . . ."[12]

The Palestinian Lobby

Little is also being said about the existence of a Palestinian lobby in many Western countries. Its official part consists of organizations and individuals who identify themselves as such. For instance, in Britain there is an organized pro-Palestinian lobby in various parties, such as the Labour Friends of Palestine and the Middle East. There is also a Palestine Solidarity Campaign.

In Norway, for instance, there is a Palestine Committee. Its official logo is a picture of what they believe to be Palestine, without Israel existing. This organization was instrumental, for example, in the invitation of Hamas representatives to Norway under the Stoltenberg government.[13] Similarly, there is a pro-Palestinian caucus in the Norwegian parliament.

Not only those who publicly identify as pro-Palestinian activists should be seen as part of the Palestinian lobby. There are also many others who in fact promote the Palestinian cause. This includes politicians, academics, journalists and media in general, trade unions, church leaders, NGOs, public intellectuals, and so on. This subject of the Palestinian lobby warrants a detailed analysis that goes beyond what is possible in this book.

Lust for Money

A derivative of the motif of "Jewish lust for power" is that Jews lust for money, and Jewish money dominates the world.

Kotek says:

> Bendib draws God holding a fat bag of dollars. On it the names of major Jewish organizations are written: "ADL, AIPAC, ZOA." God outstretches his hand to [President George W.] Bush, who slaughters a child on the altar of the Holland Foundation for needy Muslim children. The caption reads: "And the Almighty dollar [represented by God] said: 'Sacrifice me a Muslim son or else.' And George W. said: 'You've got it Lord, if this improves my chances for a second term.'"[14]

At a session of the British Liberal Democrat Party Conference, former MP and present member of the House of Lords, Baroness Jenny Tonge, asserted, "The pro-Israel lobby has got its grips on the Western world, its financial grips. I think they have probably got a certain grip on our party." She also repeated her earlier expressions of sympathy for Palestinian suicide bombers. More than twenty members of the House of Lords from the major parties condemned her language as "irresponsible and inappropriate."[15]

Lust for Blood

Another anti-Semitic motif of Jews as absolute evil is that "Jews thirst for blood, infanticide and cannibalism." While the blood libel did have precursors in the pre-Christian world, it mainly developed in Christian environments.[16] There it was claimed that Jews needed the blood of a Christian child to make unleavened bread for Passover. Although rejected and discredited, this notion has not disappeared in the West, and is presently recurring in secular forms with respect to Israel.

The blood libel in Christian Europe has its historical origins in Britain. It was invented in the twelfth century in Norwich. At that time, it was falsely claimed that Jews had killed a twelve-year-old Christian boy named William for ritual purposes. The story kept circulating. A few decades later, as in many other areas of England, all of the Jews in Norwich were murdered. From Britain, the blood libel about the Jews spread to other Christian countries. Once the first such false accusation had been made, it recurred from time to time in Europe until our days. From the Christian world, this European anti-Semitic theme spread much later to the Muslim world.[17]

The blood libel continues to appear in many forms. In the middle of the previous decade, Michael Howard, a Jew, was leader of Britain's Conservative Party, which was then in opposition. In April 2005, *The Guardian* published a cartoon by Steve Bell depicting Howard with vampire teeth, one of which was dripping blood, and holding a glass of blood. The caption read: "Are you drinking what we are drinking? Vote Conservative."[18] To add insult to injury, Annabel Crabb of the Australian Broadcasting Corporation praised Bell for this cartoon in a television interview.[19] Later Bell again drew Howard with vampire teeth in *The Guardian*.[20]

Millions of people saw a Syrian-produced movie on television that, among other things, showed a child's throat being cut. This was made to appear as being done by a Jew, and using cinematic techniques, the image showed blood streaming into a piece of matzo.[21]

The Al-Dura Blood Libel

The classic blood-libel motif has mutated in various ways from anti-Semitism into anti-Israelism. One example is the calumny that Israeli soldiers intentionally killed the Palestinian boy Muhammad al-Dura at the beginning of the Second Intifada in 2000. According to an array of researchers, if the child was even killed at all, it was done by the Palestinians. Israel has paid a very heavy price for dealing so incompetently with Arab propaganda in this case.[22]

Charles Enderlin, head of the Jerusalem-based Middle East Bureau of the French television station France 2, first broke the story, blaming Israel for al-Dura's death. Since 2000 there have been investigations of Enderlin and his sources by the Israeli government and military, in addition to independent investigative reports and documentaries on this topic. Yet the fallacy that al-Dura was killed by the IDF continues to be disseminated.[23]

In 2012 a French court overturned a libel conviction against David Yehuda, an Israeli medical doctor who was sued for libel by al-Dura's father after going public with the knowledge that wounds on al-Dura's torso were actually from a surgery Yehuda himself performed. The surgery had to be done because of a Hamas assault on the al-Dura family in 1994 for allegedly collaborating with Israel.[24]

In May 2013, an Israeli committee tasked with reviewing the al-Dura incident found that Israel was not responsible for killing or injuring the boy.[25] Yet, a month later, Philippe Karsenty, a French media analyst and leading critic of France 2's fallacious coverage of the incident, was convicted for libel by a French court for accusing Enderlin of fabricating parts of the segment.[26]

Landes remarked, "It's hard to think of a single news item that did this much damage, not only to Israel's image in the world, but to the very fabric of global civil society. It opened the door to the mainstreaming of the comparison of Israelis to Nazis."[27]

Arab Responsibility for September 11

An important indicator—not directly related to Jews—of the widespread belief in conspiracy theories among Muslims concerns the perpetrators of the September 11 attacks. In 2002, Gallup published a survey it undertook in six Muslim countries. It asked whether Arabs were responsible for these attacks.

In Turkey 46 percent of those polled believed Arabs were responsible; 43 percent believed they were not. In the other countries surveyed the figures were: 42 percent versus 58 percent in Lebanon, 20 percent versus 74 percent in Indonesia, 15 percent versus 59 percent in Iran, and 11 percent versus 89 percent in Kuwait. In Pakistan only 4 percent of those surveyed believed Arabs were responsible for September 11, while 86 percent believed they were not.[28]

In 2006, the Pew Research Center presented the same questions to Muslims in ten countries. These were both countries with Muslim majorities and countries in the West. In the Muslim world, the lowest figure of those who did not believe Muslims were responsible was now found in Pakistan, with 41 percent, and the highest was found in Indonesia with 65 percent.

High percentages of Muslims in the Western world also did not believe Arabs were responsible for the September 11 attacks. This included 46 percent of French Muslim respondents, 44 percent of German Muslims, and 35 percent of Spanish Muslims.[29]

The Norwegian Blood Libel

Another variant of the blood libel has been widely promoted in Norway. During the Israel Defense Forces' (IDF) Operation Cast Lead in 2008, two Norwegian physicians and pro-Hamas activists, Mads Gilbert and Erik Fosse, went to Gaza and took part in treating wounded Gazans. NORWAC, an organization financed by the Norwegian government, paid for their trip. Gilbert and Fosse, frequently interviewed by the international media, claimed that Israel was attacking civilians and compared it with the God of the Dead and the Underworld, Hades of Greek mythology.[30]

Although the Gazan hospital where they worked was used as Hamas headquarters, the Norwegian physicians did not mention this once in their multiple international interviews. Gilbert and Fosse did, however, develop a contemporary secular mutation of the blood libel. In their book *Øyne i Gaza* (Eyes in Gaza), they wrote that Israel entered the Gaza Strip with the goal of killing Palestinian women and children.[31] They also recounted that Labour Prime Minister Stoltenberg called them while they were in Gaza and expressed support on behalf of the government and the Norwegian people. "We are very proud of you," said Stoltenberg.[32]

Then-Labour Foreign Minister Jonas Gahr Støre wrote a back-cover blurb for this hate-mongering book, praising the authors for their role during their stay in Gaza. Former Conservative Prime Minister Kåre Willoch also wrote a back-cover blurb.[33] In 2013, King Harald V made matters even worse, awarding Gilbert and Fosse the Royal Order of St. Olav (St. Olavs Orden), which is "A reward for excellent merit for the fatherland and humankind."[34] Fosse was awarded the medal for his "medical and societal efforts";[35] Gilbert was given it for his "broad efforts in emergency medicine."[36] The Norwegian king thereby ignored the two physicians' anti-Semitic hate-mongering.

The Cannibalistic Variant

A cannibalistic variant of the infanticide motif has also emerged. In 2003, the British daily *The Independent* published a cartoon by Dave Brown depicting then-Israeli Prime Minister Ariel Sharon as a child-eater, a new mutation of the medieval blood libel. Even after receiving numerous complaints, the Press Complaints Commission (PCC) decided that the cartoon did not breach its ethical code.[37] It subsequently won the Political Cartoon Society's Political Cartoon of the Year Award for 2003. This award was presented by former Labour Party cabinet minister Clare Short at the headquarters of the prestigious weekly *The Economist* in London.

Then-Israeli Ambassador to the UK Zvi Shtauber asked *The Independent*'s Jewish editor, Simon Kelner, whether the paper had ever published a similar caricature of a public figure. Kelner had to search back eighteen years to find one.[38]

In 1994, the Jordanian paper *Al-Dustur* published a caricature of late Israeli Prime Minister Yitzhak Rabin pouring blood onto the carpet of peace.[39]

Kotek notes that Palestinians in anti-Israeli cartoons are primarily depicted as children or babies. This overlaps with the motif of the Jew as child killer.[40]

Organ Harvesting

Accusations of organ harvesting by Israel are yet another variant of this post-modern blood libel. On August 17, 2009, the culture section of the largest Swedish daily, the Social Democrat *Aftonbladet*, published an article by Donald Boström titled "Våra söner plundras på sina organ" ("Our Sons Are Plundered of Their Organs"). Boström recounted how a young Palestinian man, wanted for terrorism, was shot dead soon after the launch of a donation campaign in 1992, and how his body was returned to his family a few days later for burial. Boström then claimed there were rumors that the IDF was killing Palestinians and harvesting their organs for transplants—in collusion with the Israeli medical establishment. The article ends by saying it is time to look into this macabre activity, and urges the Israelis to investigate the allegations.[41]

Baroness Tonge has also insinuated that Israel harvests organs. She has a long anti-Israeli record. As a Liberal Democrat member of the House of Commons from 1997 to 2005, she attacked Israel on many occasions. In 2003, after visiting Gaza with Labour MP Oona King, she described the situation there: "You are almost getting a situation like the Warsaw ghetto—people can't get in or out. They can't work, they can't sell anything. There is this gradual squeeze."[42] The following year she declared that, if she found herself in a situation like that of the Palestinians, she would consider becoming a suicide bomber.[43]

When Tonge became a member of the House of Lords in 2005, she used this position as a platform for continuing attacks on Israel. In February 2010, the

Palestine Telegraph, a newspaper Tonge was a patron of, published an article accusing the IDF of harvesting organs following the Haitian earthquake.

In an interview with *The Telegraph* about this calumny, Tonge stated, "To prevent allegations such as these—which have already been posted on YouTube [sic]—going any further, the IDF and the Israeli Medical Association should establish an independent inquiry immediately to clear the names of the team in Haiti." For disseminating such notions Tonge was dismissed as the health spokeswoman for the Liberal Democrats.[44]

In February 2012, Tonge was reprimanded by her party after she attended an Israel Apartheid Week event. She had sat next to former U.S. Marine Ken O'Keefe and made no attempt to distance herself from his statements, including that "Israel must be destroyed" and that the Mossad was "directly involved" in the September 11 attacks. Following his remarks, Tonge announced to the crowd that Israel "would not last forever" and that Israelis would "reap what they have sown." Additionally, Americans would "tell the Israel lobby in the USA: enough is enough." British police investigated these remarks.[45]

Liberal Democrat leader Nick Clegg gave Tonge an ultimatum to apologize or lose the party whip. She refused and became an independent member of the House of Lords.[46]

More Blood Libels

In a cartoon that appeared in 2001 in the leading Egyptian daily *Al-Ahram*, an Arab is being put through a mill by two Israeli soldiers wearing helmets with Stars of David. The Arab's blood seeps out, and two Jews with skullcaps drink it as they laugh. This is yet another illustration of how anti-Semitism and anti-Israelism converge.[47]

A Greek cartoon also displays such convergence. It was published in the Greek daily *Ethnos* in 2002, which is close to the then-ruling, Socialist PASOK party. The caricature shows two Israeli soldiers dressed like Nazis with Stars of David on their helmets, stabbing Arabs. The text reads: "Do not feel guilty, my brother. We were not in Auschwitz and Dachau to suffer, only to learn."[48]

In 2013, the British weekly *The Sunday Times* published an anti-Semitic cartoon on International Holocaust Remembrance Day. The drawing by Gerald Scalfe showed Israeli Prime Minister Benjamin Netanyahu building a wall using what appeared to be the blood of Palestinians as cement. The caption read, "Will cementing peace continue?" Later the paper offered apologies and stated that the cartoon "was a mistake and crossed the line," admitting that it reflected "historical iconography that is persecutory or anti-Semitic."[49]

Poisoners

Another anti-Semitic submotif of "absolute evil" characterizes Jews as poisoners. This theme has been around since the early fourteenth century, when the notion that Jews were poisoning wells was propagated in parts of Germany and France.[50]

A Palestinian variant of the poisoning libel has been described by Raphael Israeli in his book *Poison: Modern Manifestations of a Blood Libel.* It analyzes the mass hysteria that erupted in the northern West Bank in March 1983. A number of girls at a junior high school in the Arab village of Arrabeh fell sick. Symptoms included fainting, drowsiness, nausea, headaches, stomach aches, and vision disturbances. Almost immediately, Palestinians accused Israel of responsibility.

During the following weeks the number of patients, mostly young women, rose to nearly a thousand in the West Bank. Investigations carried out by both Palestinians and Israelis did not find any traces of poison. Gradually it came to light that many of the later "patients" had faked their illnesses, often at the prompting of Palestinian leaders.

The Israeli authorities called in experts from the Centers for Disease Control and Prevention (CDC) in Atlanta, a world leader in epidemiology. They concluded that most of the patients' illnesses were of "psychogenic origin and induced by stress."[51] They noted that the initial Arrabeh case could have been caused by a low concentration of hydrogen sulfide gas from a poorly cleaned latrine at the school.

In one of its initial articles on the event, the Israeli daily *Haaretz* implied that there were indications Israel had used nerve gas. The secretary-general of the Arab League accused Israel of using poison gas against Palestinian students.

The Jew-as-poisoner motif also recurs in contemporary European mainstream media. A cartoon from the German *Stuttgarter Zeitung* in August 2013 shows Netanyahu poisoning the Middle East peace process. He sits on a park bench holding a piece of bread to feed peace doves, which he is poisoning with liquid from a bottle labeled "settlement construction."[52]

On November 11, 2013, the memorial day for Kristallnacht, another regional German paper, the *Badische Zeitung*, published a cartoon depicting Netanyahu as killing the nuclear talks with Iran by poison. An editor of the paper said that he saw no connection between the cartoon and the medieval accusation against the Jews of poisoning wells. Most likely he did not *want* to see it.[53]

Jews as Subhuman

Yet another extreme motif is being subhuman. The Koran calls the Jews "apes and pigs." This motif of Jews as subhuman mutated, for instance, in the Nazi accusation that Jews were subhuman and had a "severe genetic deficiency." Christian teachings said the Jew was born guilty because the forefathers of Jews were reputedly responsible for the death of their religion's originator. Christian anti-Semitism, however, had an escape clause: Jews could convert and thereby, if all went well, rid themselves of this "birth defect."

In recent decades the genetic motif has mutated even further; it is Israel that is "inhuman" or "inferior." This translates into anti-Israelism in the form of: "Israel was born in sin, and thus has no right to exist." The anti-Semitic accusation that "Israel was born in sin by driving out the Palestinians" is heard mainly from Arab and Western left-wing circles. Yet in the eyes of these accusers, all other states have the right to exist, even the most brutally criminal ones such as Syria, Iran, and so on.

This is one of many attacks on Israel's fundamental legitimacy. The Holocaust denial of former Iranian President Mahmoud Ahmadinejad stems from the fallacy that Israel's establishment was the direct result of the Holocaust. He thought that if one could undermine the European narrative about the mass murder of Jews by claiming it was a fabrication, then the basis on which the state of Israel was established would disappear.

Israeli political scientist Shlomo Avineri remarked ironically about Israel's "birth in sin": "This is in contrast to the Arab states having been immaculately conceived."[54] The anti-Semitic character of the accusation becomes clearer when one considers that if a second Palestinian state should arise in addition to the first one in Jordan, its origins will lie in genocidal propaganda, terrorism, war crimes, and corruption.

The motif of Jews as inferior beings manifests itself in various ways. One is the contemporary perception, also held by many Muslims in the West, that "Jews are apes and pigs."[55] The Simon Wiesenthal Center's list of the top ten anti-Semitic slurs in 2013 includes an example: "Iraqi cleric, Qays bin Khalil al Kalbi, said during a U.S. visit: 'Allah chose you to be the most wretched of all people. Allah chose you as the best to become pigs and apes . . . Allah chose Hitler to kill you, so who is better, you or him?'"[56] Other examples are the many, mainly Arab cartoons where Jews are portrayed as animals.

In the 2006 Iranian *Hamshahri* cartoon competition, a widespread anti-Semitic motif was the depiction of Jews and Israel as animals. The Iranian Mehdi Sadeghi drew a beetle with a Star of David on its back pushing along a giant ball of excrement with a swastika on it. It was a variation on the Nazi motif of calling the Jews "vermin." The zoomorphism theme also appeared in a cartoon by Sadic Pala of India that showed a religious Jew with vampire teeth next to a vampire bat hanging from a branch above the Al-Aksa Mosque.[57]

Kotek observed:

> Israel, an entire state of these "inferior creatures," has won military victories against the Arab world. By their logic, this was only possible, they believe, because Jews are "satanic beings." In the cartoons I collected, the Jew is depicted as inhuman and an enemy of humanity. This dehumanization is necessary to justify the hoped for elimination.[58]

The Deicide Motif

Deicide, the Jew as "murderer of Jesus," is also a hate motif used until today. In November 2013, the Anti-Defamation League released the results of a survey asking Americans about anti-Semitic attitudes. It found that 26 percent of respondents believe that the Jews are responsible for the death of Jesus. These numbers were down from a 2011 poll where 31 percent of respondents believed this fallacy.[59] The results were, however, up from 2004, when 25 percent of respondents believed this statement.[60] These findings show that demonization motifs that have permeated into societies for almost two millennia cannot be eliminated.

Kotek notes that, somewhat surprisingly, the deicide motif appears recurrently in the Arab world. In Islam, Jesus is a prophet, but not the son of God. Among the many Arab examples of cartoons using the deicide motif is a 1991 Jordanian cartoon showing Jesus on the cross, the nails through his hands dripping with blood and forming the Star of David.[61] A cartoon by the Jordanian Jihad Awrtani in the *Hamshahri* cartoon competition combined two anti-Semitic motifs by drawing a bleeding Arab crucified on a cross made of the letter T from "Holocaust."[62]

One of the European cartoons based on the deicide motif, though intended as anti-Israeli, leaves room for an anti-Christian interpretation. At the time of the Israeli siege on Palestinian terrorists hiding in the Church of the Nativity in Bethlehem in spring 2002, one of Italy's leading cartoonists, Giorgio Forattini—in what is considered one of the country's quality journals, *La Stampa* —showed the child Jesus in a manger while an Israeli tank, bearing the Star of David, waited outside. The drawing's title is "Tanks at the Manger." The child Jesus is saying, "Do you want to kill me again?"—a reference to the accusations of deicide leveled at the Jews for centuries. However, the terrorists taking refuge in the Bethlehem church were Muslims. Did Forattini imply that in his view Palestinian murderers are the sons of God? Or was he likening the founder of Christianity to these criminals?[63]

CHAPTER FOUR

Categories of Demonization

A BETTER UNDERSTANDING OF THE demonization process requires classifying the major forms of hatred promotion. Verbal demonization consists of two broad categories, false statements and distorted arguments. Pictorial demonization, of which cartoons are only one aspect, is another component of the broad array of hate-mongering. A further component is calls for action, the most extreme cases of which incite genocidal violence. Another component of demonization consists of actions taken against Israel and the Jews.

Lies are a conceptually simple form of false statements. In Christian religious anti-Semitism, the main factual lie was that "the Jews killed the son of God." Van der Horst stresses that the accusation that the Jews were responsible for the murder of Jesus could not be true, as the Jews in Roman times had no power to kill anyone. "Everything we know from other sources tells us that Pilate was thoroughly unscrupulous and ruthless. The idea that he would save a person from capital punishment because he thought him innocent is not historical and almost ridiculous."[1]

Like so many lies, this one also developed further. It brought with it the claim that *all* Jews throughout the generations were responsible for an act that their forefathers had not committed. Yet the New Testament asserts that Christians should "turn the other cheek" when attacked.[2]

During the Vatican II Council in 1965, the Catholic Church repudiated the claim that all Jews are responsible for deicide. However, some Christians continue to perpetuate this lie. The long history of the deicide charge and its murderous consequences illustrate how anti-Semitic lies are generated and how dangerous they can be for Jews.

One should add here that the concept that individuals can be held responsible for what their ancestors did—and in this specific case had *not* done—many generations earlier profoundly undermines the legal and moral functioning of any society. It is an immoral concept. In a democracy, people can only be held responsible for their own acts, not those of their ancestors.

What the concept of holding people responsible for their ancestors' crimes could mean can be illustrated with contemporary examples. German anti-Semitism did not disappear with the country's capitulation in May 1945. Sigmar Gabriel, current chairman of the German Socialist Party and deputy chancellor of Germany, has gone public about his father. He said that he was an extreme Nazi, continued to be one after the war ended, and tried to educate his son in that direction.[3] Even though Gabriel opposed his father, one wonders whether something has remained of that part of his youth. When he visited Hebron, he wrote on his Facebook page that Israeli apartheid can be seen there.[4] After that visit he remained silent, however, about the similarity between the Nazi Party's promotion of genocide of the Jews and that of the Islamo-Nazis of Hamas.

Former German President Richard von Weizsäcker incites against Israel today. One cannot see that separately from the attitude of his father, Ernst von Weizsäcker, who was sentenced as a Nazi war criminal.[5] Nor can one view the fact that 51 percent of Germans think Israel behaves like a Nazi state in detachment from the crimes of their ancestors.[6] Criminalizing Israel helps minimize the guilt of their ancestor generation.

Holocaust Denial

One extreme contemporary anti-Semitic lie is Holocaust denial. This falsehood's underlying aim is to present the Jews as extreme villains. Here anti-Semites claim that Jews invented a huge mass murder of their own people by a third party, the Nazis and their allies, which never took place. In this way, the lie continues, the Jews positioned themselves as major victims so as to gain sympathy.

This is one of the newer motifs of anti-Semitism. It developed almost immediately after World War II, mainly, though not exclusively, in France. Among its early proponents were the fascist Maurice Bardèche and Paul Rassinier, who had been a communist before the war, later became a socialist, and had been a member of the French Resistance. In subsequent years French Holocaust-denial activities often centered on Robert Faurisson, a former literature professor at Lyon University.[7]

Holocaust denial is one facet of contemporary anti-Semitism whose methodology, including motifs used by the perpetrators, their motivations, and its mode of propagation, has been analyzed in detail. This was done, for instance, by American historian Deborah Lipstadt in her 1993 book *Denying the Holocaust: The Growing Assault on Truth and Memory.*[8]

In her analysis of Faurisson, Lipstadt wrote that he

> regularly creates facts where none exist and dismisses as false any information inconsistent with his preconceived conclusions. He asserts, for example, that the German army was given "draconian" orders not to participate in "excesses" against civilians, including the Jews; consequently the mass murders of the Jews could not have happened. In making his argument, Faurisson simply ignores the activities of the Einsatzgruppen, the units responsible for killing vast numbers of Jews.[9]

As Nazis became the symbol of all evil in postwar society, their postwar sympathizers had to falsify history and claim that the Nazis were not so malevolent. In its most extreme form, this became the precursor to Holocaust denial.

Nowadays Holocaust denial is widespread in the Muslim world yet continues to occur elsewhere also in mainstream society. In 2009, the major Norwegian TV2 channel broadcast an interview of more than a quarter-hour with convicted British Holocaust denier David Irving.[10] The journalist who interviewed him displayed little knowledge of the topics discussed.

More Lies

Many of the anti-Semitic motifs described in the previous chapter are based on factual lies. Jews do not use Christian blood in any of their matzo or other rituals. On the contrary, Judaism strictly forbids the consumption of blood, even of animals. Israelis do not kill Palestinians to reuse their organs. Israel did not enter Gaza in the Cast Lead campaign to kill women and children as claimed by the Hamas-supporting Norwegian doctors Gilbert and Fosse. According to much research, Israeli soldiers did not kill the Palestinian child Muhammad al-Dura.

Jews do not aim to control the world. Unlike Christianity and Islam, Judaism does not seek to convert nonbelievers, which is a precondition for a religion or ideology if it wants to achieve global dominance. In fact, it is rather difficult to become Jewish since conversion requirements are strict. Jews did not poison wells in Europe during the Middle Ages. Jews are not pigs and monkeys or other animals. The lies about Jews are manifold.

Lies as an Instrument of Propaganda in the Arab World

Lies in the Muslim world form a category in themselves. Israeli political scientist Michael Widlanski explains:

> Palestinian leaders have developed ambiguous messages as strategic weapons to disarm, demoralize and deceive foes while gaining third-party support. They use duplicitous statements for different audiences in the tradition of taqiyya—the art of dissimulation. This is an Islam-approved application of lying to defeat enemies. When conversing in English they may sound peace-loving. Yet they simultaneously broadcast bellicose messages to Arabs in Arabic.
>
> This method of destructive ambiguity was practiced already by the pre-war Grand Mufti of Jerusalem Haj Amin al Husseini. He was heavily involved in spreading false messages about Jews "trying to conquer the Temple Mount" in the early 1920's and later in propaganda broadcasts for the Nazis. Fatah leaders, particularly Yasser Arafat and Mahmud Abbas, follow in Husseini's footsteps using ambiguity.[11]

Nadav Shragai, an Israeli journalist specializing in the history of the Palestinian-Israeli conflict regarding Jerusalem, says, "At the beginning of this century, Yasser Arafat publicly claimed that there was never a Jewish temple on the Temple Mount. Yet before 1967, Muslim sources going back centuries affirmed the existence of the Jewish Temple on the Temple Mount."[12]

This falsehood is part of a much broader structure of lies purporting that the Jewish people have no link to the Land of Israel. The Arab League's efforts to block the planned UNESCO exhibit in January 2014 on "Jews and the Holy Land" can be considered part of this approach. After various protests against the cancellation, the exhibit was rescheduled for June 2014.[13]

Accusations

A second category of false statements are unsubstantiated accusations. The line between lies and invented accusations is often very thin.

In his press conference on November 27, 1967, then-French President Charles de Gaulle made a much-publicized remark, calling the Jews "an elitist and domineering people." This is often considered the post-Holocaust reintroduction of anti-Semitism at the highest levels of mainstream European democratic society. By breaking a postwar taboo, de Gaulle paved the way for other European politicians who would go much further in later years.[14]

In 2003, then-senior Labour MP Tam Dalyell claimed that a Jewish cabal of Zionists in the United States and Britain was driving their governments into war against Syria.[15]

An extreme false accusation, particularly widespread in Europe, has already been mentioned: "Israel behaves toward the Palestinians as the Nazis behaved toward the Jews." The same goes for the related accusation: "Israel conducts a war of extermination against the Palestinians."

One type of accusation is labeling a person negatively. For instance, during the Protective Edge campaign Erdogan said that Israeli politician Ayelet Shaked had the same mentality as Hitler because she claimed that the Palestinian people were Israel's enemy.[16] Less than a week later he accused Israel of having "surpassed Hitler in barbarism."[17]

A South African example gives a combination of an accusation and labeling. The African National Congress in South Africa also compared Israel and the Nazis in a statement written by the party's deputy secretary-general Jessie Duarte, who asserted, "The State of Israel has turned the occupied territories of Palestine into permanent death camps."[18]

Venezuela also compared Israel to the Nazis in Protective Edge. President Nicolas Maduro claimed that Israel had "initiated a higher phase of its policy of genocide and extermination with the ground invasion of Palestinian territory, killing innocent men, women, girls and boys."[19]

Israel as an Apartheid State

After the 2001 UN World Conference against Racism in Durban, the "Israel is an apartheid state" lie was popularized. Israeli international-law expert Robbie Sabel notes that in South Africa under white rule, "the black population was segregated, discriminated against, and had no voting rights in general elections. It could also not participate in the government."

He contrasts that with Israel's reality:

> Israel is a multi-racial and also a multi-colored society. It has free elections with universal voting rights. Its judiciary is independent and enjoys high international standing. Jews comprise 80% of the population. Arabs, mainly Muslims but also Druze and Christians, are the largest minority. Like all other minorities, they actively participate in the political process. Incitement to racism in Israel is a criminal offense.

Sabel added:

> Since Israel became independent in 1948, there have always been Arab parliamentarians. There have been Arab cabinet ministers and deputy speakers of the Knesset. There are Arab judges on various courts including the Supreme Court. There are many Arab doctors in hospitals, as well as heads of departments. There are Arab university professors. Many Arab students study at all Israeli

> universities. The Ministry of Foreign Affairs has Arab ambassadors and other diplomats. There are Arabs among senior army and police officers and so on. This reality is radically different from the 1948 to 1994 white South African Apartheid regime.[20]

Benjamin Pogrund's book *Drawing Fire* has the subtitle *Investigating the Accusations of Apartheid in Israel.* The author, a journalist with left-wing views, is critical of Israel and gives only minor attention to the Islamo-Nazi genocidal character of the largest Palestinian party Hamas. Nevertheless, he says in a personal note in the book:

> I was treated for stomach cancer at one of Israel's leading hospitals, Hadassah Mt Scopus in Jerusalem. The surgeon (he was the head surgeon) was Jewish, the anesthetist was Arab. The doctors and nurses who cared for me were Jews and Arabs. During four and a half weeks as a patient, I watched Arab and Jewish patients get the same devoted treatment. A year or so later, the head surgeon retired; he was replaced by a doctor who is an Arab. Since then, I've been in hospital clinics and emergency rooms. Everything is the same for everyone. Israel is like apartheid South Africa? Ridiculous.[21]

Yet there is one Western country where apartheid apparently exists. After the January 2015 murders, French Prime Minister Manuel Valls said that in parts of France there is "territorial, social and ethnic apartheid."[22]

Accusations about the Future

A tool of verbal demonization that is extremely difficult to combat is that of accusations about future actions for which there are no indications. These are far more difficult to contest than lies, for instance.

One example of such an accusation about the future is that Israel intends to destroy the Al-Aksa Mosque on the Temple Mount.[23] Shragai says this canard is disseminated by leading Palestinian, Arab, and Muslim groups and individuals. "Haj Amin al Husseini, the pre-war Grand Mufti of Jerusalem was the first to promote this slander in the 1920s. It was part of the vast anti-Semitic activities of this ally of Hitler."

Shragai adds, "The 'Al Aksa is in danger' lie has expanded greatly since 1967. It is propagated by official Iranian sources—Al-Qaeda, Hamas, Hizbullah, etc. Akrama Sabri, former Mufti of Jerusalem appointed by the Palestinian Authority is another leading disseminator of the Al-Aksa libel."[24]

Another accusation about future actions to be undertaken by Israel was made by German Nobel Prize in Literature winner Günther Grass. He claimed in a hate poem—without providing any proof—that Israel is aiming to commit genocide against the Iranian people with nuclear bombs. This poem was published by major European dailies including the German *Süddeutsche Zeitung*,[25] the Italian *La Repubblica*,[26] the British *Guardian*,[27] the Spanish *El País*,[28] the Danish *Politiken*,[29] and the Norwegian *Aftenposten*.[30] Such extensive publication is so unusual for a poem that it can only be explained by the anti-Israeli attitudes of the papers' editors.[31]

Another unfounded accusation about the future was made by former French right-wing Prime Minister François Fillon. In 2014, he claimed that Israel is a threat to world peace. He formulated this fabrication by saying that Israel constitutes such a threat because it has not helped create a Palestinian state.[32]

Exaggerations

A submotif of false statements is exaggeration. One major case concerned Palestinian and other propagandists' claims about the number of Palestinian casualties resulting from Israel's military operation in the Jenin refugee camp in 2002. This intervention followed the suicide bombing by a Hamas terrorist disguised as a woman in the Park Hotel in Netanya on Passover Eve. Thirty people were killed and 140 injured.[33]

During the subsequent battle in the Jenin refugee camp, approximately fifty-five Palestinians were killed—mainly armed fighters—as well as twenty-three Israeli soldiers. Yet several Palestinian leaders, including spokesman Saeb Erekat, told the press that the number of Palestinians killed was ten or more times the actual figure. Erekat also asserted that the camp had been totally destroyed; later it could be seen that the fighting had only affected a small part of the area.[34]

In 2014, Erekat produced a new variant on the same motif. He claimed that in the fighting between Israel and Hamas only 4 percent of the Palestinians killed were militants.[35] The Meir Amit Intelligence and Terrorist Information Center examined the list of Palestinian names and concluded that 52 percent of those killed were militants.[36]

False Arguments

The use of lies, false accusations, and exaggerations as tools of demonization can be easily understood. Another type of hate propaganda, the use of false arguments, is far more opaque. These fallacies are based on distorted reasoning where the arguments presented do not support the conclusion drawn from them.

The three major categories of fallacies are emotional, ethical, and logical ones. These groups in turn have various subcategories.

One category of emotional fallacies is that of bandwagon effects. This means that people agree with the person making a statement because all others supposedly do. This can occur because of intimidation, fear, wanting to belong to a group, or opportunism. An example of the latter occurs when the most prominent scholars in an academic department are anti-Israeli. Junior scholars may consider that they will not advance without showing similar sentiments. They may then convince themselves that these are their true feelings.

It is difficult to prove the bandwagon opportunism. One suspects that various politicians take anti-Israeli positions because after their national career they look for postings at the United Nations. Another variant is that politicians take anti-Israeli positions so as to fall in line with their party.

Scare tactics are another example of emotional fallacies. An attempt is made to frighten people by threatening them with consequences of their action or inaction that are untrue, far from what may indeed happen, or by no means as harmful as they are purported to be. During the renewed Israeli-Palestinian peace negotiations in 2013, U.S. Secretary of State John Kerry warned Israel that a third intifada might break out if it made no concessions to the Palestinians. Israeli Defense Minister Moshe Yaalon responded by saying Israel would "conduct things wisely, without worrying about threats of whether or not there will be a third intifada."[37]

Sentimental Appeals

A major subcategory of emotional fallacies is sentimental appeals.

These are primarily based on feelings of pity and support for the poor.[38] Through sentimental appeals, the presenter aims to convince his audience to adopt his position by using emotional manipulation. Appealing to the audience's emotions distracts from the facts and sound logic.

Henry Silverman defines the fallacy of appealing to pity as consisting "of emotionally-charged images or language intended to evoke sympathy and manipulate an audience into adopting a partisan view or supporting an interest group."[39]

A prominent example of sentimental appeals is that "the Palestinians are weak, hence they are victims and Israel is to blame for their condition." The Palestinians have become super-victims and often can do no wrong in the eyes of many of their Western supporters.[40] These supporters frequently even look away from Hamas's genocidal intentions.

Much sentimental appeal was used when Israel acted against the Gaza flotilla. The flotilla was misrepresented as a humanitarian aid effort. Lies and false arguments intermingled. In actuality the Turkish *Mavi Marmara,* the largest ship by far, did not carry any humanitarian aid, and neither did two of the others. Some of the goods transported were for military purposes. Other items of the "aid" included pharmaceuticals that had already expired.

Furthermore, seven of the nine people killed on the *Mavi Marmara* were filmed expressing their desire to die as martyrs before setting sail. Under international law Israel had the right to impose a blockade on Gaza and thus to stop the ships from reaching their destination. Many of the worldwide reactions to the flotilla were thus a great victory of the sentimental Palestinian appeal over the legal rights of Israel.[41]

How Westerners Indirectly Promote Killing of Palestinian Civilians

It was, however, during the 2014 Protective Edge campaign that the sentimental-appeals fallacy became particularly evident. Governments knew that Hamas was making an effort to maximize the deaths of children and civilians by firing rockets from places in close proximity to them. Yet these governments reprimanded Israel for the allegedly high number of civilian deaths among the population in Gaza.

These Westerners are actually assisting the terrorist organization by using rhetoric that seeks to morally equate the two sides or posits Israel as solely responsible for all Palestinian deaths. The Palestinian civilian deaths, including children, result largely from the fact that Hamas deliberately fires rockets at Israeli civilians from heavily populated areas with a high concentration of children. Israel cannot allow itself to be fired at without reacting. Hamas does not care about civilian deaths among Gaza's population. Those foreigners who condemn Israel for firing back at Hamas and killing civilians in the process are also unpaid consultants to Hamas. Their condemnations imply that the more civilians and children are put at risk, the more they will die, and the more Israel will be condemned, rather than Hamas, for their deaths.[42]

Some Journalists Tell the Truth

During Protective Edge, Hamas frequently intimidated foreign reporters in Gaza. Nevertheless, a number of media reports clarified that Hamas was firing from near the heavily-populated areas where the reporters were broadcasting.

Sreenivasan Jain of India's NDTV reported that Hamas was launching rockets from a heavily-populated area in Gaza across from two hotels with international patrons. In his words: "But just as we reported the devastating consequences of Israel's offensive on Gaza's civilians, it is equally important to report on how Hamas places those very civilians at risk by firing rockets deep from the heart of civilian zones." The team intentionally filed the report after they left Gaza because "Hamas has not taken very kindly to any reporting of its rockets being fired."[43]

Aishi Zidan of Finland's *Helsingin Sanomat* daily reported that a Hamas rocket was fired from the parking lot of Shifa Hospital, which she reported was full of women and children injured by Israeli attacks.[44]

A Hamas rocket was also fired from behind Maha Abu al-Kas, an Arab-language reporter for France 24 news. Also reporting from a city street, she discussed civilian casualties, supply shortages in Gazan hospitals, and dangers posed to journalists by Israeli air strikes, before her report was interrupted by a Hamas rocket fired from directly behind her.[45]

Ethical Fallacies

Ethical fallacies involve attributing false authority to a person, or anyone sharing that person's thoughts, when he or she asks an audience "to agree with an assertion based simply on his or her character or the authority of another person or institution who may not be fully qualified to offer that assertion."[46]

An example of ethical fallacies is claiming that Israel is at fault because the UN General Assembly has condemned it. Such condemnations only signify that the Arab and Muslim states have so much weight in the Assembly that they can impose their opinion in the voting.

Another subcategory of ethical fallacies is dogmatism, where discussion is precluded because of the weight of the opinion of the presenter. Yet another aspect is offering personal authority as proof.

Logical Fallacies

One subcategory of logical fallacies is the inversion of cause and results; alternatively, an event can occur after another without being caused by it. Silverman cites the example of a Reuters story that paints a black picture of the Gazan economy and living conditions, particularly mentioning poverty rates,[47] while falsely portraying Israel as the culprit.[48]

Other logical fallacies include the application of double standards, the use of false moral equivalence, and scapegoating. Below we will discuss how some of these fallacies are used against Israel.

Double Standards

Cambridge Dictionaries Online defines a "double standard" succinctly: "A rule or standard of good behavior which, unfairly, some people are expected to follow or achieve but other people are not."[49]

The use of different standards for Jews compared to others has been a major tool of discrimination at the heart of anti-Semitic activities and incitement over many centuries. This was often the case, for instance, when Jews were confined to live in certain parts of a city, were not free to wear the clothes they wanted to wear, and could not work in most professions. Double standards against them thus profoundly affected most aspects of their lives. This discrimination of Jews was frequently accompanied by their demonization.

The FRA definition of anti-Semitism distinguishes "regular" criticism of Israel from anti-Semitic expressions against it. It recognizes the anti-Semitic character of double standards, noting that it is an anti-Semitic act to apply double standards against Israel by requiring of it a behavior not expected or demanded of any other democratic nation.[50] One wonders, however, why different standards should be applied for assessing democratic countries versus nondemocratic countries. That in itself seems to be a double standard.

The reactions to the Protective Edge campaign produced a slew of double standards. Just one case occurred when Secretary of State John Kerry said that Israel could do more to avoid civilian casualties in Gaza.[51] If one were to investigate U.S. attitudes toward causing civilian casualties in Afghanistan, for instance, it would emerge that Kerry's remark was misplaced and out of order. His spokesperson Jen Psaki reiterated his request of Israel. Also UN Secretary-General Ban Ki-moon and French Foreign Minister Laurent Fabius requested Israel to do more to prevent civilian casualties.[52]

It is rare that an official of an institution admits the existence of double standards against Israel. One such occasion occurred in December 2014 when

Jacques De Maio, head of the International Red Cross in Israel and the Palestinian areas, said, "Why is there so much more focus on Israel than on Syria [and] other places where many more civilians are dying? . . . In other ongoing wars, more civilians die in one week than in Israeli wars in a full year."[53]

Categories of Double Standards

The number of instances where double standards are applied against Israel is almost unlimited. To demonstrate the various aspects of this phenomenon, one can offer examples from various categories of double standards used against Israel as compared to other countries. It should be noted that as far as calls for boycotts are concerned, for instance, the use of false arguments is combined with appeals for actions against Israel.

One category of double standards applied against Israel is biased declarations or prejudiced reporting. Such declarations or reporting can come from the United Nations and other international organizations, governments, parliaments, church leaders, media, trade unions, NGOs, academic bodies, various institutions, as well as individuals.

A major case of biased declarations concerned the condemnations by many countries of the killing of Hamas leader Sheikh Ahmed Yassin by Israel in 2004. The flurry of positive international reactions to the killing of Bin Laden by the U.S. army in 2011 could have provided Israel with a major opportunity to demonstrate double standards applied against it by so many in the Western world and elsewhere. All one had to do was compare the reactions of various important leaders and institutions to this assassination with those after the killing of Sheikh Yassin. This terrorist leader was directly responsible for many lethal attacks on Israeli civilians, including suicide bombings.[54]

The United Nations' declarations in these two cases well illustrate this bias. UN Secretary-General Ban Ki-moon told reporters, "The death of Osama Bin Laden, announced by President Obama last night, is a watershed moment in our common global fight against terrorism."[55] After the killing of Sheikh Yassin, then-UN Secretary-General Kofi Annan had said, "I do condemn the targeted assassination of Sheikh Yassin and the others who died with him. Such actions are not only contrary to international law, but they do not do anything to help the search for a peaceful solution."[56]

After the Bin Laden killing, leaders of the European Council and the European Commission stated that his death "made the world a safer place and showed that terrorist attacks do not remain unpunished."[57] Following the Yassin killing, then-EU foreign policy chief Javier Solana said, "This type of action does not contribute at all to create the conditions of peace. This is very, very bad news for the peace process. The policy of the European Union has been consistent condemnation of extra-judicial killing."[58] Many other European politicians who had condemned the targeted killing by the Israel Defense Forces praised the Americans for killing Bin Laden.

Then-British Foreign Secretary Jack Straw called the killing of Sheikh Yassin "unacceptable" and "unjustified." The official spokesman of then-Prime Minister Tony Blair condemned the "unlawful attack" and observed, "We have repeatedly made clear our opposition to Israel's use of targeted killings and assassinations." British Prime Minister David Cameron congratulated President Obama on the success of the Bin Laden assassination. Cameron saw it as a massive step forward in the fight against extremist terrorism. Former Prime Minister Blair also welcomed Bin Laden's demise.[59]

Omissions

A second type of double standards, and probably their most frequent subcategory, is the omission of relevant information. One way to omit is by deleting context. For instance, media may not or barely mention the thousands of terrorist rockets fired into Israeli population centers that eventually forced Israel's army to enter Gaza in the 2008-2009 Cast Lead military campaign. That same media may then place much emphasis on Israel's military actions against Hamas.

Thomas Friedman of *The New York Times* disclosed—many years later—that Western correspondents stationed in Beirut before 1982 did not write at all about the well-known corruption of the PLO leadership there. He also noted that these correspondents judged the PLO with much more largesse than they did with the Phalangists, Israelis, or Americans.[60] One major reason was that they had to stay on good terms with the PLO; otherwise, when their foreign editor arrived, he would not be granted the much-coveted interview with Yasser Arafat.[61]

Disproportional Behavior

A third category of double standards involves disproportional behavior. One example occurs when the media report in detail on negative news about Israel and barely mention far more extreme negative news about Arab or Muslim states.

NGO Monitor has exposed how Human Rights Watch (HRW) uses disproportional behavior to demonize Israel in its publications. In 2008, NGO Monitor carried out a quantitative analysis of HRW's publications. It found that this NGO portrayed Israel as the second worst abuser of human rights in the Middle East after Saudi Arabia, but ahead of Iran, Syria, Jordan, and Egypt.

In that year, HRW condemned Israel for violations of "Human Rights Law," "Humanitarian Law," or "International Humanitarian Law" 33 times compared to 13 citations for the Palestinians, 6 for Hizbullah, and 5 for Egypt. NGO Monitor pointed out that HRW placed Israel on a par with Sudan, and with leaders of former Yugoslavia, Congo, and Uganda during that year.[62]

Interference in Israel's Internal Affairs

A fourth type of the use of double standards is interference in Israel's internal affairs. An example is a resolution unanimously adopted by the German parliament after the Gaza flotilla incident in 2010. It claimed that Israel's action did not "serve the political and security interests of Israel."

German former Social Democrat parliamentarian Gerd Weisskirchen, a leading anti-Semitism expert, wondered how the Bundestag could possibly decide what serves the interests of Israeli security. And even if it did, how could it make such a decision without an intensive dialogue with the Israeli Knesset?[63]

Discriminatory Acts

A fifth category of double standards is discriminatory acts against Israel. These may overlap with the earlier-mentioned category of biased declarations. Already a decade ago Cotler referred to the United Nations as a paradigm of double standards practiced against Israel. He said, "Despite the killing fields throughout the world, the UN Security Council sat from March to May 2002 in almost continuous sessions discussing a non-existent massacre in Jenin."[64]

Another type of discrimination that manifests double standards against Israel is the promotion of boycotts, divestments, and sanctions (BDS). One example among many is that of the Norwegian state pension fund, which divested from shares of some Israeli companies while retaining the shares of a number of highly unethical companies from other countries in its portfolio.[65]

Double Standards in Applying International Law

A sixth category concerns double standards in applying international law. International lawyer Meir Rosenne, former Israeli ambassador to the United States and France, said, "There are two types of international law. One is applied to Israel, the other to all other states. This comes to the fore when one looks at the way Israel is treated in international institutions . . ."

Rosenne mentions as a typical example the 2004 International Court of Justice advisory opinion on the Israeli security fence. "In its judgment The Hague court decided that the inherent right of self-defense is enforced only if one is confronted by a state. If this were true, that would mean that whatever the United States undertakes against Al-Qaeda is illegal. This cannot be considered self-defense under Article 51 of the UN Charter because Al-Qaeda is not a state."[66]

Humanitarian Racism

The earlier-mentioned "humanitarian racism" is yet another category of double standards. This is one of the least recognized forms of racism. As already stated, it can be defined as attributing reduced responsibility to people of certain ethnic or national groups for their criminal acts and intentions. People who engage in humanitarian racism judge misbehavior and crime differently according to the color and power rank of those who commit them. White people are held to different standards of responsibility than people of color, for example.[67] And Israelis are blamed for whatever measures they take to defend themselves.

Humanitarian racism is sometimes combined with demonization. In 1984, Swedish Deputy Foreign Minister Pierre Schori, a Social Democrat, visited Israel. He praised Arafat and his "flexible policy," claiming in an article that "the terrorist acts of the PLO were 'meaningless,' while Israel's retaliatory acts were 'despicable acts of terrorism.'"[68]

Thus the double standards used against Israel appear in a large number of fields and have permeated many aspects of Western society. The application of such double standards against Israel has a cumulative effect of demonization and a slow buildup of support for its delegitimization.

Some European politicians admit that European countries use double standards against Israel. One of these is former Dutch Foreign Minister Uriel Rosenthal. He says about the UN Human Rights Council, "The attacks on Israel have been beneficial to countries such as Iran, Zimbabwe, Cuba, and until 2011 also Syria. Unfortunately several European countries also participate in the application of double standards."[69]

That is tantamount to admitting that these countries commit anti-Semitic acts against Israel according to the FRA definition of anti-Semitism.

To better expose the bias, comparative studies should be made of the statements of leading European politicians concerning Israel and other countries in similar situations. A prime candidate to be investigated is Catherine Ashton, the previous high representative for foreign affairs and security policy of the European Union.

This author has analyzed many more examples of double standards in a lengthy essay on this subject.[70]

False Moral Equivalence

Another common type of distorted argument is false moral equivalence, a misuse of comparisons. It is the fallacious claim that there is no moral difference between two acts of greatly varying character. It is often employed to stress similarities between two evils of greatly differing magnitude. Sometimes one of the elements of the comparison is not evil, while the other is.

False moral equivalence should not be confused with moral relativism. The latter may be used to justify atrocities because they are acceptable in a specific culture's value system, or in certain periods of history. Moral relativism is frequently employed to whitewash atrocities and racism in nondemocractic societies, including Muslim ones.

Frequently, moral relativists posit colonialism, the age of globalization, the end of the Cold War, the rise of secularism, and the perceived cultural and imperial hegemony of the West over Muslim society as reasons for the rise of Islamist terror in the past twenty years. By using these factors as justifications for global terror, moral relativists rationalize the intended mass killings of civilians.[71]

False moral equivalence was also used in 1961 by Adolf Eichmann during his trial in Jerusalem. He claimed that there were no basic differences between the Allied and Axis powers during World War II. Judge Benjamin Halevi responded to Eichmann during the trial by stating:

> You have often compared the extermination of the Jews with the bombing raids on German cities and you compared the murder of Jewish women and children with the death of German women in aerial bombardments. Surely it must be clear to you that there is a basic distinction between these two things. On the one hand the bombing is used as an instrument of forcing the enemy to surrender. Just as the Germans tried to force the British to surrender by their bombing. In that case it is a war objective to bring an armed enemy to his knees. On the other hand, when you take unarmed Jewish men, women, and children from their homes, hand them over to the Gestapo, and then send them to Auschwitz for extermination it is an entirely different thing, is it not?[72]

False moral equivalence is used against Israel in many cases. It can be broken down into several categories. Some examples are categorized below. A number have already been discussed, such as Israel as a "Nazi state" and Israel as an "apartheid state."

Zionism and Racism

"Zionism is racism" is an example of false moral equivalence; it was initially promulgated to further a political agenda. There was little mention of Zionism, the ethnonationalist movement for the return of the Jewish people to their homeland, as being a racist ideology until the mid-1960s. The singling out of Zionism as a form of racism was a device created by the Soviet Union to justify its refusal to condemn anti-Semitism. Soviet leaders felt that condemning anti-Semitism would anger its Arab-world allies.

This political strategy initially was used in the 1960s to try and expel Israel from the United Nations. When it failed, the Soviet Union, its satellite states, and Arab allies instead succeeded in passing UN Resolution 3379 in 1975.[73] It determined that "Zionism is a form of racism and racial discrimination."[74] This resolution remained in place until the General Assembly officially revoked it in 1991, after the fall of the Soviet Union.[75]

The notion of Zionism as a racist ideology remains very popular in the Arab world. Particularly, Arab anti-Semitic cartoons have propagated this false moral equivalence, often using stereotypical depictions of greedy, hook-nosed Jews. In one 2001 cartoon from the Lebanese *Daily Star*, a Hassidic Jew is pictured urinating on the world, wearing a cape that says "Racism." According to Kotek, "The Lebanese [cartoonist] Stavro Jabra identifies the true cause of the evils of the world—arrogance and Jewish racism."[76]

In Egypt's *Al-Ahram Weekly*, a "quasi-governmental daily newspaper, cartoonist Gomaa is attacking Judaism: a rabbi incites racism with one of the stone tablets of the law." This tablet, meant to resemble the Ten Commandments, merely says "racism."[77]

Zionism and Colonialism/Imperialism

Related to the abusive comparison of "Zionism is racism" is another statement of false moral equivalence: that Israel represents a colonial power in the Middle East. Proponents of this theory argue that Zionism, like colonialism and imperialism, justifies the colonization of people of color in their own land by white people, who then rule the entire population and exploit their resources.

Landes exposed the hypocrisy of this false moral equivalence on his website *The Augean Stables.* He pointed out the benign nature of Zionist settlement in Ottoman and British Palestine, which sharply contrasted with the imperial aspirations of European powers at the time:

> Behind this rather blandly stated remark lies the path to a real assessment of Israeli "colonialism" and "imperialism." All other colonial projects (e.g., Spanish in Latin America, British in South Africa, French in Algeria), occurred in the wake of a conquest. The only way that the new colonists could make claims to the land was by conquest, by (at best) driving away the inhabitants, and establishing overwhelming military superiority. Political power came from victory in war. In so behaving, the European imperialist-colonialists conformed to the international norms of millennia.
>
> The Zionist project of colonization worked in a markedly different manner. Rather than arrive as zero-sum military victors, the Zionists arrived as positive-sum neighbors. Granted they had no ability to conquer, and granted they built up their defenses against predatory attacks from both Arabs and Bedouin inhabitants of the land, but they nonetheless made peace with most of those who dwelled there by offering the benefits of civil society: hard productive work made everyone better off.[78]

Zionism and Fascism

Another variant is the false moral equivalence of "Zionism is fascism." When speaking at the Fifth Alliance of Civilizations Forum in Vienna in February 2013, Turkish Prime Minister Recep Tayyip Erdogan stated, "Just like Zionism, anti-Semitism and fascism, it becomes unavoidable that Islamophobia must be regarded as a crime against humanity."[79]

This statement was criticized by U.S. Secretary of State John Kerry, UN Secretary-General Ban Ki-moon, and Israeli Prime Minister Benjamin Netanyahu. Netanyahu's office released this response to Erdogan's speech: "This is a dark and mendacious statement the likes of which we thought had passed from the world." Erdogan did not retract his comments even after the international pressure, and he did not issue an apology.[80]

Kerry said, "Obviously we disagree with that, we find it objectionable."[81] A statement from the UN secretary-general's office said, "The secretary-general heard the prime minister's speech through an interpreter. If the comment about Zionism was interpreted correctly, then it was not only wrong but contradicts the very principles on which the Alliance of Civilizations is based."[82]

The Holocaust and the Nakba

The Holocaust and the Nakba have often been compared in public discourse by Muslim inciters and their allies, but also by others. The two historical events are not equals and cannot be compared. The Nakba was a direct result of the Palestinians' refusal to accept the UN partition resolution and the subsequent Arab-initiated war in Palestine. The Holocaust was a genocide of industrial extermination planned and executed by Germany and its many allies.

Meir Litvak and Esther Webman explore the construct of the Nakba as the equivalent of the Holocaust. Like the false moral equivalence of Zionism as racism, the equivalence of the Holocaust and the Nakba was a Palestinian strategic political maneuver: "The Nakba, epitomizing the Palestinian suffering, was being reconstructed as a founding myth in the Palestinian national identity, fulfilling, wittingly or unwittingly, a similar role to that of the Holocaust, the epitome of Jewish suffering, in Israeli society."[83]

In an interview to *Haaretz* after a visit to Israel, South African Archbishop Desmond Tutu said, "The West was consumed with guilt and regret toward Israel because of the Holocaust, as it should be. But who pays the penance? The penance is being paid by the Arabs, by the Palestinians."[84]

Robert Rozett, Tutu's museum guide and director of the Yad Vashem Library, replied in the same newspaper:

> Certainly it is the Jews who paid for the Holocaust with the blood of some six million innocent victims—not the perpetrators, not the bystanders and not Arabs in Palestine or anywhere else. Saying that the Palestinians are paying for the Holocaust falsely presupposes that the Jewish tie to the Land of Israel became significant only in the wake of the Nazi attempt to eradicate the Jews. It overlooks the ancient and ceaseless connection of the Jewish people to Israel, and the modern Zionist enterprise that returned an exiled people to their ancestral home.[85]

French President Nicolas Sarkozy visited Algeria in 2007. In the town of Constantine, while lecturing to students, he said, "I appeal to progressive Islam to recognize the right of the people of Israel who have suffered so much to live freely. I appeal to the people of Israel not to inflict on the Palestinian people the same injustice that they have suffered for so many centuries."[86]

Murders and Accidental Deaths

Another category of false moral equivalence implies that the intentional murder of innocent civilians is equal to the unintentional and accidental deaths of civilians in targeted assassinations. It is often used to claim a fallacious analogy between Israeli military operations intended to target terrorists only and premeditated, cold-blooded murder.

In March 2012, Ashton compared deaths of innocent people inflicted by serial killers and brutal dictators like Syria's Bashar al-Assad to accidental deaths of civilians due to Israeli actions in Gaza. In a speech to Palestinian youth in Brussels, she said, "When we think about what happened today in Toulouse, we remember what happened in Norway last year, we know what is happening in Syria, and we see what is happening in Gaza and other places—we remember young people and children who lose their lives."

The then Israeli opposition leader Tzipi Livni responded, "There is no similarity between an act of hatred or a leader killing members of his nation and a country fighting terror, even if civilians are harmed."[87]

During the Protective Edge campaign Ashton's office once again morally equated Israel and Hamas. Speaking on behalf of Ashton, Italian Foreign Affairs Under-Secretary Benedetto Della Vedova condemned "the indiscriminate launching of rockets towards Israel by militant groups in the Gaza Strip," adding that "the Union deplores the growing number of civilian victims coming from the Israeli military operation."[88] In this statement he not only failed to specify that these militant groups were terror groups as designated by the EU, his own organization,[89] but also did not mention that terrorist rockets from Gaza indiscriminately target Israeli civilian population centers.[90]

Another example of this category of false moral equivalence occurred when U.S. Secretary of State Kerry compared the three people killed in the 2013 Boston Marathon bombing to the nine people killed on the *Mavi Marmara*, part of a flotilla that attempted to break Israel's blockade of Gaza in 2010.[91] Kerry here mischaracterized the militants on the *Mavi Marmara* as innocent activists and bystanders, like the truly innocent Boston Marathon victims killed by terrorists.[92]

Philosopher Jean Bethke Elshtain notes:

> If we could not distinguish between an accidental death resulting from a car accident and an intentional murder, our criminal justice system would fall apart. And if we cannot distinguish the killing of combatants from the intended targeting of peaceable civilians, we live in a world of moral nihilism. In such a world, everything reduces to the same shade of gray and we cannot make distinctions that help us take our political and moral bearings.[93]

Targeted Actions Against Terrorists and Intentional Killing of Civilians

The November 16, 2012 front page of the print edition of *The New York Times* also used visual manipulation to convey moral equivalence between a killed Palestinian terrorist and a murdered Israeli civilian. This cover story displays two photographs of equal size, both from funerals. The first photo is of the Gaza City funeral of Ahmed al-Jabari, a Hamas military commander killed by an Israeli airstrike at the beginning of Operation Pillar of Defense. The second image is of the funeral of Mina Scharf, the first Israeli civilian killed by a Hamas rocket during this operation.

Writing about Jabari's and Scharf's respective backgrounds, *Tablet Magazine*'s Adam Chandler demonstrates the unjustness of this comparison in an editorial:

> Jabari was killed for being a Hamas strongman, who directed terror activity for a decade and was one of the central figures in the planning of the Gilad Shalit kidnapping. Beneath his picture is the picture of the body of Mina Scharf, a 25-year-old mother of three, who worked for Chabad in New Delhi, India and who was one of three civilians killed when a Hamas rocket struck a residential building in Kiryat Malachi.[94]

In a *Huffington Post* opinion piece on the same topic, American Jewish Committee Executive Director David Harris asks, "In the same spirit, would equal and abutting space have been given to photos of the funerals of Osama Bin Laden and one of his victims?"[95]

In October 2001, Israeli Tourism Minister Rehavam Ze'evi was assassinated by Palestinian terrorists. Danish Foreign Minister Mogens Lykketoft, who later would become the leader of the Danish Socialists, said on television that there was no difference between this assassination and Israel's targeted killing of terrorists.[96]

During the Protective Edge campaign the European Council released a document stating their conclusions about the escalating conflict in Gaza. Throughout their conclusions, Israel and Hamas are called the "parties" to the conflict, and Hamas is never called a terrorist organization even though the EU added Hamas to its "blacklist" of terrorist organizations in 2003.[97]

The document concludes with the sentence: "Israelis and Palestinians need to make the strategic choice of peace in order to allow their future generations to live lives freed from past conflicts and to enjoy the stability, security, and prosperity which they are currently being denied."[98] By using the term Palestinians, the EU goes a step further by not mentioning Hamas.

Kidnapping Soldiers Versus Imprisoning Terrorists

The public debate after the kidnapping of Israeli soldier Gilad Shalit fostered a further category of false moral equivalence: its supposed analogy with imprisoned Palestinian terrorists.

In October 2011, at the time of the exchange of Shalit for 1,027 Palestinian detainees including 280 convicted of planning and perpetrating terror attacks, the expression "prisoner exchange" was used frequently. One organization that spoke of a prisoner swap was Amnesty International. In their press release titled "Israel-Hamas prisoner swap casts harsh light on detention practices of all sides," Malcolm Smart, Amnesty's Middle East and North Africa director, stated, "This deal will bring relief to Gilad Shalit and his family after an ordeal that has lasted more than five years. Many Palestinian families will feel a similar sense of relief today when they are reunited with their relatives, many of whom have spent decades under harsh conditions in Israeli detention."

In this same publication, one of the few released by Amnesty International about Shalit, and only at the time of his release, twelve paragraphs of the seventeen-paragraph text are about conditions in Israeli prisons for Palestinian detainees.[99]

Harvard law professor Alan Dershowitz deconstructed these and similar arguments:

> Every single prisoner held by Israel has judicial review available to him or her and some have won release. Every one of them has access to Red Cross visitation, can communicate with family, and has a known whereabout. Kidnapped Israeli soldiers on the other hand are kept incommunicado by criminal elements, are routinely tortured, often murdered, (as occurred recently) and have no access to the Red Cross or judicial review. Moreover, the prisoners being held by Israel are terrorists—that is, unlawful combatants. Many are murderers who have been convicted and sentenced in accordance with due process. The "women" and "children" are guilty of having murdered or attempted to murder innocent babies and other non-combatants. The soldiers who were kidnapped are lawful combatants subject to prisoner of war status.

Dershowitz noted that Hamas or Hizbullah did not treat Israeli soldiers the way Israel treats its prisoners, because "they are terrorist organizations who do not operate within the rule of the law."[100]

Legitimate Governments and Terrorists

When making statements about Israel and its terrorist enemies, officials from across the world have drawn false moral equivalence between actions by Israel's legitimate government and those of terror organizations that are illegal according to international law. At the beginning of Operation Pillar of Defense in 2012, declarations by officials representing Russia, India, Turkey, and Sweden put Israel and Hamas on the same level.[101]

Prime Minister Erdogan told a gathering of the Eurasian Islamic Council, "Those who speak of Muslims and terror side-by-side are turning a blind eye when Muslims are massacred en masse." He also said, "Those who turn a blind eye to discrimination toward Muslims in their own countries, are also closing their eyes to the savage massacre of innocent children in Gaza . . . Therefore, I say Israel is a terrorist state."[102]

David Harris responded, "Erdogan has branded Israel a 'terrorist state' for having the audacity to defend itself against a group that seeks its destruction. He has vociferously denounced Israel's use of military force, while never condemning the hundreds of missile attacks against Israel this year alone."[103]

Erdogan's extreme hypocrisy has become even clearer in view of the many murders committed by and in Muslim states, which have accelerated since the revolutions in a number of Arab countries in recent years.

Comparing Islamophobia with Anti-Semitism

In the Western world, Islamophobia and anti-Semitism are often falsely presented as equal forms of discrimination. During his aforementioned visit to Algeria, President Sarkozy declared that nothing is more similar to an anti-Semite than an Islamophobe.[104]

Anti-Semitism and Islamophobia share a common element in that many Westerners reject the "other." Yet the difference between these two types of fear and stereotyped discrimination is much greater than their similarity. Although both groups face adversity in modern Europe, the scope and styles of this persecution could not be more different. Anti-Semitism has its origins in many centuries of religious and ethnic hate propaganda. Islamophobia derives not only from perceived aggression but also from actual violence supported by many in the world of Islam in the name of religion.

In 2011, after the murders by Anders Breivik, Erna Solberg, then leader of the Conservative opposition and currently prime minister of Norway, gave an interview to the country's largest paper *Verdens Gang*. She claimed that nowadays, Muslims in Norway are treated like the Jews were in the 1930s. Solberg gave as examples discrimination in the job market, non-admission to nightclubs, along with claims that they are not really Norwegians and are frequently asked where they came from originally. She added that many individual Muslims are held collectively responsible for the actions of all Muslims.

Solberg implicitly admitted that her comparison was largely false by stating that Muslims today are not subject to brutal repression as Jews were in the 1930s. Solberg also conveniently ignored the fact that Norwegian authorities encourage Muslim participation in society. Muslims also play a significant role in Norwegian politics.

The Jewish journalist Mona Levin summed it up by noting, "Muslim-bashing is reprehensible and is neither made better nor worse by drawing parallels with Jewish history."[105] The chairman of the small Jewish community in Oslo, Ervin Kohn, reacted by asserting that Solberg's inappropriate remarks about the Jews showed that she did not understand history. During the 1930s Jews were persecuted by states and were victims of racist laws, which is not the case with Muslims in Norway.

Islamophobia and Protective Edge

In some Western countries, the reactions to the Protective Edge campaign again brought the "Islamophobia equals anti-Semitism" issue to the fore. Jewish communities have played a part in allowing this. One of these is the Board of Deputies of British Jews, which issued a joint statement with the Muslim Council of Britain (MCB).

British journalist and author Melanie Phillips analyzed this text and wrote:

> The joint statement with the MCB condemned anti-Semitism and Islamophobia as if they were equivalent forms of bigotry . . . Islamophobia is a catch-all phrase used to demonize anyone who makes a legitimate criticism of Islam or Muslims. It is not irrational to fear the murder and terrorism perpetuated in the name of Islam; it is not bigoted to warn against the steady encroachment of Shari'a law or the connections between Islamic charities and terrorist money-laundering in London; it is not demonization to condemn Muslim attacks on women and girls or on freedom of speech. Yet all such opinions are damned as "Islamophobic" in order to silence them.[106]

In the Netherlands in September 2014, Jewish-community leaders, together with their Muslim and Christian counterparts, signed a joint declaration. One of the many problematic aspects was its statement that both "hatred of Jews and Islamophobia should not be tolerated." It did not mention that a hugely disproportionate part of the aggression and incitement against Jews in the Netherlands originates from parts of the Dutch Muslim community.[107]

Condemnations

Frequent condemnations can be another form of demonization. More than ten years ago, Cotler said:

> The United Nations General Assembly annually passes some 20 resolutions against Israel, as many as are passed against the rest of the international community combined. Again, the major human rights violators escape unscathed. While these decisions are not binding, they are important representations of the political culture of the international community.[108]

One might add that this situation has not changed very much over the past ten years.

The number of condemnations of Israel by individual countries is almost unlimited. The Gaza flotilla incident, for instance, which resulted from provocations by Turkish participants, drew many condemnations. The one from the Organization of Islamic Cooperation was part of its propaganda battle against Israel. Its statement said:

> The OIC Group strongly condemns the illegal, brutal and provocative Israeli aggression carried out in international waters against the civilian convoy of ships that was carrying vital humanitarian aid to be delivered by hundreds of international peace and human rights activists to the occupied and besieged Gaza Strip. The OIC Group also condemns in the strongest possible terms the killing and injury of several civilians by the Israeli military forces that attacked the Turkish vessel in the humanitarian convoy.[109]

Sweden also took an extreme anti-Israeli position after the Israeli raid on the *Mavi Marmara*. Immediately afterward, Foreign Minister Carl Bildt met the two Swedish flotilla activists in Istanbul, where he expressed his sympathy for them and their cause and condemned Israel.[110] He also stated that Israel's Palestinian policy was "catastrophic" and "leads to one problem after another."[111]

One can indeed only regret that a detailed analysis of Ashton's condemnations of Israel has never been made. If that had been the case, one could compare that to how often she has condemned the world's major human rights violators.

Calls for Action

Part of the demonization process is carried out through public calls for acts against Israel and/or Jews. The most violent calls are those for genocide against Israel. The vast majority of these calls come from sizable parts of the Muslim world. Over the past decade, Iran has played a major role in this phenomenon. On October 26, 2005, Iran's then-president Mahmoud Ahmadinejad addressed the "World without Zionism" conference—which preceded the annual Al-Quds

(Jerusalem) Day established by Ayatollah Khomeini—at the Interior Ministry in Tehran. He stated:

> Imam [Khomeini] said: "This regime that is occupying Quds must be eliminated from the pages of history." This sentence is very wise . . . Today, [Israel] seeks, satanically and deceitfully, to gain control of the front of war . . . If someone is under the pressure of hegemonic power [i.e., the West] and understands that something is wrong, or he is naive, or he is an egotist and his hedonism leads him to recognize the Zionist regime, he should know that he will burn in the fire of the Islamic Ummah [nation] . . . Oh dear people, look at this global arena. By whom are we confronted? We must understand the depth of the disgrace imposed on us by the enemy, until our holy hatred expands continuously and strikes like a wave.

Other speakers at the event were terrorist leaders Hassan Nasrallah of Hizbullah in Lebanon and Khaled Mashal of Hamas, now living in Qatar. Before his statement, Ahmadinejad told the hundreds of students present to shout the slogan "Death to Israel!"[112]

Inciting to terror is another form of verbal aggression. Another type of call for action involves boycotts, divestment, or sanctions (BDS). All of these have a strong demonizing character.

Acts Against Israel

The most violent acts against Israel are usually accompanied by verbal demonization. The military campaigns, the suicide and other terror attacks gain, often though not always, support from the Arab propaganda war.

British anti-Semitism expert Michael Whine noted that a change has taken place in the nature of terrorist threats against Jewish communities:

> Many terrorist groups that target Jews are rooted in political ideologies that incorporate anti-Semitism into their world view. Neo-Nazi groups, for example, adhere to the view that Jews are racially inferior and conspire to destroy the

> white race. Islamist terrorists of both Shiite and Sunni varieties believe that Jews are morally inferior and conspire to undermine and destroy Islam. Leftist terrorist groups that have targeted Jews have often conflated anti-Semitism with their anti-American and anti-capitalist viewpoints. The belief in a Jewish or Zionist conspiracy is common to the ideologies that drive most terrorist groups that target Jews and Israel. The idea that Jews, Zionism or Israel are preventing the creation of a new, better world for all is also common across different extremist ideologies.

He added:

> Terrorist threats to Jews in the twenty-first century come in the main from three directions: the global jihad movement (i.e., Al-Qaeda and its affiliates and followers); Iran and its surrogates; and neo-Nazis and white supremacists. Far-left and anarchist groups carried out many terrorist attacks against Jewish communities in the 1970s and 1980s. Although some residual groups of this type remain in Germany, Italy, Greece, and Latin America, there is now less financial backing or training available for them than there was from the Soviet bloc before its implosion. Consequently, the terror threat from this quarter is currently low.[113]

Anti-Israeli demonstrations are another type of action that includes delegitimization. A substantial number of them are accompanied by anti-Jewish violence and anti-Semitic and anti-Israeli incitement. Shouts of "Death to the Jews" or "Hamas, Hamas, Jews to the gas" are heard in some of them.

BDS

The boycott campaigns against Israel must be seen in a much wider context. In the past, boycotts of different natures against other governments have not been very successful. Yet making a lasting impact is not necessarily the major aim of the boycotters. The accompanying publicity is often far more important to them as a goal.

There is another important aspect of boycotts. In complex and heavily integrated societies, the vulnerability of society increases all the time. Much more so than in the case of boycotts, this is evident from the murderous calls of the Islamic State movement. It asks supporters in the Western world to kill Westerners at random. If everybody is a potential victim, then protection for all becomes a huge problem.

In a context of general vulnerability, there is little the individual can do to protect himself. This was to a certain extent the case for Israelis during the intifadas; any Israeli could fall victim to murderous Palestinian attacks. Similarly, attacks abroad targeted Israelis at random.

The anti-Israeli Canadian Jewish author Naomi Klein admitted—while defaming Israel—that the anti-Israeli boycott is using double standards. She asserted, "The best strategy to end the increasingly bloody occupation is for Israel to become the target of the kind of global movement that put an end to apartheid in South Africa." Klein added, "Why single out Israel when the United States, Britain and other Western countries do the same things in Iraq and Afghanistan?" Her answer: "Boycott is not a dogma; it is a tactic. The reason the BDS strategy should be tried against Israel is practical: in a country so small and trade-dependent, it could actually work."[114]

This is a core case of anti-Semitism, as it singles out Israel and explains some of the instruments used in anti-Israelism and classic anti-Semitism. A key element of anti-Semitism is focusing one's actions against Jews because they appear to be an easier target than others. Once one understands that, one sees it in many other situations involving Israel and the Jews. This also explains, in part, the phenomenon that the Jews are often the first to be attacked, but never the last. It also clarifies why Jews and Israel are indicators of the nature of many phenomena in both Muslim and Western societies.

The Chief Whip of the British Conservative Party, Michael Gove, said in a 2014 speech at the Holocaust Education Trust:

> We need to speak out against this prejudice. We need to remind people that what began with a campaign against Jewish goods in the past ended with a campaign against Jewish lives. We need to spell out that this sort of prejudice starts with the Jews but never ends with the Jews. We need to stand united against hate. Now more than ever.

He continued: "We know that the jihadist terrorists responsible for horrific violence across the Middle East are targeting not just Jews and Israelis but all of us in the West."

Gove summarized:

> They hate Israel, and they wish to wipe out the Jewish people's home, not because of what Israel does but because of what Israel is—free, democratic, liberal and western. We need to remind ourselves that defending Israel's right to exist is defending our common humanity. Now more than ever.[115]

A similar argument to Klein's was offered by the president of the American Studies Association (ASA), Curtis Marez. He did not dispute that many other countries, including some of those in Israel's region, have a comparable or worse human rights record than Israel. He was reported to have said, however, that "One has to start somewhere." He added that Palestinian civil-society groups had asked his organization to boycott Israel; no similar requests had been made by groups in other countries.[116]

The BDS movement has seen increasing successes in recent years. One should add that this is partly due to the lack of professional responses by the Israeli authorities.

CHAPTER FIVE

Originators of Demonization: Muslims

THE NEXT MAJOR STEP IN deconstructing the makeup of the postmodern total war against Israel is to identify the main originators of current anti-Israelism and other types of anti-Semitism. The demonizers of Israel and the Jewish people come from many different backgrounds and fall roughly into a number of categories.

Much more information is available on hate-mongering among some originator groups than on others. For example, while much is known about anti-Semitic hate acts and incitement among European Muslims, very little has been written about the hate-mongering in Western schools. To properly analyze certain perpetrator categories requires books rather than essays. Thus hereinafter we will only offer examples of the demonization of Israel and the Jews by some major perpetrator categories.

The largest-scale, most frequent, and usually most virulent hate-mongering against Israel and the Jews comes from parts of the Arab and Muslim world. Extreme anti-Israeli and anti-Semitic incitement as well as other forms of discrimination are widespread in Arab and most other Muslim countries.

The Universal Declaration of Human Rights proclaims: "All human beings are born free and equal in dignity and rights."[1] However, many outside the democratic world disagree in practice or even also in theory with part of this statement. In 1990, the Organization of the Islamic Conference adopted the

Cairo Declaration of Human Rights in Islam.[2] Among its many human rights flaws is that it discriminates against religious minorities.[3]

For its Global Terrorism Index, the Institute for Economics and Peace conducted a survey of terror and found that Muslim terror far exceeded that by other religious groups. "In 2013, 66 percent of all fatalities from claimed terrorist attacks were caused by four terrorist groups: the Taliban, Boko Haram, ISIL and Al-Qaeda. The primary targets of terrorist attacks are citizens and private property."[4]

Anti-Semitic hatred issuing from the Muslim world comes from far wider circles than the over one hundred million supporters of the criminal Al-Qaeda and other jihadi ideologies, which seek to achieve Islamic rule over the world via jihad.[5]

Jihadis have killed many people in various countries, and they continue to do so in pursuit of their aim. A 2009 Pew study found that more than 20 percent of Muslims in Indonesia, Jordan, and Egypt had confidence that Osama Bin Laden was doing "the right thing in world affairs." Among Nigerian Muslims the total came to over 50 percent.[6]

Although support for Al-Qaeda has plummeted across the Muslim world since the death of Bin Laden in May 2011, it remains high in several places including the Palestinian territories. In a September 2013 Pew Research Global Attitudes Project poll on Muslim extremist opinions, 35 percent of Palestinians viewed Al-Qaeda favorably. These were the highest levels of favorability, by over 12 percent, compared to any other Muslim society polled. Even in Pakistan, which has heavy Al-Qaeda and Taliban influence, support was only at 13 percent, down from 21 percent the year before.[7]

The July 2014 Pew survey on concerns about rising extremism in the Middle East found that 28 percent of Palestinians believed that "suicide bombing can often be justified against civilian targets in order to defend Islam from its enemies." This figure was higher than that for any other country polled. It was twice as high as that for Bangladesh, where 14 percent agreed with this statement. The only other countries with double digits were Egypt and the Shiite population in Lebanon.

The Palestinian territories scored second in terms of aggregate total of those who often and sometimes justified suicide bombings against civilian targets so as to defend Islam from its enemies, with 46 percent of Palestinians polled displaying this attitude. They followed Bangladesh, which had 47 percent of respondents taking this stance. Third in line were Shiite Lebanese and fourth in line were Tanzanians.

As far as views about extreme organizations are concerned, the Palestinian territories also scored very high. Thirty-two percent of Palestinians viewed Hizbullah favorably, surpassed only by 86 percent of Lebanese Shiites. Next in line were 28 percent of Bangladeshis and 26 percent of Tunisians and Malaysians. Additionally, Palestinians had the highest rate of approval of Al-Qaeda at 25 percent, followed by Bangladesh at 23 percent and Malaysia and Nigeria at 18 percent.

Hamas, however, is viewed far more favorably by various Muslim populations than Al-Qaeda. In 2014 Pew found that 39 percent of Jordanians, 38 percent of Egyptians, and 37 percent of Tunisians polled had a favorable opinion of Hamas. They were followed by 32 percent of Lebanese including 55 percent of Shiites polled, 29 percent of Bangladeshis, and 28 percent of Malaysians.[8]

The Palestinian attitude toward Hamas shifts rapidly and has to be viewed separately. According to a poll by the Palestinian Center for Policy and Survey Research in September 2014, 55 percent of Palestinians polled said that if Palestinian elections were held that day they would vote for Ismail Haniyeh, the Hamas leader in Gaza. Thirty-eight percent said they would vote for the current president of the Palestinian Authority, Mahmoud Abbas. The month before, at the height of Protective Edge, 61 percent polled said they would vote for Haniyeh, while 32 percent favored Abbas.[9]

The results of a 2011 study by the Pew Research Center, "Common Concerns about Islamic Extremism: Muslim-Western Tensions Persist," reveal the magnitude of animosity toward Jews and Christians in large parts of the Muslim world. The questions asked concerned stereotypes. One was: "Who is most to blame for bad relations [between Muslims and Westerners]?" Participants could select from the options "Muslims, Western people, both, neither, Jews, or Don't know, to describe who was to blame for bad Muslim-Western relations." In some Muslim nations, Jews came in a close second to "Western people." The highest figures for Jews were found in Egypt, Jordan, and Lebanon, with 25 percent, 29 percent, and 35 percent responding respectively that Jews were most to blame.[10]

That same survey also asked participants if they had favorable views of Jews, Muslims, and Christians. Respondents in Muslim-majority countries had the least favorable opinions of Jews. Nine percent of Indonesians viewed Jews favorably, the highest number in the Muslim world. Favorability ratings for Jews were 4 percent in Turkey, 2 percent in Egypt, Jordan, and Pakistan, 3 percent in Lebanon, and 4 percent in the Palestinian territories. In sum, 96-98 percent of the Muslims interviewed in Middle Eastern countries viewed Jews unfavorably.[11]

The Muslim World

Many in the Muslim world do not differentiate in their hostility between Israel and Jews. In the Muslim world, anti-Semitism is manifested partly through state anti-Semitism.

A U.S. State Department travel advisory for U.S. citizens warns that they may not be able to enter Saudi Arabia if their passports indicate that they were born in Israel or have previously traveled to it.[12] According to ADL National Director Abraham Foxman, "Saudi Arabia also bars anyone from bringing into Saudi Arabia religious ritual objects, including religious texts, from any faith other than Islam, effectively banning religiously observant Jews from entering the country."[13]

Jordan and the Palestinian Authority (PA) are also marked by state-sanctioned anti-Semitism. Under Jordan's Law for Preventing the Sale of Real Estate to the Enemy, also adopted by the PA in 1997, a Palestinian or Jordanian can face a death sentence for selling land to a Jew or Israeli. Although nobody has been officially executed for violating this law, extrajudicial killings have occurred in the West Bank for suspected land sales to Jews.[14]

Iran still has a significant Jewish community of about ten thousand.[15] Although Jews face no legalized state persecution they are confronted with many problems because of their religion, especially in light of Iran's tensions with Israel. Jewish women are required to comply with Iran's Muslim modesty laws, and in public have to wear a *chador* and other traditional Muslim garb. Furthermore, one rabbi insists that the faces of Iranian Jews be blurred in photographs out of safety concerns.[16]

Religious anti-Semitism, media incitement against Israel and the Jews, and many other sources of hate-mongering are widespread in the Muslim world. When analyzing this sphere, one should focus separately on three different parts of it: the Muslim world at large, the Palestinian territories, and Muslims in the Western countries.

The Mahathir Affair

Just how deeply the racist attitude toward Jews has permeated the predominantly nondemocratic Muslim countries was illustrated by what may be called the "Mahathir Affair" at the 2003 Organization of the Islamic Conference summit in Kuala Lumpur. Then-Malaysian Prime Minister Mohamad Mahathir, the conference's host, portrayed relations between Muslims and Jews as a worldwide direct confrontation, offering some new examples of a "Jewish conspiracy."[17]

As he said:

> 1.3 billion Muslims cannot be defeated by a few million Jews. There must be a way. And we can only find a way if we stop to think, to assess our weaknesses and our strength, to plan, to strategize and then to counter-attack. We are actually very strong. 1.3 billion people cannot be simply wiped out. The Europeans killed six million Jews out of 12 million. But today the Jews rule this world by proxy. They get others to fight and die for them.

Mahathir added:

> We are up against a people who think. They survived 2,000 years of pogroms not by hitting back, but by thinking. They invented and successfully promoted Socialism, Communism, human rights and democracy so that persecuting them would appear to be wrong, so they may enjoy equal rights with others. With these they have now gained control of the most powerful countries and they, this tiny community, have become a world power. We cannot fight them through brawn alone. We must use our brains also.[18]

It was yet one more illustration of the classic anti-Semitic motif of the Jewish lust for world domination.

Mahathir was applauded by the attendants of the conference including top leaders of all Muslim nations. An editorial in the French daily *Le Monde* noted that "such words are common currency in the Arab Islamic world where they pass for evident truth . . . and this direct form of racism, purely and simply is practiced as a normal category of the 'political debate.'"[19]

When subsequently criticized by Western leaders, Mahathir did not apologize and many Muslim leaders supported him. Few if any dissociated themselves from his words. There was so much international public discussion of this incident that any of the attendants who had wanted to distance themselves from Mahathir's assertions had ample occasion to do so. The Mahathir Affair showed the permeation of racism and anti-Semitism into the Arab and large parts of the Muslim world at its highest levels.

Two major elements of Muslim anti-Semitism were revealed at that conference and in the remarks that followed. One is support for this racist outlook by many senior Muslim statesmen. The second is that the attack focused on the Jews and not on Israel.

Other Muslim Statesmen

There are many examples of Muslim and Arab political leaders propagating anti-Semitism, racism, and hatred. Mustafa Tlass, Syrian defense minister from 1972 to 2004, has repeatedly stated that Jews "need blood for their religious practices." The Syrian blood-libel accusations originate partly in a major nineteenth-century calumny against the Jews of Damascus, who were accused of having murdered a Christian priest, Thomas al-Kabushi, so as to use his blood for religious purposes.[20]

Major anti-Semitic incitement comes from many sources in the Muslim world, including government-controlled bodies and leaders of Egypt, which is officially at peace with Israel. In October 2012, a video showed then-Egyptian President Mohamed Morsi answering "Amen" to an imam who made a genocidal prayer request: "Oh Allah, destroy the Jews and their supporters."[21]

So far in the twenty-first century, the most extreme source of anti-Israeli hatred and incitement is Iran. Its former President Mahmoud Ahmadinejad and various other leaders promote the destruction of Israel, which can only be achieved through genocide. Yet this has not prevented Western[22] and other government officials,[23] religious leaders,[24] and academics[25] from hosting Ahmadinejad in their countries.

Comparison of the Muslim World with Nazi Germany

Some of those who compare between attitudes of the sizable extremist movements in the Islamic world and those of the Nazis present weighty arguments. Israeli Holocaust scholar Yehuda Bauer points out:

> Today for the first time since 1945, Jews are once again threatened openly by a radical Islamic genocidal ideology whose murderous rantings must be taken more seriously than the Nazi ones were two and more generations ago. The direct connection between World War II, the Shoah, and present-day genocidal events and threats is more than obvious. The Shoah was unprecedented; but it was a precedent, and that precedent is being followed.[26]

Wistrich writes that hard-core anti-Semitism in the Arab and Muslim world is comparable only with that of Nazi Germany. He explains that Muslim hatred for Israel and Jews is "an eliminatory anti-Semitism with a genocidal dimension." As for common elements between Muslim and Nazi anti-Semitism, Wistrich cites fanaticism, the cult of death, the nihilistic wish for destruction, and the mad lust for world hegemony.[27]

Richard Prasquier, then head of CRIF, the umbrella organization of French Jewry, compared radical Islam with Nazism. He noted two important common features. The first is that Jews are the prime enemy for both movements and anti-Semitism is an essential component of their ideology. The other is that both Nazism and radical Islam dehumanize Jews.[28] Landes remarked that "future historians will probably find that present anti-Semitism in Arab and Muslim societies reached an even higher fever pitch than that of the Nazis."[29]

In 2013, during an interview on the Europe1 television program *Télé*, former French Education Minister Luc Ferry compared modern Islamism with Nazism in the 1930s. He said, "Terrorism today somehow represents the equivalent of Nazism. I don't exaggerate by saying that radical Islam today, and of course I am not talking about the Muslim religion but radical Islam and anti-Semitism, are the bane of people, of human life. It is as atrocious as Nazism in the '30s." He also warned that radical Islam is not merely like an isolated "local guerrilla" but a global problem and a portent of a third world war.[30]

In 2015, before the seventieth anniversary of the International Holocaust Remembrance Day, Moshe Kantor, president of the European Jewish Congress, said, "In certain vital aspects jihadism is close to Nazism . . . one could say that they are two facets of the same evil." He added that "radical Islam is the force to blame. The features of this phenomena are well known: arrogance, unshakable belief in your own righteousness, contempt for other faiths, creeds and ideals."[31]

From time to time in anti-Israeli demonstrations, including outside of Muslim countries, swastikas can be witnessed. One such case occurred in The Hague in July 2014. Various Muslim participants carried flags and banners of the terrorist group ISIS and others, along with swastikas superimposed on Israeli flags and banners comparing Israel with Hitler. The Dutch police just stood by.[32]

World War II Nazi-Muslim Ties

Nazi Germany already attempted to gain influence in the Muslim world before World War II. German political scientist Matthias Küntzel says:

> In April 1939, Germany began to broadcast anti-Semitic propaganda in Arabic, Persian, Turkish and Hindi. Its modern shortwave station Radio Zeesen, was received in the Arab world better than any other. From 1939 to 1945, it broadcast professional anti-Semitic programs on a daily basis. They were mixed with quotes from the Koran and Arabic music. The Allies were presented as being dependent on the Jews, who were portrayed as Islam's biggest enemy. The program would announce: "The Jew is our enemy and killing him brings pleasure to Allah." In this way, German propaganda radicalized existing Jew-

> hatred among Muslims. Various testimonies from that period indicate that these broadcasts were widely heard.

He adds:

> There are many indicators which prove the continuity of influence of Nazi thinking in the Arab world to this very day. Many Arab anti-Semitic cartoons are similar to those of the Nazi era. There are numerous large edition publications of Hitler's *Mein Kampf* with the accompanying veneration of Hitler. One frequently finds denial of the Holocaust or promotion of a new one there. This Nazi influence upon the Middle East is nevertheless almost systematically overlooked by Middle East and Islam scholars.[33]

Küntzel observes that before and during World War II it was quite fashionable in certain Muslim circles to express pro-Nazi opinions. In a lecture to the imams of the Bosnian SS division in 1944, Haj Amin al-Husseini, the Mufti of Jerusalem, noted the main points of similarity between the Islamic outlook as he saw it and National Socialism:

- Monotheism—unity of leadership, the Führer principle
- Sense of obedience and discipline
- Battle for honor, to die in battle
- Attitude toward community: common interest comes before private interest
- Valuing motherhood and prohibition of abortion
- Attitude toward Jews—"In the fight against Judaism, Islam and National Socialists are very close to each other"
- Glorification of labor and creation—"Islam protects and respects labor in whatsoever form"[34]

Palestinian Anti-Semitism

Palestinian classic anti-Semitism and anti-Israelism contain many genocidal elements. These are not limited to the earlier-mentioned platform of Hamas, which emerged as the largest party in the only Palestinian parliamentary elections—those of 2006—to have been held. In Hamas circles, one regularly hears genocidal voices speaking. However, they also come out of official PA sources and are broadcast in its media.

One example among many of calls for genocide from PA circles included an appeal for a genocidal war against the Jews made in 2000 by Dr. Ahmed Abu Halabiyah, rector of advanced studies at the Islamic University of Gaza. It was broadcast on PA TV, the PA's official channel. Many similar statements can be heard or read in the Arab and Muslim world. Since Halabiyah spoke in a televised Friday sermon, his call belongs to the governmental, academic, and religious spheres of the PA and Palestinian society.

He said:

> The Jews are the Jews . . . They do not have any moderates or any advocates of peace. They are all liars. They must be butchered and must be killed . . . The Jews are like a spring—as long as you step on it with your foot it doesn't move. But if you lift your foot from the spring, it hurts you and punishes you . . . It is forbidden to have mercy in your hearts for the Jews in any place and in any land, make war on them anywhere that you find yourself. Any place that you meet them, kill them.[35]

The Mufti Muhammad Hussein is the PA's highest religious leader, appointed by President Mahmoud Abbas. In 2012 at an official Fatah celebration—a movement headed by Abbas—he called for the killing of all Jews.[36]

Hamas

Many Hamas proponents mention their movement's goal of committing genocide against the Jews. Sheikh Yunus al-Astal is a member of the Palestinian parliament and also a Hamas leader who heads the Clerics Association of Palestine, the most influential religious institution within the Hamas movement. Al-Astal also heads the Department of Islamic Law at the Islamic University of Gaza.

In 2008, for his regular column in the Hamas weekly *Al-Rissala*, he wrote an article with the headline "Suffering by Fire is Jews' destiny in this world and next." It said:

> ". . . you will taste the punishment of Scorching Fire." [Quran 3:181]
> "This [Quran] verse threatens the Jews with the punishment of Fire . . . the reason for the punishment of Fire is it is fitting retribution for what they have done . . . but the urgent question is, is it possible that they will have the punishment of Fire in this world, before the great punishment [of Fire in Hell] . . . many of the [Islamic] religious leaders believe that the [Jews'] punishment of Fire is in this world, before the next world . . . therefore we are sure that the Holocaust is still to come upon the Jews."[37]

This was not the only time al-Astal made such remarks. In 2014, he said on Hamas's Al-Aqsa TV that not only should a special discriminatory tax on Jews be imposed, but also Jews must be massacred:

> we will discuss the demand that the Palestinian people recognize Israel as a Jewish State, so that the occupation will graciously hand them out scraps. I would like to begin by quoting what Allah said about them . . . "If you gain mastery over them in war, use them to disperse those who follow them that they may remember." This indicates that we must massacre them in order to break them down and prevent them from sowing corruption in the world . . .[38]

Other Hamas representatives make genocidal statements as well. For instance, Hamas spokesman Dr. Ismail Radwan said in 2007 on PA TV:

> "The Hour [of the Resurrection] will not take place until the Muslims fight the Jews and the Muslims kill them, and the rock and the tree will say: 'Oh, Muslim, servant of Allah, there is a Jew behind me, kill him!'" We must remind our Arab and Muslim nation, its leaders and people, its scholars and students, remind them that Palestine and the Al Aqsa mosque will not be liberated through summits nor by international resolutions, but it will be liberated through the rifle.[39]

Century of Hatred

The desire to commit genocide against the Jews has an almost century-old history in Palestinian society. Haj Amin al-Husseini was the leader of the Palestinian extremists before the War of Independence and supported Hitler's actions against the Jews.

Küntzel says:

> In the mid-1930s, moderate Palestinian Arab forces which were seeking coexistence with the Zionists had not yet been marginalized. That changed with the vast Nazi support for the Islamists. The Mufti destroyed or forced out moderate Palestinians in the Arab uprising of 1936-1939. The Muslim Brotherhood in Egypt used the riots in Palestine for anti-Semitic campaigns which enabled them to become a huge organization. Their membership jumped from 800 in 1936 to 200,000 in 1938.[40]

Shragai observes, "During the Second World War, Husseini planned to build an Auschwitz-like crematorium near Nablus. He intended to have Jews from Palestine and Arab countries gassed there. Husseini also helped create Muslim SS units in Bosnia and Kosovo."[41]

For many years the leader of the Palestinian "moderates" was Ragheb bey al-Nashashibi, the mayor of Jerusalem. After the 1929 riots in Mandatory Palestine, the non-Jewish French writer Albert Londres asked him why the Arabs had murdered the old pious Jews in Hebron and Safed, with whom they had no quarrel. The mayor answered, "In a way you behave like in a war. You don't kill what you want. You kill what you find. Next time, they will all be killed, young and old." Later on, Londres spoke again to the mayor and tested him ironically by saying, "You cannot kill all the Jews. There are 150,000 of them." Nashashibi answered "in a soft voice, 'Oh no, it'll take two days.'"[42]

Incitement of Children

Incitement against Israel and the Jews in Palestinian society occurs on a major scale and is largely neglected by Western media. Psychiatrist Daphne Burdman says:

> In both the Palestinian Authority and the Hamas-ruled territory of Gaza there are carefully planned, widespread campaigns of incitement of children. Due to this indoctrination, children start viewing positively their involvement in terrorist actions in which they risk their lives. This incitement process has been poorly covered by the international media.
>
> Thus, Westerners are largely ignorant of the sinister development of these profoundly "successful" programs. These are based on both familiar and innovative techniques of persuasion and indoctrination. Similar ones were used to maximum effect by totalitarian regimes including Nazi Germany, the Soviet KGB and Chinese intelligence services. There is increasing evidence that some of these sources have inspired and trained the Palestinian Authority.

Burdman observes:

> Indoctrination in the Palestinian areas is far broader than textbook and television sources, encompassing general societal elements including newsprint, parents, teachers, methods of teaching with encouragement and praise for adherence, and strong disapproval for less devoted students. Imams are extremely influential in successfully emphasizing the goals of jihad and martyrdom. Summer camps, and the naming of streets, playgrounds, and soccer teams for martyrs, help maintain the ambience throughout society.[43]

Palestinian Media Watch (PMW) provides many examples of Palestinian anti-Israeli and anti-Semitic incitement. The PMW website divides these into categories such as "animalization," "Jews/Israelis are evil," "Jews/Israelis are cancer and other diseases," "Jews/Israelis endanger all humanity," and so on.[44]

One among many examples of extreme incitement occurred in 2013 on PA TV where two young girls recited a poem that included the lines: "You who murdered Allah's pious prophets [i.e., Jews in Islamic tradition], Oh, you who were brought up on spilling blood, You have been condemned to humiliation and hardship, Oh Sons of Zion, oh most evil among creations, Oh barbaric monkeys, wretched pigs."[45]

Doubletalk

Israeli political scientist Michael Widlanski remarks:

> Claims by many Israelis and Americans that the PLO has agreed to recognize and accept Israeli settlement blocs in return for ceding territory in Israel to Palestinian sovereignty, have been repudiated. This is also true about claims that the PLO leadership is willing to accept Israeli control of some holy places in eastern Jerusalem and that Ramallah or Al-Azzaria would serve as a Palestinian capital. Abbas repeatedly told Arab media—as late as August 2013—that there will be no Jews living in Palestinian territory and that Jerusalem will be the Palestinian capital.
>
> Abbas told an Israeli interviewer that he did not want to return to Safed. Thereafter, he declared to Arab interviewers that all Arabs could decide where and when they would go. He specifically said all refugees would have the "right" to return to their homes.
>
> Claims that the PLO has amended its charter are probably false as well. The "ceremony" in 1998 concerning this is deemed a stage act by Palestinians, even though it was sanctioned by Bill Clinton and Benjamin Netanyahu. Leading Palestinians—such as Palestinian National Congress speaker Salim Za'anoun —say that the PLO charter still stands.[46]

CHAPTER SIX

Muslims in the Western World

THE 2013 FRA STUDY AND other data show that Muslims in the European Union account for a disproportionately large percentage of anti-Semitic incidents. The study found that in the European countries surveyed, 27 percent of incidents of anti-Semitic harassment, 51 percent of negative statements about Jews heard by respondents in 2012, and 40 percent of anti-Semitic physical violence were perpetrated by someone with a Muslim extremist view.[1]

Muslim anti-Semitism is rife in Western societies. Yet European governments often avoid exposing this anti-Semitism. In colonial times, Western racism far exceeded any other form of discrimination. With these guilt feelings about the European past, it is difficult to accuse current minority immigrant groups of having a relatively high percentage of members who promote hate against another minority. The Western reluctance to confront the truth is even greater because there is substantial discrimination against Muslims in Western societies. Furthermore, officially accusing large parts of the Muslim community of anti-Semitism could disrupt a country's "social peace."

The few studies on Muslim anti-Semitism in European countries all point in the same direction. In 2011, Belgian sociologist Mark Elchardus published a report on Dutch-language secondary schools in Brussels. He found that about 50 percent of Muslim students in second and third grade could be considered anti-Semites, versus 10 percent of others.[2] It is logical to assume, in view of the age of these children, that their parents imbued them with most if not all of their Jew-hatred.

Elchardus says about the studies he undertook in Brussels, Antwerp, and Gent:

> Anti-Semitism among non-Muslims occurs mainly among the socially weaker segments of society. Yet anti-Semitism among Muslim students is not a function of social and cultural factors, such as parents' income and education, or the type of school the youths visit. The sole relevant factor is Muslim traditionalism. For instance, 12% of progressive Muslims agree with the statement "it is best to avoid Jews." Among conservative Muslims, this percentage rises to 46%. There are however few progressive Muslims. For every 8 progressive Muslims, one finds 100 conservatives.

Elchardus further observes:

> From the Muslim community, we received extremely negative reactions. The same was the case from a number of non-Muslims who present themselves as "defenders" or "spokespeople" for the Muslim communities. Some even said that I was a racist. A Muslim organization complained about me to the Center for Equal Chances and the Fight against Racism. This complaint was thrown out. Yet it took their legal expert about a month to reach that conclusion.
>
> Muslim organizations are meant to play a major role in the integration of Muslims in society. It is regrettable that none of these organizations condemn anti-Semitism, or the very negative attitudes toward homosexuals our studies in Antwerp and Gent found. Nor did any of them announce that they would provide informal education for the Muslim youngsters who have these prejudices. In short: Muslim organizations either denied our studies' findings, or remained silent about them.
>
> This denial is always expressed in the same way: "Muslims cannot be anti-Semites, as Israel's behavior justifies all Muslim attitudes toward Jews."
>
> After the publication of the second study, a new form of denial appeared concerning both anti-Semitism and hatred of homosexuals. An absurd claim was made that the findings of the studies are false, because when one talks

to Muslims, one finds that they have no prejudices and are well integrated in society. This denial of truth by Muslim leaders who are responsible for helping build society is discouraging and also alarming.[3]

More Studies

In 2011, Günther Jikeli published his findings from 117 interviews he conducted with Muslim male youngsters of an average age of nineteen in Berlin, Paris, and London. The differences in attitudes between the cities were minor. The majority of the interviewees voiced some, or strong anti-Semitic feelings. They expressed them openly and often aggressively.[4]

Although anti-Semitism cannot be eliminated, educational programs can reduce it. In thirteen Amsterdam trade schools, a pilot project with Moroccan students was carried out concerning World War II and the Middle East conflict. The aim was to counteract their discriminatory attitudes and, in particular, anti-Semitic expressions. The findings showed a decrease in such attitudes after the project. Previously, 32 percent of the young Moroccans thought Jews were "as nice as other people." Subsequently, this increased to 50 percent.[5] For others, data was only available after the project: 43 percent of Turkish students, 83 percent of Dutch students, and 77 percent of Surinamese students thought Jews were "as nice as other people."[6]

Yet after the project, only 31 percent of Moroccan students considered it a problem that Jews are discriminated against. That view was held by 43 percent of the Turkish, 58 percent of the Dutch, and 72 percent of the Surinamese students.[7]

Before the project, 39 percent of the Moroccans thought they could be friends with a Jew; afterward it increased to 50 percent.[8] The percentage of Moroccans who thought Jews wanted to rule the world was 32 percent before the project, declining to 11 percent after it. Among Turkish students 26 percent held this opinion, among Surinamese students 10 percent, and among Dutch students 3 percent.[9]

A study in France in 2005 showed that anti-Jewish prejudice was prevalent particularly among religious Muslims. Forty-six percent held such sentiments compared to 30 percent of non-practicing Muslims. Only 28 percent of religious Muslims in France were found to be totally without such prejudice.[10]

Already in 2004, Emmanuel Brenner—pseudonym for French historian Georges Bensoussan—and his colleagues had shown that Muslim anti-Semitism and many other manifestations of racism occur in French schools. Brenner does mention that some Muslims are social victims, but points out that this does not place them beyond the law, particularly when their acts have a pogrom-like character.[11]

British author and journalist Melanie Phillips notes that in 2006, a poll of Muslims commissioned by a coalition of Jewish groups revealed that nearly two-fifths believed that the Jewish community in Britain was a legitimate target "as part of the ongoing struggle for justice in the Middle East." More than half believed that British Jews had "too much influence over the direction of UK foreign policy."[12]

In 2013, the Berlin Social Science Center published a study by Ruud Koopmans titled "Religious fundamentalism and out-group hostility among Muslims and Christians in Western Europe." The study surveyed Christian natives and Turkish and Moroccan Muslim immigrants in six European countries: the Netherlands, France, Belgium, Germany, Sweden, and Austria. One of its findings was that on average, 45 percent of Muslims surveyed in these countries held the view that "Jews cannot be trusted." The highest figure was found among Austrian Muslims at 64 percent; the lowest was in Germany at 28 percent.[13]

These studies and much anecdotal information reveal that anti-Semitism among substantial parts of Muslim communities is much higher than in autochthonous populations. As it manifests itself from a very young age onward, only the extremely gullible will believe that it will disappear in the coming decades.

It may well be that during the Protective Edge campaign the percentage of anti-Semitic incidents perpetrated by Muslims increased. Although no reliable statistics are available, one indication was that Esther Voet, director of the Dutch pro-Israeli defense organization CIDI, reported an increase in anti-Semitic incidents in the summer of 2014.

The number of anti-Semitic incidents reported that summer was equal to the total number of incidents in the year 2011-2012. Voet estimates that two-thirds of these are perpetrated by non-Western immigrants or their descendants. This was a euphemistic reference to Muslim immigrants, who represent about 7 percent of the population.[14]

In view of the social climate in many European countries, Jews do not readily state publicly the disproportionately large role of Muslims in anti-Semitic incidents. One exception is Sammy Ghozlan, president of the National Bureau for Vigilance Against Anti-Semitism in France. He was quoted as saying, even before Protective Edge, that the vast majority of physical attacks in France are committed by Muslims.[15]

The 2013 Koopmans study also presents findings that should worry European society at large. It found that around 65 percent of Muslims surveyed in those six countries agreed with the statement that "Religious rules are more important than secular law." Such attitudes embody potential threats to democracies. Another worrying finding was that 54 percent of Muslims surveyed in all six countries agreed with the statement: "Western countries are out to destroy Islam."[16] This is yet one more indicator of the prevalence of conspiracy theories.

Two surveys in 2014 were conducted by the French IFOP polling company and by the Foundation for Political Innovation. One IFOP poll found that 56 percent of Muslim respondents agreed with the statement, "Jews use to their own benefit their status as victims of the Nazi genocide." On average among the French population, 32 percent agreed with the statement. Sixteen percent of the general population believed that there was "an international Zionist conspiracy," whereas 44 percent of Muslims believed this.[17]

Muslim Media Incitement

Radical Muslim hate propaganda is of a widespread and international nature outside Muslim countries as well. Some examples will illustrate this. Shimon Samuels, international liaison director of the Simon Wiesenthal Center who participated in the 2002 UN World Summit on Sustainable Development in Johannesburg, related:

> The evening before the conference we turned on the car radio and heard Radio Islam of Johannesburg (MW1548) broadcasting a hate speech against the Jews. The Imam of Johannesburg attacked the Jewish National Fund and demanded its expulsion from the conference because the JNF "is stealing land from the Palestinians."

Samuels added, "I immediately wrote a letter to the South African Minister of Home Affairs, Mangosuthu Buthulezi, protesting the Imam's position and stating that the JNF is an agency that is a model for the advancement of sustainable development."[18]

Anti-Semitism scholar Mikael Tossavainen notes that there are also a number of Muslim anti-Semitic websites in Swedish,

> the best known of which is Radio Islam. Already as a radio station in the 1980s, it broadcast Nazi-like anti-Semitism.[19] The content could have been taken from Nazi publications such as *Der Stürmer* or *Mein Kampf*, with the Jews accused of being sexually perverted, brazen and greedy, committing ritual murders, having great influence over the media and organizing a world conspiracy aimed at enslaving all other peoples.[20]

Religious Incitement

Muslim anti-Semitism also has various religious sources. After the September 11 attacks in the United States, Sheikh Muhammad Gemeaha, leader of an important mosque in upper Manhattan, made a series of anti-Semitic remarks including: "there is proof that Jews were the terrorists because only they had the capability to neutralize the automatic pilot, command the control tower, erase the black boxes and infiltrate the White House and Pentagon."[21]

Gemeaha also stated:

> Muslims do not feel safe even going to the hospitals, because some Jewish doctors in one of the hospitals poisoned sick Muslim children, who then died . . . You see these people [i.e., the Jews] all the time, everywhere, disseminating corruption, heresy, homosexuality, alcoholism, and drugs. [Because of them] there are strip clubs, homosexuals, and lesbians everywhere. They do this to impose their hegemony and colonialism on the world . . . But Hitler annihilated them because they betrayed him and violated their contract with him.[22]

In 2001, the website of the El Tawheed Mosque in Amsterdam published statements such as: "The Jews own the weapons industry and on the other hand they are the ones who make the wars," and "The Jews, the Christians and the Communists . . . are working together to destroy the Islamic community." The president of this mosque was also the principal of a Muslim elementary school.[23]

During the 2014 Protective Edge campaign there were several cases of extreme religious incitement in Europe. In a Berlin sermon the imam Abu Bilal Ismail called on Allah to "destroy the Zionist Jews . . . Count them and kill them, to the very last one."[24]

Also during the campaign Raoudi Aldelbar, an imam from Morocco employed at an Italian mosque near Venice, was filmed during a sermon saying, "Oh Allah, bring upon [Jews] that which will make us happy. Count them one by one, and kill them one by one." After a video of the sermon was released, Italian Interior Minister Angelino Alfano ordered Aldelbar's immediate expulsion for "seriously disturbing public order, being a danger to national security and for religious discrimination."[25]

Similarly, during a Friday sermon at a mosque near Madrid during Protective Edge, Sheikh Saleheoldine al-Moussaoui declared, "Oh Allah, destroy the plundering Jews . . . Oh Allah, the Most Merciful, count them one by one, and do not spare a single one of them."[26]

In November 2014 Tarek al-Swaidan, an imam from Kuwait, was denied entrance to Belgium because he had been preaching for Israel's destruction and the annihilation of Jews. According to Belgian Prime Minister Charles Michel, banning him from entering Belgium "was the only possible decision. This preacher makes unacceptable anti-Semitic statements. His presence in Belgium would represent a danger to public order."[27]

Extreme Anti-Semitic Attacks

As mentioned earlier, Muslim hate-mongers also stand out compared to native anti-Semites because of the extreme character of some of their anti-Semitic acts. This is particularly clear in France. The 1982 attack on the Jewish Goldenberg restaurant in Paris was carried out by Muslim terrorists coming from Arab countries. Six people were killed, most probably by the Arab Abu Nidal group.[28]

In the twenty-first century, Muslims living in France have committed various murders of Jews. Sebastien Selam, a Jewish disc jockey, was killed by his neighbor Adel Amastaibou in 2003.[29] In 2006, the young Jewish man Ilan Halimi was kidnapped and tortured for twenty-four days before being killed. His kidnappers, led by Youssouf Fofana, called themselves the "Gang of Barbarians." When his court trial began in 2009, Fofana shouted "Allahu Akbar" (God is great). He gave his identity as "Arabs African revolt barbarian Salafist army."[30] The 2012 murders of four Jews, three of them children, in Toulouse by Mohammed Merah were already mentioned earlier.

As also noted earlier, in 2009 during Israel's Cast Lead campaign in Gaza, the largest anti-Semitic riots in Norway's history took place in Oslo. All, or almost all, the participants were Muslims. Attackers wounded a Christian who attended a pro-Israeli demonstration. Life-threatening projectiles were thrown at pro-Israeli demonstrators.[31]

Sweden's third largest city, Malmö, is often called "the capital of European anti-Semitism." The perpetrators of many physical and verbal attacks there are all, or almost all, Muslims.[32] A record number of complaints about hate crimes in this city in 2010 and 2011 did not lead to any convictions.[33]

In 2012, Stephan J. Kramer, secretary-general of the Central Council of Jews in Germany, said that the "willingness to be violent in the Muslim camp is comparable to that in the extreme right-wing camp."[34] Those who publicly shout "Death to the Jews" in street demonstrations seem to be largely Muslim.

Protective Edge

Israel's Protective Edge campaign led to many protests and anti-Israeli demonstrations all over Europe. There were also violent attacks on Jewish institutions and individuals. Often the participants in the demonstrations were not exclusively Muslims. On some occasions Muslims, neo-Nazis, and leftists worked together. One violent demonstration in Frankfurt had a mix of Islamists and neo-Nazis.[35]

Many of these demonstrations were presented as anti-Israeli or pro-Gaza. In fact, they also often were anti-Semitic and can be regarded as demonstrations in favor of the genocidal Hamas movement.

One city where that became very clear was Utrecht in the Netherlands. The Green Left parliamentarian Judith Sargentini was unable to finish a speech where she condemned Hamas because of a roaring response of pro-Hamas slogans from the crowd. She later tweeted that she also wanted to condemn Israel but had been interrupted before she had a chance to do so.[36]

In the Netherlands, the mask also fell from a number of moderate Muslims. Dutch Labour Party politician Fatima Elatik participated in an anti-Israeli demonstration where swastikas were flaunted.[37] A picture showed her linking arms there with a person wearing a T-shirt saying "Free Palestine, stop genocide."[38]

Also in the Netherlands, Yasmina Haifi, a project manager at the Justice Ministry's Cyber Security Center, asserted on Twitter that "ISIS has nothing to do with Islam. It's part of a plan by Zionists who are deliberately trying to blacken Islam's name." She was suspended from her position for this tweet, pending further disciplinary steps.[39]

Haifi had been a candidate in a noneligible position on the Labour Party's 2012 parliamentary list. The issue would not have made many headlines were it not that Haifi worked in the main Dutch counterterrorism unit. A Facebook site was created in support of Haifi's ideas.[40] After a few days this site had more than 6,500 likes. The major Dutch daily *NRC Handelsblad* published an interview with one of the Facebook site managers in which he explained why Haifi's ideas were acceptable.[41]

Analysis

There are very strong indications that the percentage of anti-Semites among Muslim immigrants in Europe and their descendants is substantially higher than in the autochthonous populations. This disproportion is already apparent among many youngsters.[42] Furthermore, the most extreme incidents of Muslim anti-Semitism have gone beyond those of native anti-Semitism. A third reality is the unwillingness of many Muslim leaders and organizations to address this problem in their communities.

The nonselective mass immigration of Muslims into the Western world, and particularly into Europe, has been the most troubling development for Jewish communities outside of Israel over the past fifty years. This is not only the fault of segments of the immigrant communities, but also of European governments.

Many European authorities must take the blame for their attitudes toward the Jews in this context for two reasons. First, they allowed large numbers of immigrants into their countries in a nonselective way, without taking into account the major cultural differences or considering how these people would be integrated into their societies. They should have known that actively promoting anti-Semitism was part and parcel of the cultures these people came from. Allowing them in unselectively can thus be viewed as an indirect type of state-promoted anti-Semitism.

Second, over the years it has become clear that while far from *all* Muslims are anti-Semites, a large percentage are, and from a young age. Some of them openly admit that they are willing to commit violent acts. Authorities in European countries have almost intentionally neglected the need to investigate this matter in depth.

The hate phenomena among Western Muslims cannot be analyzed without focusing on the many negative characteristics and attitudes that have permeated large parts of the Islamic world. One of these is extreme anti-Israeli and anti-Jewish incitement. They often go hand in hand. This has influenced the prejudiced attitudes against Jews that many Muslim immigrants have brought with them to Europe. These attitudes have sometimes been further intensified in their countries of arrival by local inciters from different circles.

The current and often vicious anti-Jewish and anti-Israeli incitement in parts of the Muslim world also has a continuing influence on some of the immigrants and their descendants. The effect is enhanced because this ongoing incitement is conveyed from the Middle East to Western Muslims via satellite TV and the internet.

One conclusion is clear: within the framework of future efforts to address anti-Semitism and anti-Israelism in European societies, the hatred that emanates from segments of European Muslim communities must be a priority. A lengthy essay by this author in the *Journal for the Study of Antisemitism* details anti-Semitism among European Muslims.[43]

CHAPTER SEVEN

Media as Hate Promoters

IN THE POSTWAR DECADES, WESTERN media have assumed the role of a fourth force in addition to the executive, legislative, and judiciary forces in contemporary democracy. Increases in freedom of speech, press, as well as academic freedom have, however, led to a reality where in the media, many manipulators of information also have free rein.

Many media play an important role in the propaganda war particularly against Israel and to a lesser extent against the Jews. They are both perpetrators and transmission conduits for hate. Various factors interact here. To mention one, in West European countries the number of right- and left-wing voters is roughly similar. Yet there are many indications that in several countries, left-wing opinions prevail among journalists and a disproportionate number of them are extreme leftists.[1]

The media have the power to select what they publish; they can manipulate news and criticize others relentlessly. There are, however, few ways to rebut them. Their staff is mainly subject to the specific media's self-regulatory rules. Various mainstream European media have taken predominantly anti-Israeli positions. Others give space to journalists and op-ed writers who demonize Israel. As it is far easier to demonize people than to fight the demonization, this creates a structural imbalance. Media most probably make a major contribution to Israel's demonization.

It is impossible to present here a full overview of how anti-Israeli media bias functions in different Western countries. In many of them there is a large number of media. An adequate analysis would require a book dealing in far greater detail with the deconstruction of the specific methods of demonization by media in target countries. Falsification of facts and fallacious arguments abound. The various subcategories of double standards regarding Israel and its enemies, set forth earlier, are applied countless times.

Germany

The situation in Germany is particularly important in view of that country's partly undigested past. Daniel Killy, a senior German journalist, says, "In general, as in society, contemporary anti-Semitism in the media is hidden behind criticism of Israel. A study on this bias was conducted by the Berlin office of the American Jewish Committee in 2002."

It found:

> In particular, the analysis of the representation of Israel and the Israelis shows that they are portrayed in an extremely negative manner, especially regarding the depiction of the unequal balance of power between the Israeli army, which is characterized as ruthless, and the Palestinians, who are depicted as the hopeless underdogs (e.g., tanks vs. stone-throwers). The Palestinians are also viewed critically, but are clearly assigned the role of the victim.[2]

Killy remarks:

> In 2006, the "Media Tenor International" analysis of the news coverage by Germany's public TV stations ARD and ZDF regarding events in the Middle East was published. It covered the period from 21 July until 3 August 2006, during the Second Lebanon war.
>
> Its main conclusions were that an anti-Israel perspective prevailed. First, the Israeli army was primarily shown in the context of violent assaults, while Hizbullah fighters hardly appeared at all. Secondly, the victims shown were

mostly Lebanese; images of Israeli victims were rare. Furthermore, Israel was usually portrayed as the perpetrator.

The situation in two of Germany's leading dailies, the *Frankfurter Allgemeine Zeitung* and the *Süddeutsche Zeitung* is similar to that of the public broadcasting companies. There is no anti-Israel editorial policy, yet these papers are safe havens for anti-Israel writers. All vicious attacks are hidden behind a wall of "pluralism." Whenever one exposes this, one is automatically accused of attacking the "freedom of press." Thus it becomes hard to fight as one cannot publicly accuse any paper of being openly anti-Zionist or anti-Semitic.[3]

Hildegard Müller, a former high-ranking German Christian Democratic parliamentarian, observed that Israel's problematic image in Europe is partly due to media distortions. She noted that many media do not research the news they cover, and added:

Many newspapers have no editors anymore for specific topics. They take their news from press agencies, such as Agence France-Presse [AFP]. The next day one finds the same news in tens of newspapers. No journalist in any of these media has checked the truth of this information. Slowly an overall picture is created: a small Palestinian force fights against the high-tech Israeli army. This creates the distorted image of David versus Goliath.[4]

The Distorted Reporting of Protective Edge

During the 2014 Protective Edge campaign, Deidre Berger, director of the American Jewish Committee in Berlin, said that in German media it was far too rarely mentioned that:

The violence did not start with Israeli military actions but with the year-long rocket fire against Israeli civilians . . . Without mentioning this important fact, often a distortion of cause and effect takes place. Thus it is suggested to the reader, listener, or viewer that Israel and Hamas have contributed equally to the escalation of the conflict.[5]

Anatol Stefanowitsch, linguistics professor at the Free University of Berlin, undertook a study where he analyzed 170 headlines from German media during six days of the campaign. He concluded that there was a systematic asymmetry in the presentation of the actors, which was negative toward Israel.

He also concluded that: "As an actor in the conflict, Israel is mentioned far more often than its opponent." Stefanowitsch further noted that the words Israel or Israeli appeared very frequently together with "military institutions." When the word Palestinian was mentioned, it was connected to a far greater variety of issues.[6]

The distorted reporting from Israel continued after Protective Edge as well. Yet it is rare that articles by foreign journalists are analyzed anywhere in detail for factual inaccuracies. One such analysis was made about a three-thousand-word feature story in *Newsweek* on December 4 titled "The Young Woman at the Forefront of Jerusalem's New Holy Year." *Jerusalem Post* opinion editor Seth J. Frantzman devoted more than 1,400 words to illustrating the many mistakes in the article. He noted that the *Newsweek* piece was "full of errors, bias, callous discussion of Jerusalem and a dismissive attitude toward accuracy."[7]

France

French sociologist Shmuel Trigano said that in the first years of the last decade, the French elites' attitudes about Middle East politics were almost uniform. He wondered how, in a democracy, all major currents in society could propagate similar ideas: "It was frightening to turn on a television or to read a newspaper and see the same ideological discourse of disinformation about Israel."

He concluded:

> The majority of viewers have no other sources of information and cannot discern between truth, manipulation and lies. They see selective images and hear handpicked Israelis, usually very critical of their own government, express their opinions. Those with different views on Israel are considered outsiders and troublemakers. For a long time, people like myself who affirmed that there was anti-Semitism in France were considered a problem because we deviated from

> public opinion. It was psychologically difficult to live with that.
>
> What does such a reality tell about French society? I do not believe in a conspiracy. There is no commander or organization behind the multiple attacks on Israel. Yet the assaults create the feeling of a near totalitarian society regarding Israel and the Jews.

Trigano slowly started to realize that the extreme power of the media represents a major danger to Western democracy.

> Their attitude toward Israel and the Jews over the last few years has shown that they can pervert analysis, debate and criticism. We are dependent on a class of journalists with consensus political views. They read and co-opt each other's opinions, without accountability to anyone. Freedom and democracy however, cannot coexist if truth and facts are obscured.[8]

In 2002, French journalist Clément Weill-Raynal analyzed several cases of AFP's reporting. The first concerned incidents on the Temple Mount on September 28, 2000, considered the start of the second Palestinian uprising. Another event he investigated was the aforementioned death of the Palestinian boy Muhammad al-Dura, which AFP ascribed to bullets fired by Israeli soldiers, while many observers believe they were probably Palestinian ones. The debate on how the French media have treated the al-Dura affair has continued now for many years.[9]

In January 2005, *L'Express* editor-in-chief Denis Jeambar and another French journalist, Daniel Leconte, wrote that they had seen all the footage on al-Dura shot by the cameraman, including the half-hour that had not been shown on France 2 television. They concluded that many staged events were visible in the videotape, with Palestinians pretending to be wounded and being brought to ambulances.[10]

Another case studied by Clément Weill-Raynal concerned AFP's silence about Palestinian Communication Minister Imad Faloudji's declaration on March 2, 2001 that the Palestinian uprising—or Second Intifada—had been planned for more than a year, and was not caused by Ariel Sharon's visit to the Temple Mount.[11]

A major step forward in exposing the French media's anti-Israeli bias was the documentary *Décryptage* (Decoding). Its directors, Jacques Tarnero and Philippe Bensoussan, analyzed AFP's reporting of the Israeli-Palestinian conflict through interviews and scenes from the media. They said this enabled the viewers to form their own opinion on the press agency's anti-Israeli bias.[12]

The New York Times

In the United States, *The New York Times* has often been accused of anti-Israeli bias. This has been documented in much detail. Andrea Levin, executive director of the media watch organization CAMERA, says:

> Of particular concern has been *The New York Times,* which continues to be influential especially as a trend-setter for other media outlets that often echo its story choice and emphasis. As in the past, the newspaper is prone to placing the onus heavily on Israel for problems of the Palestinians and absence of peace.
>
> The role of the Palestinians in fueling conflict is slighted. In addition, *The New York Times* has been largely silent in the face of increasing global anti-Semitism, doing almost nothing to expose the biased enmity toward Israel. From the news pages to the opinion pages and even into the culture sections, *The New York Times* has an undeniable tilt against Israel.[13]

CAMERA has published a study on *The Times'* bias against Israel from July 1 to December 31, 2011. It found that when reporting on the Israeli-Palestinian conflict, "Israeli views are downplayed while Palestinian perspectives, especially criticisms of Israel, are amplified and even promoted. The net effect is an overarching message, woven into the fabric of the coverage, of Israeli fault and responsibility for the conflict." Of the 275 passages studied pertaining to Israel during this period, 187 were critical of Israel and only 88 were critical of Palestinians.[14]

Senior CAMERA analysts Ricki Hollander and Gilead Ini summarized their findings:

> *The New York Times* is guilty of advocacy journalism. Both its editorial pages and news reporting lean heavily toward an anti-Israel perspective. This is in blunt contravention of its directive to journalists in the *Ethical Journalism* handbook it publishes, "to cover the news as impartially as possible" and "tell our readers the complete, unvarnished truth as best we can learn it."[15]

In 2011, when *The Times* asked Prime Minister Netanyahu to write an op-ed for the paper, his senior advisor Ron Dermer replied by explaining why the prime minister declined the offer. Dermer wrote: "On matters relating to Israel, the op-ed page of the 'paper of record' has failed to heed the late Senator Moynihan's admonition that everyone is entitled to their own opinion, but that no one is entitled to their own facts."

Dermer noted how *The Times* had reprinted Mahmoud Abbas's falsification of history in the United Nations General Assembly about the fact that the Arabs had rejected the 1947 UN partition plan, without commenting on this. Dermer remarked that the quote "effectively turns on its head an event within living memory in which the Palestinians rejected the UN partition plan accepted by the Jews and then joined five Arab states in launching a war to annihilate the embryonic Jewish state. It should not have made it past the most rudimentary fact-checking."

Dermer added:

> The opinions of some of your regular columnists regarding Israel are well known. They consistently distort the positions of our government and ignore the steps it has taken to advance peace. They cavalierly defame our country by suggesting that marginal phenomena condemned by Prime Minister Netanyahu and virtually every Israeli official somehow reflects government policy or Israeli society as a whole. Worse, one columnist even stooped to suggesting that the strong expressions of support for Prime Minister Netanyahu during his speech this year to Congress was "bought and paid for by the Israel lobby" rather than a reflection of the broad support for Israel among the American people.[16]

CNN

The 2007 CNN series *God's Warriors* is a typical example of major media bias. Alex Safian, associate director of CAMERA, says it needs to be reassessed in light of the fact that

> religiously-based violence almost exclusively in the name of Islam, has greatly intensified since the series was first aired. The perpetrators' targets are Jews, other Muslims and increasingly, Middle Eastern Christians. One need only note the massive bloodletting in Syria to see how cloudy [Christiane] Amanpour's crystal ball was.
>
> As the title of the series suggests, it was ostensibly about the growing role of religious fundamentalism inside the world's three major religions. Amanpour's true aim however, seems to have been to propagandize by grossly exaggerating the role of Jewish fundamentalism and the incidence of Jewish-based terror, by denigrating Christian believers as backward and reactionary and by white-washing Muslim fundamentalism as mostly peaceful and only violent when provoked.
>
> At CAMERA we identified this series as "one of the most grossly distorted programs to appear on mainstream American television in many years."
>
> It relied on pejorative labeling, generalities, testimonials and a stacked line-up of guests, which are classic elements of propaganda. As such, it was the *opposite* of journalism—Amanpour's supposed profession.

Safian added:

> Amanpour was heavily criticized for her many distortions, including by other journalists. In a segment on his program titled "CNN's Holy War?" Dan Abrams of MSNBC said, "CNN should have called it what it was, a defense of Islamic fundamentalism and the worst type of moral relativism." He added, "Christiane Amanpour avoided getting bogged down in objectivity."[17]

Associated Press

In 2001, one of the recipients of HonestReporting's Dishonest Reporting Award was the Associated Press. As an example, when a Palestinian sniper murdered a ten-month-old Jewish baby in Hebron, the AP headline writers gave the article the title: "Jewish toddler dies in West Bank." They made no mention in the article of who perpetrated the murder, and readers could get the impression that the baby had died from natural causes or an accident. HonestReporting gave several other examples.[18]

Later that year American journalist Jeff Helmreich analyzed in a detailed article how AP had covered Yasser Arafat's Al-Nakba speech in May of that year. He wrote of the speech:

> By the time it reached the newspapers, entire sentences and clauses had been excluded; moderating words had been added; fiery attacks—like a slur about the United States—had been cleaned out; statements had been condensed, enhanced, or otherwise altered. In short, AP's purported "excerpts" of Arafat's remarks were at best edited, at worst fabricated. Moreover, they served to distort (and significantly soften) the message that passed through Arafat's lips.[19]

In August 2014, former AP journalist Matti Friedman wrote about his experiences at this press agency. In his words:

> Israeli actions are analyzed and criticized, and every flaw in Israeli society is aggressively reported. In one seven-week period, from Nov. 8 to Dec. 16, 2011, I decided to count the stories coming out of our bureau on the various moral failings of Israeli society—proposed legislation meant to suppress the media, the rising influence of Orthodox Jews, unauthorized settlement outposts, gender segregation, and so forth. I counted 27 separate articles, an average of a story every two days. In a very conservative estimate, this seven-week tally was higher than the total number of significantly critical stories about Palestinian government and society, including the totalitarian Islamists of Hamas, that our bureau had published in the preceding three years.

Friedman also supported his story with other quantitative examples, comparing the relatively small death totals of the Israeli-Palestinian conflict to much larger but rarely reported conflicts like the Mexican drug war and carnage in the Congo.[20]

Former AP Jerusalem bureau chief Steven Gutkin reacted. Strangely enough he chose the local Indian website *Goa Streets*, his new place of employment after leaving. Much of his article was an ad hominem attack on Friedman. He defended his actions and those of the bureau from his own perspective, with little quantitative response. Gutkin defended his reporting by claiming that Israel could become a better place.[21] This is the kind of absurd argument that can be applied to any society since paradise was lost. However, one does not see AP investing similar human resources to direct such scrutiny at other countries.

Friedman then responded to Gutkin: "We should thus believe him when he says my essay is 'hogwash,' even if he can't be bothered to actually disprove anything . . . I'm making a case about the coverage. Anyone hoping to dispute what I wrote has to provide, as I do, concrete information about the coverage."[22]

Friedman later wrote an article in *The Atlantic* titled, "What the Media Gets Wrong About Israel." In it he further exposed how AP intentionally reported stories that cast Israel in a negative light and chose not to report on reprehensible Palestinian conduct.[23]

In October 2014, a terrorist from East Jerusalem rammed his car into a crowd, killing two people including an infant and injuring several more. The terrorist was shot by police. AP reported on this incident in an article headlined "Israeli Police Shoot Man in East Jerusalem." The article also began with the words: "Israeli police say they have shot a man whose car slammed into a crowded train stop in east Jerusalem, in what they suspect was an intentional attack." Only after public outcry was the article edited to reflect what had really happened. An analysis of this case by journalist Ariel Cahana also describes how other important media distorted this incident and presented it as a road accident and not an intentional terror attack on civilians.[24]

Admitting Biased Reporting

Only in rare cases do journalists admit that they or their colleagues have been reporting in a structurally biased way. In 1989, Thomas Friedman of *The New York Times* cited a major example of such reporting in his book *From Beirut to Jerusalem*: "It would be hard to find any hint in stories from foreign correspondents stationed in Beirut before 1982 about the well-known corruption in the PLO leadership, the misuse of funds, and the way in which the organization had become as much a corporation full of bureaucratic hacks as a guerilla outfit."[25] Friedman spoke in general terms, without accusing himself.

One can only wonder that a journalist who has since spent time in so many Arab and other countries in the Middle East has abstained from an ongoing, huge indictment of the human rights situation and the massive wave of hatred coming out of these countries.

One well-known case of someone indirectly but substantially indicting himself was Riccardo Cristiano, correspondent of the Italian state network Rai in the Palestinian territories. On October 12, 2000, two Israeli reserve soldiers were lynched by Palestinians in Ramallah. The Italian network Mediaset filmed the murders and smuggled the pictures out. They included, among other things, a picture of one of the killers standing at a window with "his bloodied hands raised in triumph to signal to the crowd below that the soldiers had been killed."

As it was not known which Italian network had taken the pictures, Cristiano wrote a letter, published on October 16 in the Palestinian daily *Al-Hayat al-Jadida*, disclosing that it was Mediaset that had taken them. As a result, this network had to withdraw correspondents from the area back to Italy so as to avoid Palestinian revenge.

Cristiano also indicated that he would never have published the pictures had they been his own. In his open letter, he also offered "congratulations and blessings" to his dear friends in Palestine.[26]

In July 2014, the Dutch public-television news service NOS had to admit that it had intentionally deleted the placards bearing Israeli flags with a swastika on them from its report on an anti-Israeli demonstration in The Hague that was primarily attended by Muslims.[27]

The earlier-mentioned disclosures by former AP journalist Matti Friedman have shown how valuable the information on bias provided by a former reporter can be. Another example is Dutch journalist Hans Moll, who worked for the daily *NRC Handelsblad*. After his retirement he published a book on its anti-Israeli bias.[28] It would be advisable for Israel to systematically seek out journalists who are willing to disclose the bias of their former employers.

Lack of Transparency

The structural bias of some journalists is influenced by the information that emanates from the Arab world. One confirmation of that was given by a Dutch correspondent on the Middle East, Joris Luyendijk. He wrote about the Arab-Israeli conflict:

> The Arab countries are often dictatorships that exist thanks to lack of transparency. Everything is based on appearances. Both parties, but in particular the Arabs, lie the whole day. You really have to check their statements there on the spot. Also, reliable figures are not available: the authorities lie flagrantly in all fields. All figures are adapted to what is politically desirable.[29]

In the Netherlands, Luyendijk is considered a great expert on the Middle East. He wrote a bestselling book in Dutch in which he contributed to the bias against Israel.[30] In it Luyendijk details various news manipulations by journalists, including his own. He writes much about the tiny so-called Palestinian peace movements but remains silent about the many genocidal and inciting calls of Palestinian leaders.

In his book Luyendijk explains the essence of his work as Middle East correspondent. His editors at home sent him articles from the international press agencies; he rewrote them and they were then published under his name. These articles were supplemented with his own work. Luyendijk also relates that at the beginning of the First Iraq War, he was asked by a Dutch radio station how the Arab population would react to the American bombardments. He answered that it had emerged from conversations that they would be even more furious toward the United States.

Luyendijk admits that his sole "source" was the waiter who had brought him his room-service breakfast in the hotel in Amman, Jordan, where he was staying.[31]

During Protective Edge one of the techniques of many media was to omit incriminating information about Arabs and their supporters.

Denmark

In Denmark the Liberal daily *Politiken* has been at the forefront of anti-Israeli bias. Historian Arthur Arnheim writes:

> By the end of 2002, a violent campaign by a number of Danish media and politicians against Israel and Jews reached its peak. Many felt it especially painful that the *Politiken* newspaper took part in the slandering, because for decades *Politiken* had been seen as a leading protagonist of liberal ideas and tolerant views on public affairs.
>
> Now it appeared that the paper had changed its cause as far as Israel and the Jews were concerned. A full-page paid advertisement with more than 700 signatures—by Jews as well as non-Jews—was placed in the paper with a sharp protest under the headline: *Nu er det nok* (Now, it's enough). A few quotations from it will explain what triggered the reaction:
>
> "Over a period of time *Politiken* has contributed to aggravating moods and attitudes towards Israel and the Jews. This is apparent from editorials, articles, and letters to the editor. By comparing Israel's occupation to the Holocaust and Nazi atrocities during the war, Israel is demonized and the Palestinians raised to a symbol of suffering.
>
> "Articles in the paper have stressed that public and collective threats to Danish Jews are pardonable as long as not all Jews dissociate themselves from Israel's policy . . . We oppose that the one and only democracy in the Middle East is made an object of hatred and described as an evil empire and the root of all evil in the Middle East and the world.
>
> "*Politiken* mixes political attitudes together with conception of Jews as a minority. This fact represents a derailing of the debate and opens an opportunity

> to single Jews out and attack them in a way not seen in Europe since the Nazi and Communist campaigns against the Jews . . . it opens gates and gives free opportunities to Jew haters."[32]
>
> The response from *Politiken* appeared the same day in an editorial. If the 700 who signed the protest had expected a reaction of understanding or perhaps even remorse by the editors they were disappointed. Nothing of the kind was expressed in the reply.[33]

In 2012, *Politiken* was one of the European papers that published the anti-Israeli hate poem by Günther Grass.[34]

Pro-Israeli Media Watching

Twenty years ago, David Bar-Illan, then editor of *The Jerusalem Post*, correctly predicted that despite Israel's massive concessions to the PLO in the Oslo Accords, the strong anti-Israeli bias of the major print and electronic media would continue.[35]

The large number of journalists in the Middle East has contributed to frequent news manipulation regarding Israel. This, in turn, has led to the establishment of pro-Israeli media-watch bodies.[36] Bar-Illan was one of the pioneers of this new approach.[37] He asserted twenty years ago that the BBC was "by far the worst offender when it comes to Israel." One example he mentioned of its malice concerned a coffeehouse that collapsed in Arab East Jerusalem due to structural problems. Jews and Arabs worked together to save lives, which stunned PLO activists. The BBC did not say a word about this collaboration; all they reported was that Arabs had suffered, while repeating the libel that a bomb had been placed in the coffeehouse. Bar-Illan added that there were hundreds of examples of BBC malevolence in the political sphere.[38]

More on the BBC

Since then, analysts and media watchers have developed more systematic methods of deconstructing the work of biased media. Many years later Trevor

Asserson, a litigation lawyer, undertook some detailed analyses of how the BBC operates regarding Israel. He wrote: "Its news reports concerning Israel are distorted by omission, by inclusion, by only giving partial facts, by who is interviewed, and by the background information provided, or lack of it. I also found that there is a systemic problem with the BBC complaints system."

Among Asserson's many examples: "In Iraq, Western coalition troops are described in warm and glowing terms, with sympathy being evoked for them both as individuals and for their military predicament. In contrast, Israeli troops are painted as faceless, ruthless and brutal killers, with little or no understanding shown for their actions." He concluded that "the partiality of the BBC's reporting quite possibly infects its coverage of all politically sensitive issues."[39]

Asserson showed with this and other examples that the BBC has frequently transgressed the various legal obligations under its monopoly charter from the British government. His findings included that 88 percent of documentaries over a certain period of the Israeli-Palestinian conflict conveyed a negative impression of Israel, or a positive image of Palestinians.

Zvi Shtauber, who was Israel's ambassador in London from 2001 to 2004, said:

> The BBC is a problem in itself. Over the years I had endless conversations with them. Any viewer who for a consistent period looks at the BBC information on Israel gets a distorted picture. It does not result from a single broadcast here or there. It derives from the BBC's method of broadcasting. When reporting from Israel it usually showed in the background the mosque on the Temple Mount, which gives viewers the impression that Jerusalem is predominantly Muslim.
>
> When Sharon was elected prime minister, it struck me that the BBC spoke about him as the "military strongman." Initially I thought this expression would be mentioned only once. They continued using it for several months. I contacted them and asked whether they called Pakistan's President Musharraf a "military strongman" as he had come to power through a military coup. They did not. I then asked about whom else they used this terminology and they could not name anybody.[40]

There is much more evidence of the BBC's anti-Israeli bias. One more example occurred when Arafat was flown to Paris before his death. Barbara Plett, correspondent for BBC Radio 4, said, "When the helicopter carrying the frail old man rose about his ruined compound, I started to cry . . . without warning. In quieter moments since, I have asked myself, why the sudden surge of emotion?"[41]

The media-watch organization HonestReporting noted under the title "Weeping for Yasser": "Plett's revelation of an emotional bond with Yasser Arafat is a clear acknowledgement of her partisan stand in the conflict . . . What does it say about the BBC that they employ news reporters who are emotionally or ideologically attached to one side of the conflict?"[42]

In 2003, the Israeli government broke off relations with the BBC for several months. In 2004, in a rare reaction from Jerusalem, Minister Natan Sharansky wrote to the BBC that its reporter Orla Guerin had not only set a new standard for biased journalism but her reporting "has also raised concerns that it was tainted by anti-Semitism." Sharansky referred to the case of a Palestinian youth who was set to explode as a human bomb. Whereas other major media, in reporting on this case, focused on the use of children by Palestinian terror groups, Guerin's main item was that the Israelis had paraded a child in front of the international media. Sharansky also pointed out that he did not recall a single report in which the BBC noted "the ways and means in which the Palestinian authorities stage events for the media or direct the media to stories that serve Palestinian advocacy goals."[43]

A Journalist or a Propagandist?

For a number of years, the chairman of the Foreign Press Association in Israel was Dutchman Conny Mus, who passed away in 2010. He sometimes showed extreme anti-Israeli bias.

In one example at the end of April 2007, this veteran correspondent interviewed Hamas leader Ismail Haniyeh for the RTL television station. Haniyeh was then prime minister of the short-lived Hamas-Fatah Palestinian government, which would collapse a few weeks later amid internecine killings in Gaza.

In his broadcast Mus proudly noted that, while Haniyeh had been interviewed by Arab journalists, he was the first Westerner to be given this opportunity. He also stressed the fact that he could ask Haniyeh whatever he wanted. Mus did not, however, pose the main question that needed to be asked.

What would have been more logical than to quote a few lines from the Charter of the Hamas movement, an offshoot of the Muslim Brotherhood. For instance, Article 7:

> Hamas has been looking forward to implement Allah's promise whatever time it might take. The prophet, prayer and peace be upon him, said: "The time will not come until Muslims will fight the Jews (and kill them); until the Jews hide behind rocks and trees, which will cry: O Muslim! There is a Jew hiding behind me, come on and kill him![44]

And if this was too long a query, he could have summarized it as: "What about killing all the Jews as the Hamas Charter advocates?" This would have been a crucial question, as Haniyeh stated that two-thirds of the Palestinians supported Hamas. Mus concluded that Haniyeh's declarations about Israel were vague, an obvious outcome of his omitting to ask about the party's genocidal charter. He also said he would have liked to accompany Haniyeh on his planned trip to the Netherlands, which, however, did not take place because the Dutch government did not give him an entry visa.[45]

Mus's interview of Haniyeh is a paradigm of media distortion and unethical journalism, the more so as he had been a Middle East correspondent for over fifteen years. Mus's approach to journalism also serves to illustrate where distortion can lead. On the basis of the interview, the Palestinian Platform for Human Rights in the Netherlands claimed a few days later that Haniyeh had shown his respect for the Netherlands and its people and also had not said a word about the destruction of Israel. They avoided mentioning that he did not have to express himself on the subject because the interviewer had refrained from asking the question explicitly.[46]

Also in later years, Haniyeh had no problem promoting the extermination of Jews. PMW reported that Hamas TV broadcast statements from Haniyeh in summer 2014 such as: "We love death like our enemies love life! We love Martyrdom, the way in which [Hamas] leaders died." Hamas TV also broadcast a sermon reiterating the Hamas ideology, which claims that according to

Islam it is Muslim destiny to exterminate the Jews. PMW quotes many similar statements calling for the murder of Israelis and Jews.[47]

Cartoonists

Although cartoonists publish mainly in the media, they have to be analyzed as a separate category. The reason is that their method is so different from broadcasters and writers. Cartoons convey a message far more directly and quickly. As previously shown, one of the best methods to illustrate how anti-Israelism uses the same core and submotifs as religious and racist anti-Semitism is by analyzing contemporary anti-Israeli cartoons.

Those who create cartoons for mass media must touch upon widespread and easily recognizable stereotypes in their society. At the same time, they further strengthen these stereotypes. As the mass audience is unsophisticated, the cartoonist relies on a few recurrent subthemes in depicting Israel, Israelis, and Jews as absolute evil. These are then packaged in many diverse ways. Analyzing such cartoons allows for systematically identifying these basic themes. This, in turn, enables pointing to the same anti-Semitic motifs appearing elsewhere in society.

Arieh Stav has undertaken an important analysis of anti-Semitic imagery in Arab cartoons. He notes that he mainly focused on "how Israel and the peace process have been reflected in the mirror of Arab caricature, which is a direct, authentic and highly influential expression of views in the Arab world, where nearly half the population is illiterate."[48]

Many thousands of Arab anti-Semitic caricatures have been published. The analysis of anti-Semitic cartoons, particularly in the Arab world but also elsewhere, has been further developed by Belgian political scientist Kotek. He points out that besides classic submotifs of anti-Semitism, new ones can also be found regularly in Arab cartoons. These include that Arabs want peace and Israel does not. Another one concerns apologies for suicide bombers.[49]

In the 2006 Holocaust-cartoon competition in the Iranian *Hamshahri* newspaper, caricatures that were collected also depicted most of the ancient prejudices.[50] Among 1,100 entries from over sixty countries, over two hundred cartoons were selected for the exhibition. Several portray Israel as having taken the place of the Nazis. The Palestinians are often portrayed as suffering Nazi-like or even worse treatment by the Israelis.

Other cartoons convey the message that Israel exploits the Holocaust, either as a weapon against the Palestinians or as a tool to garner world sympathy. Still other cartoons indicate that the Holocaust is a hoax, or grossly exaggerated. Again others exploit the classic anti-Semitic motifs such as the alleged "extreme evil of the Jews," deicide, conspiracy theories of world domination, blood libel, infanticide, zoomorphism, and so on. Some contain more than one anti-Semitic motif.[51]

The *Hamshahri* cartoon collection shows once more how anti-Semitism and anti-Israelism overlap. Cartoonists commingle supposed Israeli and Jewish characteristics in their pictures. Caricaturists from Muslim countries often depict Jews as ultra-Orthodox, with black hats and sidelocks. Those from other countries frequently draw Israeli soldiers.[52]

Media and the Million Cuts

Television and written media have greatly contributed to the incitement against Israel. Many media do so "drop by drop." The recurrent manipulation of TV news gives relatively major attention to negative items about Israel, while a vastly smaller proportion of the far more frequent and far more violent negative news items about Arab and Muslim countries are shown. The media category of Israel-hate perpetrators offers one of the best illustrations of how the million-cuts method of delegitimization works.

Shtauber summarized his experience with British media when he was Israeli ambassador to the UK: "In the media there is no limit to the idiocies one is confronted with. Many young journalists do not listen to what they are told. The reports they prepare are often unprofessional."[53]

In this cultural atmosphere, journalists themselves start to believe the false image built up by their colleagues. Shtauber observes:

> Shortly after I arrived in London, the board of an association of journalists came to visit me. One of the five respectable visitors, a very important jour-

> nalist, asked me: "We want your assurance, Mr. Ambassador, that it is not the official policy of the government of Israel to shoot journalists." I looked at him and hardly knew what to say.

The tools to analyze media bias against Israel have been developed by a variety of experts. It is now up to the Israeli government to ensure that such investigations are carried out on a large scale and provide the funding for them.

CHAPTER EIGHT

Christian Inciters—Roman Catholics

The analysis of the current demonization of Israel by Christian organizations, preachers, and individuals is a complex issue. Various factors contribute to this complexity. One is the lengthy history of Christian anti-Semitism. A second is the huge number of Christians, with Christianity fragmented into many denominations. A third is the absence of systematic monitoring of Christian anti-Semitism and anti-Israelism. One cannot do justice to the subject in this chapter and the next; it requires an entire book. Hence, only a number of important issues will be discussed.

For many centuries, Christian demonization of the Jews was the main thrust of European anti-Semitism. Even today the hate motif of the Jews being responsible for the killing of Jesus is widespread, as earlier-cited statistics have shown. Multiple remnants of Christian anti-Semitism are found in many denominations of that religion to which new elements of anti-Israeli hate-mongering are added.

Christianity permeated European society with anti-Semitism for many centuries. Numerous leading figures and others within church movements were promoters of Jew-hatred. The main hate message, among many others, was the deicide accusation. Its means of dissemination were preaching and religious education. Christian intellectuals also brought European types of anti-Semitism to the Middle East while teaching in churches and European schools there.[1]

Meir Litvak, an expert on Arab anti-Semitism, said:

> European anti-Semitism was brought to the Middle East by Christian intellectuals who taught in Church and European schools. Christians initiated the 1840 blood libel in Damascus by accusing Jews of murdering a Capucine monk and using his blood for ritual purposes. The local government under Mohammed Ali—Egypt's ruler on behalf of the Turks—arrested several Jewish community leaders. When they were tortured, two of them confessed to a crime they had not committed. However, they were freed under pressure from the European powers.[2]

The severity of anti-Semitic propaganda differed historically between various Christian societies. Catholicism played a major role in the massive demonization of Jews over the centuries. Yet there are also deep roots in segments of Protestant anti-Semitism. A major role was played here by the reformer Martin Luther. Disappointed by the fact that the Jews did not want to convert, he wrote an extreme anti-Semitic book about the "Jews and their lies." Luther called them "live devils" and recommended burning synagogues in honor of God and Christianity.[3]

The longtime diffusion of this extreme loathing of Jews by many Christian churches made the hatred not only very powerful, but also persistent. These churches kept defining absolute evil in theological terms, suggesting that because many tens of generations ago some forefathers of Jews had allegedly killed God's son—a false accusation—Jews were capable of all imaginable evil. Nor did they explain how Jesus, if he *were* God's son, could be killed against his own will. Once one falsely accused people of being Satan's representatives on earth, it was easy to scapegoat them as being responsible for many disasters they had nothing to do with.

The infrastructure laid by Catholicism, Lutheranism, and so on fostered a large part of the European mindset that later on made the Holocaust possible. Nineteenth-century European nationalist movements adopted the same core motif of the Jew's ultimate wickedness. Hand in hand with the religious variant, ethnic anti-Semitism developed as a second major form of extreme Jew-hatred. German and Austrian Nazism, along with its many supporters elsewhere, took this anti-Semitic worldview to its genocidal consequence.

More Reasons for Jews to Hate Christians?

As powerful institutions and elites promoted ideas of hatred over a very long period, they became an integral part of cultures. In the 1960s, James Parkes analyzed the conflict between Christians and Jews during the first eight centuries of the Christian era. Concerning that period he concluded, "There was far more reason for the Jew to hate the Christian than for the Christian to hate the Jew—and this on the evidence of Christian sources alone."

Parkes also came to the conclusion that the Christian theological concept of the first three centuries created the foundations for the hatred, on which an "awful superstructure" was built. The first stones for this were laid at "the very moment the Church had the power to do so, in the legislation of Constantine and his successors."

Regarding modern anti-Semitism, Parkes asserted, "If on the ground so carefully prepared, modern anti-Semites have reared a structure of racial and economic propaganda, the full responsibility still rests with those who prepared the soil, created the deformation of the people and so made these ineptitudes credible."[4]

Change in the Catholic Church

The Catholic Church changed its attitude toward the Jews with the *Nostra Aetate* declaration by Pope Paul VI at the Second Vatican Council in 1965.[5] Wistrich commented:

> At the Vatican II Council (1962-1965), the charge of deicide was removed from the Jewish people as a whole. *Nostra Aetate*, the document that embodies this, was published in 1965 under the papacy of Paul VI who was much more lukewarm on these issues than his predecessor. The document that John XXIII and Cardinal Bea originally wanted had been significantly diluted by more conservative circles within the Church.
>
> *Nostra Aetate* was not a complete exculpation of the Jews. It said that the guilt for the death of Jesus belonged to the Jewish leadership of two thousand years

> ago but did not carry through to the Jewish people of today. It has nonetheless been a crucial instrument in the fight against Catholic anti-Semitism. This type of anti-Semitism, after all, was the most powerful and extensive or pervasive form of hostility toward Jews, at least before the Russian pogroms and the Nazi mass murder of the Jews in the twentieth century.[6]

Aharon Lopez, former Israeli ambassador to the Vatican, summarized the changes made by *Nostra Aetate*:

> This text eliminated the Jews' collective guilt for Jesus' crucifixion and stated that "Jews were most dear to God" and that "the great spiritual patrimony was shared by Christians and Jews." Hatred of the Jews thus became incompatible with formal Church doctrine.
>
> Until then Church doctrine had asserted that, due to Jesus' execution, God had removed the covenant from the people of Israel and transferred it to the Church, the "true Israel" (Verus Israel). Now the Church accepted the existence of an ongoing covenant between God and the Jewish people, which constituted a major theological breakthrough in its relationship with it.

Yet changes are slow in a huge organization such as the Catholic Church. Lopez observed: "The major turnaround at the highest levels has yet to permeate the entire Church, which is quite extensive . . . It remains, however, difficult for the Church to reverse its 2,000 year-old position. This may take another generation or two."[7]

Almost fifty years after the *Nostra Aetate* declaration, Catholic anti-Semitism continues in many places. The Vatican and many senior Catholic leaders make efforts to fight it, but these do not necessarily focus on the most severe cases.

Prejudices Reemerge

From time to time, even at Vatican-sponsored events, the old prejudices reemerge in various forms. In October 2010, a Synod of Bishops for the Middle East took place at the Vatican. One hundred and eighty-five bishops and patriarchs who had full voting rights participated, representing mainly the declining number of Catholics in the Middle East. Under the sections dedicated to relations with Jews, the synod said in its final statement that "recourse to theological and biblical positions which use the word of God to wrongly justify injustices is not acceptable."

Thereafter, the Melkite Bishop Cyrille S. Bustros of the United States, who had attended the conference, said, "For us Christians, you can no longer speak of a land promised to the Jewish people." He added that the coming of Christ shows that Jews "are no longer the chosen people; all men and women of all countries have become the chosen people." He further remarked that the theme of the Promised Land cannot be used "to justify the return of Jews to Israel and the expatriation of Palestinians."[8]

Israeli Deputy Foreign Minister Danny Ayalon was quoted as saying that the synod had become "a forum for political attacks against Israel in the best tradition of Arab propaganda." He added that the synod had been hijacked by an anti-Israeli majority.

Rabbi David Rosen, director of interreligious affairs for the American Jewish Committee, was the only Jewish representative to address the synod. He said that it was "appalling that in their final statement . . . the bishops did not have the courage to address challenges of intolerance and extremism in the Muslim countries in which they reside and rather chose to make the Israeli-Palestinian conflict their first focus." He added that Bishop Bustros's statement reflected "either shocking ignorance or insubordination in relation to the Catholic Church's teaching on Jews and Judaism flowing from the Vatican II Declaration 'Nostra Aetate.'"

Mordechai Lewy, Israeli ambassador to the Vatican, said about Bishop Bustros's remarks, "The Vatican should take a clear distance from them because it will give every Jew a reason to be suspicious of rapprochement with the Catholic Church." He added that he disagreed with several points in the synod's final message and observed, "The Israeli government doesn't use the Bible to determine our political borders."[9]

The Vatican spokesman, Father Lombardi, reacted to the Jewish criticism rather opaquely: "There is a great richness and variety of contributions offered by the Synod fathers, however, that should not be considered the voice of the

Synod in its entirety." He then added that the overall assessment of the synod was largely positive according to Pope Benedict XVI.[10]

The Failed Historical Commission

Pope Pius XII's attitude toward the Holocaust has been a subject of much debate. Wistrich was a member of the International Catholic-Jewish Historical Commission, which was supposed to scrutinize the documents in the Vatican's archives relevant to this subject. The commission suspended its work after two years. Wistrich remarked:

> The stark truth is that in two years we received no material assistance, no real encouragement, and above all, not one single new document from the Vatican. On the other hand, we did receive our fair measure of denigration, insinuation, and false rumors from persons attached to, or even speaking in the name of, that powerful and august institution. This negative response to its own initiative stands in striking contrast to the positive reception that the Commission's work received from most enlightened opinion in the world, from many liberal and lay Catholics, and from much of the scholarly community, which sincerely hoped that we would succeed in our efforts to open up the archives.[11]

Wistrich also observed:

> A judgment on Pius XII's attitude during and after the war should not be limited to his silence on the genocide of the Jews. The pope remained largely neutral about the German atrocities against the Polish people. Nor did he condemn the genocidal Catholic Croatian fascist state and its leader Ante Pavelić. This state massacred 350,000 non-Catholics, including thirty thousand Croatian Jews. There is compelling evidence that the Vatican was instrumental in permitting Pavelić to escape from Italy to Argentina in 1947.[12]

The yet unadmitted links between the Holy See and the Ustasha-led Croatian regime have never been clarified. These mass murderers of Serbs, Jews, and others were one of the cruelest Nazi allies in World War II. There is proof that the Vatican has assisted Croatian Nazis in hiding funds and helped them escape Europe.[13]

Another issue that merits a detailed investigation is how much attention the Vatican's paper *Osservatore Romano* gives to Israeli actions in the Middle East compared to the widespread persecution of Christians in Muslim lands.

Contemporary Catholic Inciters

In the margins of the official Catholic Church, the traditionalist Society of Saint Pius X (SSPX) often adheres to ancient dogmas. One of its bishops, Richard Williamson, who is British, is a Holocaust denier but was only expelled from the society in 2012. According to the Anti-Defamation League, "In sermons, writings, Web sites and publications, SSPX representatives have charged contemporary Jews with deicide, have endorsed *The Protocols of the Elders of Zion*, and have claimed that there is factual basis for the Blood Libel. One of its bishops has also denied the Holocaust."[14]

There are also new elements of anti-Israeli hate-mongering in Catholic environments. In October 2003 the Jewish Telegraphic Agency published a series of articles, called "Funding Hate," about the Ford Foundation's contribution to anti-Israeli hate groups. As a side note, the article mentioned that there was an even bigger donor to the leading Palestinian hate group behind the Durban anti-Israeli hate campaign: the Dutch Catholic charitable NGO Cordaid, which had contributed $1.5 million.[15]

In 2007 Cordaid together with another pro-Palestinian Roman Catholic group, Pax Christi, initiated a pro-Palestinian public statement in the Netherlands calling on the Dutch government to break the stalemate in the Palestinian-Israeli conflict. The statement complained about forty years of "occupation" but remained silent about seventy-five years of genocidal intent and murderous attacks by the Palestinian Arabs.[16]

Yitzhak Santis of NGO Monitor says:

> Cordaid's biased activities are illustrated by their funding decisions, publications and political positions. It is a joint member with other Dutch-based organizations of the United Civilians for Peace organization, which advocates Boycotts, Divestment and Sanctions (BDS) against Israel. Cordaid Director René Grotenhuis, argued during a 2011 panel in the Dutch parliament, that BDS is a defensible tactic because, "it is important that people in Palestine look for ways to resist occupation, and this is a non-violent way to do so."
>
> In 2012, Cordaid joined a coalition of 22 European NGOs in producing a report titled *Trading Away Peace: How Europe Helps Sustain Illegal Israeli Settlements.* It promotes the BDS agenda, calling on the EU and national governments to wage political warfare through economic sanctions against Israel. Cordaid also joined in a 2009 report titled *Failing Gaza: No rebuilding, no recovery, no more excuses.* The report falsely claims that Gaza remains occupied. The organization also funds various anti-Israel NGOs in Israel and the Palestinian Arab territories.
>
> Cordaid is regularly subsidized by the Dutch government. Funding amounts vary. From 2007 to 2010, Cordaid received 422 million Euros. Due to a reduction in government subsidies, it received 69 million Euros in 2011.[17]

There are also Catholic politicians who incite against Israel. Former Dutch parliamentarian Wim Kortenoeven says:

> The major Dutch agitator against Israel is former Prime Minister Dries van Agt, a Catholic Christian Democrat. Initially, Van Agt's organization for his personal crusade against the Jewish State was the "International Forum for Justice and Peace" (IFJP).
>
> It included Swedish anti-Semite Jöran Jermas, who posed as a Jew using the alias Israel Shamir. I was involved in unmasking this "Swedish connection" when I worked for [the Dutch pro-Israeli defense organization] CIDI. After the ensuing scandal, Van Agt terminated the IFJP. He then established a new crusade medium—The Rights Forum.
>
> At the 2007 Palestinian-European Conference in Rotterdam, Van Agt said that the three Western demands of Hamas were extremely unreasonable. They are: abandoning violence, recognition of the State of Israel and of Palestinian agreements with the State of Israel.[18]

Ancient Anti-Semitic Rituals Continue

In several Christian countries as well as elsewhere, anti-Semitic rituals continue. In Greece, that concerns the main church of the country, the Greek Orthodox Church. In 2004 the Simon Wiesenthal Center (SWC) of Los Angeles wrote to the newly elected Greek prime minister, Kostas Karamanlis of the New Democrat Party, that the country's National Tourist Organization was promoting the Easter ritual of "burning [the effigy] of Judas" as a tourist attraction. Hundreds of local ceremonies include this ritual, which is sometimes described as the "Burning of the Jew."[19]

As Rabbi Mordechai Frisis of Salonika noted in 2004, "Greece is a very traditional society, and they blame the Jews for killing Jesus. There are still people who believe that Jews drink the blood of Christians on Passover." Frisis said that when he was a student at a Greek high school, "There were people who said this openly to me."[20]

Although the Greek Orthodox Church has in the past officially condemned the "Burning of the Jew" ritual, it has had little influence. The late archbishop of Athens, Christodoulos, made occasional negative statements about the Jews. In 2003, he visited the Majdanek extermination camp in Poland; but his speech made no reference to the Holocaust even though the great majority of the victims there were Jewish. He also did not mention the 1,500 Greek Jews murdered there.[21]

In 2001, Christodoulos falsely accused the Jews of being behind the Greek government's decision to abide by EU rules that oppose including one's religion on state identity cards.[22] In 2004 he congratulated George Karatzaferis, leader of the xenophobic anti-Semitic right-wing party Laos, on his "deserving election" to the European Parliament, and added that Karatzaferis would "bring to the broader European family the other intellectual values that spring out of your Christian and Greek soul."[23]

CHAPTER NINE

Incitement in Christian Institutions—Protestant Churches

THERE ARE A VARIETY OF strong Protestant pro-Israeli movements. Yet one also finds many active anti-Israeli currents in some of the mainstream Protestant denominations. Several Protestant organizations in the Western world and developing countries play an important role in anti-Israeli activities. They often propose discriminatory measures against Israel, without suggesting taking any action against countries that are extreme human rights abusers.

U.S. scholar Eugene Korn summarizes the history of anti-Israelism in Western liberal churches:

> This harsh anti-Israeli attitude had long been building in America and Europe. Since the First Intifada in the late 1980s, the liberal churches have become increasingly hostile to the Israeli understanding of the conflict, viewing Palestinian violence as a legitimate grassroots rebellion by oppressed natives against Israeli colonial conquerors of Palestinian lands. Moreover, during this period the World Council of Churches—which never had great sympathy for Israel—became an unabashed apologist for Palestinian rejectionism, even refusing to condemn Palestinian terror.[1]

Major battles against Israel have taken place in the Presbyterian church in the United States, says CAMERA analyst Dexter van Zile:

> The protagonists are a relatively small number of so-called peace activists, some with ties to the Middle East, who seek to put the Jewish state in the judgment seat. Leveling chimerical accusations at Israel in the name of peace, these activists seek to enlist their fellow Presbyterians—and the church's bureaucracy—into their efforts to banish the modern state of Israel from the community of civilized nations and portray it as uniquely worthy of criticism and condemnation.[2]

The danger, however, is that while initially anti-Israeli incitement in such organizations starts at the top, it filters down over time to the rank and file.

Van Zile notes:

> For the past several years, a group of five Protestant churches—the Presbyterian Church USA, the United Church of Christ, the United Methodist Church, the Episcopal Church, and the Evangelical Lutheran Church in America—have legitimized the increasingly virulent anti-Israel movement in the States . . . They still enjoy a considerable influence on the American scene, particularly on the left thanks to their role in American history and the affluence of their members.[3]

Much hate-mongering against Israel also comes out of smaller Protestant communities such as the Mennonites[4] and the Quakers.[5]

Rabbi Yitzchok Adlerstein of the Simon Wiesenthal Center observed, "The leadership of most American 'mainline' Protestant churches is top-heavy with anti-Israel agitation, especially among those on mission committees. By now, a substantial number of their members have been influenced by anti-Israel rhetoric."[6]

The IPMN Hate-Israel Guide

Yet another anti-Israeli action occurred in 2014 when the Israel/Palestine Mission Network (IPMN) of the Presbyterian Church released a study guide called "Zionism Unsettled" accompanied by a DVD. The president of the Jewish Council for Public Affairs, Rabbi Steve Gutow, said that the guide was "worthy of a hate group, not a prominent American church."

It was not only condemned by Jewish organizations but also by Presbyterians involved in dialogue with Jewish organizations. The Reverend Katharine Rhodes Henderson, president of the Presbyterian Auburn Theological Seminary in New York, said that "this document purports to be about love, but it actually expresses demonization, distortion and imbalance."

John Wimberly, a co-convener of Presbyterians for Middle East Peace, a group that has been fighting against the anti-Israeli groups in the church, said that the study guide expresses "the desire to eliminate Israel as a Jewish state." He observed, "We have always been dealing with a small group of activists who know how to manipulate the system and intimidate people. Now that will blow up in their face because very few people share their agenda."

Major Jewish groups have rejected the church's efforts to disclaim responsibility for the guide. Ethan Felson, a vice-president of the Jewish Council for Public Affairs, said that the IPMN is not a separate entity and received contributions through the church.[7]

Audience Remains Silent

A more general problem, not limited to Protestant churches, occurs when organizations give inciters a platform to promote their hate and then remain silent about the slander. One such case was the 2012 General Convention of the United Methodist Church in the United States.

At this convention, a resolution was adopted calling for the boycott of Israeli products made in the West Bank. Subsequently another resolution, proposing that the denomination's board of pensions and health benefits sell its stock in three companies doing business with Israel, Caterpillar, Hewlett-Packard, and Motorola, was defeated.

A woman named Margaret Novak then said to the assembly, "I would just ask us all to imagine we were United Methodists in the 1930s and 40s [and] that our board of pensions held stock in the very successful manufacturing firms in Germany that bid and received the bids to manufacture the ovens for concentration camps. At what point would we decide it was time to divest? How much evidence would we ask for before it was time to stop the wholesale destruction of people?"

CAMERA remarked:

> Margaret Novak compared Israeli policies in the West Bank to the destruction of Jews in Europe. She made this statement in front of several hundred people and the moderator of the assembly let her statement pass unchallenged. Novak's comparison between current Israeli policies and that of the Nazi regime falls under the working definition of anti-Semitism issued by the European Forum on anti-Semitism. This definition warns against "drawing comparisons of contemporary Israeli policies to that of the Nazis." Novak's suggestion that the Israelis are perpetrating a genocide ("wholesale destruction of people") is defamatory. The population of the Palestinians has grown four-fold in the decades since the 1948 war.[8]

A key figure in the Anglican anti-Israeli campaigns is Reverend Stephen Sizer. Anglican writer Margaret Brearley observes:

> His book, *Christian Zionism: Road-map to Armageddon?* (Inter-Varsity Press, Leicester 2004) is endorsed by many leading British and American bishops, theologians and clergy, who share his views . . . It is worth briefly examining Sizer's ideology, on account of its influence and because it typifies a major strand of Christian hostility to Israel. Sizer utterly opposes Christian support for "Rabbinic Judaism" and for Israel . . . Like other anti-Zionists, he ignores the devastating consequences of both Christian and Arab anti-Semitism, and decontextualizes Israel politically.

She adds:

> Sizer's own theological position is, in essence, pre-Vatican II, and seems unaffected by mainstream post-Holocaust Christian theology. While he does not explicitly affirm "replacement" theology ("the idea that the spiritual church, as the 'new Israel' has replaced physical Israel within God's purposes"), nevertheless his theology of "covenantalism" is indeed essentially anti-Judaic replacement theology: "Covenantalism affirms that the church is Israel renewed and restored in Christ but now enlarged to embrace people of all nations."[9]

In autumn 2014, Sizer participated in a conference in Iran where claims of Zionist involvement in 9/11 were promoted. Sizer said that he was there to present a Christian point of view. The Board of Deputies demanded an investigation by the Church of England.[10]

Canada

Professor Ira Robinson of Concordia University (Montreal) says:

> The United Church of Canada has a five decade-old history of anti-Israel rhetoric. In 2012, it backed a campaign titled "Unsettling Goods" to boycott a list of items made by Israeli firms in the West Bank. In 2009, Canadian Immigration Minister Jason Kenney from the Conservative party ended governmental funding—which had lasted 35 years—to the NGO KAIROS. Kenney did so because of its leadership role in the BDS campaign against Israel. KAIROS has been supported by the United Church, as well as Canadian Catholic, Anglican, Presbyterian, Evangelical Lutheran and Mennonite churches.[11]

A lengthy battle between anti-Israelis and their opponents has been going on in Canada. Historian Paul C. Merkley says, "Mainline Canadian churches, like their counterparts in the United States, have addressed petitions seeking commitment to the Durban indictment against Israel."

He summarizes the situation as: "The laity of Canadian Protestant churches is generally pro-Israel and they, along with pro-Israel Jewish organizations, are ultimately a stronger factor than these churches' often anti-Israel leadership."[12]

European Churches

Similar developments have occurred in various European countries, says Eugene Korn.

> In 2000, the churches of the Anglican Communion sent a fact-finding group to the Middle East to examine the Israeli-Palestinian conflict. When they returned to England they published a report containing twenty-two recommendations for peace. Tellingly, not a single recommendation demanded anything substantive of the Palestinians. All were directed at what Israel needed to do for peace in the Middle East. It was eminently clear from the Anglican perspective that Israel was the root of the problem, and so they placed the blame on it exclusively.[13]

In 2013, the General Assembly of the Church of Scotland adopted a document that aimed to discredit the Jewish attachment to Israel from a theological standpoint. It proposes that the Jews' claim to the Land of Israel could be invalidated by their treatment of the Palestinians and suggests that the church consider boycotts and sanctions against Israel.[14]

In 2014, the Methodist Church in the UK issued a report on the BDS movement. Although it did not recommend that the church join the boycott, its tone was such that the Israeli embassy condemned it as an attempt to "legitimize the extremist BDS political campaign." The Jewish umbrella organization Board of Deputies also criticized the document.[15]

Sweden

Zvi Mazel was Israel's ambassador to Sweden from 2002 until 2004. In 2008, he reminisced in an interview about that period and said:

> For about a decade the Lutheran Church has no longer been the state church. Its former head, Archbishop Hammar, is a well-known Israel-hater. In January 2003, he gathered seventy Swedish intellectuals to sign a petition to boycott Israeli goods, particularly those that come from the territories . . .
>
> The Lutheran Church also has a theological institute in Jerusalem that is led by a pro-Palestinian director. When a delegation of all parliamentary parties in Sweden came to Israel in 2006, I was invited to address them. It turned out the director had arranged matters so that, besides me, they would only meet

> with Palestinians and extreme-Left Israeli organizations. They visited Ramallah but not Tel Aviv.
>
> The church has been sending Swedish youth to the Palestinian Authority with the aim of accompanying Palestinians to school or work so as to "document infringements of international law." These youngsters do not document the Palestinian Authority's infringements of international law or the crimes against humanity by Hamas in Gaza.
>
> The activists of the Christian branch of the Social Democratic Party continue to strengthen their links with the Palestinians and Israeli left-wing organizations. Their representatives visit the Palestinian territories regularly and their impressions are published in their newspaper, which is characterized by defamation of Israel.
>
> In autumn 2007 the daily *Göteborgs-Posten* published four articles by journalists who had visited Israel and the territories under the sponsorship of the Swedish church. They harshly attacked Israel, portraying it as a colonial state and its inhabitants as a race of rulers operating an apartheid system.

To put matters in historical perspective, Mazel added: "A study by a researcher at Lund University notes that from 1937, well before World War II, Swedish Lutheran pastors would not perform marriages between Germans of Aryan blood and anyone with a Jewish grandparent.[16] This racist position was adopted on the advice of the Swedish Foreign Ministry."[17]

Norway

Odd Sverre Hove, former editor-in-chief of the Norwegian Christian daily *Dagen*, says about the situation in Norway:

> The present generation of Lutheran bishops in Norway is dominated by pro-Palestinian liberation theology, as well as replacement theology. The latter claims that God's Covenant with the Jews has been "replaced" by one with Christians.
>
> Oslo's Bishop Ole Christian Kvarme lived in Israel for several years and speaks excellent Hebrew. His impact was crippled by a hostile campaign waged by the

> media and leftists before his consecration into the bishop's seat. Kvarme is a friend of Israel, but knows how harsh media criticism will be if he states it too loudly in public.

Hove adds:

> The Ecumenical Council (MKR, Mellomkirkelig Råd) of the Church Synod is a strong advocate of Palestinian theology, maintaining connections to the World Council of Churches in Geneva. The presently elected Church Synod, together with the Synod Council, is often more moderate in questions concerning "political" theology. In September 2013, the MKR sent a liturgical text on Palestinian occupation theology to all local churches to be used for one week on a voluntary basis. The MKR was subsequently criticized by the Church Synod, which argued against political statements within church liturgy.[18]

In early 2014, the Young Men and Women's Christian Association (YMCA-YWCA) in Norway came out in favor of a total boycott of goods and services not only from the settlements but also from Israel itself. It justified this decision "because a long series of U.N. resolutions and negotiations for decades have not yielded results. We believe it is now appropriate to initiate an economic boycott of Israel to put increased pressure on the Israeli authorities." The organization has thirty thousand members in more than five hundred chapters and affiliated scouts groups.[19] Shortly thereafter the Oslo branch of YMCA-YWCA distanced itself from the boycott motion.[20]

The Netherlands

The PKN is the umbrella organization of Dutch Protestants and represents the vast majority of them. Its church order mentions an unbreakable connection with the "People of Israel," that is, the Jewish people. That, however, is often a mask for actions to the contrary. The PKN's duplicitous attitude became much clearer when it sent its preachers and lay people "Kairos—A Moment of Truth—Document 2009."

There was no valid reason to do so, as its authors were mainly minor figures in the Palestinian churches. The document had been prepared by Palestinian Christians who espouse either replacement theology or liberation theology. The former has contributed greatly to almost two thousand years of Christian hatred and continues to do so.

Rabbi Tzvi Marx, who is involved in dialogue with Christians, said:

> By de facto accepting the Kairos document, the PKN has undermined 60 years of efforts to create a new relationship with the Jewish people. Liberal and Orthodox Jews feel hurt and shocked by this open support of this large Protestant organization for a document that in fact aims to eliminate Israel from the Middle East.[21]

Later it turned out that the original text had been made even more radical in its Dutch translation.[22]

In early 2010, the PKN leadership also sent the Israeli ambassador to the Netherlands a letter of accusations against the Israeli government.[23] A few weeks later the Simon Wiesenthal Center (SWC) sent a sharp response to the PKN leadership. It said, among other things, "This Kairos document is nothing less than a frontal attack on the legitimacy, viability and existence of the State of Israel." The SWC gave a detailed argumentation.[24] There was a further exchange of letters between the PKN[25] and the SWC.[26]

Dutch organizations criticize others quite often. It was, however, a rather unusual experience for them that the PKN had to answer foreign accusations. In 2010 the former theological adviser of the Dutch Reformed Church in Jerusalem, Geert Cohen Stuart, wrote an open letter to the PKN leaders in which he said:

> The justified criticism of the Wiesenthal Center merits being taken seriously. You have opened a Pandora's box and the liberated Christian anti-Judaism, anti-Zionism and anti-Israelism has justifiably been exposed by the Wiesenthal Center. It is shameful to give a possible Jewish dialogue partner a slap in the face on the basis of "an unbreakable connection with the People of Israel."[27]

The PKN's dubious attitude toward Israel and the Jews requires a detailed study. It must also be noted that the PKN leadership frequently looks away when Palestinian Muslim human rights violations and severe crimes against Palestinian Christians are publicized.[28]

In March 2014 Arjan Plaisier, secretary of the PKN, refused to oppose the BDS movement. He wrote that companies and consumers have to make their own decision. It was yet one more example of the PKN's hypocrisy in claiming an "unbreakable connection" with the "People of Israel."[29]

World Council of Churches

An example of a Christian international body that is heavily anti-Israeli is the World Council of Churches (WCC). As Van Zile noted, "WCC institutions demonize Israel, use a double standard to assess its actions, and from time to time, delegitimize the Jewish state."[30]

In 2005, former Dutch European parliamentarian Rijk van Dam visited the WCC with a delegation of pro-Israeli Christians. He related that they asked the WCC representatives they met:

> "Why doesn't the WCC condemn what goes on in Darfur, or in North Korea?" They replied: "In Africa and Asia we have member churches. They will object if we take a stand on their countries. In Israel we do not have influential churches." We told them our conclusion: "What you in fact say is that you take a one-sided, biased action against Israel because you get no protest."[31]

Evangelical Christians

A variety of factors play a role in Christian attitudes toward Israel and Jews. David Parsons is media director of the International Christian Embassy Jerusalem. He said that, on the one hand, there remain Christians who wish to stick to the classic theology of "rejected Israel." Parsons added, "Replacement theology, also called supersessionism, is the main theology of Israel's Christian foes." On the other hand, there are the Christian Zionists. Parsons stressed that the Protestant Evangelicals number perhaps as many as six hundred million in the world.[32]

Yet it is becoming increasingly clear that a major pro-Palestinian effort is underway in the United States to draw Evangelical Christians into the pro-Palestinian camp. The American evangelical author and researcher Jim Fletcher says:

> A massive effort is going on in the heart of the American Evangelical Church to lure its members to the Palestinian side. There are approximately 100 million self-identifying Evangelicals in the U.S, of which a much smaller number is actively connected with their faith. There are probably about 15 million engaged Evangelical Millennials.
>
> It is severely mistaken to think that all Evangelicals are pro-Israel. Millennials are constantly being targeted with the Palestinian narrative through media, conferences, mentoring relationships, book publishing and social networks. Frequently shown films are: *Little Town of Bethlehem* and *With God on Our Side.*

Fletcher adds, "The top power centers within American Evangelicalism are already committed to spreading the Palestinian version of the conflict. These pro-Palestinian leaders currently control the narrative within the Church."[33]

Van Zile observes:

> The beginnings of what some commentators have called the "Evangelical Intifada" can already be seen in 2010. This was the year that *With God on Our Side* (an anti-Zionist film) . . . was released. It was also the year of the first Christ at the Checkpoint conference that took place in Bethlehem. This event, which was attended by approximately 250 people from 20 different countries, was organized by the Bethlehem Bible College (which at the time was led by Bishara Awad) and the Holy Land Trust, a so-called peacemaking organization led by Bishara's son, Sami Awad.
>
> The conference, which was targeted at evangelical Protestants, presented messages that undermined the legitimacy of the Jewish people and of their state. For example, Mitri Raheb, a Lutheran pastor in Bethlehem, reported that "Israel represents Rome of the Bible, not the people of the land" and that Israeli President [sic] Benjamin Netanyahu really is not a Jew with legitimate ties to Israel, because he "comes from an East European tribe who converted to Juda-

> ism in the Middle Ages." . . . Manfred Kohl, a supersessionist theologian from Germany, told the audience that Palestinians are experiencing a "holocaust action" at the hands of Israeli Jews who, because of their tribal self-understanding, think they are "superior, better, or even 'chosen' by God."
>
> . . . the 2010 conference received sparse coverage, but the 2012 Christ at the Checkpoint Conference can be legitimately described as a watershed moment for the cause of anti-Zionism in American Evangelicalism. The March 2012 conference attracted approximately 600 attendees, including a contingent of 35 students from Wheaton College, which has been referred to as the "Evangelical Vatican."[34]

About the 2014 conference Van Zile wrote:

> If the testimony offered at the Christ at the Checkpoint (CATC) Conference . . . in Bethlehem is reliable, Christianity is a religion that allows—and encourages—its adherents to malign the Jewish homeland while behaving in a submissive manner toward Muslim extremists who are oppressing and killing Christians in Muslim countries in the Middle East, North Africa and Asia.

He added:

> But instead of holding Muslims directly accountable for the violence they perpetrated, speakers directed their ire at Israel, its Christian supporters and at Christians in both the West and the Middle East who have allegedly failed to be loving enough to Muslims who oppress and murder Christians. The conference gave its audience a heavy dose of magical thinking in which authentic expressions of Christian love toward Islamists could bring about peace and justice.[35]

Palestinian Christians

Palestinian Christians play an important role in the demonization of Israel. Van Zile sums it up:

> Arab Christians, especially those living in the West Bank and East Jerusalem, have had a corrosive and narcotic effect on church and para-church organizations in Europe and the United States. These Christians successfully portray Israel as the worst human rights abuser and singular threat to peace in the Middle East. Often they falsely depict Christian-Muslim relations in the region as good. In those instances when they are willing to acknowledge that there is a problem between Christians and Muslims, they blame these difficulties on Israel.[36]

One institution promoting hatred of Israel is the Sabeel Ecumenical Liberation Theology Center in Jerusalem. It was established in 1994 by the Reverend Naim Ateek. Van Zile says:

> This Anglican priest who holds Israeli nationality, and his associates, portray the Palestinians as victims like Jesus in his time. In a text published in 2005, the Sabeel Center equates the situation in the Gaza Strip with Christ being nailed to the cross. They compared the construction of the West Bank security barrier with Christ's crucifixion. Sabeel also promotes the idea that Israel insists on repeating the sins of the ancient Israelites as detailed in the Old Testament.
>
> Ateek has created a powerful international anti-Zionist infrastructure. On various occasions, he has influenced church-wide assemblies in the United States. Sabeel has succeeded in turning anti-Zionism into a competing religious practice in American mainstream churches and a persistent element in Protestant thought. This has even occurred in a number of churches where anti-Zionist activists have not been the majority at national assemblies.[37]

Fletcher considers Sami Awad another important Palestinian Christian inciter against Israel. The Holy Land Trust "is a Bethlehem-based Palestinian Christian organization with close ties to the Sabeel Center and other Israel-hate groups. Awad has perfected the model of bringing the Palestinian narrative into American churches."[38]

The Kairos Document

The Kairos Document plays a major role in the demonization of Israel. This paper was published in 2009 by some Palestinian Christians. Its official title is "A moment of truth: A word of faith, hope and love from the heart of Palestinian suffering."

Dutch Protestant theologian Hans Jansen comments: "In many countries, the media has greatly overstated the relevance of the signatories. It has also understated the importance of the major opposition against the document."

Jansen gives this summary:

> The central argument of the Kairos document is that only Israel is responsible for the problems in the region. The document called for considering the Israeli occupation policy as "a sin." The main aim of the document is to call for an international economic boycott against Israel.
>
> Later it became known that the Kairos document had been promoted in various countries as a declaration of the most prominent Palestinian Christian leaders such as the Greek Orthodox, the Roman Catholics, the Lutherans, the Anglicans and the Baptists. This was entirely false—not a single leader of these churches signed the document.

Jansen says:

> The document had been signed by only one church leader, Monib Younan, Bishop of the Evangelical Lutheran Church in Jordan and the Holy Land. He later retracted his signature. This church has a few hundred members in the areas under the Bishop's authority and was founded in 1959 by German Lutheran missionaries. Its membership is miniscule compared to the 400,000 Christians who live in these areas.[39]

Muslim Persecution of Palestinian Christians

A factor that should be considered as well in the context of Christian demonization of Israel is the widespread persecution of Christians in many Muslim-dominated countries. This issue is greatly underreported. The same is true for the situation of Christians in the Palestinian territories.

International human rights lawyer Justus Weiner said in 2008:

> The disputed territories of the West Bank and the Gaza Strip have been administered by the Palestinian Authority (PA) and in more recent years, in part, by Hamas. Under these regimes, the resident Christian Arabs have been victims of frequent human rights abuses including intimidation, beatings, land theft, firebombing of churches and other Christian institutions, denial of employment, economic boycott, torture, kidnapping, forced marriage, sexual harassment, and extortion.
>
> Muslims who have converted to Christianity are the ones in the greatest danger. They are often left defenseless against cruelty by Muslim fundamentalists. PA and Hamas officials are directly responsible for many of the human rights violations. Christian Arabs also fall victim to the semi-anarchy that typifies PA rule.

Weiner concludes:

> The human rights crimes against the Christian Arabs in the disputed territories are committed by Muslims. Yet many Palestinian Christian leaders accuse Israel of these crimes rather than the actual perpetrators. These patriarchs and archbishops of Christian Arab denominations obfuscate the truth and put their own people in danger. This is often for personal benefit or due to intimidation. This motif has been adopted by a variety of Christian leaders in the Western world. Others who are aware of the human rights crimes choose to remain silent about them.[40]

In 2014, Weiner presented additional examples: Steve Khoury, pastor of the First Baptist Church of Bethlehem, said in May 2013 that Christians are facing continuous harassment. Because of this many of them refrain from bearing crosses in public and carrying Bibles. He added that they are often told by Muslims to "convert to Islam. It's the true and right religion." Khoury's church has been fire-bombed fourteen times.

In December 2013 Samir Qumsieh, a Christian community leader from

Beit Sahour near Bethlehem, provided several examples of the intimidation the Christian community faces. He showed some examples of souvenirs sold by Christians around Bethlehem's Manger Square, including T-shirts of the Church of the Nativity that do not bear crosses as would be customary. On another occasion Qumsieh stated: "We are harassed but you would not know the truth. No one says anything publicly about the Muslims. This is why Christians are running away."[41]

A Different Voice

In October 2014 Father Gabriel Naddaf, a Greek Orthodox priest from Nazareth, spoke to the UN Human Rights Council on behalf of UN Watch. He began his speech with the statement: "while I stand before you today, the earth of the Middle East is soaked with the blood of Christians being killed daily."

He then offered examples, such as how 20 percent of the Middle Eastern population was Christian at the turn of the twentieth century compared to 4 percent today, and how the Syrian Christian population has shrunk from two million to 250,000. He mentioned the exodus of 77 percent of Iraq's Christian population in 2000 alone.

Naddaf followed these statistics by observing:

> If we look at the Middle East, Mr. President, we realize there's only one safe place where Christians are not persecuted. One place where they are protected, enjoying freedom of worship and expression, living in peace and not subjected to killing and genocide. It is Israel, the country I live in. The Jewish state is the only place where the Christians of the Holy Land live in safety.

Yet, according to Naddaf, by demonizing Israel the global community is complicit in assisting the groups that want to destroy their Christian minorities.

He concluded his speech with the statement:

> I, Father Gabriel Naddaf of Nazareth, stand before you and plead: O world leaders and supporters of peace, stop those who want to destroy the only free

> Jewish state in the region. It is the only refuge welcoming and protecting all of its citizens. It is the only place that does not attempt to push out Christians, forcing them to leave their land in search of security.[42]

Father Naddaf has faced criticism for his pro-Israeli views in the past, in particular his support of Israeli Christians enlisting in the IDF. In May 2014, the Greek Orthodox leadership removed him from his church for his political involvement.[43] His pro-IDF views also endangered his son, who was severely beaten by an activist from Hadash, the Arab-Jewish political party in the Knesset, because of his father's stance on enlistment.[44]

Complacent about Genocidal Intentions or Accomplices to It?

Are those Christians who look away from the glorification of murderers at the highest level in the Palestinian Authority just complacent about the frequent absence of basic moral values at the top echelon of Palestinian society? Or are they accomplices to people who consider murderers of civilians praiseworthy, provided the victims are Israelis? This question is even more emphatic concerning those who criticize Israel and omit the genocidal intentions of Hamas.

These questions can be posed justifiably about many of the other hatemongers against Israel and the Jews. Yet, in view of the lengthy, violent, and murderous history of parts of Christianity, the anti-Israeli hate mongers among Christians are in a different league because of the many crimes committed by adherents of the religion against Jews over many centuries.

The Palestinian Jesus

The distortion of the historical background of Jesus does not necessarily originate in Christian circles, yet has to be mentioned. It is an important element of the PA's propaganda strategy. It has depicted Jesus as a Palestinian liberator, the "Palestinian" prophet, and even "the first Palestinian." Many of these claims add Palestinian identity to ancient fallacious anti-Semitic motifs, such as "Christ . . .

is a Canaanite Palestinian . . . killed by the Jews."

According to Palestinian Media Watch, the PA tries to "hide from Palestinians that Jesus was a Jew who lived in the Land of Judea/Israel. PA leaders repeatedly define Jesus as a Palestinian who preached Islam, thus denying not only Jewish history, but also the history and legitimacy of Christianity."[45]

This distortion of Jesus' historical background has important precedents. Nazi Germany before and during World War II propounded the propagandistic fallacy that Jesus was not a Jew but an Aryan. The Nazis' Institute for the Study and Eradication of the Jewish Influence on German Church Life intended to "redefine Christianity as a Germanic religion, whose founder, Jesus, was no Jew but rather had fought valiantly to destroy Judaism, falling victim to that struggle." The image of Jesus as an Aryan hero was disseminated by the Nazis throughout Europe, and was widely accepted by lay leaders and churchgoers alike.[46]

CHAPTER TEN

Academics Against Israel and the Jews

IN A NUMBER OF COUNTRIES, campuses have become one of the prime battlefields against Israel.[1, 2, 3, 4, 5, 6, 7, 8, 9] This is partly related to many other problematic characteristics of contemporary academia. Academic freedom in many places is abused so extensively that new standards are required.

The prevailing concept in the past was that academic freedom fosters knowledge and through it, science advances. Nowadays one can investigate a number of universities where the Palestinian-Israeli conflict is taught, for instance. One can then check the literature list given to the students and record what is said by the teachers in the classes. In the United States, one could start with some of the campuses of the University of California, which have particularly bad reputations because of numerous incidents of anti-Semitism and anti-Israelism there.

One is likely to discover from time to time that the so-called knowledge taught about the Middle East includes propaganda, sometimes even mixed with hatred. This reflects a larger reality. One then understands that academia cannot be fully self-governing, though it will fight tooth-and-nail to retain its privileges. There are many indications that in several countries attitudes toward Israel have become a sensor of what is wrong with academia at large.

Going Back Decades

There had already been anti-Israeli manifestations at universities almost fifty years ago. For instance, in 1969 left-wing students verbally attacked Asher ben Nathan, Israel's first ambassador to Germany. When he was shouted down at Frankfurt University by the left-wing alliance, it was a portent of what would happen many years later. The aggressors at that time were a mixture of Germans, Palestinians, and Israelis. When Ben Nathan spoke in Munich in 1969, a poster in the auditorium proclaimed, "Only when bombs explode in 50 supermarkets in Israel will there be peace."[10]

Years later, the vice-chancellor of Hebrew University addressed a meeting at Kiel University in Germany. Before his arrival, a left-wing group distributed a leaflet with the slogan "Beat Zionists dead, make the Near East red."[11]

Major anti-Zionist activities also took place at British universities decades ago. Wistrich says:

> In the 1970s . . . I wrote my doctorate at University College, London. The campus war had heated up and was at full blast in 1975 after the UN "Zionism is racism" resolution. There were efforts to ban all Jewish societies on British campuses. This was stopped by a militant and determined campaign. The time was not yet ripe for the brazen anti-Semitism of the kind we find today in Britain and much of Europe, but it was certainly there beneath the surface.[12]

The Current Century

A major campaign against Israeli universities began in the current century and developed in many places. It was initiated in Britain by two British professors, Steven Rose (who is Jewish) and his wife Hillary. In April 2002, an open letter appeared in *The Guardian* that gained signatures from scholars in various countries. It called for a moratorium on all cultural links with Israel at European or national levels, until the Israeli government abided by UN resolutions and opened "serious" peace negotiations with the Palestinians.[13]

Since then many attempts to discriminate against Israel, its academic institutions, and its scholars have been made in several Western countries. Initiatives have multiplied in recent years. Campaigns frequently employ anti-Semitic motifs and sometimes also involve violent anti-Semitic acts. Although the phenomena on campus are heterogeneous, assailants mainly come from two specific segments of the academic world: the extreme left and Muslims.

It is often difficult to get a clear view of widely dispersed, multifaceted phenomena. Academic measures against Israel involve many countries, each with its own peculiarities as far as academia's functioning and organization are concerned. The process of defaming and demonizing Israel has many aspects, as do reactions to it by administrators, faculty, students, and nonacademic bodies and individuals.[14]

The Portfolio of Anti-Israeli Activities

Anti-Israeli and anti-Semitic activities in academia take the form of biased teaching, initiatives for divesting Israeli securities by university funds, discrimination against Jews identifying with Israel and sometimes classic anti-Semitic acts, proposals to cut ties with and boycott Israeli universities, ostracizing Israeli academics, refusing to publish or review Israeli academic papers, hampering the careers of pro-Israeli scholars, and so forth. Several of these campaigns have strong anti-Semitic motifs. Many actions are initiated by university lecturers.

Such initiatives recur on a number of campuses in certain countries. Among the main ones are Britain, Canada, and the United States. Anti-Israeli educators often cluster within certain disciplines worldwide, some of which are Middle Eastern studies and linguistics.[15]

There are also academic whitewashers of hatred. In Sweden, for example, Ahmed Rami, the man behind Radio Islam, was convicted of hate crimes because of the anti-Semitic content of his broadcasts in 1989 and again in a court of appeals. Nevertheless, influential journalists and politicians supported him and even denied or exculpated his anti-Semitism.[16] Jan Bergman, professor of theology at Uppsala University, testified in Rami's defense and claimed among other things that for Jews it was indeed a religious duty to kill Gentiles.[17]

Extreme Examples

There are many extreme examples of Israel-hate promoted by academics in several countries. In Italy, National Holocaust Remembrance Day on January 27 is often abused by left-wing academics for anti-Israeli hate-mongering.

Italian journalist Angelo Pezzana says:

> Marking the 27th of January as a day of remembrance has turned it into a national event where everyone can express his opinion, however miserable. The latter happens mostly in schools. Meetings are held with hundreds of students present where extreme leftist professors are invited to speak. They present the Shoah in a distorted way. This leads thereafter to a public debate usually linking the crimes of the Nazis to Israeli policies.
>
> These hate preachers are so verbally violent that moderates can not state their opinions. I have participated in a number of these meetinjgs. The horrific past was quickly forgotten in order to express hatred of Israel. The most recurrent sentence was, "Israel is doing to the Palestinians what the Nazis did to the Jews."[18]

In a 2007 essay, Alan Goldschläger noted that Canadian "universities do not object when the very legitimacy of the existence of the Jewish state is rejected, as has been the case during Israel Apartheid Week events held in 2006 on campuses in Toronto, Kitchener, Waterloo and Montreal."[19]

Goldschläger also quoted an email from Michael Neumann, a Jewish professor of philosophy at Trent University in Ontario, who wrote that his sole concern was to "help the Palestinians." Neumann continued:

> I am not interested in the truth, or justice, or understanding, or anything else, except so far as it serves that purpose . . . If an effective strategy means that some truths about the Jews don't come to light, I don't care. If an effective strategy means encouraging reasonable anti-Semitism, or reasonable hostility to Jews, I also don't care. If it means encouraging vicious racist anti-Semitism, or the destruction of the State of Israel, I still don't care.[20]

It was a blatant example of how deceitful the concept of academic freedom has become.

The medical journal *The Lancet* gave a platform to a number of anti-Israeli inciters during Protective Edge. It published a letter by doctors, including Mads Gilbert, who claimed that Israel had created a false state of emergency to "masquerade a massacre" of the Gazan people, particularly civilians. Additionally, they accused Israeli academics of complicity in the massacre because only 5 percent of Israeli academics signed an appeal to the Israeli government to cease military operations in Gaza.[21] The letter made no mention of Hamas's atrocities.

Violence

As far as threats of violence are concerned, in February 2009 Jewish students at York University in Toronto—which has gotten an increasingly bad name as a center of campus anti-Semitism—were forced to flee to the Hillel office after they had participated in a press conference. Anti-Israeli protesters banged on the doors chanting "Die bitch go back to Israel" and "Die Jew get the hell off campus."[22]

A few months later, an anti-Israeli propaganda conference called "Models of Statehood in Israel/Palestine" took place at the same university. Speakers demonized Israel. Dr. Na'ama Carmi from Israel, who gave a talk, said that "anyone who challenged the Palestinian perspective was intimidated or even labeled a racist . . . At times, those presenting a different view were subject to abuse and ridicule." She added: "Never before in my whole academic career have I encountered the rudeness that I experienced at this conference."[23] This is just one example of academia as a tilted playing field in the battle of ideas, or, less politically correct: academia as a provider for hate promotion.

Support for terrorism was on display at the University of Toronto in 2005. A former student, Avi Weinryb, recounted: "A mock refugee camp constructed in the school's Sydney Smith Hall foyer was adorned with Arabic language posters calling on camp residents to support or join the terror group Islamic Jihad. This group had been banned by the government of Canada in November of 2002."[24]

Outright incitement to murder occurred at the same university in 2002. As mentioned earlier, Ted Honderich, a Canadian-born philosophy professor at

University College in London, gave a lecture at the University of Toronto. In it he said the Palestinians had a moral right to blow up Jews, and even encouraged them to do so.[25]

At one point Concordia University in Montreal also became known abroad for physical violence against Jews on campus. In an incident that reached the international media, in September 2002 then former Israeli Prime Minister Benjamin Netanyahu was scheduled to speak there, but the event had to be canceled.[26]

Recommendations of the CPCCA Inquiry Panel

The Inquiry Panel of the Canadian Parliamentary Coalition to Combat Anti-Semitism (CPCCA) devoted much attention to anti-Semitism and anti-Israelism on campus as it saw this as a major problem. It concluded:

> Universities have a responsibility to uphold the rights to free and critical academic inquiry and to free political expression that have so long been a feature of the university experience. The Inquiry Panel recognizes that by doing so, universities serve the broader polity through the introduction of new ideas and theories concerning the world around us. However, the Inquiry Panel also concludes that these rights must be balanced with the responsibility of ensuring academic rigour in both research and teaching and with the provision of a learning environment in which all students feel safe and accepted and able to focus on their studies.[27]

The panel also presented recommendations for universities:

- First and foremost protect the safety of students by implementing and enforcing strict student codes of conduct, which among other things, prohibit and enforce academic (or legal) penalties for harassment of other students. They must also ensure that proper security and police are allowed to monitor events that have potential to turn violent;
- Designate certain "student spaces" on campus which should be reserved as a sanctuary from advocacy for various causes;
- Protect the equal right to freedom of speech for all students, by applying the

same standards to both pro- and anti-Israel events and promoting academic discourse on campus;

- Exercise their own rights of free speech, and their responsibilities as academics by condemning discourse, events and speakers which are untrue, harmful, or not in the interest of academic discourse, including Israeli Apartheid Week;
- We recommend that student unions operate in the interest of the broad campus community;
- We recommend that the Federal Government and/or the Inquiry consider offering assistance sponsoring conferences and other similar initiatives, or the issuance of statements of principle to help combat hate on campus;
- We recommend that the Federal Government and/or the Inquiry work with the provinces to help administrators develop suitable tools and structures to deal with this burgeoning problem in an effective and principled manner;
- We recommend that students be permitted to opt-out of non-union organizations that take positions on partisan issues;
- We further recommend that when student fees are automatically directed to campus organizations, that students be able to opt-out of such fees online and prior to paying them, rather than in person and by way of refund;
- We recommend that university administrations support programs aimed at elevating the academic discourse surrounding contentious issues and fostering programs aimed at achieving real dialogue; and
- We recommend that professors be held accountable for academic rigour of their curricula.[28]

Norway

In spring 2009, a group of lecturers at the Norwegian University of Science and Technology (NTNU) in Trondheim called for an academic boycott of Israel.[29] At the same university in April 2005, the student organization SIT, of which membership is obligatory, had declared a boycott of Israel that lasted close to a year.[30]

After the 2009 boycott call, NTNU launched a seminar on the Middle East. It consisted of a series of six lectures over a few months. Three were presented by prominent anti-Israelis: the Israeli extremists Ilan Pappe and Moshe Zuckerman and the American scholar Stephen Walt. The other three lectures were by Norwegian anti-Israeli academics. The main organizers of the series had all signed the call for an academic boycott of Israel.

From an international perspective, the new element of anti-Israeli hate was that the seminar series received financial support from the university rector, Torbjørn Digernes. Never before had the top management of a university in the Western world supported a series of anti-Israeli propaganda lectures. This is yet another example of the pioneering of hatred that occurs in Norway.

Leslie Wagner, who has headed universities in the United Kingdom, wrote on Digernes's blog:

> Dear Rector, I write to you as a former vice chancellor (rector) of 2 British universities. That universities have meetings, lectures and debates which are one sided is unfortunate but not new. But that these activities take place under the patronage of the Rector is in my experience unprecedented. We must assume from this that you support the clear one-sided nature of the debate. In doing so you besmirch the name of your university, and its reputation for scientific objectivity. The international academic community is aware of your activities and is watching carefully. I understand that further anti-Israel actions are being considered, and I urge to think very carefully before you completely obliterate whatever international reputation Trondheim currently enjoys.[31]

During the lecture series, the NTNU board decided to discuss a proposal brought to it for the boycott of Israeli academia. This request was condemned by leading academic and other bodies abroad. Later, articles opposing the boycott appeared in leading Norwegian newspapers. Under this pressure the Norwegian government came out against the boycott, after which the board unanimously voted against the proposal.[32]

Biased Teaching

In several academic fields there is major anti-Israeli bias in teaching. One example is Middle Eastern studies in the United States. The field of Palestinian studies has expanded disproportionately to its academic relevance. Thanks to scholars' bias, there are taboo subjects that are never studied in the framework of Middle Eastern studies, including both Palestinian and Al-Qaeda terrorism.

Martin Kramer, then at the Moshe Dayan Center for Middle Eastern and African Studies at Tel Aviv University, played a major role in exposing distortions in Middle Eastern studies in the United States. The tragedy of academia, he asserted, is that it has become home to countless people whose mission is to prove the lie that "Zionism is colonialism." Research is undertaken, books are written, and lectures are presented to establish this falsehood.[33]

In his 2001 book *Ivory Towers on Sand*, Kramer concluded that since the 1980s, American academic centers in Middle Eastern studies had been factories of error.[34] Scholars in this field were so biased that they failed to analyze or forecast all major developments in the Middle East. He pointed out that had one relied only on the analyses of academics, one would not have anticipated the emergence of Al-Qaeda or the possibility of an event such as 9/11. Kramer described the situation as even graver in light of the discipline's heavy funding by the U.S. government.[35]

American Boycotts

In 2013, three associations of American academic teachers decided to cut ties with Israeli academic institutions. One of them was the American Studies Association (ASA). Although it voted in December 2013 to boycott Israel, the motion was supported by less than a quarter of its members. The organization said that 1,252 of its approximately 5,000 members had cast electronic ballots over the last several days, a rate of participation it termed an all-time high. Sixty-six percent of the voters favored the boycott.[36] Among the many reactions was a letter to the ASA by the Israeli NGO Shurat Hadin threatening legal action.[37]

The ASA boycott was preceded by that of the Association for Asian American Studies (AAAS) from May 2013. Only 10 percent of the AAAS membership was present for the vote, but protest was minimal compared to the ASA boycott vote. Using false moral equivalence between Israel and apartheid-era South

Africa, the AAAS said American civil-society organizations had to boycott Israel because of the United States' ongoing ignorance of "illegal actions of Israel with respect to the Palestinians' right to education," while offering no specific examples.[38]

In an open letter on December 15, 2013, the Native American and Indigenous Studies Association (NAISA) also announced a boycott of Israel. Like the ASA and the AAAS, the NAISA declared that it would boycott Israeli academic institutions. Their open letter drew false parallels between the discrimination of Palestinians by Israel and the historical plight of Native Americans.[39]

The AMCHA Initiative

One of the most active fighters against the academic boycott of Israel has been Tammi Rossman-Benjamin, a lecturer in Hebrew at the University of California Santa Cruz. She is a founder of the AMCHA Initiative.

AMCHA has understood that a first step toward fighting the anti-Israelis on campus is to compile their names. In September 2014, AMCHA published a list of 218 professors who identify themselves as Middle East scholars and call for the academic boycott of Israel.

In the same vein, University of California Los Angeles emeritus professor Leila Beckwith explained how detrimental professors who engage in boycotting are to academic freedom:

> It's bad enough that these professors have revealed themselves to be wildly biased against one, and only one, Middle Eastern country. Even more troubling, however, is the fact that many of these patently biased boycotters of Israel are affiliated with government-designated, taxpayer-funded National Resource Centers (NRC) on their campuses. Clearly NRC-affiliated faculty who have publicly vilified Israel and committed themselves to refusing "to collaborate on projects and events involving Israeli institutions" have violated both the letter and spirit of the federal law which funds their teaching and research.[40]

Israel and the Jews as Sensors of Academic Decay

Israel as well as the Jews can often serve as sensors of both the moral and professional decay in many ways. One place where that is particularly clear is in the academic world. Examples are numerous. Within the framework of academic freedom, any absurdity including conspiracy theories can be proclaimed by seemingly respectable scholars.

Some remarks by the Norwegian scholar Johan Galtung provide an illustration. Galtung is considered one of the founders of a discipline called "Peace Studies and Conflict Resolution." He also established the International Peace Institute in Oslo.

After the Breivik murders in 2011, Galtung claimed there was a possible connection between this killer and the Israeli Mossad. He said, "I consider the Mossad highly unlikely, but it is illegitimate to eliminate it as a hypothesis with no evidence." In line with such an absurd approach, one can claim a possible connection between Galtung's own institute and the murderer, or the Norwegian government and Breivik, as there is no evidence to the contrary.

Galtung, a part-time anti-Semite, claimed that the murderer had ties to the Freemasons organization, which had Jewish origins. On other occasions, he said one of the factors behind the anti-Semitic sentiment that led to Auschwitz was that Jews had influence in German society. One might as well say that the far larger influence of the trade union in Norway could lead to the extermination of trade union members.

Galtung also held a discussion on *The Protocols of the Elders of Zion*, probably the best-known anti-Semitic forgery. According to Galtung, "It is hard to believe that the Russian secret police were able to be so specific." In a correspondence with *Haaretz*, he later toned down his remarks and wrote, "I don't know exactly who wrote *The Protocols*."[41]

This author has provided a far more detailed analysis of anti-Semitism and anti-Israelism on campus in the book *Academics against Israel and the Jews*.[42]

CHAPTER ELEVEN

Schools and Hatred

ANTI-SEMITISM AND ANTI-ISRAELISM IN SCHOOLS or places related to them constitute significant problems in a number of Western countries. Another issue concerns Holocaust education. When these studies are part of the curriculum in some schools, problems may arise with students.

Little is known about anti-Israeli incitement in schools in the Western world. Hardly any statistics are available. Because of the fragmented nature of the problems, many vignettes will be offered here to indicate in what areas far more detailed information is needed. A major study on this issue is called for and would require significant funding.

In some schools in a number of countries, a new young generation of Israel-haters and anti-Semites is being nurtured. There are only a few studies on some subtopics of this phenomenon in several countries. Some of these concern aspects of hatred related to Jews and Israel in schools. For instance, in the United States and France, bias in textbooks has been analyzed. A study in the Netherlands has dealt with anti-Jewish prejudice in Amsterdam schools. A 2011 study in Norway shows major ongoing anti-Semitism in Oslo high schools.[1] As mentioned previously, in Brussels,[2] Antwerp, and Gent, studies of Dutch-speaking schools found that Muslim students are far more anti-Semitic than other students.[3]

Anti-Semitism in primary and secondary schools also extends to incidents in the United States. Pine Bush School District in upstate New York was sued by three Jewish families. In January 2014, federal authorities announced that evidence "is sufficient for a jury to find that the district failed to respond to pervasive anti-Semitic harassment in its schools." The children from these families, who attended schools in the district, complained of anti-Semitic harassment in recent years, including seeing swastikas drawn on school property and students chanting "white power" and making Nazi salutes with their arms on school buses. In the worst anti-Semitic incident, a Jewish student was punched repeatedly by other students on a school-sponsored ski trip after he responded "yes" when his peers asked if he was Jewish.[4]

Textbooks

School textbooks are a major source of biased anti-Israeli teaching in several countries. In the 1990s Mitchell Bard published *Rewriting History in Textbooks*, a study of eighteen of the most widely used history textbooks in American high schools. He found them "full of factual errors, oversimplification, omission, and distortion. All these are consistently to the detriment of Jews and Israel. This inevitably leads to the conclusion that the authors are prejudiced."[5] Bard concluded that American "high schools are, as far as anti-Israeli teaching is concerned, even worse than universities."

Gary Tobin and Dennis R. Ybarra's book, *The Trouble with Textbooks: Distorting History and Religion*, confirmed Bard's findings.[6] They reviewed twenty-eight high school textbooks in the U.S. from major publishers, focusing on four main subjects: Jewish history, theology, and religion; the relationship between Judaism and Christianity; the relationship between Judaism and Islam; and the history, geography, and politics of the Middle East.

Tobin and Ybarra found that Arab and Muslim interest groups try to whitewash and glorify all things Islamic, while promoting Islam. These organizations attempt—sometimes successfully—to advance the Palestinian narrative. Their discourse promoting a whole array of lies has permeated American textbooks. Several of these obfuscate, minimize, or even justify Palestinian terrorism. One book invests great effort in delegitimizing Israel as a Jewish state.

Another textbook states that Jesus lived in "Northern Palestine," even though the term Palestine came into use much later. Tobin and Ybarra correctly viewed the inappropriate use of the term "ancient Palestine" as a red flag indicating distortion. The myth that Jesus was a Palestinian is also presented. Regarding the refugee issue, one text falsely states that Israel put the Palestinians into refugee camps, when in reality this was done by the Arab states that occupied parts of the former Palestine Mandate and those to which the refugees fled.[7] Most books do not mention the Jewish refugees who came to Israel.[8] Several textbooks state that the Second Intifada was a spontaneous uprising, despite all the evidence from the Palestinian side that it had been planned long before.[9] The major lies and omissions are far too numerous to itemize.

Tobin and Ybarra wrote: "Historical revisionists and their anti-Western, anti-American and pro-Palestinian perspectives have found their way into textbook content and are largely consonant with the Arab narrative." They also noted that "Some textbooks enthusiastically recommend [these revisionists'] works to students."[10] One of the authors' major conclusions is that, during a period of increased need for better information about the Middle East, many publishers and educators disseminate politics and propaganda disguised as scholarship.

France

Barbara Lefebvre and Ève Bonnivard analyzed a number of textbooks used in French high schools and their teachings about contemporary affairs.[11] Before that, Lefebvre contributed to a book by Emmanuel Brenner that exposed multiple manifestations of anti-Semitism, racism, and sexism in French schools.[12]

Nowadays there is a considerable amount of current affairs studies in French high schools. Yet Lefebvre and Bonnivard show that providing students with more information may actually cause them to become misinformed.

One of their important conclusions is that in many textbooks, criticism of the Taliban and other terrorists is restrained. When discussing 9/11, with only one exception, textbooks remain silent about the ultimate aim of the Arab hijackers—namely, global Islamic rule. Most of the textbooks treat terrorism as a symptom rather than a structured strategy of war, and they hardly refer to the terrorism of the extreme left in the 1970s.

Palestinian terrorism in particular is barely mentioned, "despite its contribution to shaping contemporary terrorism." Lefebvre and Bonnivard ask: "Does not limiting Palestinian terrorism only to the course concerning the Israeli-Palestinian conflict reveal a desire to turn it into something different [from general terrorism]?"[13]

Another book edited by Lefebvre and Shmuel Trigano analyzed the image of the Jew in elementary and high school textbooks, as well as in dictionaries.[14] In one essay on teaching about Jews and Judaism in high school history classes, Joëlle Allouche-Benayoun points out that these textbooks do not include Jews at all:

> Not a single textbook mentions that Jews have lived on French soil for many centuries. In this light, it cannot be easy to understand that Jews were deported and murdered in the 20th century in Europe, because students have not learned that Jews even lived there at all! Nor is it mentioned that from time to time, they were the subject of hate and discrimination.[15]

Allouche-Benayoun adds:

> To quickly summarize—who are the Jews in these history textbooks for children? One could answer with a caricature: in ancient times, they were the Hebrews whose religion, Judaism, was significantly improved by Jesus, the founder of Christianity. At the end of the 19th century, a Jewish French officer [Dreyfus] was accused of treason, dividing the country until the beginning of the 20th century. In the middle of the 20th century during the Second World War, Jews were exterminated, and subsequently others who created Israel carry on an unjust war against the innocent Palestinians.[16]

Belgium

Often a single sentence in a textbook can expose the bias of its authors. For instance, in a Dutch-language sixth-grade textbook in Belgium, students were asked to read sentences with the correct intonation. One of these was: "When a

Palestinian child in Jerusalem saw a Jewish soldier arriving, he shrank in fear."[17]

This sentence has both anti-Semitic and anti-Israeli elements. It is anti-Semitic because not all Israeli soldiers are Jewish. It is anti-Israeli because for a child, such a sentence helps lay the infrastructure of a negative image of Israel.

One only has to imagine what the reactions would be if a Belgian textbook had included an intonation exercise with the sentence, whose truth can easily be verified: "After a Palestinian suicide terrorist killed many Jewish children and adults, the Belgian press gave most of its focus to Israel's military response to it."

Jehudi Kinar was Israel's ambassador to Belgium from 2003 to 2007. He says that his embassy protested when

> the Walloon and Flemish governments subsidized anti-Israeli educational material for schools. While our complaints against these publications were given attention, nothing was done about the problems even though some of the prime ministers of those governments wrote to the ministers concerned. Among these were, for instance, Flemish Prime Ministers Bart Somers in 2003 and Yves Leterme in 2006.[18]

Britain

In Britain, there is proof that anti-Semitism is far more prevalent in Muslim schools than in other ones. A *Panorama* TV program aired by the BBC in November 2010 dealt with what is taught in Saudi-run Muslim schools in Britain. It found that these schools used textbooks from Saudi Arabia that teach children from age six and up that Jews are descendants of monkeys and pigs. After-school programs catered to about five thousand children from the ages of six to eighteen and were overseen by the cultural bureau of the Saudi embassy in London.

The *Panorama* program also noted that one textbook stated, "Jews are cursed by God" and asked children to list the Jews' negative traits. Teenagers who follow the Saudi national curriculum are being taught that "Zionists aim to take over the world for Jews and that the fabricated text of *The Protocols of the Elders of Zion* is real."[19]

Germany

In 2008 during a presentation to the Interior Committee of the German parliament, Deidre Berger, director of the American Jewish Committee in Berlin, said that school curricula needed to improve the knowledge of Jewish life and history, and also provide information about modern Israel. She remarked, "The material should take into account that up to a third of today's students are of immigrant background with little or no knowledge of Judaism or even of the Holocaust."[20]

An article by Gideon Böss in the German daily *Die Welt* accused the three major German textbook publishers of presenting Israelis as perpetrators and Palestinians as victims.[21]

Biased Teaching

Another topic for investigation is biased teaching. However, no detailed studies are available. The information on this topic is largely incidental and anecdotal in character. In the United States, one source of indirect information on biased teaching in schools comes from the youth group of the Orthodox Union (OU). The National Conference of Synagogue Youth (NCSY) has developed culture clubs in over 150 public schools across the country and reaches thirty thousand Jewish youngsters. Former OU Chief Executive Rabbi Tzvi Hersh Weinreb said, "We find that many children are very anti-Israeli. They have been very much brainwashed by an extremely anti-Israeli educational establishment."[22]

In October 2011, it became known that the German EVZ Foundation had financed two high school programs that promoted hatred of Israel. This state foundation was created to compensate Holocaust slave workers and fight contemporary anti-Semitism.[23] In one program a Dutch Jewish anti-Israeli extremist, Hayo Meyer, visited the Anne Frank High School in Gutersloh. There he equated Palestinian suffering with the mass murder of Jews in the Holocaust and termed Israel a "criminal state."[24]

At a high school in the village of Nesbru in Norway, an exhibition sponsored by Norwegian Church Aid was held on "Palestine." It included a picture of a crossed-out Israeli flag with "Murder" written in reverse underneath it. An Israeli student at the school protested and there was some negative media publicity.[25]

After even more negative publicity, the school finally decided to remove the exhibit. The student who had complained said her reaction was not at all supported by the school's administration.[26]

The Netherlands

Dutch Holocaust scholar Johannes Houwink ten Cate remarks:

> The anti-Israeli viewpoints in the Netherlands are even transmitted via elementary education. At the end of 2006, I was watching the news together with an 11-year-old child. The news showed that an error had been made and the Israeli army had inadvertently caused civilian casualties. The child didn't believe that it was a mistake.
>
> This seemed strange to me and I said: "Listen, you know that in general, the Israeli army tries to avoid civilian casualties." He replied, "I don't believe that. My teachers told me otherwise in school." He did not want to accept my viewpoint. And that was a Dutch child of 11.[27]

In June 2010, the umbrella body of Dutch Jewry, Centraal Joods Overleg (CJO), wrote a letter to the Dutch parliament. Its main point was a request to pay attention to what was taking place in the educational system. One issue raised was that "No school in the Netherlands should be prevented from teaching about the Holocaust—a pitch-black period in Dutch history."[28]

In February 2011, the CJO prepared another document on anti-Semitism in the country. It was sent to the Dutch parliament on the occasion of the plenary debate on anti-Semitism, which would take place there a few days later. One of the issues addressed was education in schools. The new text stated again:

> No school in the Netherlands should be prevented from teaching about the Holocaust, an extremely dark period in Dutch history. Holocaust memorialization and education should no longer one-sidedly emphasize the similarities

> between the Holocaust and other serious matters in today's world. It should be made clear that genocide is something fundamentally different from a political conflict where there are victims, however terrible one might find that.[29]

During and after Protective Edge fifteen Jewish families took their children out of Amsterdam Jewish schools and placed them elsewhere due to fear of attacks. It also became known that Jewish parents pay about ten times more for tuition at Jewish schools than at other schools. Half of this money is used for security.[30]

In autumn 2014, a delegation led by UK Labour parliamentarian John Mann visited a Jewish high school in Amsterdam. Afterward he said, "We were surprised that so many pupils said that they want to leave the country and go to Israel." He added that he was surprised that the Dutch government remained silent about this issue.[31] To be fair, one has to mention that also in the past many alumni of this school have left the Netherlands for Israel or elsewhere.

Sweden

Oredsson and Tossavainen wrote in 2003:

> Teachers in Swedish suburbs report widespread and brazen hostility toward Jews among groups of Arab and Muslim students. This hostility is expressed by refusing to concern oneself with anything that can even be considered as Jewish. Students may sabotage or skip classes on religion when Judaism is the subject, or skip homework, books, or examinations on courses about Judaism.
>
> During history lessons, confrontations arise between teachers and students who may on the one hand say that the Holocaust never happened—instead dismissing it as Zionistic propaganda—or on the other hand, express their admiration for Hitler and regret that he didn't succeed in killing more Jews.[32]

In 2008, Tossavainen returned to the issue:

> In Swedish schools, religious studies are a mandatory subject. Students are taught not only about Christianity but also about other religions such as Islam,

Judaism, Buddhism, and Hinduism. The purpose of these classes is not—as when Protestant Christianity was the only religion in the curriculum—to spread a certain creed, but to provide a deeper understanding of other cultures and worldviews and foster tolerance. Some suburban schools, however, have a majority of Arab and Muslim students and they object to the teaching of one specific religion—Judaism. Some of them decline to participate in classes on this subject, some actively sabotage them, and others do not show up at all. Such students may refuse to do their homework or take tests on Judaism, or go on field trips to local synagogues.[33]

Sometimes students react very strongly when Islam is described as a religion that grew out of a tradition largely inspired by Judaism, rejecting the notion that there could be any connection between the two religions. As a consequence, these students' knowledge of Judaism is usually very limited and their prejudices are rife. They may "learn" about Judaism only in the mosques, where apparently they are mostly told that Jews are infidels who will burn in Hell.[34]

Another subject that sometimes causes trouble in these schools is the Holocaust. The Arab and Muslim students often express either some form of Holocaust denial or an appreciation for the genocide of European Jewry. Sometimes they profess both opinions simultaneously. While saying on the one hand that the Holocaust is a lie, or at least has been largely exaggerated by Jews to extort reparations or build sympathy for Israeli policies, they also state that it was a pity that Hitler did not kill more Jews.

One Holocaust survivor who gives lectures at schools all over the country about his experiences during the Shoah, tells of Arab and Muslim students who stay away from his talks, sometimes at their parents' request. Students who do attend, he says, rarely express hostility, but those who do are exclusively "of Middle Eastern origin." After his lectures he asks for the listeners' evaluations, and once a student from an Iraqi family wrote:

> What happened in the Second World War, I think it was a good thing that Hitler treated the Jews that way, because I hate Jews. After the war they tried to get a country because they didn't have a country and so they took a part of Palestine and they created little Israel because Hitler threw them out of every country and that thing today [the lecture by the survivor]

> was only crap. The film was bad and I think what Hitler did to the Jews served them right and I don't care what you [the survivor] talked about and I wish that the Palestinian people would kill all the Jews. Jews are the most disgusting people in the world and the biggest cowards and because of what happened today, I wasn't going to come to school because an ugly Jew comes to school.[35]

> Other lecturers and teachers have similar experiences, with students expressing their hatred of Jews in the same kind of terms. They rarely make any distinction between Jews, Israelis, or Zionists, and have very clear opinions about Jewish behavior or characteristics, despite having had little or no interaction with Jews.

Tossavainen observes:

> Teachers tend to point to the home environment as an explanation for these attitudes. In the segregated suburbs, immigrants live isolated from Swedish society, culture, and values, while staying in touch with the discourse of their countries of origin. Hence, Iraqi, Lebanese, and Palestinian students tend to be more anti-Semitic than those from Bosnia or Turkey, for example.[36]

Harassment of Jewish Students

Harassment of Jewish students occurs, although there is scant information about its statistical frequency. Until recently no statistical data on any aspect of anti-Semitism were available in Norway. In June 2011, the Oslo municipality published a study on racism and anti-Semitism among eighth- to tenth-grade students in the city's schools. The results came as a shock to many people. The study found that 33 percent of the Jewish students regularly experience bullying at school. According to the definition used, this means that at least two or three incidents of verbal or physical abuse target these Jewish students per month. These data seem extreme for Western Europe. The study also made it difficult to blame anti-Semitism on Muslim children exclusively, as it turned out that autochthonous Norwegian students are also heavily involved.

After the Jews, the next most harassed group was the Buddhists, with 10 percent experiencing bullying; "Others" were at 7 percent and Muslims at slightly over 5 percent. Fifty-one percent of all students believe the word Jew is used pejoratively, 41 percent had heard ethnic jokes about Jews, and 35 percent had heard insulting comments. Close to 5 percent had been present when the Holocaust was denied in class. Only 25 percent of students had never witnessed anything negative involving Jews in school.[37]

These findings should have come as no surprise. Already in 2002, Martin Bodd, a representative of the Jewish community in Oslo, reported at an international conference of the Anti-Defamation League that there had been more harassment of Jews in the preceding two years than at any time since 1945.

Bodd noted that "most of the incitement and harassment against Jews has not been reported. Hardly any of the children or the adults offended by anti-Semitic statements or the like is willing to come forward publicly." He said there had been approximately fifteen incidents in which ten children had been harassed.[38]

A year later, Irene Levin, professor of social work at Oslo University College, observed:

> Some Jewish children were told they would not be allowed to attend a birthday party because of the Israeli army's actions. When there were anti-Semitic incidents at school, Jewish parents discussed this with some school principals who supported the harassment. One told a Jewish girl to remove her "provocative" Magen David [Star of David]. These incidents are important, but at present, remain exceptions.[39]

In 2010, journalist Tormod Strand of the state TV channel NRK broadcast a program about anti-Semitism in primary and other schools. It focused mainly on bullying of Jewish students by Muslims.[40] The teachers and parents who discussed the repugnant facts did so, with one exception, on condition of anonymity. This was another significant indication of Norwegian reality.

The widespread anti-Semitism in Oslo schools is most probably linked to the extreme anti-Israeli hate-mongering in Norway as practiced for years by ministers from the previous Labour-dominated government, politicians, media, trade unions, academics, church leaders, and others. One important issue not investigated in the Oslo study is how many teachers discuss the Israeli-Palestinian conflict in class and to what extent their remarks are biased. Though not stated explicitly, to several Jewish parents who did not wish to be quoted, it is obvious that hostile leftist teachers make remarks in school that put Israel in a very negative light. This, in turn, fuels negative attitudes toward Jewish children. In addition, efforts to blame the harassment primarily on Muslim students do not reflect the full truth; most of the aggression comes from autochthonous Norwegian children. Once again, however, it seems that the Muslim share in the harassment is probably far larger than their share in the student population.

All this happens in a country where the organized Jewish community numbers only eight hundred among a general population of about five million. The total number of Jews in Norway, which includes Israelis who often leave after a few years, is estimated at two thousand at most.

The Netherlands

The Center for Information and Documentation on Israel (CIDI) has already reported for over a decade about the harassment that Jewish schoolchildren encounter. It publishes annual reports on anti-Semitism that include many specific cases.[41]

Some authorities have also made efforts to pinpoint problems. In 2003 the Amsterdam municipality wrote to the city's seventy high schools asking to report on problems of anti-Semitism, hatred of homosexuals, or other forms of discrimination. This was in response to reports from various teachers that they did not dare teach about the Holocaust for fear of aggressive reactions from, in particular, Moroccan students. Only one school replied. Alderman Rob Oudkerk considered the schools' attitude unacceptable. It seems that the schools tried to conceal these incidents so as to avoid a negative image or further escalation of the problems.[42]

In 2003, the Anne Frank House in Amsterdam organized a meeting of Holocaust survivors who visited schools to speak about their wartime experiences.

What prompted the meeting was that one of the survivors had been confronted by anti-Semitic remarks on one occasion and the teacher present had not intervened. Those invited said that most of their experiences were positive. One, however, mentioned that she had been asked by a Moroccan girl whether she didn't think that "Sharon was worse than Hitler." In another school, a student asked her why this specifically happened to the Jews. One student responded: "Because they killed Christ."[43]

In 2005, media reported that the Amsterdam municipality was investigating hatred of Jews at the Het Mozaïek Elementary School. Several students had pictures of Mohammed Bouyeri, the Islamist murderer of the Dutch media maker Theo van Gogh, in their backpacks. After a visit to the Anne Frank House, some eighth-grade students said that what had happened to Anne was "good," or "They should have killed more Jews."[44]

During the same year, the teachers organization Algemene Onderwijsbond (AOb), together with the Amsterdam TV station AT5, undertook a study on radicalization in schools. Two hundred and thirty-nine teachers answered the questionnaire. Forty-seven percent of them confirmed that they had experienced the radicalization and two-thirds of them were worried about the incidents. One-third of those who answered said that they often or sometimes experienced anti-Semitic remarks. The same percentage found that some students had anti-Western views. More than a third considered that they got too little support from the school board on this matter. A quarter said they were not sufficiently equipped to react.[45]

Henri Markens, director general of the Jewish school system (JBO) in the Netherlands, relates:

> Students who transferred to [the Jewish high school] Maimonides from other schools would tell us about the anti-Semitism they had experienced. Every year we had a few children who transferred to us. This was usually because students in their previous school had made anti-Semitic remarks and the school had not done enough—or anything—about this matter. Other parents and children apparently considered the anti-Semitism normal.

Markens adds: "Often the students themselves informed . . . CIDI that they had experienced anti-Semitism. This organization also asked me from time to time whether I had heard stories from our students that were of interest to them."[46]

During a four-day evening walk in 2010 in the southern part of Amsterdam, participants from the Jewish elementary school Rosh Pina were harassed and cursed at. The paper that reported this said they had already been having similar experiences for five years.[47]

France

Emmanuel Brenner (a pseudonym) and his associates have done groundbreaking work on describing anti-Semitism and other racism in French schools. Their work had some impact in France. The title of the book Brenner edited at the beginning of the previous decade translates as *The Lost Territories of the (French) Republic.*[48] It refers to the breakdown of law and order in various domains of French society. This manifests itself, for instance, in the fear of the police to enter certain areas in and around major cities throughout the country. These "no-go" areas are largely populated by North African immigrants and their descendants. Many are Arabs, others Berbers.

Brenner and his collaborators describe and analyze this breakdown of French society in parts of the school system where anti-Semitism, racism, and sexual discrimination have emerged. On various occasions, these issues have not been dealt with appropriately by teachers and the authorities. In schools with large Muslim majorities, individuals from other groups often find themselves so intimidated that they try to hide their identity.

Brenner's book also contains testimonies by teachers describing many cases of extreme—mainly Muslim—racism. An English extract dealing with anti-Semitism in French schools has been published under Brenner's real name —Georges Bensoussan.[49]

Testimonies in the book indicate the serious plight of French democracy. Many teachers close their eyes to the violence, intimidation, and racism. Others describe the perpetrators as "hooligans" or "hoodlums," in denial of the fact that there are elements in the French Muslim community as well as foreign TV stations that systematically incite against others. Some teachers try to maintain "social peace" by appeasing the bullies and withholding sympathy from their victims.

As noted, the cases described do not only concern Jewish victims. Some Christian students are so intimidated by the Muslim majority in their classes that they have considered converting to Islam. Teachers have been harassed as well. Some Muslim students expressed joy about 9/11, and many regard Bin Laden as a hero. It would be mistaken to think the hatred focuses exclusively on Jews and Americans; the more extreme Muslims' main target is French society.

Beyond the many stories of violence, threats, insults, and harassment, there are other major problems in the schools. The testimonies mention teacher-arsonists who introduce politicized views of the Middle East conflict into their classes.[50]

Germany

Berger said in her presentation to the Interior Committee of the German parliament, "Jewish children transfer, on a regular basis, to the Jewish school in Berlin in order to escape anti-Semitism at their public school." She also remarked, "German school officials have alerted us to the fact that many incidents are not reported to either school authorities or justice officials for lack of definition and an effective monitoring system, as well as insufficient knowledge about Jewish life, history, culture and the Mideast conflict on the part of some teachers."[51]

At a Berlin high school, a student said in class, "All Jews must be gassed." In German schools, "Jew" is often used pejoratively. The educator Peter Wagenknecht said that Jewish students increasingly conceal their background: "They don't want to present themselves as Jewish. In such cases, the class often doesn't know about their background, and the teachers keep mum." He added that "the students are often acting on advice from their parents, who want to spare their children conflicts and exposure to aggressive behavior."[52]

At the beginning of 2006, *Der Spiegel* reported:

> The Jewish High School in Berlin's central Mitte district resembles a high-security fortress. Those who want to access the imposing old building on

> Grosse Hanburger Strasse have to pass through a meticulous security check. The building is surrounded by a fence several meters high and video cameras record every move. Policemen stand guard in front of the building.

Around that time two Jewish girls transferred to this Jewish school from the public Lina-Morgenstern High School in Berlin's Kreuzberg neighborhood. One of these girls had suffered anti-Semitic insults from youngsters with an Arab background. After some time, the police had to protect her on her way to school.[53]

Sometimes non-Jewish students also become victims of anti-Semitism. In 2006 a sixteen-year-old high school student in the town of Parey, in Eastern Germany, was forced by other students to wear an anti-Semitic sign in the schoolyard that read: "In this town I'm the biggest swine because of the Jewish friends of mine."[54]

Harassment of Teachers

Harassment of teachers occurs as well. In its report on Dutch anti-Semitism in 2003, CIDI quoted Oudkerk, who had told a newspaper that several teachers had informed him that the subject of the Holocaust had become almost impossible to teach. He noted that this not only created an intimidating atmosphere but, in some cases, led to telephone threats to the teachers such as: "We know where your child goes to school." As a result, Jewish teachers are inclined to conceal their Jewish identity.[55]

A Gentile teacher with a Jewish name reported that when he passed some students in school, they called him a "dirty Jew." Another teacher was quoted as saying: "In my previous school . . . I sometimes said so as to confront pupils about anti-Semitism, that part of my family is Jewish. Now I don't dare do that anymore . . . this is how one must have felt at the end of the 1930s."[56]

This teacher was wrong, however. At the end of the 1930s in democratic Netherlands, before the German occupation, Dutchmen were not intimidated to such an extent that they feared revealing that members of their family were Jewish.

In Sydney, Australia, at the beginning of 2011, there were reports of a Jewish teacher being harassed by Muslim students in class. Two Jewish substitute teachers were told by other staff members that, to avoid being harassed, they should not mention that they were Jewish.[57]

A Jewish high school teacher in France, Catherine Pederzoli-Ventura, who taught history at the Lycée Henri-Loritz in Nancy, was suspended in September 2010 for four months. She was accused of devoting too much time to teaching about the Shoah. A report by school inspectors observed that she was using the word Shoah instead of genocide.[58]

The teacher's suspension sparked a major debate and a support committee was established. The suspension was subsequently overturned, and in February 2011 Pederzoli-Ventura submitted an official complaint as a discrimination victim to the French prosecution office.[59]

The JTA reported in 2011:

> David Katzenelson, an Israeli transplant who has lived in Norway for 15 years, said that Norway is not known as a particularly hospitable place for Jews. A high school math and science teacher who also runs the small Society for Progressive Judaism there, Katzenelson said that a swastika was once spray-painted on his mailbox and that Jewish students of his have been afraid to publicly disclose their faith.[60]

Extremism and Terrorism

Extremism and terrorism against schools are yet another problem.

Hugo Deckers, secretary of the Belgian Socialist teachers trade union (ACOD), threatened Jewish schools. He sent a letter to the Flemish Jewish paper *Joods Actueel* about an announced expansion of Israeli settlements after the Palestinian Authority had gained membership in UNESCO. Deckers wrote, "If this is the [Israeli] reaction, I will, as union leader of the ACOD, bring the situation of Jewish schools in Antwerp to public attention. I suspect you will be frightened."[61]

Over the decades there have been a number of violent attacks on Jewish schools. Several of these were in Muslim or Latin American countries. In most cases there was property damage but no casualties. In 1969, there was an explosion in the Jewish school in Tehran.[62] In 1970, a bomb caused extensive damage outside the Khaddouri-Louise Zilkha School in Beirut.[63]

There were bomb attacks on Jewish schools in 1951 in Lima, Peru,[64] in 1976 in Cordoba, Argentina,[65] and in 1976,[66] 1979,[67] and 1980 in Buenos Aires.[68] In 1992, gunshots were fired at a bus of Jewish schoolchildren returning to Buenos Aires.[69] In 1995, a car bomb exploded outside a Jewish school in the French city of Lyon, wounding fourteen people.[70]

In 2004, an arson attack took place at the United Talmud Torah Elementary School in Montreal. A letter left at the scene claimed it was a retaliation against Israel's assassination of Hamas founder Sheikh Ahmed Yassin.[71]

In 2006, there was a firebombing at the Skver-Toldos Orthodox Jewish Boys School in Outremont, Montreal. In February 2009 the perpetrators, an Algerian Muslim and his Kazakh-born accomplice, were sentenced, for this and the bombing of a Jewish community center in the town, to seven and four years in prison, respectively.[72] In 2011 windows were broken at six Jewish institutions in Montreal, including four synagogues and the United Talmud Torah.[73]

The most serious terrorist attack has already been mentioned: in March 2012 Mohammed Merah killed a teacher and three children at a Jewish school in Toulouse, France.[74]

These bombings and other terrorist attacks on Jewish communities have created a situation where major security measures have been taken at many Jewish schools in the Western world.

CHAPTER TWELVE

Lawfare

Lawyers, mainly among those who specialize in international law, have also been at the forefront of anti-Israeli incitement.[1, 2] The United Nations is one place where this has happened frequently. As already mentioned, Israeli international lawyer Meir Rosenne said, "There are two types of international law. One is applied to Israel, the other to all other states. This comes to the fore when one looks at the way Israel is treated in international institutions . . ."

Yehuda Blum, a law professor and former Israeli ambassador to the United Nations, remarks that some fields of international law have greatly assisted society at large. He mentions as examples the law of diplomatic relations, the Law of the Sea, and the Law of Treaties.

Blum adds:

> One field where international law has failed in recent years, especially since World War II, is where it relates to the use of force. Its main weakness concerns the law of peace, belligerent occupation, and so forth. Since these are usually acute problems, such instances highlight contemporary international law's weakness.
>
> Another major failure of international law concerns recent international terrorism. International law is premised on the existence of states, which are bound by its norms. In this particular case, we are confronted with a different

> phenomenon: armed groups perpetrating many crimes without any state taking responsibility for their actions.
>
> There is no ability to hold any particular state accountable for these actions. Al-Qaeda is like an octopus, which has spread its tentacles all over the world. It was headquartered in Afghanistan where it has been disposed of. International law has been unable to develop the necessary adjustments to this novel situation.[3]

In view of these extremely weak elements of international law, the discipline itself has become a dubious one and easily lends itself to corruption in many areas. Harvard law professor Alan Dershowitz was quoted as saying that international law is "a construct in the mind of a bunch of left wing academics." He said this in a lecture at the Institute for National Strategic Studies in Tel Aviv in 2013. He added, "There is no basis for international law in any reality. It's not based on legislation. Much of it is not based on treaty. It is the ultimate exercise in elitist non-democracy."[4]

Lawfare

Dubious and false interpretations, as well as the use of international law against Israel, have become major tools in the anti-Israeli struggle. The term lawfare is now commonly employed for the aggressive aspects of this endeavor.[5]

Anne Herzberg, legal adviser of NGO Monitor, explains how lawfare is used against Israel:

> Lawfare cases cover areas of international law including international human rights law, laws of armed conflict, laws of statehood, borders, sovereignty, and treaty law. Lawfare against Israel takes many forms. First, it involves the distortion of international law and use of legal rhetoric, accusing Israel of "war crimes," "ethnic cleansing," "crimes against humanity," "collective punishment," "apartheid" and so on.
>
> Second, lawfare refers to co-opting and abuse of the United Nations and other international frameworks like the U.N. Human Rights Council and the human rights treaty bodies to issue *sui generis* condemnations against Israel. It

> also involves pressing for quasi-judicial investigations and international "fact-finding" missions like the Goldstone one.
>
> Third, lawfare involves exploiting international courts such as the International Court of Justice and the International Criminal Court as well as taking advantage of universal jurisdiction statutes in foreign—mostly European—courts to bring civil and criminal "war crimes" cases against Israeli officials, or those doing business with Israel.[6]

She recalls:

> An important part of the lawfare strategy was developed at the World Conference Against Racism in 2000 in Durban South Africa. This "Durban Strategy" operates as follows: Palestinians launch mass terror attacks on Israeli civilians such as waves of suicide bombings in March 2002, or rocket attacks from Gaza. As the attacks escalate and Israel employs increasingly intense counter-terror measures to prevent those attacks, NGO's begin a public relations blitz by issuing countless press releases and reports under a façade of research, condemning Israel for alleged "war crimes" and other violations of international law.
>
> These claims are then picked up in the media without any independent verification. In conjunction with the Arab League, these NGO's then lobby various U.N. bodies to issue condemnations, to establish "fact-finding" investigations and to hold "war crimes" trials. These groups also lobby the European Union and other governments, primarily European ones, to impose sanctions on Israel. They also file lawsuits seeking to have Israeli officials arrested abroad, or to have high criminal and financial penalties imposed on corporations for aiding Israel's military.[7]

Baseless Legal Arguments

International law expert Jacques Gauthier, a Canadian, has spent twenty years investigating the legal aspects of the status of sovereignty concerning Jerusalem. He states:

> Declarations relating to the status of Jerusalem should clearly distinguish between the legal aspects of the issue and political claims. U.N. Secretary General Ban Ki-moon and other political leaders frequently employ baseless legal arguments when they make statements concerning Israel's sovereignty over Jerusalem and the West Bank.

Gauthier remarks:

> The Balfour Declaration was a statement by the British government. In November 1917, Great Britain however, did not have military control or the legal authority to give rights over Palestine to others.
>
> To understand the legality of Israel's sovereignty in Palestine, we have to begin with the Paris Peace Conference in 1919 which took place at the French Foreign Office on the Quai d'Orsay. Both Arabs and the Zionist Organization presented their cases concerning the future of Palestine there. The Zionist Organization asked for the recognition of "the historic title of the Jewish people in Palestine and the right of Jews to reconstitute their national home." It demanded that the borders of Palestine—for which a map was presented—broadly follow the biblical territory on both sides of the Jordan River. It proposed that "the sovereignty of Palestine shall be vested in the League of Nations and the government will be entrusted to Great Britain acting as Mandatory of the League."
>
> The Paris Conference led to various treaties with nations defeated in the First World War. They transferred title of many territories they had lost in the war to the five Principal Allied and Associated Powers, the United States, the British Empire, France, Italy and Japan.

Gauthier adds:

> The Paris Conference was followed by the San Remo Conference, which took place in April 1920 at the Villa Devachan. There, the Supreme Council of the Principal Allied Powers adopted a resolution on 25 April concerning Palestine. It stated that its administration would be entrusted to a Mandatory which they would select. It also said: "The Mandatory will be responsible for putting into effect the declaration originally made on the 8th [2nd] November 1917 by the

British government and adopted by the other Allied Powers, in favor of the establishment in Palestine of a national home for the Jewish People. It being clearly understood, that nothing shall be done which may prejudice the civil and religious rights of existing non-Jewish communities in Palestine, or the rights and political status enjoyed [by] the Jews in any other country."

This resolution is the legal foundation of the rights under the Law of Nations granted to the Jewish people in respect to Palestine.

In San Remo, the Principal Allied Powers approved British mandates over Palestine including Trans-Jordan (East-Palestine) and Iraq, as well as the French Mandate over Syria and Lebanon. The Arabs acquired huge territories as a result of the San Remo Conference. However, there were crucial differences in the texts of the Mandate treaties for Syria and Lebanon, as well as the one for the Mesopotamia (Iraq) Mandate on one hand and the Mandate for Palestine on the other. In the former, it said that the organic law will be "formed in agreement with the native authorities and shall take into account the rights, interests and wishes of all the population inhabiting the mandated territory." In the Mandate for Palestine, there is no such formula. It stated that the Mandatory will be responsible for creating the conditions to "secure the establishment of the Jewish National Home." It also said that recognition was given "to the historical connection of the Jewish People within Palestine and to the grounds for reconstituting their national home in that country."

The Council of [the] League of Nations approved the British and French Mandates in July 1922. In the 1923 Treaty of Lausanne, Turkey renounced all rights and title on the aforementioned territories. In international law, once the title to Palestine was given to the Jewish people, this cannot be nullified retroactively as a result of the introduction of new principles of international law several decades later. In fact, the rights granted to the Jewish people are protected under Article 80 of the UN Charter. This preserves intact all the rights granted to Jews under the Mandate for Palestine, even after the Mandate's expiry in May 1948.[8]

The EU Directive on Settlements

In reaction to the EU directive regarding settlements promulgated in July 2013, more than a thousand attorneys from many countries signed a detailed letter to Catherine Ashton.[9] Its initiator was retired Israeli ambassador Alan Baker, an international law expert. The letter asked the European Union to revoke the directive as it was based on "legally flawed and incorrect assumptions regarding both the legality of Israel's settlements and the status of the pre-1967 Armistice Lines as Israel's border." Although the letter did not explicitly call the EU directive "lawfare," it accused the EU of "misreading the law" which can be considered a euphemism for that term.

The letter furthermore said:

> The long-held view of the EU as to the illegality of Israel's settlements is a misreading of the relevant provisions of international law, and specifically Article 49 of the Fourth Geneva Convention, which is neither relevant to the unique circumstances of Israel's status in the area, nor was it ever applicable, or intended to apply to Israel's circumstances in Judea and Samaria.
>
> The EU together with other international bodies has consistently ignored authoritative sources, including the 1958 official commentary by International Committee of the Red Cross, as well as the published opinions of prominent international jurists, all of which explain the provenance of Article 49 in the need to address deportations, forced migration, evacuation, displacement, and expulsion of over 40 million people by the Nazis during the Second World War. This has no relevance to Israel's settlements in Judea and Samaria.[10]

The letter added that the issue of settlements was agreed in the 1995 Israeli-Palestinian Interim Agreement to be an issue for negotiation between the parties. The EU is a signatory to that agreement as a witness, and its "determinations . . . undermine the negotiating process and run against the EU's status as signatory."

The letter also pointed out that the legality of Israel's presence in the area "stems from the historic, indigenous and legal rights of the Jewish people to settle in the area, as granted in valid and binding international legal instruments recognized and accepted by the international community." It further notes that the EU is predetermining the outcome of the negotiations concerning Israel's borders by calling the Armistice Lines borders, even though they were never considered to be such. This is the more so as the EU in its 1980 Venice Declaration called for "secure and recognized boundaries" that would replace the Armistice Lines.[11]

The EU and Anti-Semitism

This EU directive can be considered an example of anti-Semitism according to the FRA definition. American international law expert Eugene Kontorovich has exposed the EU's double standards concerning Israel and Turkey. The EU funds Turkish-occupied Northern Cyprus. Yet "Turkey's invasion and occupation of Cyprus in 1974 was condemned by the UN Security Council and the EU's official policy is that the Turkish occupation is illegitimate and Turkey must completely withdraw. The EU does not recognize the Turkish government in Northern Cyprus."

Kontorovich remarks that the EU

> maintains an entire separate program to direct funds to Northern Cyprus. This program accounts for about 0.8% of Northern Cyprus's GDP. Projects include study abroad scholarships for students at the numerous Northern Cyprus universities . . .; developing and diversifying the private sector through grants to small and medium-sized businesses; various kinds of infrastructure improvements (telecom upgrades, traffic safety, waste disposal); community development grants, funding to upgrade "cultural heritage" sites, and so forth. They even put on a concert. The program basically gives grants to the Turkish business and private entities, and builds the infrastructure of the occupying government. The EU is doing exactly what it claims, in the settlement guidelines, international law prohibits. The relevant EU resolutions and reports make no mention of any international legal question about such funding.[12]

Lessons from the Ukrainian Conflict

In the 2014 Ukrainian conflict, further elements of the West's selective application of international-law concepts came to the fore. Western powers accused Russia of violating international law by annexing Crimea. This implies that the United States and the European Union uphold international law.

This argument was greatly weakened by Gerhard Schröder, former German Socialist chancellor and a friend of Putin. He stated that he himself was one of many Western leaders who violated international law with regard to Kosovo. Schröder compared the referendum conducted by the government of Crimea with Kosovo's declaration of independence from Serbia.[13]

The EU has consistently claimed that Israel's settlement policy in the territories—which previously did not legally belong to any sovereign state—contravenes international law. This argument has been contested by many prominent legal scholars. Schröder's remarks undermine the EU position even further. If the EU behaved much worse than what it falsely condemns Israel for, this is yet one more example of the double standards that are part of the FRA definition of anti-Semitic acts.

CHAPTER THIRTEEN

The United Nations, a Purveyor of Hate

Dore Gold's book *Tower of Babble* focuses on the functioning of the United Nations. Its subtitle is *How the United Nations Has Fueled Global Chaos*. The book's final paragraph reads:

> This deficiency in the UN is hard for many to admit. The UN is protected by a very high wall of political correctness that makes criticism of it tantamount to an attack on all of mankind. But it is time to recognize that it has utterly failed to achieve its founders' goals: to halt aggression and assure world order. With determined leadership, the United States can lead its allies in creating a safer and freer world. Perhaps in the long term they can reinvigorate the UN and make the organization's system of collective security a viable option. But that day is a long way off.[1]

More than fifty years ago Ben-Gurion called the United Nations "the theater of the absurd." Since then the organization has largely proved that this is true. Its attitude toward Israel is one of the best indicators of this.

One rather typical example occurred after the Protective Edge campaign at the October 2014 meeting of the Cairo Conference on Palestine. This gathering had the goal of amassing financial commitments to rebuild Gaza. UN Secretary-General Ban Ki-moon spoke there a number of times. In one statement he said, "Yet we must not lose sight of the root causes of the recent hostilities: a restrictive occupation that has lasted almost half a century, the continued denial of Palestinian rights and the lack of tangible progress in peace negotiations."[2]

Not a word was said about the rockets aimed at Israeli civilian centers by Hamas or its advanced network of terror tunnels used to plan an attack on Israeli civilians as the main root causes of the conflict. Ban Ki-moon also said nothing about the fact that Hamas aims to commit genocide against Israel. By ignoring this, Ban Ki-moon shows his indirect support for this Palestinian terrorist movement.

In 2004, Cotler summarized the UN's attitude toward Israel: "The United Nations is singling out Israel and the Jewish people for differential and discriminatory treatment in the international arena. It purports to protect international human rights, but instead gives anti-Jewishness a protective cover."

He added:

> A similar attitude can be found in the resolutions of the United Nations' specialized agencies such as the International Labor Organization (ILO), the World Health Organization (WHO), UNESCO, etc. The ILO holds Israel to be the enemy of labor, claiming it suppresses Palestinian trade unionism. The WHO considers Israel the enemy of health, arguing it violates the health of Palestinian inhabitants. UNESCO accuses Israel of being the enemy of culture because of alleged desecration of historic sites. Elsewhere Israel is charged with being the enemy of women and children because of its supposed suppression of Palestinian women and children, and Israel is the only country which has been declared a "non-peace loving nation."

Cotler called the United Nations Relief and Works Agency (UNRWA) a "corrupted dimension of the United Nations." He said, "This institution is supposed to work for the relief of refugees. Under its supervision and management, the refugee camps became part of the culture of incitement as well as bomb factories."[3]

Ten years later during Israel's Operation Protective Edge in July 2014, UNRWA had to admit that it discovered rockets on the premises of its Gaza schools.[4]

The Leading Global Purveyor of Anti-Semitism

The United Nations is both an anti-Israeli player and an important conduit of the new anti-Semitism. Extreme attacks on Israel are a regular feature of its gatherings. Anne Bayefsky, senior fellow at the Hudson Institute, has made major contributions to analyzing the methodology of the anti-Israeli and anti-Semitic forces at this supranational body and its affiliated organizations.

At the first UN Conference on Anti-Semitism in New York in June 2004, Bayefsky asserted, "The United Nations has become the leading global purveyor of anti-Semitism—intolerance and inequality against the Jewish people and its state."[5] "The UN also encourages terrorism directed at Israelis."[6] Her writings frequently contrast the EU's strong support for condemnations of Israel with its rather negligent attitude toward anti-Semitism at the UN.

Assessing the UN's anti-Israeli methodology, Bayefsky said that the organization "delegitimizes the self-determination of the Jewish people, denies Israel the right to defend itself and demonizes it in the framework of the international regime of human rights protection."

Bayefsky summarizes her view: "The evil of anti-Semitism today moves through its UN host like an opportunistic pathogen. First, discrimination of Israel followed by its demonization; the deification of the enemies of the Jewish state; the denial of Jewish victimhood; denunciation of the Israeli who fights back; and finally, the refusal to identify the assailants."[7]

Europe and the United Nations

One strong gauge of Europe's negative political attitude toward Israel is its voting record in the United Nations. These democracies express biased judgments about another democracy. The argument that Israel's attitude toward the Palestinians is responsible for the conflict is easily refuted. After the 1993 Oslo agreements, Europe's voting pattern at the UN did not change.[8]

Dore Gold, former Israeli ambassador to the UN, notes many aspects of consistent European anti-Israeli bias in various institutions of the UN. In condemning Israel, Europe has frequently sided with the world's most abject dictatorships. Gold has drawn attention to Europe's consistent and longstanding anti-Israeli bias at the world body. He says that according to the UN, Israel behaves demonically. He points to the possible consequences of this process, for which the European Union has helped lay the attitudinal groundwork. "From Israel's distorted record at the UN to demonizing the entire Jewish people is then a short step. This process binds anti-Zionism, the attack on the legitimate rights of the Jewish people, with anti-Semitism."[9]

Gold notes that the UN is often unwilling to take measures against genocide. For instance, it did not manage to convene the Security Council or Emergency Special Sessions of the General Assembly for Rwanda, or Darfur in the Sudan. He adds:

> Yet such sessions are used, with European support, to discuss issues of infinitely less gravity for international peace and security that involve Israel.
>
> For instance, in July 1997 the Arab states successfully convened an Emergency Special Session of the General Assembly, dealing with Israeli building practices in East Jerusalem at Har Homa, a barren hill . . . In the entire UN history, perhaps nine or ten Emergency Special Sessions have been convened. Sometimes the same session was reconvened a number of times. Almost all dealt with the Middle East and Israel.[10]

Samuels stressed that the UN is a vital arena and that its international conferences will increasingly be held in Third World countries. "It is there that we face multiplier effect problems. Our enemies may not have the power to destroy us, but in the world's chambers of diplomatic rhetoric, they conduct a war of attrition that leads to confrontations on campuses, boycotts, lawsuits and media campaigns."[11]

The UN Human Rights Council

Extreme examples of double standards against Israel come from the UN Human Rights Council (UNHRC) in Geneva. According to a former Israeli ambassador to the UN in Geneva, Itzhak Levanon, the UNHRC "has focused on Israel to the exclusion of other pressing human rights needs."[12] He added that the council, for instance, had not passed a resolution condemning the over two hundred thousand deaths in Darfur, nor dealt with major human rights violations in countries such as China, for example.

The UNHRC is largely dominated by Arab and Islamic states. Hillel Neuer, executive director of UN Watch, says, "The United Nations Human Rights Council . . . has a standing agenda item against Israel. It is the only country specifically targeted at every meeting. Not even major human rights abusers like China, Cuba, Pakistan, Saudi Arabia, Sudan, Syria or Zimbabwe are subjected to such treatment."

He adds:

> The UNHRC adopts more resolutions condemning Israel than it does for the rest of the world combined. In its March 2013 session, there were six politicized resolutions against Israel—and only four against all other countries. The vast majority of the world's victims of gross and systematic violations failed to merit a single resolution. The UNHRC turns a blind eye to mass killings in Iran, Syria, Iraq, Egypt and elsewhere, a clear denial of international due process.
>
> Furthermore, Israel is also the object of more emergency sessions than any other country in the world. One product of these sessions was the 2009 Goldstone Report, which excoriated Israel and exonerated Hamas.[13]

Lawfare: The Goldstone Report

Herzberg says:

> After Israel's Cast Lead campaign in 2008, the United Nations Human Rights Council assigned a highly biased mandate to a commission headed by Judge Richard Goldstone. It read: "to dispatch an urgent, independent international fact-finding mission, to be appointed by the President of the Council, to investigate all violations of international human rights law and international humanitarian law by the occupying Power, Israel, against the Palestinian people throughout the Occupied Palestinian Territory, particularly in the occupied

> Gaza Strip, due to the current aggression, and calls upon Israel not to obstruct the process of investigation and to fully cooperate with the mission."
>
> This mandate thus called for an exclusive investigation of Israel. In addition, it included several statements that pre-judged the investigations such as claiming that Israel had indeed committed violations of human rights and humanitarian law, that Israel was an "occupying power" and that it had engaged in "aggression." This manifest prejudice is why earlier former United Nations Human Rights Commissioner Mary Robinson refused to head up the Commission.[14]

The Goldstone Report is a prime example of lawfare against Israel. The Israeli government refused to cooperate with the commission. The resulting report fit the biased assignment.

Only several years later the commission's chairman, Richard Goldstone, made partial amends for what must be considered a "hate-Israel" document prepared under his and his colleagues' supervision. In April 2011, Goldstone wrote in *The Washington Post*:

> If I had known then what I know now, the Goldstone Report would have been a different document . . . The allegations of intentionality by Israel were based on the deaths of and injuries to civilians in situations where our fact-finding missions had no evidence on which to draw any other reasonable conclusion . . . [T]he investigations published by the Israeli military and recognized in the U.N. committee's report . . . indicate that civilians were not intentionally targeted as a matter of policy . . .[15]

A book titled *The Goldstone Report "Reconsidered": A Critical Analysis* contains a large number of damning condemnations of the text written by the Goldstone Commission, which is sometimes referred to as a kangaroo court.[16] Dershowitz titles his chapter "The Case against the Goldstone Report: A Study in Evidentiary Bias." Giving tens of examples, he says, "The Goldstone Report is, to any fair reader, a shoddy piece of work, unworthy of serious consideration by people of good will, committed to the truth." He adds, "The Irish member of the mission, Colonel Desmond Travers, refused to believe evidence that undercut

Hamas' position, even when it was on videotape and utterly uncontradicted." Dershowitz also notes, "The British member, Christine Chinkin, had already decided the case before hearing one bit of evidence." Dershowitz brings proof for these statements and many others that illustrate the commission's bias.[17]

The book also contains a letter by lawyer Trevor Norwitz to Goldstone, with whom he is on a first-name basis. He calls the report "deeply flawed," "unbalanced and inflammatory," "a procedurally deficient rush to judgment, and incapable of producing any meaningful findings."[18] The resolution that had given the Goldstone Commission its mandate, Norwitz notes, was in Goldstone's own words "very lopsided" and "unfair." It authorized Goldstone's commission to demonize Israel while legitimizing and even whitewashing Hamas.

In several subsections, Norwitz exposes the report's fallacies. These subsections have titles such as: "Your procedurally flawed investigation," "Failure to investigate critical facts," "Use of hearsay and anonymous accusations as evidence," "More prejudice than proof," "Double standards in assessment of credibility of evidence and intentions," "Seeking political impact rather than truth," "Lawmaking Rather than Fact-Finding," "Piling on Gratuitous anti-Israel criticisms," "Legitimizing Hamas," "Your ahistorical context," and "The language of your report illustrates its bias."[19]

Herzberg remarks, "If one accepts the Goldstone report, terrorists in future asymmetric conflicts can learn from it that it is worthwhile to deliberately operate in areas where civilian harm is greatest. Damage to international humanitarian law is of lesser concern, as almost all credible legal experts in the field have rejected the report's terribly flawed legal analysis."[20]

Deliberately operating in areas where civilian harm is greatest was indeed what occurred in 2014. In its reaction to Israel's Operation Protective Edge, Hamas made an effort to put civilians at risk. It is not far-fetched to conclude that the Hamas leadership, thanks to the writings of Goldstone and his colleagues, understood what crimes one can get away with in the international sphere.

Regarding Goldstone's partial retraction of the report in 2011, Herzberg comments, "Goldstone admitted in a *Washington Post* article that the central premise of the report, that Israel deliberately targeted Palestinian civilians, was wrong. He falsely claimed however, that his commission had reached erroneous conclusions based on evidence it had at the time. The truth is that it willfully ignored evidence which was already right in front of them."[21]

There is not enough space here to discuss the various authors' criticisms of the Goldstone Report in more detail. Any reader of some of the chapters must come to the conclusion that if this report is a legitimate expression of international law, this is indeed a very warped and dangerous discipline for democratic societies.

Another important point is that the Goldstone Report, even if criticized, is a further sign that in this profession, apparently, anything goes. It is a further indication of international law's dubious character. One conclusion could be that there is an urgent need for a new academic discipline called "manipulations of international law."

In summer 2014, the UNHRC repeated its previous biased operations. It appointed Canadian lawyer William Schabas to head yet another commission investigating Israel's actions against Hamas in summer 2014.[22] Neuer of UN Watch published a large amount of evidence that Schabas had shown bias against Israel and was not fit to adjudicate in this case because of his past statements calling to indict Israeli leaders.[23]

UNRWA

The continued existence of UNRWA is an indication of the United Nations' extreme bias in the Palestinian-Israeli conflict. Kenneth Bandler of the American Jewish Committee wrote:

> UNRWA is the only international refugee agency dedicated to exclusively benefit one population group, the Palestinians. All other refugees worldwide are covered by the U.N. High Commissioner for Refugees (UNHCR), which not only provides sustenance but, importantly, also strives to resettle them, to ensure that their refugee status is not a permanent condition.
>
> Originally envisaged as a temporary agency, UNRWA's mandate, which does not call for resettlement, has been regularly renewed. UNRWA's original roll of 700,000 refugees grew to include children, grandchildren, and great-grandchildren, some 4.7 million Palestinians living in Gaza, the West Bank, Jordan,

> Lebanon and Syria. The agency's staff, some 27,000, is four times the size of the UNHCR workforce, deployed in every other conflict where refugees need help.

As for the financing of this greatly oversized agency, Bandler observes:

> The Arab world's refusal to integrate Palestinian refugees and the generosity of Western governments in providing more than 95 percent of UNRWA's funding has assured its existence. The United States provides more than 25 percent of UNRWA's $500 million annual budget. Arab nations, often first to rally for the Palestinian cause, account for about one percent, which speaks volumes about their genuine concerns for Palestinian well-being.[24]

In May 2014, Ron Prosor, Israeli ambassador to the UN, spoke in its building at a gathering of the International Association of Jewish Lawyers and Jurists and the American Association of Jewish Lawyers and Jurists, and said, "UNRWA fuels false promises and gives grievance to dangerous myths. We have heard time and again that settlements are the major hurdle to peace. In these halls, no one will admit that the real obstacle is the so-called 'claim to return.'"

Prosor added that the right of return "would flood Israel with millions of refugees and drown the Jewish state by sheer numbers." He called it a euphemism for the destruction of Israel. Prosor remarked that "UNRWA is responsible for helping fuel this 'fiction' of the right of return to Palestinian children through their textbooks and schools." He observed that the UNRWA mandate to resettle refugees was removed in 1965. This means that UNRWA has perpetuated the refugee problem instead of solving it. When comparing UNRWA to the UNHRC, he noted, "In addition to the right of return, the fact that the UN puts Palestinian refugees in a class of their own, separate from those elsewhere in the world, has also fueled the problem."[25]

In 2013, a group of congressmen demanded that the State Department investigate and justify U.S. financial aid to UNRWA. They did so in view of accusations that the organization incites and radicalizes Palestinian refugees.[26]

UNESCO

Yet another UN organization biased against Israel is UNESCO. UN Watch notes that "Since 2009, UN Watch has counted no less than 46 UNESCO resolutions against Israel, one on Syria, and zero on Iran, North Korea, Sudan or any other country in the world."

The current head of UNESCO, Irina Bokova, made major efforts to indefinitely delay an exhibition in Paris on the Jewish people and Israel, under the pressure of Arab states. According to UN Watch's Neuer, "Bokova justified her cancellation of Monday's Jewish exhibit by invoking UNESCO's alleged concern not to endanger the fragile Israeli-Palestinian peace negotiations. Yet somehow this noble principle of caution for peace never stopped UNESCO from excoriating Israel incessantly."[27]

Ultimately, partly due to pressure from the United States, Canada, and others, the exhibition went ahead in June 2014.[28]

In August 2014, Bokova issued a statement condemning the killing of Palestinian journalist Abdullah Murtaja. The statement said: "I condemn the killing of Abdullah Murtaja. Journalists must be able to carry out their work in safe conditions and their civilian status needs to be respected at all times. Society needs to be kept informed of events, never more so than when living in the shadow of conflict . . ."

However, bloggers revealed that Murtaja was a member of Hamas's Al-Qassam Brigade. Following his death, a picture of him in Hamas logos and a video of him with Hamas were released.[29] This evidence forced Bokova to correct her statement. She now admitted that Murtaja was a member of an "organized armed group," without specifically mentioning that the group was Hamas.[30]

The UN Division on Palestinian Rights

Yet another example of the extreme bias of the United Nations is the existence of the United Nations Division on Palestinian Rights (DPR) and the Committee on the Exercise of the Inalienable Rights of the Palestinian People (CEIRPP).

Daniel Mariaschin, executive vice-president of B'nai B'rith International, describes this reality:

> Both the division and the committee were established by the UN in the wake of the infamous "Zionism is Racism" resolution, which itself followed on Yasser Arafat's appearance before the UN General Assembly in 1974. Together with another body, the Special Committee to Investigate Israeli Practices, these committees serve as an in-house public relations operation for the Palestinian side in the conflict with Israel . . .
>
> On its website, the CEIRPP states that together with the DPR, the "secretariat" for Palestinian matters, the General Assembly "has gradually expanded the committee's mandate." Indeed, the DPR is the only bureau in the UN's Secretariat to be dedicated solely to one group, sitting aside, as it does, bodies devoted to geographically-based divisions for Africa, the Americas, Asia and Pacific, Europe, Middle East and West Asia.[31]

In sum, the United Nations assists in promoting anti-Semitism whenever its organizations and staff members discriminate against Israel.[32, 33, 34]

CHAPTER FOURTEEN

Social Democrat Inciters

SOCIALISM FREQUENTLY DEFINES ITS MAJOR characteristic as "solidarity with the weak." In today's confused situation, this often means that in the Palestinian-Israeli conflict Social Democrats avert their gaze from the genocidal incitement of Hamas and the glorification of murderers by the Palestinian Authority. It is a major example of a structural ideological problem of substantial segments of socialism. Those socialists who are not careful, showing near blind solidarity with those declared as victims, may become allies of potential or real murderers and even of planners of genocide.

There is probably no other issue where one can see how many leading Social Democrats have gone down a slippery moral slope as in the case of the Middle East conflict. Once one is confronted with extreme cases, one can better discern the lesser ones.

In a study on Greek anti-Semitism published almost twenty years ago under the pen name Daniel Perdurant, Moses Altsech wrote that at the end of 1988 during the Socialist PASOK party's rule,

> following a judicial investigation, the Athens Court of Appeals and the Greek Supreme Court decided that Abdel Osama Al-Zomar, an alleged Palestinian terrorist apprehended in Greece, should be extradited to Italy to face charges of bombing the synagogue of Rome in October 1982, injuring thirty-four people

> and killing a three-year-old child. Greek Justice Minister V. Rotis used his authority to overrule the court decisions, stating that Osama's acts were part of the "Palestinian struggle for liberation of their homeland, and, therefore, cannot be considered acts of terrorism."[1]

Altsech commented, "Rotis compared these deeds to the acts of terrorism as part of anti-Nazi resistance during World War II. Osama could choose a country to fly to and went to Libya. *The Washington Post* wrote that Greece had rolled out a red carpet for terrorists."[2]

Altsech remarked elsewhere:

> In 1986, a regular session of the Athens City Council received national—and international—attention because of comments made by the Socialist mayor, Dimitris Beis. At one point during the session, there was some noise and confusion, which the mayor described as "*havra*"— an insulting term which equates noise and tumult with Jews praying in unison in the synagogue. The mayor defended his remarks, and mocked those who protested.
>
> An article in *Apoghevmatini* noted that at the time when Jews were being blamed for everything from forest fires to the Chernobyl meltdown, the mayor could expose his prejudice openly without concern about losing votes from a few Jewish citizens.[3] New York Mayor Ed Koch, referred to Beis' comments in a *New York Post* article about Greek anti-Semitism.[4]
>
> In 2002, Theodoros Pangalos, a former Pasok foreign minister and EU commissioner led a protest march to the Israeli embassy. The embassy was closed because it was the Saturday of Passover. Pangalos then suggested that since the embassy was in Greece, it should respect the customs of its host country, and that not receiving the protest on the Sabbath of Passover was an insult to Greece.
>
> After Pasok's electoral defeat to New Democracy in 2004, the outgoing Prime Minister Costas Simitis, was accused of not having handed power over to his successor, George Papandreou, early enough to give his party a better chance at victory. He was referred to as "the Jew Simitis" in a derogatory front page article of the pro-Pasok daily *Avriani* on March 11.[5]

The word Jew was used as invective, the more so as Simitis is not Jewish.

Sweden

In Scandinavia one can find many examples of Social Democrat direct or indirect support for Palestinians while looking away from their multiple, extreme criminal activities. The anti-Israeli double standards are not only linked to election opportunism. Anna Lindh, who was Sweden's foreign minister and destined to be prime minister before being assassinated, was known for her anti-Israeli bias.

Ambassador Mazel says:

> The late foreign minister Anna Lindh usually made the most vicious attacks on Israel. Her hatred of Israel can only be described as almost pathological. Under her leadership Sweden published the greatest number of one-sided condemnations of Israel of any EU country. Lindh was stabbed to death in 2003 by a mentally disturbed Swede of Serbian origin.[6]

Lindh's successor as foreign minister Laila Freivalds, also a Social Democrat, visited Yad Vashem in June 2004 to honor murdered Jews. She then heavily criticized Israel at a meeting in the Israeli Foreign Ministry. Freivalds remained silent on the extensive anti-Semitism in Sweden, much of which is of Muslim origin. This phenomenon of paying honor to dead Jews, criticizing Israel, and ignoring or belittling one's own country's major delinquencies toward living Jews is common in Europe. Freivalds's behavior was subsequently exposed by four former chairmen of the Swedish Jewish community, who wrote about the rampant racism and anti-Semitism in the country.

They sent a letter to the editor of *Haaretz* in which they summarized contemporary Swedish anti-Semitism. The letter first praised Sweden for having received Jews fleeing the Holocaust during World War II, and Prime Minister Göran Persson for initiating the Living History Project.

The four then went on to say:

> The number of verbal and physical attacks against Jews has increased in Sweden. Youngsters in schools give evidence of how they hide the fact of being Jews, as they are attacked both verbally and physically. Teachers testify that students

> refuse to participate in classes when Judaism is studied. Survivors report feelings of fear. The police stand passively by when extremists attack pro-Israel and anti-racist manifestations.

They added:

> Over the last decades, Sweden has become a center of racist and anti-Semitic White Power music, and several anti-Semitic groups have established Swedish websites spreading anti-Semitic propaganda. The Swedish Church has just recently initiated a boycott campaign [against Israel], a reminder of the commercial boycott of Jews in various societies in the past.[7]

When the new Swedish Social Democratic government consisting of Social Democrats and Greens started activities in October 2014, Social Democrat Prime Minister Stefan Löfven announced that his government intended to recognize the Palestinian state. He did not mention any conditions.[8] This was done at a time when there were many indications from polls that if there were Palestinian elections, Hamas leader Ismail Haniyeh would defeat the incumbent Fatah president Mahmoud Abbas.

On October 30, 2014, Foreign Minister Margot Wallström announced that Sweden had recognized Palestine as a state.[9]

Malmö's Inciting Mayor

On January 27, 2010, International Holocaust Remembrance Day, *Skånska Dagbladet* interviewed the Social Democrat mayor of Malmö, Ilmar Reepalu.[10] He condemned anti-Semitism by saying, "We don't accept Zionism nor anti-Semitism. That's extremes that put themselves above other groups and think that they are worth less." He furthermore condemned the alleged Israeli human rights violations and abuse of the civilian population in Gaza. Reepalu added, "I wished that the Jewish community would distance itself from Israel's violations of the civilian population in Gaza." Such a statement is anti-Semitic according to the FRA definition. Typically, this part-time anti-Semite has never held the

Muslim population of Malmö responsible for the huge and often unequaled crimes in parts of the Muslim world.[11]

There were large anti-Israeli demonstrations in Sweden during Israel's Operation Cast Lead. Thanks mainly to Swedish bloggers, it is known that prominent members of the Social Democrats—then the country's largest party—took part in hate demonstrations against Israel. Mona Sahlin, the party's leader, participated in a rally in Stockholm[12] where Hizbullah and Hamas flags were flown and an Israeli flag was burned.[13] Jan Eliasson, the former foreign minister,[14] and Wanja Lundby-Wedin, chair of the Swedish Trade Union Confederation,[15] also took part in that event.

In Norrköping another senior Social Democrat, Lars Stjernkvist, spoke at a demonstration with a Hizbullah flag as well as swastikas in the background. A blogger captured this with his camera.[16] When it became news, the local Social Democrat newspaper *Folkbladet* criticized the blogger for making an issue out of it.[17] In Göteborg, white cloths with Israeli symbols were burned. In Malmö another Social Democrat parliamentarian, Luciano Astudillo, spoke as someone next to him held up a picture of Hizbullah leader Hassan Nasrallah.[18]

Norway

In April 2006 two Hamas representatives, spokesperson for the Hamas bloc in the Palestinian Legislative Council Salah Mohammed el-Bardawil and Mohammed el-Rantisi, were invited to visit by the Norwegian Palestine Committee. They claimed it was "important" to invite representatives from the new Palestinian government.[19] El-Rantisi was given a Schengen visa by Norway, allowing him entry into any of the fifteen member countries, while el-Bardawil received a national visa as his previous Schengen application had been denied by France.[20, 21]

The entry permits were given only a few weeks after a major suicide bombing took place outside a fast-food restaurant, the Mayor's Falafel, in Tel Aviv, which claimed nine lives and left more than seventy wounded.[22] The Islamic Jihad movement claimed responsibility. Hamas called the attack a legitimate response to "Israeli aggression." Even though el-Bardawil said that he did not condemn the suicide bombing, Foreign Minister Støre—also from Labour—welcomed the Hamas representatives to Norway.[23, 24]

In the following months, Hamas parliamentarian Yahya al-Abadsa and Refugee Minister Atef Adwan were invited by the same organization. During his week-long visit al-Abadsa met with Amnesty International Norway and the Labour Party head of the Parliamentary Standing Committee on Foreign Affairs, Olav Akselsen.[25] Adwan attended a meeting with the head of the Middle East section of the Foreign Ministry, Kåre Eltervåg.[26] He also met with parliamentarians from both the Labour and Socialist Left parties.

Norway was the first Western government to recognize the short-lived 2007 Hamas-Fatah unity government, which was led, as mentioned, by Ismail Haniyeh.[27] Norwegian Deputy Foreign Minister Raymond Johansen, a Labour politician, became the first senior European official to hold talks with Haniyeh in March 2007. Several media displayed a picture of the two shaking hands.[28] After meeting Haniyeh, Johansen said, "We hope that all the European countries and even other countries will support this unity government."[29, 30] Israel thereupon canceled all planned meetings between Johansen and Israeli officials.

Denying the Truth

In an interview with Norway's commercial channel TV2 in 2011, Norway's then-Labour Party Foreign Minister Støre initially denied that he had spoken directly with Hamas leader Khaled Mashal several times on the phone.[31] The interviewer replied that Mashal had confirmed that he had been in contact with the foreign minister at the time. Støre then asked to stop the tape and restart the interview. He explained that the contacts with Mashal were made upon a request by Palestinian Authority president Mahmoud Abbas.

Then-opposition leaders Erna Solberg of the Conservative Party (Høyre), Siv Jensen of the Progress Party (FrP), and Knut Arild Hareide of the Christian People's Party (KrF) reacted strongly to this information. Jensen accused Støre of lying to the parliament.[32]

In April 2011, Støre published an article titled "Why we must talk" in the *New York Review of Books*.[33] He argued for the use of dialogue as a tool of conflict resolution in the Middle East. Støre cited the international intervention in Afghanistan as an example of why dialogue with hostile and violent groups, such as the Taliban, is a crucial element of dealing with the increasing problem of terrorism. He wrote: "While a military presence is still needed, Afghans and their international partners must find a way forward through diplomatic dialogue with the Taliban."[34]

In 2011, the Norwegian government claimed on its official website that it had assisted in bringing Fatah and Hamas together in their short-lived unity government in 2007. At the request of Abbas, Støre had approached Mashal to convey expectations of the international community that the two movements join in a unity government. The Norwegian government also asserted that it had never recognized Hamas or established political contact with it.

The then U.S. ambassador to Norway, Benson K. Whitney, saw it differently. In a note he sent home in 2009, he said, "Even though they would deny it, there are clear signs that the contact with Hamas is not just a tactical need for dialogue, but that they also support Hamas's position on some level."[35]

Operation Cast Lead

During Israel's Cast Lead campaign against the Hamas-ruled Gaza Strip in 2008-2009, the Norwegian government's position toward Israel was among the most negative in Europe. Pretending to serve the interests of the civilian Palestinian population—which had voted a parliamentary majority to the genocide-promoting Hamas—the Norwegian attitude benefited the terrorist rulers of Gaza.

Støre stated, "The Israeli ground offensive in Gaza constitutes a dramatic escalation of the conflict. Norway strongly condemns any form of warfare that causes severe civilian suffering, and calls on Israel to withdraw its forces immediately." He added, "Gaza is the world's most densely populated area, and the effects of a ground invasion on a long-suffering civilian population that has endured a strict closure regime for many years, and now many days of military attacks, will be extremely grave."[36]

In his condemnation of Israel, Støre made use of a recurrent lie. The Gaza Strip is far from being the world's most densely populated area. Singapore,

Hong Kong, and even the Tel Aviv metropolitan area are more crowded than Gaza.[37] Such lies are repeated often by many pseudo-humanitarian critics of Israel. Yet, once again, Støre criticized Israel without offering any practical alternative for it to protect its population against Hamas's indiscriminate attacks.

Other Northern Countries

In May 2004 the chairman of the Danish Social Democrats in the European Parliament, Torben Lund, published an article in the daily *Politiken*. Proposing a complete economic boycott of Israel, he stressed the responsibility of the Jews for the policies of the Israeli government and asserted that if criticism of murder was anti-Semitism, "then call me an anti-Semite." Chief Rabbi Emeritus Bent Melchior responded with an article in the same newspaper titled "Congratulations Lund, You Are an Antisemite."[38]

Finland's Foreign Minister Erkki Tuomioja, who has compared Israeli policies with those of the Nazis, also engaged in distorting facts. In a 2005 interview he said that, since Abbas's election as Palestinian Authority president at the beginning of that year, "There are approximately as many roadblocks as before and all political prisoners that were promised to be freed have not been freed . . ."

Political scientist Efraim Karsh commented:

> There are no political prisoners in Israeli jails. All Palestinian prisoners whose release is demanded by the PA are either convicted terrorists, or suspected terrorists awaiting trial, or planners and perpetrators of other acts of violence. Of these, 500 were released on 21 February 2005, while another 400 were released four months later, on 2 June 2005.[39]

A British Holocaust Distorter

During Israel's Protective Edge campaign a former British deputy prime minister from the Labour Party, John Prescott, wrote a column condemning Israel. In his words:

> Compare . . . the toll in Gaza. Of the 1,000-plus to die, more than 80 per cent were civilians, mostly women and children. But who is to say some of the other 20 per cent weren't innocent too? Israel brands them terrorists but it is acting as judge, jury and executioner in the concentration camp that is Gaza.

He added, "What happened to the Jewish people at the hands of the Nazis is appalling. But you would think those atrocities would give Israelis a unique sense of perspective and empathy with the victims of a ghetto."[40]

Prescott exaggerated the percentage of civilian casualties and did not mention Hamas's interest in having as many civilians killed as possible, or the similarity of Hamas's aims to those of the Nazis. That is just a small selection of the many distortions in his column.

The Netherlands

The party platform of the Dutch Labour Party (PvdA) for parliamentary elections in 2010 contained a section on unstable regions in the world. One sentence was devoted to the many conflicts in Africa: "The situation in the Horn of Africa and the Great Lakes there, remains very precarious."[41] There was no mention of anything else, including Darfur, where already more than three hundred thousand people had died in previous years.

There were and still are many unstable regions in Asia where Muslims murder, mainly, other Muslims. A partial daily update is available on a website.[42] The war in Afghanistan, concerning which the PvdA caused a cabinet crisis that led to new elections, did not merit a single word in the entire party program. Iran and the genocidal threats emanating from that country were not mentioned either. There was no word about the more than one hundred million Muslims who share—the since killed—Osama Bin Laden's murderous outlook on the world. According to leaders of the Dutch Labour Party, this was apparently not something that warranted concern.

The only other conflict to which the PvdA devoted specific attention was the Palestinian-Israeli conflict. They claimed in their program that their only standard was international law, and made demands of Israel based on it. Their only specific demand of the Palestinians was that the "shooting of rockets from Gaza into Israel has to be stopped."

An intelligent Martian who landed on Earth and read the international section of the PvdA's program would have understood that the problems of the entire world could be solved if Israel withdrew from the disputed territories. A Martian who had arrived in the Middle Ages and heard preachers in Catholic churches would have understood that the pest epidemic would end if there were no more Jews. If it had been the same Martian who had recently returned to Earth, he could have concluded, "People have become more hypocritical in the course of the centuries, but the motif is still the same."

There were some other potential targets for the application of what is called international law in the Middle East. The UN Genocide Convention posits that incitement to commit genocide, even before actual genocide is carried out, is punishable under international law. That convention has been signed by 130 countries, among which are the Netherlands and Iran. Until the beginning of 2010, the PvdA was still part of the Dutch government and should have ensured that the Netherlands brought Iranian President Mahmoud Ahmadinejad before an international court.[43] But when it came to this issue, the Dutch Labourites ignored international law.

Belgium

Jehudi Kinar was Israel's ambassador in Belgium from 2003 to 2007. In 2013, he described the negative attitude toward Israel of several leading Socialist politicians from Wallony:

> After the kidnapping of Gilad Shalit in 2006, Di Rupo came out with a press release claiming Israel used this as a pretext to start a war against Lebanon. [Di Rupo would be Belgian prime minister from 2011 to 2014.] The embassy responded by pointing out that the PS [Wallonian Socialist Party] had never condemned the rocket attacks from Gaza on the citizens of Sderot. Di Rupo referred to this in the summer university, an annual political gathering of the party, where he declared that he would continue his political line toward

> Israel "despite the arrogant letter from the Israeli ambassador." That letters of the Israeli ambassador did not deserve a response was a trademark of the PS.
>
> . . . André Flahaut, then defense minister, was particularly problematic. He is currently chairman of the Chamber. Flahaut was always available for meetings yet came out with very strong anti-Israeli statements. In later years he also took part in anti-Israeli demonstrations. Meetings with him were important because Belgium had soldiers in the UNIFIL force in Lebanon.
>
> Many politicians were surrounded by anti-Israeli advisers. This was not only the case with Flahaut but also, for example, with a Liberal like Louis Michel. He had a number of close advisers with Muslim backgrounds.
>
> A case apart is Philippe Moureaux, a former Belgian deputy prime minister and now mayor of St.-Jans-Molenbeek. For years he asked the Israeli embassy to provide Palestinian children from Bethlehem and Ramallah with exit visas so they could spend their vacations in Belgium. When I asked Moureaux why he did not organize a common visit for those children together with Jewish children from Sderot, he did not answer. A year later when he repeated his request, we asked the same question and got no reply. In June 2010, the not-so-young mayor (seventy-two) married Latifa Benaicha, who is of Muslim background.
>
> The most extreme anti-Israeli in the PS is Senator Pierre Galand. He has initiated many anti-Israeli motions in the Senate. He also heads various anti-Israeli organizations such as the Belgian-Palestinian Association and the Lay Action Center. Galand was also secretary-general of OXFAM Belgium during the period 1967-1996. Veronique De Keyser, a European PS parliamentarian, once declared that she wanted to strangle the Israeli ambassador. Many people thought she meant me. As she is a member of the European Parliament, I can clarify that she referred to my colleague who was the Israeli ambassador to the EU.[44]

After Protective Edge, the Socialist former secretary-general of NATO Willy Claes attacked Israel. He said, "Israel has to realize that the enormous historical credit that Judaism has built up after the Second World War has now been exhausted." He also claimed that Russian immigration to Israel is the cause of the political center moving to the right.

It apparently did not dawn on Claes that the extreme ideological violence and criminality widespread in Palestinian society has convinced many Israelis that peace with the Palestinians is at present impossible. Claes also mentioned another of his fantasies: "I am afraid that more Israelis think the Palestinians should be expelled from what remains as autonomous Palestinian territories." He added, "I do not say that all Israelis want that, but I fear that it is the wish of a new majority in the country."[45]

Pleasing Muslims

Some British Labour politicians favor extreme anti-Semites so as to please Muslims. While he was mayor of London, Labour politician Ken Livingstone gave a cordial welcome and appeared jointly with the Egyptian cleric Yusuf al-Qaradawi,[46] who had praised Palestinian suicide bombings. In 2003, senior Labour MP Tam Dalyell claimed that a Jewish cabal of Zionists in the United States and Britain was driving their governments into war against Syria.[47]

An adviser of the French Socialist Party, Pascal Boniface, told the party before the 2002 elections to become more pro-Arab because there were many more Muslims than Jews in France.[48] In a 2004 lecture in Alexandria, former French Prime Minister Michel Rocard, also a Socialist, called the Balfour Declaration that led to Israel's creation "a historic mistake."[49]

Rocard also once banalized the Holocaust knowing well what he was doing. He said that he and his followers in the French Socialist Party said among themselves that they had a status in the party "like those wearing the yellow star, this comparison may be repugnant but it describes the atmosphere well."[50]

Boniface's calls encountered substantial resistance. In 2014, there was a similar occurrence in the United Kingdom. As noted, in October of that year the new Swedish Social Democrat Prime Minister Stefan Löfven announced that his government would recognize a Palestinian state, and it soon did so. Shortly after the initial Swedish announcement the British Labour Party initiated a vote in the House of Commons on recognition of a Palestinian state.

The Jerusalem Post wrote that Shadow Foreign Sectary Douglas Alexander, also the head of the Labour Party's election strategy team, "has done the math, noting that he has to make sure his party is attractive to the 3 million Muslims in the UK, a large number of whom reside in marginal, inner city constituencies. They far outweigh Britain's roughly 280,000 Jews, only a small number of whom reside in similarly marginal constituencies."[51]

During Protective Edge, French Socialist Interior Minister Bernard Cazeneuve said that he would have participated in the pro-Gaza demonstrations had he not been a government member.[52] In other words, he would have participated in supporting the genocidal Hamas movement, in demonstrations where most probably there were anti-Semitic acts.

Samuels's Intentional Mistake

At an OSCE meeting in Berlin in 2004, Samuels "exposed" a Socialist-terrorist collaboration. He referred to a fictitious congress on creative solutions for immigration into Europe in which Jean-Marie Le Pen and the Russian anti-Semitic leader Vladimir Zhirinovsky were to participate; it was to be financed by the Konrad Adenauer Foundation, associated with the German Christian Democrats. This caused an uproar. Samuels apologized for his "mistake" and said he had intended to refer to a conference held in Beirut, funded by the German Socialist Friedrich Ebert Foundation, with speakers from the terrorist Hizbullah and Hamas.

The Wiesenthal Center noted on its website that participants at this conference, funded by the "flagship of Germany's ruling Social Democratic party," included

> Shaykh Naeem Qasim from Hizbullah; Azzam Tamimi, from the Institute of Islamic Thought in London, who presents himself in the Arab press as a counselor to Hamas; Tariq Ramadan, from the University of Fribourg, a Muslim Brotherhood ideologue, notorious for his public incitement to anti-Semitism in France; Ibrahim al-Masri, vice president of Lebanon's al-Jama'a al-Islamiyya, a group linked by terrorism experts to al-Qaeda; and Munir Shafiq, a leading Hamas ideologist and former activist in Islamic Jihad.[53]

We have earlier noted how various leading Socialists, including Palme and Andreas Papandreou, compared Israeli policies with those of the Nazis.

CHAPTER FIFTEEN

Jewish and Israeli Inciters

A FREQUENT MISUNDERSTANDING IS THAT Jews cannot be anti-Semites. Yet it can easily be explained why this is erroneous. Any text can be analyzed as to whether it is anti-Semitic or not according to the FRA definition of anti-Semitism. If it is, it becomes irrelevant what the religion or nationality of the writer is. If that author is Jewish, he is an anti-Semitic Jew. The same goes for the anti-Semitic element of anti-Israelism, as that is included in this definition. Anti-Semitic Jews often offer some indication of their Jewish background, such as they had a bar mitzvah, visited Israel, and the like.[1]

In an essay in 2006, American academic Alvin Rosenfeld exposed various Jewish inciters against Israel in the English-speaking world such as Jacqueline Rose, Michael Neumann, and Daniel Boyarin. About the historian Tony Judt, he noted that he

> has published a series of increasingly bitter articles over the past three years in *The Nation*, the *New York Review of Books*, and *Ha'aretz*, in which he has called Israel everything from arrogant, aggressive, anachronistic, and infantile to dysfunctional, immoral, and a primary cause of present-day anti-Semitism. "Israel today," Judt avers, "is bad for the Jews," and it would do them and everyone else a service by going out of business. "The time has come to think the unthinkable," he writes, and that is to replace the Jewish state with "a single,

integrated bi-national state of Jews and Arabs."[2]

Far from being new, this is an old idea and, by now, a properly discredited and discarded one; everyone knows that such an entity, were it ever to come into being, would before long be an Arab-dominated state in which a residual Jewish presence would, at best, be a tolerated minority. In promoting such an obsolescent scheme, which would spell an end to a territorially-based Jewish national existence, Judt, as Benjamin Balint persuasively argues, unwittingly aligns himself with older forms of Christian opposition to Jewish particularism: "Israel is merely the new ground upon which the old battle over Jewish distinctiveness is being waged."[3] Nevertheless, Judt has his followers, and talk of dissolving the Jewish state and replacing it with a binational state is once again in the air in certain intellectual circles.[4]

Another Jewish inciter against Israel is Judith Butler, an American academic. Historian Landes and journalist Benjamin Weinthal write:

> Participating in an "Anti-War Teach-In" at Berkeley in 2006, Ms. Butler answered a question about Hamas's and Hizbullah's place "in the global left." These are two of the most belligerent movements within the warmongering, anti-Semitic, homophobic and misogynistic world of Islamist jihad. Yet while criticizing violence and "certain dimensions of both movements," Ms. Butler told the students that "understanding Hamas [and] Hizbullah as social movements that are progressive, that are on the left, that are part of a global left, is extremely important."
>
> For Ms. Butler, anything that opposes Western power can be defended. It does not seem to concern her that in so doing, she betrays every constituency she claims to celebrate—lesbians, gays, women, Jews and other diasporic minorities. Their problems, it seems, are always the fault of oppressive "colonial" powers.[5]

In 2007, Dutch law professor and poet Afshin Ellian attacked the national anti-Israeli Jewish organization Een Ander Joods Geluid (Another Jewish Sound). He said:

> For me, this is a movement that falsifies history with the aim to minimalize Nazism. If one gives to the behavior of Israel in Jenin the same weight as what

> the Nazis had done in Warsaw, then one trivializes historical reality. Jenin continues to exist. It's a busy town. The ghetto of Warsaw has been totally destroyed. These anti-Jewish propagandists want to create the impression that everything the Nazis wrought is now being done by Israel. They are the same falsifiers of the heritage of the Holocaust as regular Holocaust deniers.[6]

Leon de Winter, a bestselling Jewish Dutch novelist, offered another perspective on the same group:

> They constantly proclaim: "We Jews have experienced the Shoah and should apply the highest morals." They present the Shoah as an educational institute for Jews to teach Jews morals. In other words, the Nazis held courses in the concentration camps to imbue Jews with humanity. These are Jews who pervert the memory of the Shoah. It is a noisy group that gets much media attention because they proclaim a message that many non-Jews like to hear.[7]

One small group of Jewish anti-Israeli inciters had a success in the Netherlands when in autumn 2013 then-Israeli President Shimon Peres visited as a guest of King Willem Alexander. The king gave a dinner in honor of Peres, and several Jews were invited. Among them was the head of the small organization Another Jewish Sound. However, the head of the Jewish umbrella group CJO, and those of the two largest Jewish communities, the Ashkenazi Orthodox NIK and the liberal LJG, were not invited.

Jewish self-hate and anti-Semitism are ancient phenomena. Converted Jews were among the most fanatic inciters against Judaism in the Middle Ages. One example among many was Paulus de Santa Maria, who in 1405 became bishop of Cartagena in Spain.[8]

Part-Time Anti-Semites

Postwar Austrian Jewish Chancellor Bruno Kreisky was a typical example of a part-time anti-Semite. Wistrich describes him as "the one Jew who could grant gentile Austrians full exculpation from a latent sense of guilt over their prominent role in the Holocaust. Kreisky was destined to become the '*Entlastungsjude*.' This might be translated as, 'The Jew who frees from guilt'—in other words, freeing Austrians of the burdens of complicity in the German mass murder."[9]

Kreisky came out in favor of former Nazis who were ministers in his cabinet.[10] He called Simon Wiesenthal a "Jewish fascist."[11] Wistrich quotes an interview in which the Socialist Kreisky made a racist remark: "The most-hated diplomats are the Israelis . . . They are as bad as the Africans who are also intolerable people."[12]

Jewish self-hate has been studied by various scholars. American historian Sander L. Gilman wrote:

> Self-hatred results from outsiders' acceptance of the mirage of themselves generated by their reference group—that group in society which they see as defining them—as a reality . . . "Jewish self-hatred" (a term interchangeable with "Jewish anti-Judaism" or "Jewish anti-Semitism") is valid as a label for a specific mode of self-abnegation that has existed among Jews throughout their history.[13]

In his book *The Oslo Syndrome: Delusions of a People under Siege*,[14] psychologist Kenneth Levin explains the attitude of Israeli self-haters:

> This phenomenon reveals great similarity at the level of human psychology to the response of children subjected to chronic abuse. Such children tend to blame themselves for their suffering. In their helpless condition, they have two alternatives: they can either acknowledge they are being unfairly victimized and reconcile themselves to being powerless, or they can blame themselves for their predicament. The attraction of the latter—"I suffer because I am bad"—is that it serves the desire of being in control, fantasies that becoming "good" will elicit a more benign response from their tormentors. Both children and adults invariably seek to avoid hopelessness.[15]

In *Post-Zionism, Post-Holocaust: Three Essays on Denial, Forgetting, and the Delegitimization of Israel*, philosopher Elhanan Yakira elaborates on the role of Jewish and Israeli self-haters:

> It seems as if Israel's main ideological adversaries outside the Arab and Muslim world are Israelis and Jews abroad. These people are much appreciated by Israel's non-Jewish enemies. The self-appointed Israeli true left takes positions that are commonly referred to as post-Zionist. In fact, they are anti-Zionist. This ideology refuses to grant the Jewish people the right of self-determination and thus Israel's right to exist as the Jewish state . . . Leading intellectuals, both Jewish and non-Jewish, play a major role in this new mutation of anti-Semitism.[16]

Contemporary anti-Semites find a Kreisky-type Jew quite useful in absolving themselves of criticism, as they can point to Jews who share their opinions. Yakira addresses a related issue. Post-Zionist Jews—in fact, *anti*-Zionist Jews —demonize Israel. In this way they become members of "an intellectual community of similar-minded distorters." Yakira adds, "The best way to advance internationally in academic circles is to be part of a system. One is then frequently invited abroad and gets published, even if one's work has no significant substance."[17] The ways of anti-Israeli perpetrators are indeed multiple and only some examples can be given.

The Finkelstein Case

A different issue is that when Jews defend their interests, in almost every field there are some Jews who help their enemies by assigning major blame to the Jewish side. One example is Norman Finkelstein, who published a book about "the Holocaust industry."[18]

Israeli historian Ronald W. Zweig wrote in a review of Finkelstein's book:

> Finkelstein argues that the contemporary use of the Holocaust has created an entire "industry" which, in the best manner of exploitative capitalism, is not only politically useful but also financially rewarding. Himself Jewish and the son of Holocaust survivors, Finkelstein could allow himself to articulate what many people believe but do not dare say in public. This is especially true in Britain, where socialist circles are anti-Zionist and pro-Palestinian *de rigeur* but struggle to avoid being tarred with the brush of anti-Semitism.

The core of Finkelstein's argument is that a cabal of Jewish leaders conspired to extort money from European governments, under the pretext of claiming material compensation for the losses of the Holocaust and for the benefit of the survivors. Once their claims were successful, these organizations then kept the money to themselves and paid the survivors only a pittance. Summarized in this form, the accusation is so unbelievably and totally without foundation that I looked once again at the third chapter of *The Holocaust Industry* to ensure that I had not parodied Finkelstein's argument. But the summary fairly represents what he wrote.[19]

Exploiting "Survivors"

During the Protective Edge campaign a group of 359 people claiming to be Holocaust survivors gained much publicity in the West. They condemned Israel's actions in a paid ad in *The New York Times* and *The Guardian* and asked for a full boycott of Israel, as a response to Holocaust survivor Elie Wiesel in support of Israel. In *The New York Times* they stated that they belonged to the International Jewish Solidarity Network (IJSN) and in *The Guardian* they called themselves the International Jewish Anti-Zionist Network (IJAN).[20]

Rosenfeld criticized the ad:

> What makes the IJSN statement noteworthy . . . is not the litany of emotionally-charged accusations against Israel but the identities of those making these accusations. They present themselves as "Survivors," "Children of survivors," "Grandchildren of survivors," "Great-grandchildren of survivors," and "Other relatives of survivors" . . . their endorsement of the most reckless charges against Israel—e.g., Israelis are like Nazis and are carrying out a genocide against Palestinians—by members of a people who themselves were victims of the twentieth century's most determined attempt at genocide is unprecedented and can be hugely harmful unless it is seen for what it is: an unseemly exercise in the spread of propagandistic lies.

Additionally, in Rosenfeld's words, "Sanctioning such propaganda by stamping it with the moral authority that supposedly belongs to Holocaust survivors does not turn these lies into truth. What it does instead is expose as fraudulent the claims of certain Holocaust survivors and their kin to possessing an enlarged moral and political consciousness."[21]

An Alibi Jew

Much insight into how Jewish self-haters are used by Israel's enemies can be gleaned from an interview that Belgian ex-Trotskyist Nathan Weinstock gave to *Haaretz* writer Adi Schwartz in 2014. He said that he was an anti-Zionist and pro-Palestinian. In 1967, shortly before the Six Day War, he went to speak before the Palestinian Students Association in Paris. Weinstock remarks that he was convinced that the Palestinians would embrace his pacifist message.

In retrospect, he admits that he was a "useful idiot" and adds, "They had better things to do: they listened to Cairo radio in ecstasy, savoring every word and absorbing the messages, bragging about Arab armies soon throwing the Jews into the sea."

In 1969, Weinstock published a book in French, *Zionism—False Messiah.* He then received many invitations because people wanted to hear him condemn Israel. He found that there was "total support of the public actions of the worst of the Palestinian terrorists and boundless hatred of Israelis, no matter who they were."

It took a long time until Weinstock understood that the attacks on Israel had an anti-Semitic nature: "Initially they denounced the 'Zionists,' then the 'Zionist takeover of the media' and finally the 'Zionist control of the banks.' . . . When I was quoted the least criticism I had of the Palestinians was always omitted . . . I was for them an anti-Jewish 'alibi Jew.'"[22]

One particularly active alibi Jew is Max Blumenthal. His book *Goliath: Life and Loathing in Greater Israel* includes chapters titled, "The Concentration Camp," "The Night of Broken Glass," "This Belongs to the White Man," and "How to Kill Goyim and Influence People."[23] In autumn 2014 the Left Party in Germany canceled a meeting where Blumenthal and another speaker were to feature, under the auspices of party parliamentarians. It caused substantial discontent within the party.[24]

Jewish Voice for Peace

According to their mission statement, the American group Jewish Voice for Peace (JVP)

> opposes anti-Jewish, anti-Muslim, and anti-Arab bigotry and oppression. JVP seeks an end to the Israeli occupation of the West Bank, Gaza Strip, and East Jerusalem; security and self-determination for Israelis and Palestinians; a just solution for Palestinian refugees based on principles established in international law; an end to violence against civilians; and peace and justice for all peoples of the Middle East . . . We are among the many American Jews who say to the U.S. and Israeli governments: "Not in our names!"

Yet, while claiming to oppose anti-Jewish bigotry, the organization overlooks the genocidal statements of Hamas. For instance, after Netanyahu's speech to the UN General Assembly in September 2014, they published a blog post asserting, "In equating Hamas, ISIS, Iran and the Nazis, Netanyahu attempted to paint a black and white picture of global evil in order to clear Israel of responsibility for human rights violations and war crimes." JVP claimed in this post that Operation Protective Edge was not just, because "Hamas has responded with vastly less ineffective [sic] weaponry."[25]

JVP also went to the 2014 Presbyterian General Assembly in Detroit where they urged divestment from three companies that "profit from operations in occupied Palestinian territory, Caterpillar, Motorola Solutions and Hewlett Packard."[26]

Haaretz

Jonathan S. Tobin, the senior online editor of *Commentary*, wrote about the newspaper *Haaretz* on *Commentary*'s website. According to Tobin:

> The fact that the Israeli newspaper *Haaretz* is a major source of incitement and often misinformation about the Jewish state and the Middle East is not news.

> Some of its columnists are fervent anti-Zionists . . . and provide a steady source of material for Israel-bashers. Israel is a free country and if a formerly Zionist newspaper wants to play this role that is its right. But sometimes, even *Haaretz* goes too far and not only feeds the anti-Israel propaganda machine but steps over the line into material that aids and abets anti-Semitism.

Tobin wrote this in October 2014 when *Haaretz* published a cartoon by Amos Biderman that showed an Israeli plane piloted by Netanyahu on the verge of crashing into the World Trade Center. It thus compared Netanyahu's policies to the murderous behavior of the September 11 terrorists and Bin Laden. There was much criticism but Biderman and *Haaretz* refused to apologize.[27]

Jewish anti-Semites fulfill a special role in the war of a million cuts because non-Jewish anti-Israelis use them as a fig leaf for their delegitimization campaigns against Israel. The same is true of articles in Israeli papers that have a distinct anti-Semitic character of the anti-Israeli type.

CHAPTER SIXTEEN

Other Originators of Hatred and Incitement

In addition to the groupings of hate-mongers mentioned in previous chapters, there are several other disparate originator categories of incitement against Israel and the Jews. All of these need far more attention than can be given here.

The explosive rise in internet usage in this century has brought with it new ways of transmitting a wide range of often well-known anti-Semitic messages. In addition to promoters of incitement belonging to the main categories of hate-mongering, there are hate promoters who are not members of any group.

One out of an almost unlimited number of examples occurred in May 2014 after the Maccabi Tel Aviv basketball team defeated Real Madrid in the Euroleague final. Nearly eighteen thousand offensive messages were posted on Twitter by Spanish supporters.[1] Several of these called for a second Holocaust.

The Euroleague condemned the anti-Semitic outburst on the internet. Jewish organizations in the Catalonia region announced that they would lodge a complaint.[2] The damage, however, was done.

The Multiplication of Internet Anti-Semitism

Rabbi Abraham Cooper, associate dean of the Simon Wiesenthal Center, has been a pioneer in analyzing the development of hate-mongering on the internet. He said:

> Terrorist, racist, bigoted and anti-Semitic sites have emerged in large numbers and are sometimes connected. Traditional hate groups, such as neo-Nazis, the Ku Klux Klan and skinheads proliferate on the web. Very different activist groups have built coalitions in the name of anti-globalization, anti-Americanism and attacks on Israel. The Internet is also a tool used to raise money, recruit new terrorists and coordinate terrorist communications for such groups.
>
> One can put up any website on the Internet, resurrecting and dressing up any idea, while focusing one's message on specific audiences. In this medium one can even say that the Jews drink the blood of their victims and not be challenged or rebuked by anyone. Major anti-Semitic themes are September 11 mythology, Holocaust denial and *The Protocols of the Elders of Zion*. The Internet provides a new face for well-known anti-Semitic themes and forms part of a much bigger problem. If we want to confront this type of anti-Semitism, we have to understand the nature and scope of its challenge.
>
> Lies are difficult to fight on the Internet because it's not a fair game. One could spend 10 million dollars on a website proving that *The Protocols of the Elders of Zion* is a fraud, without necessarily reaching any of the people who are swayed by the book's fraudulent allegations.

Cooper observed about the Internet:

> It is a propaganda tool par excellence to get one's message out to supporters and potential recruits, as well as a powerful way to denigrate one's enemies. Thus, the Internet is a natural venue not only for amateurs, but also for organized extremist groups and terrorists. The latter category, in particular Al-Qaeda, utilizes the Internet not only for propaganda, but also for the transmission of messages.
>
> A number of factors make the Internet attractive to hate promoters. It is

> cheap, difficult to monitor and virtually impossible to keep a message off the Internet. Furthermore, it knows no borders; so consequently, a minor local player in a hate movement can now become a global operator. From a propaganda point of view, there is no quality control on the Internet, no librarian, no censorship and no analysis. In some attractive web sites, racist groups aim at women's hearts and minds—and if possible, their money.[3]

In 2013 Cooper added:

> In 1995 there was one hate site, Stormfront. It is still active and has hundreds of thousands of postings. The Simon Wiesenthal Center's *Digital Terrorism and Hate Project*, in its fourteenth year, currently monitors over 15,000 hate and terror-related sites. The exponential growth of viral social networking however, makes the numbers game increasingly irrelevant, as a single posting, image, song or YouTube video can reach untold thousands and beyond.[4]

Young Israelis Confront Hatred

In 2014, the Anti-Defamation League released a survey showing that more than half of Jewish Israeli teens have reported being attacked online when they identified themselves as Israelis. Five hundred Jewish Israeli teens aged fifteen to eighteen participated in the poll. Fifty-one percent said they had encountered hatred on the internet for being Israeli. An identical poll in 2013 found the figure to be 31 percent.

The anti-Semitism figures were even worse. The poll found that 83 percent of teens had been exposed to anti-Semitism on the web, compared to 69 percent in 2013. Sixty-one percent reported an increase in online anti-Semitism during the Protective Edge campaign in the summer of 2014.

"The more teenagers in Israel are using the internet to connect with friends and share social updates, the more they are coming into contact with haters and bigots who want to expose them to an anti-Israel or anti-Semitic message," said ADL National Director Abraham Foxman. "But Israeli teens do not feel powerless to act. In fact, a significant majority of those polled indicated that they had initiated action to respond to anti-Semitic content by reporting it to administrators or requesting its removal."[5]

The Problems for Jews and Israel

Andre Oboler, an Australian analyst of cyberhate, says, "The rise of social media has caused multiple problems for Jews and Israel. Many of them manifest themselves in ways that concern society at large. Jews and Israel however, often seem to be the first ones negatively impacted."

He remarks:

> The first issue we face is ideological. The internet grew out of a lawless environment. This tradition of "internet exceptionalism" continues, even if it is increasingly challenged. A clash of cultures exists between the Americans who operate many of the global service providers, and the rest of the world. The Americans want complete freedom in their operations.
>
> Outside America however, the common position is that hate speech is highly undesirable. The public there has a legitimate expectation that the state will take steps to prevent and perhaps even criminalize it. This is in light of how hate speech played a significant role in enabling the Holocaust.

Oboler goes on to note:

> Another major issue concerns flaws in the systems of service providers such as Facebook, YouTube and Twitter. They can relate to the software, processes and sometimes also the people involved . . . Yet another major concern is the companies' lack of understanding about anti-Semitism's nature. This oldest form of hatred which has existed for millennia, has been studied well. In most forms, it is easily and consistently identified by scholars and experts. The providers however, want to create their own definitions and understanding of anti-Semitism. They clearly lack the expertise, skill or even a desire to do so properly.[6]

In autumn 2014 John Mann, chairman of a British parliamentary group on anti-Semitism, criticized Twitter in a speech to the House of Commons for failing to deal adequately with people posting anti-Semitic abuse on social media. He added, "Where individuals set up multiple accounts, Twitter finds it impossible to deal with that. That shows a lack of will."[7]

Political Blogs

Yet another problematic area is political blogs. Adam Levick, who has analyzed three major American blogs, concludes:

> Progressive blogs and news sites in the United States are a new field where Jew-hatred, in both its classic and anti-Israeli forms, manifests itself. This incitement is hardly monitored, as many of the most popular blogs are only a few years old and it seems counterintuitive that such anti-Semitic expressions would be found in this political milieu.
>
> Monitoring the media for anti-Semitic and anti-Israel bigotry has so far almost exclusively consisted of reading the major American newspapers, magazines, and journals and attending to the three major news networks, as well as radio broadcasts. However, the huge amount of content in the political blogosphere makes such monitoring—which is increasingly necessary—much more difficult to achieve with any degree of thoroughness.[8]

Levick has also researched hate cartoons against Jews in progressive blogs. He comments that this is a yet uncharted field:

> Anti-Semitic cartoons found—and seemingly tolerated—on progressive blogs such as Daily Kos, MyDD, Mondoweiss, and Indymedia are mainly expressions of anti-Israelism, a more recent category of anti-Semitism than the religious and ethnic-nationalist versions . . .
>
> The cartoonist most frequently appearing on the progressive blogs analyzed here is Carlos Latuff. He is an extreme left-wing political activist who won second place in the notorious Iranian Holocaust Cartoon Competition. Latuff

is one of the more prolific anti-Semitic cartoonists on the web, with a staggering amount of work dedicated to advancing explicitly anti-Semitic political imagery.[9]

Not Prosecuting Israel-Haters

Ronald Eissens, director-general of the Dutch NGO Magenta Foundation, which focuses on international human rights and combating racism, says:

> We have to mark the difference between legally punishable postings and those which are discriminatory yet not illegal. The percentage of punishable postings on anti-Semitism is high. This is because most anti-Semitic postings are extreme and of a "classic" nature. Regarding these there is a large Dutch jurisprudence.

He continues:

> Anti-Semitism on the internet in the Dutch language is strongly developed in three major areas—North African websites, extreme Rightwing sites and talkbacks on mainstream sites. The Dutch prosecution department of the Ministry of Justice is willing to prosecute expressions of anti-Semitism. If one writes, "All Israelis in the Netherlands have to be killed," the prosecution may also act because it is a call for violence in the Netherlands. But if one writes, "All Israelis have to be killed," or "Ahmadinejad should launch a nuclear bomb on Tel Aviv so that all Israelis will be fried," the prosecution office will do nothing.
>
> The reason is that Israelis are not Dutchmen and therefore anything can be written about them. This may be in breach of the International Convention on the Elimination of All Forms of Racial Discrimination of which the Netherlands are a signatory. However, the Dutch legal position is ambiguous on this issue and this enables prosecutors to ignore it.[10]

State Anti-Semitism

Both in the 1930s and in the more remote past, European countries frequently established discriminatory laws against Jews. When this legislation was later abolished, de facto discrimination often remained. Over a long period of time, Jews have been demonized. This has laid the ideological basis for murder on a huge scale, culminating in the Holocaust. A similar defamatory approach is now being applied to Israel, aiming in its more extreme forms at its total elimination as a Jewish state.

Since the demise of communism in the former Soviet Union and its satellites, state-promoted or state-sponsored anti-Semitism has largely disappeared there. It now mainly occurs in Arab and Muslim countries to varying degrees. However, in a number of other countries, anti-Israeli positions of governments foster a societal climate conducive to anti-Semitism.

The government of the late President Hugo Chavez of Venezuela is one such example. Sammy Eppel, a member of the governing body of Venezuelan Jews, says that Chavez had close relations with the anti-Semite and Holocaust denier Norberto Ceresole, an Argentinean sociologist. Eppel comments:

> After Chavez became president, Ceresole published a "bible" for all revolutionaries. It was titled, "'Caudillo, Ejercito, Pueblo' La Venezuela del comandante Chavez," which translates as "'Boss, Army and People,' the Venezuela of Commander Chavez."
>
> The first chapter began with "The Jewish Problem." Due to its anti-Semitic nature, it only had one printing. Yet the text remained available on government-sponsored websites until 2009. It was downloaded by hundreds of thousands of Chavez's followers. Not surprisingly, relations between the Jewish community and the Chavez government remained difficult throughout.[11]

Letting Anti-Semites Immigrate

In postmodern societies there are several modes of behavior that can be defined as state anti-Semitism. A major one is letting in immigrants who are disproportionately anti-Semitic and whose anti-Semitism is more extremely violent compared to that of the native population.

Governments must assure the wellbeing of all citizens. They should thus take measures to prevent discrimination against minority groups. In this new century, many European governments have often failed to do so concerning individual Jews and the Jewish community, as well as concerning others.

As mentioned previously, many European authorities must be held accountable for what they have done, or not done, for the Jewish communities. They allowed immigrants into their countries in a nonselective way without examining the cultural differences, or considering how these immigrants would be integrated into their societies. They should have known that active promotion of anti-Semitism was part and parcel of the Muslim cultures many of these people came from. Allowing them in unselectively can thus be considered an indirect type of state anti-Semitism.

Several government-owned media in Europe discriminate against Israel and the Jews. Sometimes they even incite explicit hatred. Allowing them to do so is an indirect manifestation of government anti-Semitism. These attacks frequently come from left-wing journalists.

There are many discriminatory gradations on the left side of the political spectrum. The BBC is a public service broadcaster financed by government-controlled license fees, which households pay. Asserson has revealed systematic anti-Israeli bias in its reporting on the Middle East. His conclusion that the distorted reporting creates an atmosphere in which anti-Semitism can thrive is convincing.[12]

Norway, Denmark, and Ritual Slaughter

It is rare that a Western state discriminates against Jews within its laws. In Norway, however, there is an example of state anti-Semitism in this context. Jewish ritual slaughter has been forbidden there since several years before this occurred in Nazi Germany. On the other hand, except for Norway, Japan, and Iceland, no countries allow whaling. In 2013 the Norwegian minister of fisheries and coastal affairs set the country's whale quota at 1,286, the same as it was in

2012. Only half of the quota is usually realized.[13] These mammals are harpooned and often die in an exceptionally cruel and barbaric way.[14] This shows the discriminatory character of the prohibition of ritual slaughter.

Seal hunting is currently practiced in six countries: Canada, where most of the world's seal hunting takes place, Namibia, Greenland, Iceland, Norway, and Russia. Canada's largest market for seal products is Norway. In 2013, the aforementioned minister increased the price of seals as an incentive to combat the waning interest in seal hunting.[15] The quota for harbor seals in 2012 was 435, but the final result was 355; while the quota for grey seals was 460 and only 64 were harvested in the end.[16] These seals are also killed in a barbaric way, being bludgeoned to death.

In 2014, Denmark forbade ritual slaughter. At the same time, the country is well known internationally for allowing sex with animals. Denmark even has animal brothels, which are permitted under the law and freely promote their activities.

The Extreme Right

Another perpetrator category is the extreme right, which is enjoying a revival in Europe. In several East European countries, this trend is partly stimulated by reactions to the communist past combined with economic problems.

In Western Europe, right-wing radicalization involves, on the one hand, a reemergence of Nazi and related movements. On the other hand, it is fostered partly by problems related to mass immigration such as poor government policies for integration of these immigrants and anti-Western racism among some Muslim immigrant groups.

The two EU countries where neofascist parties have entered the parliament in a significant fashion are Hungary and Greece. The neofascist and anti-Semitic Jobbik Party received nearly 17 percent of votes in Hungary's 2010 parliamentary elections and became the country's third largest party. Their anti-Semitism is a regular component of Hungarian public debate.

In Greece the Golden Dawn Party, which has neo-Nazi leanings, has become more powerful in recent years. It entered parliament after both 2012 elections. By autumn 2012 the party received 14 percent of the votes in opinion polls. Once such parties enter a country's parliament they also gradually attain positions in international or representative organizations.

The Extreme Left

The Soviet Union played a key role in the promotion of anti-Israelism. Dutch scholar of Russian studies André Gerrits says:

> Anti-Zionism became a significant element of the Soviet Union's foreign policy toward the end of the 1940s. The Soviet leadership had supported Israel's creation at the United Nations General Assembly in November 1947. They believed that Israel could become an ally in the Middle East. It rapidly turned out that this would not be the case.
>
> The initial anti-Zionism of the Soviet Union was also based on other considerations. The undesirable popularity of Israel among many Jews there became obvious in their enthusiastic welcome for the first Israeli ambassador to Russia, Golda Meir in 1948. Furthermore, from an ideological viewpoint communism was against every form of nationalism including Jewish versions, Zionist or not.
>
> Communists have always seen Zionism as a petty-bourgeois deviation, as well as an expression of Jewish nationalism. The emphasis anti-Zionism received in the Soviet Union and other communist countries during various periods depended mainly on international developments.
>
> . . . Anti-Zionism was also a factor in the Soviet Union's relations with the United States and its efforts to strengthen relations with Arab countries and Iran. Only late in the 1980s, when Gorbachev changed the overall direction of foreign policy, did anti-Zionism largely stop being a Soviet political propaganda tool . . . One might say that anti-Zionism is a traditional ideological motif that has been mainly used and manipulated as an international political instrument.[17]

Norway as a Paradigm

Currently politicians and others from the extreme left, and often politicians of Socialist parties, continue to play a major role in the demonization of Israel. In Norway, Kristin Halvorsen, then leader and a government minister of the Socialist Left Party (SV), even participated in an anti-Israeli demonstration.[18]

In 2006, Halvorsen—then SV leader and finance minister—endorsed a consumer boycott of Israel. The SV program for the period of 2005-2009 did not directly advocate a consumer boycott. It stated that SV would work for a weapons boycott and embargo "as long as the state [Israel] continues to breach international law in dealings with the Palestinians."[19] Halvorsen was probably the first Western government minister to promote a boycott.[20] She later apologized to her government.[21]

Halvorsen published her memoirs in 2012. She wrote that her initiative to boycott Israel while holding a ministerial position was her "greatest political blunder."[22] Halvorsen noted that both Prime Minister Stoltenberg and Støre had made it clear that this was contrary to government policy. That forced her to publicly retract her statement.

Before she became Norway's deputy environment minister, Ingrid Fiskaa of SV said in 2009:

> When, for example, the Palestinians are exposed to a slow genocide and the UN does not get much done, this discussion does not appear. Why not? Because it is not in the U.S. interest. In some dark moments, I might wish that the UN would send some precision-guided rockets at selected Israeli targets, but of course that wouldn't be relevant and probably wouldn't solve any problems either.[23]

Fiskaa's statement about Israel committing genocide against the Palestinians was an explicit illustration of what 38 percent of adult Norwegians think about Israel, as an aforementioned study has found.

Trotskyites in France

Simon Epstein, a Hebrew University expert on anti-Semitism, states that Trotskyism in France has become a larger anti-Zionist force than communism. He says furthermore that "the suffering of the Jews has become an instrument in an extreme leftist strategy of attracting, recruiting and mobilizing Arab and Muslim populations in France." Epstein also observes:

> For many decades after the Second World War, the Communists were the main promoters of anti-Zionism in France. Their decline in the last 20 years ran parallel with the amazing electoral growth of another major anti-Zionist force, the Trotskyites. Today, even though divided, they are the most important component of the French extreme left.
>
> French Trotskyites promote an anti-Zionism which originated in the 1920's. It has never been tempered by a pro-Israel phase similar to the one which the Communists underwent in 1947 and 1948 and they have never accepted Israel's existence. For the same reasons as the Communists, they are trying to seduce —by any means—the Arab and Muslim sectors of French society. Their goal is clear. They want those sectors to replace the traditional French working class which is rapidly vanishing for sociological and other reasons, as their main electoral and political basis. This strategy engenders a vicious anti-Zionism which often surpasses that of the Communists.

He adds:

> Leftist militants dug up the Shoah during the first and even more so, the second *Intifada*. This time they did so in order to give articulation to their radical anti-Zionism, claiming that Israelis were doing to the Palestinians what the Nazis did to the Jews. In this way, the German crimes fulfilled a new historical function. They enabled the Trotskyites to turn the Shoah against the Jews, and demonize the Israelis by promoting a totally distorted picture of the Middle Eastern conflict.[24]

Trotskyites in the United Kingdom

Wistrich says:

> It is a curious fact that Trotskyites have been influential in left-wing circles in the UK—at least in comparison to other European countries. Only in France does one find anything equivalent. There seems to be no obvious reason connected to British society or culture. Perhaps it is related to the weakness of the Communist Party, which faded quickly in the 1950s in Britain. Unlike in France and Italy, communism was never very powerful on the British Left. Trotskyism could therefore fill the vacuum. It is an alternative form of communism that bears many parallels with the Stalinism that the Trotskyites love to hate and vilify. Of course, the Trotskyites were hunted down in the Soviet Union and eliminated by Stalinist communists. This persecution had antisemitic undertones.
>
> Trotskyites have been characterized by an intense polemical energy and have often been in the forefront of the "anti-imperialist struggle." With the collapse of official communism after 1990 in most parts of the world, they saw a chance for themselves to become what they call a "revolutionary vanguard."
>
> In their concept of the world, Zionism has for decades been inextricably linked with global capitalism and American imperialism. These were also the hackneyed phrases of Soviet propaganda. The communist empire has collapsed, of course, but the Trotskyites are still running with the ball. Their numbers are small but they have tenacity, ideological discipline, and use clever tactics of infiltration. They have practiced these more effectively in recent decades in the UK than perhaps anywhere else. Trotskyites infiltrated the Labour Party and the trade unions in the pre-Blair era. We see the bitter fruits in boycott actions today against Israel, sparked by people who went through this anti-Zionist indoctrination and have passed it on.[25]

Muslims and the Extreme Left

Taguieff has pointed out the similarity of the Islamist approach that the end justifies the means to Lenin's and Trotsky's doctrine. He posited that for the

"Marxist orphans," that is, the Leninists, Trotskyites, and Third Worldists, as well as for the anarchists, new mutations of Judeophobia—an expression he prefers to anti-Semitism—meet their demand for meaning in life.[26]

In 1954, historian Bernard Lewis wrote a seminal article on "what qualities, what tendencies exist in Islam, in Islamic civilization and society, which might either facilitate or impede the advance of Communism."

Lewis pointed out that communist propaganda against the West could always rely on a positive response from the Muslim world when it attacked imperialism. There, communism also found a source of sympathy because of the extreme juxtaposition of the poor masses and the few very wealthy people in Muslim countries. Lewis noted that the communist doctrine of the state controlling economic life was not so alien to the world of Islam. He also asserted that attempts to show that Islam and democracy were identical were based on "a misunderstanding of Islam or democracy, or both."[27]

Almost sixty years later Wistrich analyzed the issue of communism and the world of Islam. To Lewis's assessment he added the more recent collaboration between the extreme left and radical Islamists. He quoted Arab Palestinian Marxist terrorist leader George Habash, who stated that his wing of the PLO drew equally on Soviet and Iranian fundamentalist sources of inspiration. "Beyond ideology, we have in common anti-imperialist, anti-Zionist and anti-Israeli elements."[28]

Wistrich wrote that many Shiites also share the Leninist principle that "whatever promotes the revolution is good and whatever opposes it, is bad."[29] The Supreme Guide of the Iranian Islamic Republic, Ayatollah Khomeini, was partly influenced by the Iranian Islamo-Marxist Ali Shariati, a theoretician of "Red Shiism." Like the Nazis, the communists saw Muslims as potential allies.[30] Iraqi Baathism, according to Wistrich, presented "an eclectic mixture of Arab-nationalist, socialist, Nazi and Stalinist themes," and found expression under Saddam Hussein.[31]

Among the promoters of the leftist-radical Islamic alliance one finds such diverse figures as the late Venezuelan President Hugo Chavez, the British leader of the Respect Party, George Galloway, and the terrorist Carlos. On the other side, Muslim philosopher Tariq Ramadan maintains links to the antiglobalist left through his hostility to neoliberal economics. He is supported by neocommunists, Trotskyites, and Third World circles in France.[32]

Radical left-wing anti-Semitism is often connected with Arab and sometimes even with extreme right-wing anti-Semitism. They usually work independently toward similar goals. During Israel's 2014 Operation Protective Edge in Gaza, this occurred, for instance, in Germany. The Israeli ambassador to Germany, Yakov Hadas-Handelsman, observed that "the protests against Israel are attracting an 'unholy alliance' of Islamists, neo-Nazis and extreme leftists."[33]

A November 2001 article in the French progressive weekly *Le Nouvel Observateur* included a claim that Israeli sodiers rape Palestinian women at checkpoints so that the women will later be subjected to "honor killings" by their families. The author, daughter of the paper's Jewish editor Jean Daniel, thus reiterated Palestinian hate propaganda. After protests the paper was forced to admit that the allegation was untrue, but tried to belittle its importance.[34]

NGOs

Nongovernmental organizations (NGOs) are in the forefront of attacks on Israel. A number of political and humanitarian NGOs have an anti-Semitic character. Part of the power of these organizations derives from the huge funding they have available, over which there is little external control. The research organization NGO Monitor provides ongoing documentation on these NGOs as anti-Israeli hate-mongers.[35]

Gerald Steinberg, who has headed NGO Monitor since its founding in 2002, remarks:

> Among Israel's many attackers, non-governmental organizations . . . are the least subject to external monitoring. These anti-Israel NGOs claim to promote human rights and humanitarian aid, yet are characterized by a lack of professionalism and a post-colonial ideological agenda. In some cases, theological anti-Semitism is an additional factor.

Steinberg, who has studied this issue in detail, cites various reasons why NGO bias against Israel often reaches such heights. He says that heads of international NGOs are often anti-Western ideologists. Furthermore, it is beneficial to them to focus on the Palestinian-Israeli conflict because of its high media visibility. For international NGOs, it is important to be in line with the UN Human Rights Council in Geneva, which is controlled by Arab and Islamic blocs. For some, classic Christian replacement theology plays an important role. The situation is further complicated by the fact that many diplomats and politicians in the UN rely on these NGOs.[36]

Human Rights Watch

The aberrations of Human Rights Watch in its criticism of Israel went so far that its founder, Robert L. Bernstein, wrote in *The Washington Post*: "Most shockingly, human rights groups have become the unwitting accomplices of the United Nations as almost every mainstream human rights group has ignored hate speech and incitement to genocide, not only against Israel but against all Jews."

Bernstein observed more specifically:

> Human Rights Watch, which I founded 33 years ago, continues to attack many of Israel's defensive measures during war, yet it says nothing about hate speech and incitement to genocide. To cite just one example, the speaker of the Hamas parliament, Ahmad Bahr, called in April 2007 for the murder of Jews, "down to the very last one." Imagine what leading human rights groups would say if this same speech and incitement were coming from Israel, aimed at the Palestinians.[37]

What is true for international organizations is equally valid for several ones with a national character. Some of these Israel-hate organizations even receive substantial financing from the Dutch government. As former Dutch parliamentarian Wim Kortenoeven put it:

> A number of Dutch anti-Israel NGO's are partly financed by the Dutch government for their general activities. Three of them, the Protestant ICCO, the Catholic Cordaid and the general Oxfam Novib, have created an anti-Israel front organization called United Civilians for Peace (UCP). An additional part-

ner is the Christian peace movement IKV Pax Christi, which is also subsidized by the Dutch government.[38]

Edwin Black, who has published extensively on the Ford Foundation's funding of anti-Israeli hate groups, reports that it gave more than $1 million to the Palestinian Committee for the Protection of Human Rights and the Environment (LAW), which was a key organizer of the anti-Semitic hate campaign in Durban. He notes that the Dutch charity Cordaid and the Grand Duchy of Luxembourg were other major funders of LAW.[39]

The NGOs at the Durban Conference

At the 2001 Durban Conference, major anti-Israeli actions by many NGOs suddenly became visible internationally. Samuels noted that the steering group of the NGO Forum was dominated there by SANGOCO (South African NGO Committee), which played a leading role in attacks on Israel. It had developed an eight-point plan against Israel that clarifies many aspects of the total-propaganda-war approach.

Samuels summarized this program:

> The first point: to launch an educational program to create worldwide solidarity against Israel, the last bastion of "apartheid." The second point: to use all legal mechanisms in countries of universal jurisprudence against Israel. The third and fourth points of attack were to discredit the Law of Return—the foundation of Zionism and Israel, and replace it with a Law of Return for all Palestinian refugees in order to create moral equivalence.
>
> The fifth point: to reinstate the Arab boycott out of Damascus, combined with a secondary boycott, as in the 1970s and 1980s. The sixth point: to impose a sports, telecommunications, academic, scientific and military embargo on Israel. Points seven and eight encapsulate their broad goals: the eventual rupture of all diplomatic relationships with Israel and measures against any state that does not accept ostracism of Israel. All of these eight points were to be carried out over a five-year program.[40]

The World Social Forum

Samuels observes, "The Durban agenda was gradually developed further in a much broader way within the framework of the World Social Forum. This was created one month after the Durban 'anti-racism' conference in 2001 by the Brazilian Labor Party." He says:

> The Palestinian cause has gradually taken over the agenda of the World Social Forum (WSF). Currently it is almost the WSF's sole subject. Its meeting in November 2013 was entitled, "WSF Free Palestine." There were 127 seminars and workshops on how to cause damage to Israel. From the WSF, regional forums such as the North American, Latin American and Asian Forum emerged. The one which is most poisonously anti-Israel is the European Social Forum (ESF). Its first gathering took place in Florence, Italy in 2002. This forum has a more operational role than the WSF.

Samuels adds:

> At the 2006 Athens ESF, a handbook describing how to promote BDS was distributed, illustrating how individuals, civil society and businesses can support the refusal to buy or sell Israeli products. The book explained that the main aim of these actions is to create a critical mass in public opinion so that governments will eventually follow its lead. The book also recommended "smart boycotts" such as academic targets. Proponents claimed that even if boycotts are reversed by "Zionist pressure," their real goal is the publicity engendered.
>
> The handbook also proposed withdrawal of investments from companies directly or indirectly involved with Israel. Emphasis was laid on divestment by churches. It stressed that the measure of success is not the amount of money withdrawn, but the repercussion on the public's concepts and attitudes. Instructions were also offered on advancing sanctions such as governmental restrictions on travel, communication, trade, finance and arms sales.
>
> The Official Reference Document of the Palestine National Committee and the WSF promotes 16 issues on the Palestinian-Israeli conflict. They include dismantling of the "apartheid wall," ending of the "apartheid regime," the right

of return of Palestinian refugees from both 1948 and 1967, the advancement of a military embargo on Israel, the development of BDS campaigns and strategies, the promotion of academic and cultural boycotts, the intensifying of the struggle to lift the siege on Gaza, support for the release of Palestinian prisoners, as well as to bring Israel before the International Court of Justice. Other issues are designed to support anti-Zionist Jews everywhere, assist in the electronic or real intifada, alert media to "Israel's crimes" and to attack "distortions of history" by Israel.[41]

International Committee of the Red Cross

The International Committee of the Red Cross's (ICRC) attitude toward Israel requires a far more detailed analysis than can be offered here. NGO Monitor notes that it showed little interest in kidnapped Israeli soldier Gilad Shalit.

NGO Monitor states, "In fact, while Shalit was held in Gaza without access to the Red Cross, the Red Cross sheltered Hamas officials in its East Jerusalem offices for more than a year, in violation of the organization's alleged mandate of political neutrality."[42]

Alan Baker discusses other aspects of ICRC that diverge from its proclaimed neutrality, which, it says, is the basis of its operations. In an article about the neutrality of the ICRC, Baker demonstrates that the organization refers to all land controlled by the Palestinian Authority in the West Bank and by Hamas in Gaza as the "occupied territories," even though legally these areas never were occupied territory and Israel is not even the governing authority in them.[43]

Trade Unions

In some countries, trade unions are at the forefront of the anti-Israeli battle. They promote discriminatory actions against Israel while abstaining from activism against notorious human rights offenders in many countries. One will usually hear little if anything from them about the widespread murderous criminality in parts of the Muslim world. This happens, for instance, in Britain,

Ireland,[44] Belgium, Norway, Canada,[45] and South Africa.

Calls for boycotts of Israel by Norwegian and Danish trade unions in 2002 were among the first by such organizations in the Western world. In that year, Gerd-Liv Valla was among the first important trade-union figures to call for a boycott of Israel.[46] Valla was a former Stalin supporter who was then leader of the Norwegian Confederation of Trade Unions (LO). On May 1, 2002 (Labor Day), the LO's main agenda was a call to boycott Israel.

The annual First of May celebration in Norway concerns not only the International Workers' Day. For Norwegian trade unions, its second role might be called Israel Hate Day. The main coordinator of these events is the LO. Before each major gathering, texts and topics are agreed upon locally. They then usually appear on banners or posters. Most highlight Norway's domestic problems. Concerning foreign issues, the most dominant focus is on Israel-hate.

Prime Minister Stoltenberg spoke at the main First of May celebration in Oslo in 2013. The speaker immediately before him was the invitee Salma Abudahi from the Union of Agriculture Work Committees (UAWC) in Gaza. She called rockets a "symbol of resistance" and said that occupied people have a right to defend themselves. Abudahi added, "It is important to understand the proportions, the Israelis are killing our loved ones all the time."[47] Stoltenberg remained silent. At this gathering the only international issue referring to a country read: "Support the state of Palestine—Boycott Israel."[48]

The Trades Union Congress, the umbrella organization of British trade unions, had a record of support for the Jews of Palestine and Israel. In 1982, however, the annual TUC Congress adopted a resolution condemning Israel's invasion of Lebanon. It also recognized "the national rights of the Palestinian people to self-determination with an independent, sovereign state."[49] Thereafter the situation deteriorated. Ronnie Fraser has researched UK trade-union incitement against Israel.[50]

A variety of trade unions have passed motions to boycott Israel. For example, in 2006 the Ontario division of the largest Canadian trade union, the Canadian Union of Public Employees (CUPE), voted to boycott Israel for its treatment of Palestinians.[51] A few weeks later the Congress of South African Trade Unions (COSAFU) published a letter expressing enthusiastic support for the CUPE boycott.[52]

André Gantman, author of a book on Belgian anti-Semitism, says, "The

Socialist Trade Union (ABVV) is a major initiator of anti-Israelism. The ABVV wants to exclude the Israeli Histadrut from the international trade union organization."[53]

The Interaction of the Perpetrators

One of the most complex elements of the propaganda war against Israel is interaction between the various perpetrators. To study this effectively, many more case analyses of anti-Semitic attacks against Israel need to be undertaken. The usefulness of such studies can be demonstrated by a detailed example: the previously mentioned research about the 1983 mass hysteria in the West Bank undertaken by Raphael Israeli in his book *Poison: Modern Manifestations of a Blood Libel*. It shows the interaction between Arab hate propaganda, the media, and the United Nations.

Israeli also analyzed the reporting of various media on the case. Among the worst distorters of the truth were French dailies such as the Communist *L'Humanité*, the Socialist-inclined *Libération*, and *Le Monde*. None of these apologized after the facts became known. *The New York Times* was one of the few media outlets that did so, yet even that was only on an inside page.[54]

Nonsocialist Mainstream Politicians

In 2002 Norbert Blüm, a former German Christian Democrat minister of labor, charged that the Jewish state was conducting a "*Vernichtungskrieg*"—a "war of destruction" against the Palestinians. This is the Nazi expression for a war of extermination.[55]

In 2003 the Christian Democrat Party expelled parliamentarian Martin Hohmann, months after he called Israelis a nation of criminals. He used the expression "*Tätervolk*"—"a nation of perpetrators"—a term commonly reserved for Nazi Germany.[56]

Karel de Gucht, the European Union's chief negotiator and a Belgian Liberal, said in 2010, "Don't underestimate the power of the Jewish Lobby on Capitol

Hill . . . You shouldn't underestimate the grip it has on American politics, no matter whether it's Republicans or Democrats."[57]

Kåre Willoch

In 2004 Jo Benkow, a former speaker of the Norwegian parliament and former leader of the Conservative Party, called former Conservative Norwegian Prime Minister Kåre Willoch—in part because of his opinions on Israel—"the most biased person participating in the public debate in this country."[58]

Willoch insists that he is merely criticizing Israel and denies any accusations of being anti-Semitic. However, in a 2009 radio interview, when asked what he thought of the chances for advancement of peace in the Middle East with the new administration of Barack Obama, Willoch said that he was not optimistic. To substantiate this pessimism he pointed to the fact that Obama had appointed a Jew, Rahm Emanuel, as his chief of staff.[59]

Mona Levin, a cultural journalist, responded that with this statement Willoch had crossed a line, and his words would lead to increasing anti-Semitism. She added that, as a former top politician, he knows the importance of words and needs to understand that he is responsible for the opinions he generates.[60]

Fellow Travelers, Opportunists, Business Leaders, and Hired Guns

A separate category of hate originators is fellow travelers who occasionally may play a minor role in campaigns. Others are opportunists, such as some Western politicians who make pro-Palestinian statements to attract Muslim voters in their countries or constituencies.

Yet another category of those working against Israel consists of some business leaders and employees who have financial or commercial interests in the Arab world. Various oil companies have often been mentioned in this context.

Among the promoters of anti-Israeli interests are also public relations firms, lawyers, former diplomats, and so on paid with Arab money. Some of this is exposed in Bard's book *The Arab Lobby*.[61]

The Jews First, Others Later

A major ramification of the total propaganda war concerns the significance to others of what happens to Jews and Israel. The de facto function of the Jews and Israel in many societies has been compared to that of a canary in an underground mine. A common mining practice was to send canaries into mines so as to assess environmental hazards. When the bird stopped singing, the miners knew they were in danger. This comparison should be avoided as the canary had to die so that the miners could live. This is not the role Jews wish to fulfill again.

Others can, however, often learn what is awaiting them from what has first happened to Jews. Anti-Semitism is a construct that takes aim at the Jews initially. The aggressor first looks for what seems an easy target; thereafter he upgrades to more difficult ones. This phenomenon has often been described regarding authoritarian societies, but it also exists in democracies. The perpetrator's aggression subsequently extends to others and endangers them as well. In the 1930s, the Jews were a prime target for Hitler and his adherents. Later tens of millions of others would also perish or suffer.

This functional role has nothing to do with how Jews and Israel see their contribution to society. The distorted image, constructs, discrimination, and attacks on the Jews and Israel are rather an indicator of substantial problems of contemporary Western society at large. Although today the Jews and Israel are prime initial and visible targets, they are rarely the sole ones.

In other words, what may manifest itself initially as scapegoating the Jews is often revealed later as a precursor of attacks on many others. A few disparate examples indicate that the Jews' and Israel's functioning in a precursor role for other democratic societies is a wide-ranging phenomenon.

Israel and Jews as a Prism

The fact that so many Europeans totally falsely think that Israel is conducting a war of extermination against the Palestinians or behaves toward them as the Nazis did toward the Jews provides a prism on the widespread decay of Europe.[62] It is also an indicator of how deeply irrational many Europeans are.

Israel and Jews as well as Holocaust and post-Holocaust issues can serve as prisms for many more aspects of societies, not only Western ones. As far as the Holocaust is concerned, using it as a looking glass can show how easy it is to propagate extreme lies at the highest level in the Arab and some other parts of the Muslim world. A few examples: in these societies, Holocaust denial is rife, Palestinians and many other Arabs compare the Nakba to the Holocaust, and cartoonists of many leading papers draw Israeli prime ministers as Hitler.

Israel is also a useful prism for quickly understanding what is wrong with the United Nations and many of its associated bodies. At the UN Human Rights Council, Israel is condemned more than all other nations put together, including the most criminal ones in the world. By using Israel as an ongoing prism, we are regularly reminded to what extent this UN human rights body, while supposedly antiracist, includes many racists among the representatives of its member countries.

Israel is also a more general sensor of racists in the ostensibly antiracist camp. Probably no event shows racism in the antiracism camp better than the NGO Forum at the 2001 Durban Conference. The NGO Forum included many thousands of participants from a multitude of major humanitarian bodies. The extreme anti-Israeli resolution adopted there made it clear that it was a gathering of racists claiming to be antiracists.

Another example of racism in the antiracist world emerged after the Breivik murders at Utoya Island in Norway. It turned out that the camp of the Labour youth movement AUF was to a substantial extent a hate seminar against Israel. Children from fourteen years old were indoctrinated against Israel there.

Western postmodern societies are complex and opaque. They have a huge number of interrelated and difficult-to-analyze elements. The Jews constitute such a good prism for these countries because of their lengthy and checkered history in Europe. In recent decades Israel has also become a very good prism on European societies because of its multiple interactions with them.

There are many other realities that can be analyzed much better by using Jews and Israel as prisms. Yet another example concerns the attacks on Israel in a given society by mainstream Christian organizations, together with their relative silence about violence, and ethnic cleansing, against Christians in large parts of the Muslim world. This is an indication of many highly disturbing phenomena in contemporary Western Christendom. Many more examples of this "barometer role" of Israel can be given.[63]

CHAPTER SEVENTEEN

How Hatred Is Transmitted

There are many conduits available and used to transmit hatred and incitement. The major mechanisms of doing so have already been discussed in previous chapters. We will thus only group these here summarily. Before that, however, attention has to be given to what is often poorly understood: language is not neutral, as the choice of words is a tool to convey messages, including hatred.

Semantics

Semantics have long been an important method of transmitting anti-Semitism, and they remain so in our time. The use of the word Jew as an invective is widespread in many European countries. Norwegian Jewish community leader Ervin Kohn said in 2014 that "Jew" is one of the most common curse words in Norwegian schools.[1]

In the propaganda war, semantics are also an important method of transmitting hate messages. If one uses the term "occupied territories," one employs language that bends international law—which, as mentioned before, is a dubious field in itself—because these are "disputed territories."[2] Most Palestinian "refugees" are not true refugees. They did not flee from Israel, though their parents, grandparents, or great-grandparents may have done so and are genuine refugees. Another abuse of language is to call Israelis "colonists" if they live a few tens of kilometers from where they resided before.

The semantics of anti-Israelism often include terminology with an anti-Semitic undertone. Israeli policies are defined as an "eye for an eye" approach, an expression rarely used about far more severe actions taken by other countries. The word revenge is also associated much more with the IDF than with other armies, such as the Allied forces in Iraq or Afghanistan.

"Peace" with Israel is seen by many Arabs as an intermediate stage toward its total destruction. In the context of the Israeli-Palestinian conflict, the distorted use of terms such as "peace movements" and "peace activists" requires an in-depth investigation. Some of the more extreme peace organizations might perhaps be described more accurately as "allies of Arab and Palestinian murderers" or "indirect genocide promoters," or "inexplicit helpers of Islamo-Nazis."

There are many other disparate uses of semantics against Jews and Israel. In some European countries, typical "code words" for Jews in the United States are, for instance, "East Coast intellectuals" and "neoconservatives."

Politicians and media often use the term borders for what were "armistice lines" between Israel and Jordan. All of these examples are just a small selection of a far larger arsenal of semantic distortions concerning Jews and Israel.

Introducing Ideological Views in Language

Several authors have noted the use of semantics against Jews and Israel. French linguist Georges-Elia Sarfati undertook a detailed analysis of the phenomenon. He pointed out that discourse is formulated on the basis of the ideological views of those who engage in it. "Rather than words being neutral, they serve to introduce a certain vision of the question they address."[3]

This is simple to understand. An extreme case is how the Nazis contaminated the German language and how, after the war, the expressions they had coined entered the lexicon of other languages as well. One example among many is the expression "war of extermination," which is a literal translation of the German *Vernichtungskrieg*. This expression has now entered the minds of many Europeans who believe that Israel is conducting such a war against the Palestinians.

Sarfati remarked that anti-Zionism's major "canonic" texts are primarily Soviet fabrications. A key role was played by Trofim Kitchko, a major ideologist who published several anti-Semitic books over a twenty-year period starting in 1963. "His first book, *Judaism Unembellished*, was sponsored by the Soviet Academy of Sciences."

The term anti-Zionism came into systematic use only after the Six Day War. This was first done by the Soviet Union's Information Ministry and thereafter by the media of France's extreme left. Sarfati noted that anti-Zionism has by now become an "ideology"—a system of ideas—that has permeated specific groups in society. He added, "A number of key equations dominate the anti-Zionist discourse. The master one—which transversally commands all others—is 'Zionism equals Nazism.' This also demonstrates how this conduit is used to propagate the notion that Jews are the most evil people in society."

Sarfati summed up by saying that the equivalences used against Israel "are so evil because they attach the four major negative characteristics of Western history in the last century—Nazism, racism, colonialism and imperialism—to the State of Israel. They relate to a collective memory and are easily memorized."[4]

Calling Up Associations with George Orwell

There are also a large number of other linguistic distortions that in part call up associations with George Orwell's *1984*, and works by other authors. Raphael Israeli described the

> Kafkaesque world where there is no cause and effect; when you achieve peace it does not mean reconciliation; when you wage hostilities that is not called war, when you massacre civilians that is not terrorism; when you make concessions, that does not mean that you cannot go back on them once you have achieved your goals; and when you pledge something it obliges you only as it is convenient to you.[5]

Susanne Urban discussed a book by another German historian, Jörg Friedrich, whose revisionist works have become bestsellers.

> He uses terms that for decades were associated with Nazi persecution and the Shoah; thus, cellars and air-raid shelters in which Germans died are "crematoria," an RAF bomber group is an "*Einsatzgruppe*" [task forces which became known as mass murderers of Jews], and the destruction of libraries during the bombings constitutes "*Bücherverbrennungen*" [burning of books]. In this way the Shoah is diminished through language.[6]

Samuels drew attention to yet another aspect of the use of language. He noted that at the 2001 Durban Conference, terms such as "genocide," "Holocaust," "ethnic cleansing," and even "anti-Semitism" were hijacked by the defamers and used against the Jews—who have historically been the main victims of these phenomena.[7]

Steinberg said:

> Many in European politics, academia, the media and the NGOs use almost identical semantics. These four elements of society parallel each other and work together as well, reinforcing each other in the overall attack on Israel. Analysis can start with any one of them. When various European Union representatives and diplomats condemn Israel they use standard vocabulary such as "excessive force," "violation of human rights," or "violation of international law."[8]

Operation Protective Edge

During the 2014 Operation Protective Edge, one saw the recurring use of other false semantics. One of these was the mention of "tension between communities." It suggested that two communities, the Muslim and the Jewish ones, were aggressive toward each other. The reality was very different. The root cause of these "tensions" was the aggression and hatred toward the Jewish community that originated mainly from parts of the Muslim community.[9]

A second recurrent expression was that one did not want to import the

Israeli-Palestinian conflict into European countries. This was said, for instance, by both French President François Hollande and Prime Minister Manuel Valls.[10] It would have been much more correct to say that their predecessors imported the conflict as a byproduct of letting millions of people from Muslim countries into France.[11]

There are many other cases where as a result of the massive immigration, different groups of immigrant descendants have fought with other such groups. For instance, in August 2014 in Herford, Germany, three hundred Yazidi immigrants from Syria and Iraq protested ISIS actions against their communities. During the demonstration they were attacked by ISIS supporters. Earlier that day a Yazidi restaurant owner and a sixteen-year-old boy were injured by ISIS supporters for displaying a poster for the demonstration.[12]

Similarly, in October 2014 there were violent clashes in the German cities of Hamburg and Celle. In Celle there was fighting between Yazidi Germans and Chechen Muslim immigrants. In Hamburg an initially peaceful protest by Kurdish immigrants turned violent when Salafist Muslims confronted them.[13]

There are related protests as well. In October 2014, sixty to seventy Kurdish protesters occupied part of the Dutch parliament in The Hague, demanding international action to defend the Syrian town of Kobane against Islamic State fighters.[14] In the same month under the banner "Hooligans against Salafists," four thousand soccer fans and members of a neo-Nazi organization confronted the police in major riots in Cologne, Germany. The authorities had great difficulty containing the situation.[15]

Obama's Strange Statement

During Protective Edge U.S. President Barack Obama strangely remarked that he had "no sympathy for Hamas." If he had said "I have no sympathy for Al-Qaeda" or "I have no sympathy for Nazism" he would justifiably have come under heavy criticism.[16]

Obama frequently reiterates that the status quo of the Israeli-Palestinian conflict is not sustainable, an expression borrowed from the environmental discourse.[17] He said this several years ago and repeated it during Protective Edge.[18]

If one looks at the reality in the Middle East and North Africa, there are many situations that are chaotic and thus unsustainable. The U.S. president, however, seems to prefer the use of the expression for the Israeli-Palestinian conflict.[19]

Masking the Truth

In the case of anti-Semitism and anti-Israelism, the biased use of semantics is sometimes accompanied by what might be called "expressions that try to mask the truth." A frequent one is "I'm an anti-Zionist, not an anti-Semite." The denial of the Jewish people's right to their own state and self-determination is an anti-Semitic act according to the FRA definition.

A second, frequent masking expression is the denial that anti-Semitic acts are anti-Semitic. A third is the claim that anti-Semitic acts are for the benefit of Jews or Israel. An extreme case where the two were combined occurred in the Netherlands in 2005 and 2006. In 2005, the pastor Kees Mos spoke in the town of Wassenaar at a church belonging to the Protestant umbrella organization PKN. He said, "The Jew in us is a traitor, says Matthew. . . The sin of the Jew is that he refuses to be human . . . We have painted Hitler in the past decades as a monster, but monsters don't exist . . . But the Jew we do not recognize. He is a silent killer." Thereafter, the community was split into supporters and opponents of Mos.

In 2006, another pastor named Van Veen, who did not belong to the community, preached in the same church. He spoke about the persecution of the Jews and said, "We have to be careful that our guilt feelings about genocide won't lead to an attitude of lack of criticism toward Israel. That doesn't help Israel and the Jews." He added, "In that way, Jews remain in their victim role and see anti-Semitism in everything."[20] A year and a half after his hate sermon, Mos withdrew the text. The PKN had remained silent.[21]

The Changing Use of "Palestinians"

A complex semantic issue that is difficult to categorize concerns the word "Palestinians." Before the creation of Israel it was mainly the Jews in Palestine who used "Palestinian" as a way to describe themselves. They were "Palestinian Jews."

This gradually changed after the establishment of the Jewish state. Jews now called themselves Israelis or, more rarely, Israeli Jews. Gradually, "Palestinians" became the term with which the inhabitants of the West Bank and Gaza identified themselves. So did some of the Israeli Arabs, and the refugees were now called "Palestinian refugees."

These usages have helped foster the misleading image in the Western world of the Palestinian Arabs as the native population of both Israel and the territories. This, in turn, has engendered many distortions, historical and others.

Word of Mouth

In previous centuries, word of mouth was a dominant means of transferring messages. Many Christian preachers and teachers spread the hatred of Jews, mentioning their alleged role in the alleged deicide of Jesus for centuries. They did so from the pulpit and in religious education.

Word of mouth remains a widespread means of gossip, slander, and incitement. One small illustration: Jeffrey Gedmin described typical dinner conversations in Berlin a number of years ago, in which most of the conversation partners attacked his pro-Israeli positions. There were others at the table who agreed with him, yet remained silent. Some of these called him the next day and expressed their empathy.[22]

A Jewish nurse who worked at an Amsterdam hospital was willing to be interviewed only by using the pseudonym Carla because of how she saw the current situation in the Netherlands. She said:

> I worked at that hospital for more than ten years. My coworkers knew that my son had served in the Israeli army. I sometimes heard remarks like: "They only kill Palestinians there." Doctors and psychologists often said this too. The head

> of a medical department frequently and casually discussed "the suffering of the Palestinians." He always attacked me directly when something was published on Israeli politics.
>
> Whenever the Dutch media wrote something about Israel, several people started a political discussion with me. They behaved as if I shaped Israeli politics. No one would ever say to someone with family in Italy, "What crazy thing has Berlusconi done this time?"[23]

Those who demonize Israel and the Jews by word of mouth have a number of public-domain "channels" at their disposal to transmit their hate messages. Among these are shouts of "Death to the Jews," which have been heard during anti-Israeli demonstrations in various European cities.

The JTA reported from an anti-Israeli demonstration in The Hague: "Holding up the black ISIS flag, the crowd chanted in Arabic, 'Jews, remember Khaybar, the army of Muhammad is returning.' The cry relates to an event in the seventh century when Muslims massacred and expelled Jews from the town of Khaybar, in modern-day Saudi Arabia."[24]

Abuse of the Holocaust

Abuse of the Holocaust is a special category of transmitting hatred. The main abuse of Holocaust memory has long been Holocaust denial. Additional categories such as Holocaust justification, inversion, and obliteration are, however, becoming important as well.[25, 26, 27]

These sometimes appear together with the promotion of alleged "Jewish conspiracy theories." This author's 2009 book, *The Abuse of Holocaust Memory: Distortions and Responses* analyzes these issues in detail.[28]

Teaching

Another category of word of mouth is teaching at universities and high schools. This has been discussed in two earlier chapters.

As aforementioned, sometimes anti-Semitic concepts are conveyed in schools. Some university teachers promote anti-Israeli ideology instead of advancing knowledge. At some universities Jewish students feel physically and verbally threatened.

Conferences with an anti-Semitic character take place at several universities—for instance, questioning Israel's right to exist as a state. Similar discussions do not take place regarding any other nation. This indicates the highly discriminatory nature of such gatherings.

Popular Art

Art and popular art are also vehicles of transmitting hatred. Though often debated, Shakespeare's character Shylock is a classic example. Wistrich says that during his high school years there were few British authors he had to read who were devoid of anti-Semitism. Regarding Shakespeare and Shylock he remarks:

> This Shylock image influenced the entire West because it fits so well with the evolution of market capitalism from its early days. Shakespeare portrayed the subject in a way that is to a certain extent realistic, reflecting the rise of a commercial society in Venice and of economic competition. But Shylock has come to embody an image of the *vengeful*, *tribal*, and *bloodthirsty* Jew, who will never give up his pound of flesh. Rightly or wrongly, this is what most people remember. Shylock is the English archetype of the villainous Jew. Those who talk about how humanistic, universal, and empathetic his portrait is, are ignoring not only how it was perceived at the time but its historical consequences.[29]

There are several examples of hatred of Israel expressed through art. Altsech related:

> In October 2003, [the important daily] *Ta Nea* interviewed the artist Alexandros Psychoulis, who was organizing an exhibition in Athens concerning the heroism of an Arab female suicide bomber who blew herself up in a Jerusalem supermarket in March 2003. The artist said "that the title 'Body Milk' brings

together both female cosmetics and the human milk of an 18-year-old Palestinian girl bomber in an Israeli supermarket . . . A very beautiful girl, educated, in love . . . of an army of women in the women's space of the supermarket . . . the supermarket is a super female provider. If she blows herself up there, she is magnifying her existence and her act." *Ta Nea*[30] wrote that the pink lace embroidery montage displayed an Arab woman with a bomb belt, who was "heroically obliterating an Israeli supermarket."[31]

In 2004, then-Israeli ambassador to Sweden Zvi Mazel damaged an art exhibition in a Stockholm museum that glorified suicide bombing.[32]

Performing Artists

During his 2013 world tour, musician Roger Waters equated the Jews with dictatorial regimes and unethical corporations. He appeared on stage simultaneously with a floating pig covered in Stars of David, in addition to symbols such as dollar signs, while wearing a costume reminiscent of a Nazi uniform.

In a statement released by the Simon Wiesenthal Center, Rabbi Abraham Cooper responded to these visual displays: "Waters has been a supporter of the anti-Israel BDS (Boycott, Divestment, Sanctions) movement. Forget Israel/Palestine. Waters deployed a classic disgusting medieval anti-Semitic caricature widely used by both Nazi and Soviet propaganda to incite hatred against Jews."[33]

When not using his own music and stage shows to denigrate Israel, Waters also devotes much time to encouraging other entertainers to boycott Israel. In 2014 he publicly urged musician Neil Young to cancel a scheduled concert in Tel Aviv, and actress Scarlett Johansson to step down as spokesperson for the Israeli company SodaStream.[34]

The French anti-Semitic comedian and inciter Dieudonné behaves somewhat similarly. He managed to remain in the French news for several years. As the BBC describes it:

> He now openly attacks the "Zionist-American axis of power" and named [the extreme rightist anti-Semitic politician] Jean-Marie Le Pen as godfather

> of his child. He has been condemned on seven occasions for anti-Semitic remarks—at one point describing Holocaust commemorations as "memorial pornography"—and counts as allies a motley mixture from Shiite radicals to shaven-headed far-right ultras.[35]

In 2013, Dieudonné invented a new salute called the quenelle. It emulates the Nazi salute yet does not violate France's law against displaying Nazi symbols. This salute was then adopted by many in France, among them extreme right-wingers. It also went international when the French soccer player Nicolas Anelka performed it at an English soccer game of the club he plays for there. So did the French NBA basketball star Tony Parker.

One picture shows a man doing the quenelle in front of the Jewish Ohr Torah school in Toulouse, where Mohammed Merah murdered four Jews in 2012. The man is wearing a shirt with a picture of Yasser Arafat.[36]

Social Media

With its massive number of surfers, the internet has become a major instrument for disseminating anti-Semitic ideas and promoting the delegitimization of Israel. Using this medium for these purposes becomes increasingly effective. It may well lead to a culture where anti-Semitism becomes socially acceptable on it and thereby permeates society even further. New internet media such as Facebook, Twitter, and YouTube serve various originators of hate-promotion.

Creating Israel-hate or anti-Semitic sites on the internet is a simple method of transmitting demonizing statements in many ways through social media. Tens of thousands of such hate sites exist.

For Dieudonné, social media plays a major role. As the BBC puts it:

> But despite (or maybe because of) his estrangement from the establishment — and these days he is now more or less totally boycotted by the media—Dieudonné retains a wide appeal in France. Thanks to the internet, he speaks regularly to his tens of thousands of fans via Twitter and Facebook. And his videos on YouTube, which appear every week or so, can draw up to 2.5 million hits.[37]

Media

Anti-Israeli media are, besides originators of Israel-hatred, instruments of anti-Semitism and the delegitimization of Israel. They can be an "originator" through their editorials. Their choice of news items can also be biased and create hatred.

Such media become transmission instruments of incitement when they provide space for hate-promoting opinion articles. A further element is talkbacks in those media that have internet sites. Some media eliminate talkbacks from their site that do not meet certain criteria; others do not.

Cartoons are concentrated tools for transmitting anti-Semitic messages. Many originate from Arab and Muslim sources, including in countries that are at peace with Israel. They also appear in government-owned journals. Many extreme anti-Semitic cartoons have also been published in Europe, primarily in Greece and Norway but in other countries as well.

TV stations can be originators of hatred through their choice of items, the ways these are structured, and the language used. By their choice of interviewees they can become transmission channels.

The United Nations

The United Nations is sometimes an originator of hatred when the secretary-general or others use double standards against Israel. The General Assembly's resolutions against Israel show that it is a transmission medium for hatred. This has been possible because the Arab states can count on almost automatic support from a majority of states. The same is true for other UN bodies, among which the UNHRC is probably the most prolific.

Lawfare[38, 39]

In recent years, the interpretation of international law in an anti-Israeli fashion has become a major tool in the battle against Israel. In 2004, the International

Court of Justice (ICJ) released an advisory opinion that the separation barrier between Israel and the Palestinian territories was "contrary to international law." The ICJ was not the initiator of this opinion; it became in part a transmission tool. The opinion was given at the request of the UN General Assembly.

With fourteen votes in favor and one against, the ICJ concluded that Israel is obligated to cease construction on the barrier, which is intended to prevent terrorists from entering Israel, and dismantle it in areas where it was already built.[40] Although this is the only case submitted to the ICJ specifically applying to Israel, in other cases the Arab bloc in the United Nations has distorted international law to demonize Israel.

According to Israeli legal expert and former ambassador to Canada Alan Baker:

> Arab states initiated an alteration in the text of the Court's statute listing as a serious violation of the laws of armed conflict the war crime of "transferring, directly or indirectly, parts of the civil population into the occupied territory." The deliberate addition of the phrase "directly or indirectly" to the original 1949 text was intended by them to adapt the original 1949 Geneva Convention language in order to render it applicable to Israel's settlement policy.[41]

Intimidation in the Public Square

Intimidation in a public domain or in private is also a way of transmitting "messages." It can take the form of actual violence or threats. It occurs in many places including on a number of campuses in the Western world.

During the IDF's Operation Cast Lead, a new phenomenon merited particular attention. Groups, often dominated by violent Muslims, tried to conquer the public square in Europe and at the same time, tried to remove Jewish and Israeli symbols from it. Sometimes the authorities assisted in this process, such as in cities like Duisburg, Germany and Malmö, Sweden.

Muslims have attacked pro-Israeli demonstrators in various places, as well as Jews in the streets. There were also arson attempts against Jewish institutions. After some anti-Israeli demonstrations, Muslim prayer services were held in public places in Europe and the United States. The roles played by Muslim organizations in these activities have not been sufficiently investigated. Attempts to remove Jewish and Israeli symbols from the public square have occurred in the past, mainly on an individual basis (e.g., attacking people carrying Israeli flags or wearing kippas or Stars of David). In those cases, the perpetrators were not necessarily mainly Muslims.

Physical Attacks

A substantial number of physical and verbal attacks on Jews take place in the public domain in various countries. Only a few examples can be given here.

In 2012, a German rabbi was attacked in Berlin for wearing a kippa by four Arab youths in front of his six-year-old daughter, who was also threatened.[42] In response, a German rabbinical college advised against wearing kippas in public.[43]

Perpetrators of these anti-Semitic and anti-Israeli attacks are often but not only Arabs. Also in 2012 in Kiev, an ultra-Orthodox man was in critical condition after an assault by Ukranian neo-Nazi skinheads.[44] These are just some examples out of many.

Sometimes non-Jews are attacked because of pro-Israeli actions. In 2013 Mats Green, mayor of the Swedish city of Jönköping, was physically assaulted outside his home. Although he could not identify his attackers, police believe the attack was motivated by his attempts to stop the sale of "Burn, Israel, burn" shirts at a Socialist shop operating in a city-owned cultural center.[45]

It was to be expected that during Operation Protective Edge there would be anti-Semitic incidents in Malmö, where the hatred of Jews is so widespread.

CHAPTER EIGHTEEN

Demonization's Impact on Jews

THE RISING ANTI-SEMITISM AND THE demonization of Israel, particularly in Europe, have led to a change in behavior and attitudes of large segments of the Jewish population there. While this change has taken place over a longer period, much of it occurred in this century. Some of these changes, however, such as thinking about whether to emigrate, are not necessarily linked exclusively to an unattractive national environment for conscious Jews, but also to more general factors such as the economic situation, secularization, new European values, and so on.

As shown previously, much but not all of current European anti-Semitism is closely linked to the demonization of Israel. Other factors are in play as well. The quantitative impact of each of them cannot be ascertained. One of them is classic religious and ethnic anti-Semitism. The existence of above-average numbers of aggressive anti-Semites among the Muslim immigrant community is another one. A further factor is the ineffectiveness of the fight against anti-Semitism by the authorities of various countries. Yet another one is the secularization of Europe, which facilitates public attacks on core Jewish rituals such as circumcision and ritual slaughter.

The impact of anti-Semitism on Jewish attitudes is manifested in many ways. They include increased fear of anti-Semitic attacks, the hiding of Jewish identity in the public domain by many Jews, increased security measures for Jewish institutions, changes in one's social contacts, no longer informing authorities or monitoring organizations about anti-Semitic incidents, moving out of certain cities, emigration or considering it, as well as community leaders wondering whether there is a future for "conscious" Jews in Europe. An issue apart is how to react to attempts to prohibit Jewish rituals.

Much anecdotal material on these subjects has been available for many years. The 2013 FRA study provides insight into the quantitative importance of several of the changes in attitudes. The study confirms the impact of anti-Semitism on Jewish communities.[1] Yet what is true for one community is not necessarily true for another, even in the same country. In France, for instance, Jews live rather undisturbed in the affluent Paris suburb of Neuilly sur Seine, which has a significant Jewish population. In other suburbs—for instance, some with many Muslim inhabitants—the situation may be very different.

One of those who consider that "normative Jewish life in Europe is unsustainable" is European Jewish Congress President Moshe Kantor. He said so in April 2014 when presenting the results of a study on worldwide anti-Semitism in 2013 by the Kantor Center for the Study of Contemporary European Jewry at Tel Aviv University. He cited increasing anti-Semitism and "fear and insecurity" as reasons.[2]

A month earlier Prasquier said in London, "Today, much more acutely than when I left my position as President of CRIF ten months ago, the question of our lasting presence in France is raised . . . Today in the Jewish community, there is hardly a conversation when the subject of leaving [France] is not brought up." He added that the Jewish Agency and Israeli authorities expect about forty thousand French Jews to immigrate to Israel in the coming years.[3]

Wistrich says that the atmosphere in Europe is such that Jews will not be able to stay there much longer: "Any clear-sighted and sensible Jew, who has a sense of history, would understand that this is the time to get out." He adds that in two to three decades, the Jews' history in postwar Europe will have come to an end: "It's finished . . . It's a slow death . . . The many efforts to counter anti-Semitism are important yet Sisyphean in that there is no chance for them to overcome the ever-strengthening forces of hatred . . . These trends are far more powerful than people even begin to understand."[4]

Ira Forman, the U.S. State Department's special envoy to monitor and combat anti-Semitism, saw the situation somewhat differently. He said, "It's hard to empty half a million Jews out of France in any short period of time, but I do think the viability of communities is a concern." He added, "If current trends continue or get worse, I can see some of the smaller communities essentially disappearing."[5]

Operation Protective Edge: A Selection of Incidents

The anti-Semitic eruption during Operation Protective Edge evoked additional remarks on the future of Jews in Europe.

The most severe of a limited selection of incidents took place before the campaign started. Four people were killed in an attack on the Brussels Jewish Museum at the end of May. The person charged with this crime is Mehdi Nemmouche, a French volunteer who had spent a year as a jihadi in Syria. The weapons found in his possession were wrapped in a cloth bearing the sign of ISIS.[6] He was later identified by a former ISIS captive as his torturer in Syria.[7]

The most violent attacks during Protective Edge were in France. Two synagogues in Paris were attacked by Muslim mobs after an anti-Israeli demonstration. A grocery store owned by Jews in the Paris suburb of Sarcelles was burned.[8]

In Frankfurt the police succumbed to pressure and lent their megaphone to a leader of a pro-Palestinian crowd. He used it to shout anti-Semitic slogans.[9] In Copenhagen a school was vandalized with the slogans "No peace in Gaza" and "No peace to you Zionist pigs," in addition to having its windows smashed.[10] In Belfast, Northern Ireland, a synagogue was vandalized a number of times.[11]

Some Jews were attacked. In Amsterdam, a Jewish woman was severely beaten. In some countries there were shops, restaurants, and others who denied entrance to Israelis or to Jews. In the Belgian town of Liege, a shop put a sign in its window that said in Turkish, "Dogs are allowed in this establishment but Jews are not under any circumstances."

At the end of July in Malmö, Sweden, stones were thrown through the windows of the synagogue. A few days later various objects, including a glass bottle, were thrown at the rabbi and a congregant.[12]

In Antwerp a Flemish doctor broke his Hippocratic Oath. A family member of a ninety-year-old Jewish woman, who had fractured a rib, called a medical hotline. The physician who answered refused to come and attend to the injured woman, and said that she should go to Gaza and after a few hours she would feel no pain.[13]

In Iceland a caravan company refused to rent to Israelis. Earlier it had called its low season "Jew Season."[14] In Hungary an extreme right-wing mayor hanged effigies of Israeli Prime Minister Benjamin Netanyahu and of former President Shimon Peres in a mock execution.[15]

Though many of the incidents took place in Europe, there was also violence in other continents. In Calgary, Canada, peaceful pro-Israeli demonstrators who came to protest a pro-Palestinian march were injured and verbally harassed by pro-Palestinian demonstrators. One pro-Israeli demonstrator was punched in the face trying to protect her younger brother, and another was dragged several feet with an Israeli flag tied around his neck while pro-Palestinian demonstrators shouted "Kill the Jews" and "Hitler was right."[16]

Anti-Semitic attacks and vandalism increased elsewhere in Canada during Protective Edge. In Montreal a man was punched in the face while walking out of a kosher restaurant, a Hasidic woman was slapped in the face, and a dog was ordered to attack a Jewish boy.[17]

In Sydney, Australia, during this time a bus full of elementary-aged Jewish children was boarded by drunken teenagers. They spent about forty-five minutes shouting "Heil Hitler" and "Kill the Jews" while threatening the young children.[18]

Protective Edge: Are Jews Secure?

British Jews, like their conationals, often prefer the understatement to express their opinions. During the Protective Edge campaign journalist Hugo Rifkind of *The Times* wrote of his discomfort with being a British Jew: "Never before have I felt that attitudes towards Jews in Europe—and even, albeit less so, in Britain—could grow far, far worse before a whole swathe of supposedly progressive thought was even prepared to notice."[19]

In a conversation with Israel's Channel 2, BBC Television Director Danny Cohen said, "I've never felt so uncomfortable being a Jew in the UK as I've felt in the last 12 months. And it's made me think about, you know, is it our long-term home, actually. Because you feel it. I've felt it in a way I've never felt before actually."[20]

Roger Cukierman, president of the French Jewish umbrella organization CRIF, said regarding the anti-Israeli protests in France during Protective Edge, "They are not screaming 'Death to the Israelis' on the streets of Paris. They are screaming 'Death to Jews.'"[21]

The only resident chief rabbi in the Netherlands, Binyomin Jacobs, said on a television program that Jews feel unsafe in the Netherlands and are being threatened and insulted on the streets. He noted that he himself also wonders whether or not it is safe for him to remain in the Netherlands. Jacobs has, however, come to the conclusion that he has to stay—because the captain is the last one to leave the ship.[22]

David Beesemer is the chairman of Maccabi in the Netherlands. He was quoted by the Jewish weekly *NIW* as saying, "I am now constantly busy with wondering whether I can offer my children a safe future here. Before the summer of 2014 I did not even think about this."[23]

David Serphos, former director of the Ashkenazi community in Amsterdam, wrote:

> I don't dare trust the authorities after the mayor of The Hague, and now even of Amsterdam do not interfere when Jews and Judaism are threatened . . . Often I spoke jocularly with friends about reliable addresses to go into hiding [like in the Second World War] if it would ever be necessary. In recent times I look far more seriously at that very short list.[24]

Dieter Graumann, head of the Central Organization of Jews in Germany, observed, "These are the worst times since the Nazi era." He continued:

> On the streets, you hear things like "the Jews should be gassed," "the Jews should be burned"—we haven't had that in Germany for decades. Anyone saying those slogans isn't criticizing Israeli politics, it's just pure hatred against Jews: nothing else. And it's not just a German phenomenon. It's an outbreak of hatred against Jews so intense that it's very clear indeed.[25]

In an interview with the *Rheinische Post* Graumann noted the solidarity of the churches and political elites with the German Jews. He added, however, that Jewish citizens felt left alone by ordinary citizens. He said that hundreds of Jews had asked his organization whether they should stay in Germany or leave.[26]

In July 2014, after firebombs were thrown at a synagogue in Wuppertal, Germany, Graumann's predecessor Charlotte Knobloch said that Jews should, at least for the moment, hide their identity. Otherwise the risk of an attack would be too great.[27]

In Frankfurt the Jewish community left the Council of Religions because of anti-Semitic and anti-Israeli statements by Muslim representatives. One of the Jewish leaders, Leo Latasch, said that these "people are not the ones we can work with."[28]

In an article the German Social Democrat Foreign Minister Frank-Walter Steinmeier expressed solidarity with the country's Jews. He wrote—even though it is doubtful that this was true—that in the present situation, the whole country stands behind its Jewish fellow citizens. He added, "We are grateful that after the Shoah so many Jews once again live here." That is far from self-evident.[29]

German Chancellor Angela Merkel showed her solidarity with German Jewry in a rally in Berlin where she said that "the hundred thousand Jews living in Germany are a national treasure." She also noted that there was not a single Jewish institution in the country that did not require police protection in the current climate. She asserted that it was every German's duty to take a stand.[30]

As aforementioned, Moshe Kantor, president of the European Jewish Congress, summed it all up: "Normative Jewish life in Europe is unsustainable."[31]

At a conference held by the Organization for Security and Cooperation in Europe, the U.S. ambassador to the United Nations, Samantha Power, addressed the European problem. She said that the growing number of anti-Semitic acts "are not only a threat to the Jewish community, they are a threat to the larger project of European liberalism and pluralism." She added that "rising anti-Semitism is rarely the lone or the last expression of intolerance in a society." In particular, she singled out Merkel as among the political leaders who have stood strongly against anti-Semitism.[32]

During Protective Edge it also became clear that in many places the police and the authorities simply looked away from anti-Semitic expressions by demonstrators.[33]

Stephan Kramer, director of the American Jewish Committee's European Office on anti-Semitism, said in an interview during Protective Edge that it appeared inciters from Hamas and other organizations in Germany were trying to escalate the situation. He added that his impression was that the police were no longer masters of the situation in certain places. In Kramer's view the deescalation strategies were leading to appeasement, but not to the understanding that violence should not be permitted. When asked about it, he said that he doubted whether the Jewish minority in Europe is secure.[34]

As early as 2012 Kramer, then secretary-general of the Zentralrat, said that he no longer trusted the Germans. "Only the Jews can save themselves." He added that he always carried a gun, which he had to show to someone who had harassed him on Yom Kippur so as to frighten him away.[35]

Natan Sharansky, chairman of the Jewish Agency, wrote in the *Jewish Chronicle*: "I believe we are seeing the beginning of the end of Jewish history in Europe. What makes the situation in Europe unique in history is the fact that Europe has become very intolerant of identities in a multicultural and post-nationalist environment."

He added:

> This new antisemitism is very connected to Israel—demonization, delegitimization and double-standards—and is now so deep in the core of European political and intellectual leaders that practically every Jew is being asked to choose between being loyal to Israel and loyal to Europe. That insecurity is due to Muslim immigration and the rise of the classical right, which sees the Jews as the "other."[36]

Many European politicians condemned the anti-Semitic demonstrations. A joint statement by Steinmeier, Italy's Federica Mogherini, and France's Laurent Fabius declared, "Anti-Semitic rhetoric and hostility against Jews, attacks on people of Jewish belief and synagogues have no place in our societies." Similarly, French President Hollande met with Jewish and Muslim leaders to declare that fighting anti-Semitism would become a "national cause."[37] French Prime

Minister Manuel Valls stated in response to the surge in anti-Semitic violence: "What's happened in Sarcelles is intolerable: attacking a synagogue or a kosher grocery, is quite simply anti-Semitism, racism."[38]

Valls's attitude was very different from that of the Jospin Socialist government at the beginning of this century. It, along with the president, Jacques Chirac, tried to conceal as much as possible the massive outburst of anti-Semitic incidents in France at that time. Shmuel Trigano said:

> The official version propagated by the Jospin Government can be summarized as saying that if Jews were attacked, this was not anti-Semitism, but a reflection of a social problem. The socialist policy aimed to obscure, with this mechanism, the terrorist menace against France. It resulted in the Jews seeing themselves as the country's scapegoat and safety barrier—as they had received the main blows, which targeted French society at large.[39]

However many condemnations of anti-Semitism there were in summer 2014, in practice it does not mean that the authorities managed to prevent anti-Semitic incidents.

Experiencing Anti-Semitism

There is a significant quantity of data about Jews experiencing anti-Semitism. One example is a survey conducted by and for the Norwegian Jewish community (DMT) in 2011. It was based on a questionnaire sent to members in Oslo and Trondheim.[40]

When asked about the level of anti-Semitism in Norway, 72 percent of respondents from the Jewish community in Oslo and 55 percent from the Trondheim community saw an increase. Half of the respondents said that they had personally experienced anti-Semitism. One-fifth reported having experienced anti-Semitism in 2011.

Hiding Identities

The hiding of identities by Jews has several aspects. One often hears that many Jews conceal their Jewishness at their workplaces or in public as much as possible. Information about this was mainly anecdotal until the 2013 FRA study was published. In 2011, Islin Abrahamsen and Chava Savosnick conducted a qualitative study for the Norwegian Jewish community of Jewish children and young people's experiences with anti-Semitism in the country. Twenty-one young Norwegian Jews from school age to twenty-five were interviewed. The study found that young Jews often do not reveal their religious identity and some have even changed schools, or their parents have even changed residences because of the anti-Semitism they have experienced.[41]

In the earlier-mentioned interview with the Jewish nurse Carla, who worked at an Amsterdam hospital, she said remarks were made to her about Jews such as "You Jews have acquaintances everywhere" or "You Jews are rich." She observed, "As I publicly expressed my Jewish beliefs, I was seen by many as 'stereotypically Jewish.'"

Regarding her subsequent job she said:

> I do not speak about my religion there and give minimal information about my background. For Jews in the Netherlands, it has become increasingly difficult to openly reveal our religion. There are several factors at play: the increase in the Muslim population, the right-wing turn in society, and increasing intolerance in the Netherlands. Other factors are the decline in knowledge of history and the erosion of Dutch norms and values.[42]

Another aspect of Jews hiding their identity is avoiding wearing items in public that make one recognizable as a Jew. This also has to be seen in a wider context. Whereas many members of the Muslim community insist on making their identity publicly visible, anti-Semitic incidents lead many Jews to conceal their identity in the public domain. Statistics often show that in these incidents, Muslims are far more involved than their share in the population.

The 2013 FRA study, which was undertaken in France, Belgium, Hungary, Denmark, Latvia, Italy, Sweden, and the United Kingdom, found that on average 20 percent of the Jews in the countries surveyed said they always avoided wearing, carrying, or displaying things that might help people identify them as Jews in public. Eighteen percent said they do this frequently; 30 percent said they occasionally avoided religious symbols because of safety concerns.[43]

The country surveyed with the highest percentage of Jews avoiding being recognizable as Jews is Sweden, with 34 percent of those interviewed stating that they avoided such identification most of the time.[44] This cannot solely be explained by the massive anti-Semitic incidents mainly perpetrated by Muslims in Malmö, as the Jewish population in that city represents far less than 10 percent of Swedish Jewry.

Jewish Leaders' Reactions

Jewish leaders have made various recommendations that Jews hide their identities in public. In a radio interview in 2003, French Chief Rabbi Joseph Sitruk told French Jews to wear hats rather than kippas so as to avoid being attacked in the streets.[45]

In 2014, Dutch Chief Rabbi Jacobs reacted to the publication of the 2014 ADL global survey by saying, "Today, if you are a visible Jew in the street, it's common to be heckled as 'Dirty Jew' . . . This was not possible in Holland 40 years ago. Today's [sic] it's normal."[46]

Several years ago Henri Markens, director-general of the Organization for Jewish Education (JBO) in Amsterdam, said:

> For a number of years already we have been telling our students to "put a cap over your kippa." In principle one shouldn't have to do this, but the circumstances in Amsterdam leave you no choice. One must draw logical conclusions from one's experience. In recent years, perceptions in the Netherlands have changed and some people now regard the kippa as a provocation. If one holds such views, a woman wearing a burka is far more provocative. She doesn't allow any social contact. If I wear a kippa you can look me in the eye and talk to me. This is a major difference.[47]

Motti Wolf, a young man who left the Netherlands to study at the Hebrew University of Jerusalem, told how in 2007 at the Amsterdam South train station, a group of Dutch Moroccans followed him while shouting "Jews to the gas." He mentioned that one always had to be alert when wearing a kippa in certain parts of Amsterdam. Wolf also noted that when he was a student at the Jewish high school, he preferred not to visit certain areas where many Muslims lived. If he had to go there, he put on a cap instead of a kippa.[48]

Chaim Nisan, who now lives in Israel, tells about his experiences in an Amsterdam supermarket where he worked:

> In the supermarket, most of the anti-Semitic incidents were caused by our Moroccan patrons. They made insulting remarks or called me names. Sometimes they were physically intimidating. They shouted a variety of curses such as "cancer Jew" and "Hamas, Hamas, Jews to the gas." Some Moroccans made the Hitler salute at me. Others said nothing, but followed me around annoyingly. There were on average two or three such incidents per week. During the less than a year that I worked in the store, these incidents occurred at least 100 times.
>
> The number of incidents increased greatly, in particular during the Sugar Festival (Eid al-Fitr) holiday. That's when Moroccans came in festive clothing to the store. I was insulted continuously and complained a number of times to my boss. He was always friendly and accommodating and he hired me knowing I wore a yarmulke. When a situation became threatening, he put someone else in the same aisle where I worked. It never came down to physical confrontations, however, because there are security people who immediately intervene when something happens and my attackers knew this.[49]

Security Measures

Increased security measures have to be employed for Jewish and Israeli institutions. It often also includes institutions other than places of worship and schools. This problem already existed in part before the Second Intifada, which led to a huge outburst of anti-Semitic violence in Europe. There were terrorist attacks against Jews and Jewish institutions in Europe well before that time, however. The perpetrators were usually Arabs who came from outside Europe.

Increased Fear

The 2013 FRA study asked Jews across the eight European countries surveyed if they were concerned about future encounters with anti-Semitic insults and harassment. Forty-six percent of respondents worried that they would encounter anti-Semitic verbal harassment in the next twelve months. Thirty-three percent were concerned about future physical anti-Semitic attacks. France had the greatest share of respondents who worried about both. Seventy percent of French Jews surveyed worried about future anti-Semitic verbal harassment, and 60 percent worried about future potential physical attacks.

Fifty-two percent, or over half of all respondents across Europe, worried about a family member being a victim of a verbal anti-Semitic attack, and 41 percent expressed fear over the potential of an anti-Semitic physical attack in the next twelve months. The figures in France were the highest, with 76 percent of French Jews surveyed concerned about the potential of a family member being verbally attacked for being a Jew, and 71 percent concerned about physical attacks.[50]

Another question of the FRA study was presented to parents and grandparents surveyed in all eight countries. One in ten respondents (11 percent) with at least one child or grandchild thought their children or grandchildren had experienced either anti-Semitic physical or verbal harassment, or an anti-Semitic physical or verbal attack in the past twelve months. Sixty-six percent of respondents were concerned that they would be verbally attacked in the future, and 52 percent were concerned about future physical anti-Semitic attacks. Sixty-one percent of respondents who assessed themselves as being very religious were concerned about future attacks, and 37 percent who self-identified as Jewish but were not religious were worried about anti-Semitic physical and verbal harassment in the next twelve months.[51]

There is also a direct correlation between respondents who choose not to wear Jewish symbols in public and respondents who fear anti-Semitic attacks.

> Of those respondents who are worried (both "very worried" or "fairly worried") about becoming a victim of antisemitic verbal insults or harassment in the next twelve months, more than three quarters (76%) at least occasionally avoid wearing, carrying or displaying items in public that might identify them as Jewish ("all the time"—27%, "frequently"—22% or "occasionally"—27%). Of those respondents who do not worry ("not very worried" or "not at all worried") about becoming a victim of antisemitic verbal insults or harassment in that same period, about three in five (59%) at least occasionally avoid wearing, carrying or displaying items in public that might identify them as Jewish. This suggests that some respondents feel compelled to hide their Jewish identity in public in response to safety concerns, limiting the extent to which they are able to live an openly Jewish life.[52]

This attitude is manifested in other ways, too. Some Jewish organizations do not put identifying signs on the outside of their buildings. During one visit to the Netherlands, I attended synagogue services in a provincial town. That synagogue—where its community office is also located—had existed for many decades. It was in a building that possibly was used as a private home in the past. It would have been appropriate if a text from the Hebrew Bible had been posted to indicate that a synagogue was now housed there. That was not the case, nor was there a nameplate.

The Impact of Violence

The murders in Toulouse in 2012 by Mohammed Merah were the worst acts of violence against Jewish schools anywhere in Europe in past decades.[53] Their impact went far beyond France. Jewish communities all over Europe implemented increased security measures. Ervin Kohn, head of the Jewish community in Oslo, told the daily *Dagbladet*, "This could just as easily have happened in Norway. We do not feel safe." He added that the Jewish community is a vulnerable group and would like to see permanent police protection at its institutions.[54]

Additional security measures for Jewish institutions were put in place in the Netherlands as well. This seemed to end a lengthy conflict between the Jewish community and the Dutch government about the latter's unwillingness to contribute to the community's large expenses incurred for security.[55] In Belgium, Britain, Italy, and other European countries, Jewish communities expressed their fears after the Toulouse murders.[56] Even in New York enhanced security measures were put in place.[57]

Adopting Low-Profile Attitudes

Many Jewish communities try to adopt low-profile attitudes. A major reason—as far as anti-Semitic incidents are concerned—is that it is often assumed that authorities are incapable of protecting Jewish institutions sufficiently. It is hoped, then, that by remaining silent one can at least avoid "copycat" attacks.

Some Jewish community leaders, including many British ones, have frequently thought that the way to promote the interests of their organizations' members and protect the country's Jews is to have good relations with the authorities. Leaders of the small Oslo Jewish community told me in 2010 that the community must have good relations with whatever government is in power. This may be true, but it is rarely enough.

For a number of years until 2013, Norway had a left-of-center government that included the extreme Socialist Left Party, and this caused substantial difficulties. When I first drew attention in 2008 to the fact that in Norway there were pioneering acts of anti-Semitic and anti-Israeli behavior, the then head of the Jewish community told a newspaper that I had greatly exaggerated the situation and there were very few problems.

When I published my book *Anti-Semitism in Norway* in Norwegian at the beginning of 2010, the Jewish community was already much less critical of my positions. In the following years they had no choice but to confirm all of my earlier claims to the newspapers. They did so without mentioning that I had stated the same much earlier.

In Morocco a number of years ago, Jews told me that they keep as low a profile as possible whenever there are important negative news items about Israel. This is more understandable because Morocco is not a democracy.

Rifat Bali, an expert on Turkish Jewry, says:

> If one examines the manner in which Turkey's Chief Rabbinate and the community's only remaining press organ, *Şalom*, have responded to the series of crises that have beset the community over the past half-century, two things are readily apparent. First, the community's leaders have regularly had only limited options both socially and politically. Second, the only solution they have found is simply to continue their traditional low-profile policy and wait for the various storms to pass.[58]

Sometimes there are very good reasons for Jews who live in democracies to keep a low profile. During the autumn 2005 riots in France, the government lost control of the situation. It later emerged that the authorities had advised the Jewish community to maintain a low profile because the French government could not protect them.[59]

The low-profile policy is problematic, however, because problems ultimately rise to the surface and in the meantime increase. To understand this better, one only has to look at how some segments of Muslim societies behave in Europe and how problems with them have intensified over the years. One sees Muslim women walking around in head scarves and sometimes even hiding their faces. One sees men with beards and *jalabas*, all indicating that they want to express their personal identity in public.

One can also see Muslim prayer services in the public square in European countries. One can sum all this up by saying that some Muslims are a major cause of Jews avoiding self-identification in public, while many Muslims in general have become more visible. Mainly since the summer of 2014, in some countries that also includes adherents and supporters of Islamo-Nazi movements.

The one Jewish movement that intentionally tries to create a Jewish presence in the European public square is the Chabad Hasidic organization. For decades after the war, it was unthinkable that Jews would publicly light the candelabrum at Chanukah festivities in Dutch towns. Nowadays there are many towns where it is lit publicly in central locations. The same occurs in many other countries.

Social Contacts

"Salon anti-Israelism" is a widespread European phenomenon. In 2004, Trigano mentioned that he frequently heard French Jews say things like: "We don't go to dinner with our non-Jewish friends anymore, nor do we see them." He explained that at many dinners, people would talk aggressively about Israel and, thus, about Jews—who then felt the need to defend Israel against the excessive criticism. They were then accused, however, of being supporters of Sharon and violence. Hence, Jews would decide to avoid such meetings and discussions.[60]

Around the same time, U.S. journalism professor Ari Goldman wrote about his visit to Greece:

> As an American Jewish academic traveling in Europe, I expected that I would get angry questions about U.S. foreign policy, especially the war in Iraq and President George W. Bush's support for the Israeli government of Ariel Sharon. But I didn't expect the anger would be directed toward Jews.
>
> "Don't you think that American Jews have too much power?" one well-dressed man challenged me at a university-sponsored dinner in Athens. "They control everything. They control Bush. They control America. It's got to be stopped."

Goldman added that when he was in Salonika, "another professor called the Christian Zionists hypocrites for their support of Israeli policies. 'How can they profess a religion of love and at the same time support "targeted killings" of Palestinians?' he asked."[61]

This question gains ironic force if one considers that Greece's primarily Greek Orthodox population overwhelmingly supported the Serbs in the murderous Yugoslav wars; the Serbs probably carried out even more mass murders than the other parties to the conflict. The Greek viewpoint appears even more ironic if one considers the multiple atrocities committed by government units and the communist revolutionaries in the Greek civil war of the mid-1940s.

Emigration

In the new century there has been significant Jewish emigration from Europe. The French Jewish community is by far the largest in the continent, and it has seen the most significant emigration. Part of French Jewish emigrants leave for the Western Hemisphere where Montreal, for instance, has gained a sizable French-speaking community. Other emigrants have left for Israel.

One should not only attribute this emigration to the increased anti-Semitism in France. The economic situation in the country also plays a role in such decisions. In 2013, emigration from France to Israel increased by 63 percent, from 1,916 in 2012 to 3,120.[62] In 2014, the figure rose further to over seven thousand.[63]

The Jewish Future in Europe

France was the country in which the new century's outbreak of anti-Semitism began the earliest and most massively. Many conscious Jews started to view their future in France as uncertain. This later spread to other countries in Europe.

It should be noted that in the large-scale autumn 2005 riots in France, almost all or all rioters were Muslims. Although religion did not play a role in these riots, many Frenchmen wondered what their future was. They feel uncomfortable with parts of the non-Western immigrant communities. A poll in 2005 showed that 45 percent of Frenchmen no longer feel entirely at home in France.[64] In some cases this has led to bizarre remarks that Jews have heard in some other Western countries as well: "You at least have Israel to emigrate to."

The FRA study proves that the uncertainty about the future is Europe-wide among many Jews. The situation could radically change, for instance, if in some countries circumcision is forbidden. Those who advocate such a ban come from various circles such as members of the medical profession, child-protection agencies, and anti-Islam politicians. Some Jews also play a role in this campaign.[65] Various Jewish organizations are fighting the trend.[66]

For these various reasons, the future of Jews in Europe has once again become an important topic of discussion in a number of European Jewish communities.

Of the Jews surveyed in the FRA study, 4 percent have moved from their neighborhood because of anti-Semitism and 7 percent have considered doing so. Most surprisingly, 29 percent of those surveyed have considered moving in the past five years because they did not feel safe as a Jew in the country where they live. In three of the eight countries surveyed, France, Hungary, and Belgium, 40–48 percent of Jews have considered emigrating to somewhere more secure because they did not feel safe as Jews in their current residence.[67]

Of the Jews in the eight surveyed nations who have experienced prior anti-Semitic harassment, both physical and verbal over the past five years, 34 percent stated that the most serious form of harassment they have encountered has led them to consider emigrating.[68]

In the Netherlands much public discussion took place in 2010 when this author quoted senior Dutch liberal politician Frits Bolkestein, who said that Jews have to realize "that there is no future for them in the Netherlands, and they can best advise their children to emigrate to the United States or Israel." He supported this statement by pointing to the unsuccessful integration mainly of many Muslim immigrants in the Netherlands and the problems this would pose for conscious Jews in the future.[69]

Several of those Jewishly active in the Netherlands share this view, yet few say so publicly. In 2003, psychologist and Auschwitz survivor Bloeme Evers-Emden wrote in the Jewish weekly *NIW*: "I strongly advise my children to leave the Netherlands."[70] Seven years later she made a similar statement and added her grandchildren to those she advised to leave.[71]

Other Aspects

There are many other aspects of the current reality of Jews in Europe. Jews often do not complain about anti-Semitic incidents because they expect the authorities to do little or nothing. Jewish communities attempt to avoid conflict with authorities who take discriminatory positions against Israel. Sometimes there is also whitewashing of anti-Semitic events by Jewish leaders.

Anti-Israelis—often but not always Muslims—have attempted to change the content of Holocaust Memorial Day, for instance, by trying to include mention of the nonexistent Palestinian genocide. Holocaust Memorial Day plays an important role in Jewish communities and such actions have an impact on them.

Some Jews try to become acceptable to anti-Israeli elites by attacking Israel. They remain silent about the massive extreme crimes in many Arab and Muslim countries. In other cases they will claim that hatred of Muslims in the Jewish community is similar to hatred of Jews in Muslim communities. To avoid exposing the truth they remain silent about the violent anti-Semitic incidents perpetrated by Muslims.[72]

Some Jewish leaders are in the forefront of fighting against public campaigns aiming at Muslims, without making demands on Muslim leaders to fight the major anti-Semitism found among Muslims.

Some Jews distance themselves as much as possible from the Jewish community, saying that identifying as a Jew today only has negative consequences in the circles they frequent. Close to a quarter (23 percent) of the Jewish respondents in the FRA survey stated that they avoid attending Jewish events, visiting Jewish sites or certain parts of their neighborhood because they do not feel safe there as Jews. The highest percentages of respondents who avoid these places were found in Belgium (42 percent), Hungary (41 percent), and France (35 percent).[73]

A very different issue is that Jews abroad are being held responsible by various societal actors for Israel's acts. This phenomenon manifests itself in various ways. In the summer of 2014, during demonstrations against Israel in several places, "Kill the Jews" and similar expressions were heard.[74]

In Turkey *Yeni Akit*, a paper affiliated with Erdogan's party, wrote an open letter to Turkey's chief rabbi accusing Turkish Jews of killing Muslims in Gaza. According to the letter, written by *Akit* correspondent Faruk Köse, "You have lived comfortably among us for 500 years and gotten rich at our expense. Is this your gratitude—killing Muslims? Erdogan, demand that the community leader apologize!"[75]

CHAPTER NINETEEN

Demonization's Impact on Israel and Israelis

THE ONGOING PHYSICAL AND VERBAL attacks against Israel have had a gradual negative effect in a variety of areas. Several years ago there were already indications of how far its demonizers had succeeded in damaging Israel's image.

A 2006 report on Israel's international image by the Anholt Nation Brand Index concluded that: "Israel's brand is, by a considerable margin, the most negative we have ever measured in the NBI, and comes in at the bottom of the ranking on almost every question."[1]

Israel has invested substantially over the past few years in improving its image. Despite the negative publicity it gets in many media, it has risen in ranking. In the 2014-2015 Future Brand Country Brand Index, Israel was ranked twenty-sixth out of seventy-five.[2]

A more professional overview of the success of delegitimization attacks against Israel and of discrimination against Israelis is required. Here a number of major categories will be mentioned, with some examples.

Discrimination within United Nations Bodies

Discrimination against Israel at the United Nations is widespread. As Cotler noted already a decade ago:

> [Israel] has been excluded from its proper geographical location, Asia and is a limited member of the Western European and Other Group (WEOG). Its status does not grant it the right to participate equally in the deliberations of the UN or to be nominated and elected to international bodies. While the UN Charter requires it to operate pursuant to principles of the equality of nations large or small, Israel is disenfranchised.

He added that a similar attitude prevailed in the UN's specialized agencies.[3]

Need for Security Measures

Israeli institutions abroad including embassies and consulates have been attacked and have had to take major security measures. In addition to their own guards, they are often guarded by the local police. Terrorist attacks have been perpetrated against Israeli institutions from time to time, several with lethal results. Some Israeli diplomats have been killed outside of embassies.

The most lethal attack against Israeli diplomats abroad was the 1992 car bombing of the Israeli embassy in Buenos Aires. More than twenty people were killed and close to 250 wounded. Gustavo Perednik, an expert on Latin American Jewry, says, "The judicial investigations have shown convincingly that Iran was behind the AMIA attack [a Jewish communal institution in Buenos Aires] and the 1992 car bombing of the Israeli embassy . . . Yet, Argentina never severed diplomatic relations with Iran."[4]

In 2012, twin car bombs targeted employees of the Israeli Foreign Ministry in Georgia and India. Intelligence demonstrated that Iran was behind these attacks. They are believed to have served as retribution for the killing of a senior Hizbullah official, Imad Mughniyeh, one day after the fourth anniversary of his assassination. In the attack in New Delhi, India, the wife of an Israeli defense attaché was moderately injured. In Georgia, the car of a Georgian national who worked for the Israeli embassy was targeted. However, the bomb was neutralized by Georgian police.[5]

Various websites give overviews of the main terrorist attacks against Israelis abroad.[6] In 2003, Israel's former ambassador to the United Kingdom Shlomo

Argov died from wounds sustained twenty-one years earlier. In 1982 he was shot in the head by terrorists from the Abu Nidal Organization, resulting in a three-month coma and lifelong paralysis. This assassination attempt was also one of the deciding factors in the Israeli government's launching of the 1982 Lebanon War.[7]

From 1969 to 2011 there were a total of ninety-two attempted and successful attacks and assassinations on Israeli embassies and diplomatic staff. In some cases local people were the sole victims. For instance, in 1988 in a bomb detonation by terrorists a few hundred meters from the Israeli embassy in Nicosia, Cyprus, several local police officers were killed. Perpetrators of attacks have ranged from locals, as in the 2011 attack on the Israeli embassy in Cairo, to neo-Nazis, Palestinians, Iranians, and other Muslims.[8]

Airline Security

Israeli airlines have been attacked as well and require special protection. In many airports El Al is the only airline where security personnel, both Israeli and local, specifically protect the travelers. Terrorist attacks have taken place over the past decades on Israeli planes and at various airports.

A few examples will illustrate this. On December 27, 1985, there were terrorist attacks at the Leonardo da Vinci Airport in Rome and the Schwechat Airport in Vienna. Thirteen people were killed in the Rome attack and seventy-six injured. Three of the terrorists were killed by Israeli security staff.

At the Vienna airport on the same day, terrorists attacked the ticket counters of El Al. Two Austrian passengers and an Israeli were killed and forty-four people were injured. After Israeli security guards and Austrian police gave chase, one terrorist was killed and two were wounded. In 2002, an Egyptian terrorist killed two at the El Al counter at the Los Angeles International Airport.[9]

Entebbe

The best-known airline attack by terrorists against Israelis and Jews abroad involved a foreign airline. An Air France flight left Tel Aviv on July 27, 1976 for

Paris. It was hijacked by pro-Palestinian terrorists after an intermediate stop in Athens and flown to Entebbe in Uganda. An Israeli-army rescue mission ended the hostage crisis. Several hostages were killed as well as IDF officer Yonatan Netanyahu, brother of current Israeli Prime Minister Benjamin Netanyahu.[10]

Israeli tourist groups have also been attacked abroad on various occasions. In 2002 in Mombasa, Kenya, terrorists fired shoulder-launched missiles at an Israeli passenger plane. They missed their target. Shortly afterward, three suicide bombers detonated explosives close to the Israeli-owned Paradise Hotel there. Twelve people, primarily Kenyans and the three terrorists, were killed and dozens were wounded.[11] In February 2012, four Iranian suspects were arrested in Thailand for explosions targeting Israeli nationals.

In 2012, two terrorists carried out a bus bombing in Burgas, Bulgaria. Five Israelis and a Bulgarian bus driver were killed, and thirty-two Israelis were wounded. Later the Bulgarian government published names of two terrorists who were Lebanese citizens; one of them also had Canadian and the other Australian citizenship. There are strong indications that Hizbullah was behind the bombing.[12]

Sports

Sport is an area where Israelis have been affected in many ways for a long time. It should therefore be analyzed separately. In various sports, Israel is excluded from Asian competitions. It has instead, however, been welcomed in various European competitions, including for soccer and basketball. Israeli sportsmen and trainers have been actively recruited abroad. An estimated forty Israeli soccer players played for teams abroad as of 2012.[13]

Individual Israeli players have been excluded from some international competitions.[14] In February 2009, internationally-ranked Israeli tennis player Shahar Peer was refused a visa to the United Arab Emirates for the Women's Tennis Association (WTA) Tour. Emirati officials cited "security concerns" following Israel's Operation Cast Lead in Gaza. In response to this unprecedented measure in the world of tennis, the WTA stipulated that Dubai could only stage tournaments with written confirmations that they would issue visas for all Israeli athletes.[15]

Peer also faced hostility for being an Israeli in New Zealand only a month before being excluded from the WTA Tour in Dubai. In January 2009, she faced a "small but noisy" protest of about twenty people against Operation Cast Lead outside of a stadium where she played in Auckland. Peer rejected calls to withdraw from the tournament. In her words, "I am not the government of Israel and I am not representing Israel in politics. I am a tennis player and that's what I represent now."[16]

Violence in Sports

Aggression and insults have often been directed at Israeli teams and players in Europe. A much-publicized murderous case was the killing of eleven Israeli athletes by Palestinian terrorists at the Munich 1972 Olympics.[17]

Israeli players and teams have been assaulted abroad on a number of occasions. One large-scale incident took place in Turkey's capital Ankara in January 2009 at the time of Israel's Cast Lead campaign. The Israeli basketball team Bnei Hasharon was supposed to play against the local club Turk Telekom.

Before the game started, many of the three thousand Turkish fans shouted "Allah Akbar" (God is great). Some fans threw bottles at the Israeli players and stormed onto the court, forcing the Israeli players to flee to the dressing rooms.[18]

In July 2013, Austrian police canceled a friendly soccer game between Maccabi Tel Aviv and the German team Energie Cottbus. In this case the threats came from extreme rightists.[19]

During Operation Protective Edge, the Israeli Maccabi Haifa soccer team was attacked in Austria by Turkish hooligans.[20] In Poland, near Warsaw, the Israeli Ashdod soccer team was attacked by skinheads.[21]

The under-nineteen players of Maccabi Netanya were insulted by shouts during a game in Dortmund, Germany. Fourteen neo-Nazis shouted "Jews out of Palestine," "Never again, Israel," "Israel: international murder center of people" and waved the Palestinian and Nazi flags until the police removed them from the stadium.[22]

Academics

Various actions in the academic domain have affected Israel and Israeli academics. Although some wide-ranging boycotts have been announced, these are mainly cases that affect individuals rather than Israeli academia at large.

In April 2013, the Teachers Union of Ireland (TUI) became the first European educational trade union to call for an academic boycott of Israel. It was to include "the exchange of scientists, students and academic personalities as well as cooperation in research programs."[23]

In 2013, similar efforts intensified in the United States with three organizations deciding to sever links with Israeli academic institutions. These were the Association for Asian American Studies, the American Studies Association, and the Native American and Indigenous Studies Association (NAISA). The practical impact of these actions remains limited.

Publications

There have been some reports of academic journals refusing to publish articles by Israeli scholars. *The Guardian* wrote in 2002 about Professor Oren Yiftachel, a left-wing Israeli academic at Ben-Gurion University who has made extreme anti-Israeli statements such as, "Israel is almost the most segregated society in the world." He submitted an article that was coauthored with an Arab scholar, Dr. Asad Ghanem of the University of Haifa, to the left-leaning journal *Political Geography*.

Yiftachel had claimed to *The Guardian* that his article was returned unopened, with a note attached explaining that the journal could not accept a submission from Israel.[24] In a subsequent clarification, *The Guardian* reported that *Political Geography*'s editor had asked for revisions and thereafter would have referred the article for review without guaranteeing that it would be published.[25]

Similar difficulties may affect authors who are not willing to distort their work so as to make it more pro-Palestinian. Publishers have many ways to compel authors to compromise on the truth. American psychologist Steven Baum relates that he had proposed his book *Antisemitism Explained* to Cambridge University Press. In one chapter he illustrated how Muslim propaganda had promoted hatred of Israel.

He recounts:

> While originally Cambridge University Press had liked the book, a new editor came in. He didn't like this explanation of the anti-Israel sentiment, even though it was consistent with the main theme of my book. He wanted me to focus on context, i.e., the Palestinian point of view. I asked what this had to do with a book on anti-Semitism. The reply came down to "fix it or walk." I did not want to distort my opinions, whereupon the editor rejected my book.

Baum added:

> Several other academics told me that they had a difficult time publishing articles which put Israel in a favorable light. I realized then that there were no academic journals which were specifically devoted to investigating anti-Semitism. Pro-Palestinian academics, however, encountered no such problems. By contrast there is a *Journal of Palestine Studies* which is available in many libraries.[26]

Yet another discriminatory action is the refusal of some anti-Israeli foreign academics to review works by Israeli scholars. Israeli universities often ask scholars abroad to review the work of Israeli academics with regard to promotion. Professor Paul Zinger, a former head of the Israel Science Foundation, told the *Sunday Telegraph* that about seven thousand research papers are sent out each year for review. In 2002, about twenty-five came back from scholars who refused to look at them.[27] Similarly there are efforts to convince academics not to visit Israel.

Another development is that Israelis are not invited to international conferences or to lecture at foreign universities. In Italy, David Meghnagi of Rome 3 University organized a group of hundreds of Italian academics who see to it that a certain number of Israeli scholars are invited each year to teach at Italian universities.[28]

There are some known cases of academics refusing to publish in Israeli publications. In 2006, for instance, Professor Richard Seaford of Exeter University refused to review a book for the Israeli journal *Scripta Classica Israelica*.[29]

The April 2002 letter in *The Guardian* organized by the Rose couple was the first public call in Europe to discriminate against Israel. Its aim was to prevent Israeli academics from obtaining grants. Whether it has had any impact is not known.

Sometimes on campus there are campaigns to get university foundations to divest from Israeli securities, or from those of American suppliers of weapons to Israel. This is a particularly American phenomenon.

The impact of anti-Israeli academic-boycott activities is unknown. Those who instigate them know that they mainly have a public relations effect. However, the longer they continue, the more the anti-Israelism also penetrates into academic society.

The Economic Area

There are boycott attempts against Israeli firms abroad, people who sell Israeli goods, or supply to Israel. Many of these attempts are primarily against firms in the disputed territories, but this is far from exclusive. No overview of these anti-Israeli activities exists. Much information can, however, be gained from various BDS websites.

One firm that has suffered from this is Ahava Cosmetics, an Israeli firm located in Mitzpe Shalem in the West Bank. In 2011, for instance, it had to close its London store because of frequent activity by pro-Palestinian boycotters.[30] In 2012, the major Norwegian pharmaceutical retail firm VITA stopped selling its products.[31]

Another firm located in the territories that is often subject to boycott attacks is SodaStream. Companies and shops that sell Israeli products are also targets of violence. The United Church of Canada, for instance, has called for the boycott of products of Ahava, SodaStream, and Keter Plastics.[32]

Music and Other Performances

The issue of artistic boycotts of Israel has two major aspects. First, there is increasing pressure on international artists not to perform in Israel. Second, Israeli artists and their audiences face aggressions and pressures by boycott advocates when these artists perform abroad.

Individual international artists who choose to perform in Israel face boycott pressures. When singer Alicia Keys made the decision to perform in Israel, writer and BDS activist Alice Walker responded with an open letter urging her to cancel her performance. However, Keys ignored pressures and continued with her scheduled concert. Other international musicians like Bon Jovi and the Pixies have bowed to intimidation by BDS activists and canceled concerts.[33] The Pixies, however, decided in June 2014 to ignore BDS pressures and perform in Tel Aviv.[34]

Israeli artists also feel these pressures when performing abroad. On March 15, 2013, pro-Palestinian vuvuzela-blowing protesters stormed a concert and interrupted a performance by Israeli-born pianist Yossi Reshef in Johannesburg. Although Reshef has been living abroad for many years and has given recitals across the globe, protesters accused this recital of being an intentional rejoinder to Israel Apartheid Week, coincidentally occurring at the same time. They claimed this concert was "a direct attempt to undermine the campaign."[35]

The Israeli Batsheva Dance Company faced a similar fate during their performances in the United Kingdom. Although they were not outright banned from appearing at the 2012 Edinburgh Fringe Festival, the renowned and well-reviewed contemporary dance company performed to half-empty houses. Performances were also interrupted by protesters. In one case at the festival, protesters interrupted a performance four times with chants of "Free Palestine."[36] Notwithstanding Batsheva choreographer Ohad Naharin's statement that he is "in disagreement" with his government, the troupe has been protested against globally merely for its nationality.[37] In other words, the choreographer could learn from this that he was not heckled for what he thought, but for what he was.

Israeli groups were similarly boycotted at the Edinburgh Fringe Festival in the summer of 2014. A Jerusalem-based theater company and Ben-Gurion

University's dance troupe were forced to cancel performances at the festival. Protesters claimed that they were targeting these performances and not two other Israeli ones at the festival because they received public funding from Israel.[38]

Protests against Israeli musicians abroad have occasionally grown so threatening that some Israeli musicians have even had to cancel performances out of safety concerns. In June 2011 award-winning composer Yuval Ron, whose musical ensemble includes Christian and Muslim members, had to cancel an Istanbul concert because of death threats. Some of these threats were allegedly connected to the IHH Humanitarian Relief Foundation, the Turkish NGO that led the 2010 Gaza flotilla.[39]

In 2010, a Jewish dance group was attacked while performing during a street festival in Hanover, Germany. Members of the Haverim dance group were pelted with stones as they took the stage, and one dancer was injured. The youthful stone-throwers screamed "Juden raus!" (Jews out). Six suspects ranging in age from nine to nineteen were identified; five of the six were Muslims.[40]

Brand Israel was a campaign launched by the Israeli Foreign Ministry. Although it succeeded in attracting some positive attention to Israel, it also served as a rallying cry for Israel's opponents, leading to protests against pro-Israeli events. This included both Foreign Ministry-sponsored events and some that were not, like the 2009 Toronto International Film Festival, which highlighted Israeli achievement in film.[41]

Legal Action Against Israelis

On various occasions, attempts have been made to cause the arrest of Israeli authorities or former officials on the basis of alleged war-crime accusations against them. Court cases have also been brought.

The most far-reaching legal case concerned then-Prime Minister Ariel Sharon. In June 2001, a number of survivors and family members of Palestinian victims of the 1982 murders by Lebanese Christians in the Sabra and Shatila refugee camps submitted a complaint to a Belgian court under the country's universal-jurisdiction law. It was not, however, directed against the Lebanese murderers, many of whom had been identified. The claim was instead against Sharon, defense minister during the 1982 First Lebanon War; Rafael Eitan, chief of staff during the war; and Amos Yaron, head of Northern Command during the war.

Irit Kohn was head of the International Department of the Israeli Justice Ministry at the time and led the Israeli defense team. She recounted:

> This complaint seemed a politically motivated act. The complainants waited until Sharon became prime minister of Israel. They wanted to subject him to criminal prosecution for alleged war crimes. They claimed that as Sharon was Israeli defense minister in 1982 and collaborated with the Christian militias, he should have known that if they came to the Palestinian refugee camps, there would be a massacre.[42]

Contrary to the expectations of Sharon's Belgian lawyers, the process went ahead. In its course, however, in 2003 a further complaint was brought under Belgium's universal-jurisdiction law against former U.S. President George Bush, Sr., then-Secretary of State Colin Powell, and retired General Norman Schwarzkopf concerning the Gulf War in Iraq. The United States thereupon informed the Belgian government that if the process were to go ahead, NATO's headquarters would be moved away from Brussels.

Kohn observed that the Belgian parliament

> rushed to change the law, and amendments to it were passed that would create obstacles for future plaintiffs. These included provisions that a plaintiff or victim would have lived in Belgium for three years. There would also have to be real linkage between the alleged crime and Belgian interests and several other such clauses.

Kohn remarked:

> Initially they wanted to exclude the United States from the universal law but not the three Israelis. Till the last moment there was a major Belgian parliamentarian effort to retain the original complaint as to them having committed a war crime. That, however, would have proved that the entire motivation of the process against Sharon was political. It would also have shown that the

Belgian parliament could legislate against a particular country, which would have publicly revealed their one-sidedness toward Israel. In the end they also understood that such a move would not hold up judicially.[43]

Arrest Warrants

On a number of occasions, attempts were made to arrest leading Israelis abroad. For example, in 2008 a British district judge ordered the arrest of General (res.) Doron Almog. Having arrived in London, he decided to remain in the El Al plane and returned to Israel.[44]

In 2009, a British court issued an arrest warrant for Tzipi Livni concerning her responsibility for alleged war crimes while she was Israel's foreign minister during Operation Cast Lead in Gaza that year. The warrant was later withdrawn when it turned out that she was not in the UK.[45] Similarly, in 2011 an arrest warrant was issued against former Israeli Defense Minister Amir Peretz. It was withdrawn when he supposedly canceled his trip; he came to the UK later on.[46] In 2011, Israeli General (res.) Danny Rothschild broke off a visit to London after the Israeli embassy warned him he was in danger of being arrested if he remained in the UK.[47]

In 2010, Intelligence and Atomic Energy Minister Dan Meridor canceled a planned visit to London. The Israeli Foreign Ministry and the Justice Ministry warned Meridor that he might face an arrest warrant connected to his alleged role in the IDF raid on the Gaza-bound ship *Mavi Marmara* earlier that year.[48]

In 2014, Karmi Gilon, former director of the Israel Security Agency (Shin Bet), left Denmark after a police complaint was filed against him. It was unclear what the consequences would be. The Danish legal authorities decided to reject the complaint.[49]

In 2010 the Israeli Reut Institute stated that in the UK, the Netherlands, Spain, Belgium, and Norway, a network of lawyers existed that aimed to compile a list of IDF officers who should be charged with war crimes. The sources for this information apparently came from pro-Palestinian activists who track invitations extended by pro-Israeli organizations abroad to IDF officials and Israeli politicians.[50]

Concealed Boycotts

The abovementioned cases were all in the public domain. Yet unofficial or concealed boycotts also exist. Little is known about them because the boycotters do not announce them, or give reasons other than the real ones for their actions. This was a common phenomenon under the initial Arab economic boycott. Investment proposals involving Israeli firms and projects, or collaborations, were suggested to Western firms. When they were turned down by such firms wishing to comply with the boycott, they often gave a variety of reasons other than their main motivation.

This is a subject to be studied in more detail. This author experienced several cases of this firsthand in the last decades of the previous century.

Almost a decade ago, this author was told by several Israeli academics that some colleagues abroad with whom they had long-term contacts had severed them without explanation. In 2002, Hebrew University lecturer Aaron Benavot was quoted saying there was anecdotal evidence of this type of boycott. Two colleagues in the Geography Department, for example, received a letter from the section editor of an international journal who said he was unable to consider their papers because he was a signatory to the boycott. Another Israeli scholar in London was told by his coordinator that he could "foresee problems" with colleagues in Europe if the Israeli joined an EU-funded research team.[51]

Miscellaneous

There are also various issues that do not come under any of the aforementioned headings. The Tricycle Theater in London, longtime host of the UK Jewish Film Festival, decided to rescind its role as the festival venue in the summer of 2014. In light of Operation Protective Edge, the theater asked the festival to "not accept funding from any party to the current conflict." The festival instead searched for alternative venues, refusing to decline a grant it receives from the Israeli embassy in London. The Tricycle Theater later withdrew this demand, but the 2014 festival was still held elsewhere.[52]

The sole MP from the British Respect Party, George Galloway, was interviewed by police in August 2014 after complaints over a speech he gave. In it he stated, "We don't want any Israeli goods, we don't want any Israeli services, we don't want any Israeli academics coming to the university or the college, we don't even want any Israeli tourist in Bradford, even if any of them had thought of doing so."

This dispute escalated when, following these remarks, Israeli Ambassador to the UK Daniel Taub visited Bradford and met with local Jewish leaders. According to the embassy, Taub arrived at their invitation despite Galloway's assertions that he was unwelcome.[53]

The Impact of Anti-Israeli Actions

All in all, the combined impact of various anti-Israeli actions is not huge so far. This may change in the future if counteractions by Israel and its allies remain haphazard instead of systematic.

Anti-Israeli actions have, however, a number of other aspects. The boycotts receive publicity, which often damages Israel's image. They are even frequently undertaken mainly for their public relations aspects rather than to make an actual impact.

For some corporations and individuals, however, divestments and boycotts may be more problematic than for Israeli society at large. Sometimes, but far from always, they turn into an occasion to mobilize Israel's friends. The potential of this is rarely fully utilized.

CHAPTER TWENTY

Those Who Fight Against the Demonization

THE FIGHT AGAINST ANTI-SEMITISM HAS been waged for a long time. Established Jewish organizations have been active in this field for decades. Some are international such as the World Jewish Congress, which created a European associate, the European Jewish Congress a number of years ago. Nowadays the two seem to operate rather independently of each other.

Another one is B'nai B'rith International. Yet others are American organizations that are also active internationally. The two major ones that go back well before prewar days are the Anti-Defamation League and the American Jewish Committee. The Simon Wiesenthal Center joined them a few decades ago. Much information on the activities of these well-known organizations can be found on their websites.[1]

Many other organizations fighting and exposing anti-Semitism have a national character. An important example is the Community Security Trust, the defense organization of British Jewry. Such organizations exist in several countries. Sometimes the fight against anti-Semitism is dealt with by an umbrella body of the national Jewish community or its associates.

The rapid increase in anti-Israelism and the recognition of its major anti-Semitic aspects has led to many organizations having added this issue to their activities. Sometimes the reverse has also taken place. In the Netherlands, CIDI was founded to serve as an Israel defense and information organization. With the increase of anti-Semitic incidents in the country over the past decade, the fight against anti-Semitism has become an important activity for it.

Of a different nature yet important in the exposure of Arab hate-mongering by documenting it, is the Middle East Media Research Institute (MEMRI), founded in 1998. Its focus is global and not confined to the Palestinian-Israeli conflict. It translates media material from the Arab world into English, and occasionally from other Muslim countries as well. MEMRI also deals with the two Palestinian entities. One also finds case studies at MEMRI on specific issues in several Arab and Muslim countries. Its website provides much informative material.

Grassroots Organizations

The rapid growth in anti-Israeli activity has led over the past decades to the emergence of grassroots organizations that fight this trend. Most of them have specific targets. They mainly combat one type of anti-Israelism in their specific country.

It is impossible to give an overview of all the organizations in the various fields. A few examples will illustrate how such organizations function. This can best be done by analyzing them according to categories of perpetrators of anti-Israelism and anti-Semitism.

Several grassroots organizations view spreading information about Israel as a major task. One example is StandWithUs, an international nonprofit organization that was founded in 2001 and says it believes that "education is the road to peace."

It writes about itself:

> StandWithUs is dedicated to informing the public about Israel and to combating the extremism and anti-Semitism that often distorts the issues. We believe that knowledge of the facts will correct common prejudices about the Arab-Israeli conflict, and will promote discussions and policies that can help promote peace in the region. Through print materials, speakers, programs, conferences, missions to Israel, campaigns, and internet resources,

> we ensure that the story of Israel's achievements and ongoing challenges is told on campuses and in communities, the media, libraries, and churches around the world.

Based in Los Angeles, StandWithUs has offices across the United States and in various countries abroad, including Israel.

To those who want to combat anti-Israeli activity in their own communities, StandWithUs offers the services of its professional staff members and volunteers. It says that it will work with students on college and university campuses throughout North American to provide them with training and education, resources, and funding for events.[2]

Media Watching

As biased anti-Israeli media hold such a prominent place in the demonization of Israel, the monitoring of media bias has acquired a prominent place in the fight against anti-Israelism. The more general organizations fighting anti-Israelism and anti-Semitism frequently criticize the media, but they often do not do so systematically.

Currently, several organizations monitor the foreign media's reporting on Israel-related matters systematically. Most pro-Israeli media watchers write in English and mainly deal with media in that language. There are also some in other languages. Already in the mid-1970s Si Kenen, editor of the AIPAC-affiliated, Washington-based *Near East Report*, initiated a media-monitoring column titled "The Monitor."[3]

Pro-Israeli media monitors typically have several of the following characteristics:

- They focus on the Arab-Israeli conflict.
- They supply otherwise inaccessible information—for instance, from Arabic sources —to policymakers and stimulate activists to react to the media concerned. Their ultimate aim is to remove the media bias.
- They have websites where their material is published.

- They regularly publish their findings, either on their website or via emails to their subscribers.
- Media watchers may speak behind the scenes to a media organization that has published biased material and seek to reach an agreement.
- Some also lobby foreign governments and authorities.[4]

These monitors have also become a counterweight to pro-Palestinian media watchers who claim that the media is biased against the Palestinians.

Among the major pro-Israeli media watchers are CAMERA and HonestReporting. Both organizations search for inaccurate information in coverage of Israel, or doctored photos incorrectly portraying Israelis—particularly the IDF.

CAMERA also operates a second website, *Camera on Campus*, and a blog called *In Focus*. Both of these sites focus on correcting falsified information demonizing Israel that is disseminated on college campuses. These internet resources also offer students one-on-one assistance in directly combating anti-Israeli bias on campus. CAMERA covers a wide range of media in the United States and is also active to some extent outside of it. It methodically monitors TV, radio, and newspapers and obtains part of its "media raw material" by subscribing to databases. CAMERA places advertisements in newspapers and frequently issues requests to its email lists of thousands of activists to send letters and op-eds to the media.

HonestReporting grew out of a private British initiative after the second Palestinian uprising began. In 2001, it became an independent foundation. It has defined seven categories of media bias: misleading definitions and terminology, unbalanced reporting, opinions disguised as news, lack of context, selective omission, using true facts to draw untrue conclusions, and distortion of facts.

Because of the anti-Israel campaigns, pro-Israeli media watching has also become an example for general media watching. As so many media are biased, there is a need for systematic media watching in many places on multiple issues, unrelated to the Arab world. Thus this pro-Israeli media watching can serve as a model for other monitoring groups that are unrelated to the Palestinian-Israeli conflict or to Jews.

Individual Media Watchers

There have been and still are individual media watchers as well. One of the early ones was the late David Bar-Illan, former editor of *The Jerusalem Post*.[5] Nowadays Tom Gross regularly informs about the media.[6] Individual studies have also been undertaken on specific media. A prominent example is Asserson's multiple studies on the BBC's manifold biases. Others include analyses of the Australian daily *The Age*,[7] the *Philadelphia Inquirer*,[8] and the French press agency L'Agence France Presse.[9]

Over the past decades various individuals have made important contributions to pro-Israeli media watching. Sergio Minerbi, former Israeli ambassador to the European Community, analyzed six documentaries focusing on the Middle East of the French-speaking Belgian TV station RTBF from 1979 to 1982. In 1985, his findings were published in a book.[10]

In 1987, Henry Weinberg devoted an entire chapter of his book *The Myth of the Jew in France* to the anti-Israeli bias of the French leftwing daily *Le Monde*.[11] In 1980 this leading French paper had published an article by the academic M.L. Snoussi, titled "Double Nationality, Double Allegiance," which "openly leveled the charge of treason against French Jewry." Weinberg remarked that the article "contained phrases which in other democratic countries would be considered as incitement to racial violence."

After terrorists bombed a synagogue on Rue Copernic in Paris in October 1980, *Le Monde* published an article by Jean-Marie Paupert on its front page. Weinberg noted that it was full of anti-Semitic clichés. *Le Monde* at the time already used several of the techniques that have become so familiar today. Much of its coverage of the Middle East was assigned to pro-Arab Jewish journalists. Frequently when citing Israeli "sources," they quoted Israeli extremists such as Felicia Langer, Uri Avneri, and Matityahu Peled without mentioning their isolation from the Israeli mainstream.

Weinberg summed this up by saying that the paper expressed "consistently unfair and excessive criticism of the Jewish state and made for the acceptance of anti-Semitic expression as a legitimate means of public debate."[12]

NGOs

NGO Monitor analyzes the international NGO community. The organization's primary goals, as postulated in its mission statement, are to provide information and analysis, promote accountability, and support discussion of the reports and activities of NGOs claiming to advance human rights and humanitarian agendas.

NGO Monitor achieves these goals by producing reports and analyses of NGO bias. In particular, it exposes NGOs working in the Middle East that often distort "universal human rights" to promote partisan and ideological agendas not included in their mission statements.[13]

The organization also states that it aims to "end the practice used by certain self-declared 'humanitarian NGOs' of exploiting the label 'universal human rights values' to promote politically and ideologically motivated agendas."[14]

NGO Monitor's monograph series, which is not only devoted to issues concerning Israel, includes titles such as: *Second Class Rights: How Amnesty International & Human Rights Watch Fail Women in the Middle East*; *NGO Malpractice: The Political Abuse of Medicine, Morality, and Science*; *Spanish Government Funding for NGOs: 2009-2011—Assessing Transparency, Accountability, and Impact on Israel*; *NGO "Lawfare": Exploitation of Courts in the Israeli-Arab Conflict*; *The Politics of Canadian Government Funding for Advocacy NGOs*.[15]

Muslims

A number of organizations watch and expose negative developments in the world of Islam. They usually do not focus on matters concerning Israel specifically, though they may mention hate attacks against Israel or Jews.

One organization that specifically addresses Palestinian hate-mongering is Palestinian Media Watch (PMW). It was established in 1996. PMW monitors the Palestinian Arabic-language media and scrutinizes the Palestinian Authority's culture and society from many perspectives, including studies on summer camps, poetry, schoolbooks, religious ideology, crossword puzzles, and much else. As it is so common in Palestinian and other Arab societies to make radically different statements in Arabic and, to foreign audiences, in English, PMW sees documenting these disparities as an important task.

PMW has exposed the fact that, although the PA appears to recognize Israel's existence to foreign media, it does not do so in its domestic media or school systems. Another example of PMW's activities is that it has exposed internationally a video of a song that was taught on children's shows aired on PA state TV on eight different occasions. This song names Israeli cities as being part of "greater Palestine."[16] In addition, PMW has translated Palestinian schoolbooks that call all of Israel "Palestine" and make no mention of Israel's right to exist.[17]

Academics

The main international group acting against academic demonization of Israel is Scholars for Peace in the Middle East (SPME). It was founded in 2002. SPME strives to counter the anti-Semitism and anti-Israelism that now pervade college campuses globally, especially in "intellectual debate" and in the classroom. SPME strives for academic discourse on the Middle East in which Israel is acknowledged as a sovereign Jewish state that needs secure borders. In addition to fighting distortions about Israel in classrooms, SPME also tries to stop anti-Semitic and anti-Israeli events on campuses.[18]

Its cofounder and first president, Edward Beck, considered that one of SPME's major achievements was the signing by more than ten thousand academics from over one thousand institutions worldwide of a statement written by Professor Alan Dershowitz and Nobel Laureate Steven Weinberg, which expressed solidarity with Israeli academics. Among the signatories were thirty-three Nobel Laureates and fifty-eight college and university presidents. Its essence was: "if one boycotts Israeli academics and professionals, one boycotts us."[19]

Later, SPME played a major role with the same approach in the fight against the proposed boycott of Israeli academia by the Norwegian University of Science and Technology (NTNU) in Trondheim, Norway. On this issue it also mobilized thousands of academics and a number of Nobel Prize winners who made a similar statement.

The Fight Against Academic Bias

For a few years in the past decade, Bar-Ilan University was active in fighting foreign boycott attempts against Israeli universities. It also had a Bar-Ilan University-based International Advisory Board for Academic Freedom (IAB).

In 2007, a full-page ad sponsored by the American Jewish Committee was published in *The New York Times* in which close to three hundred American university and college presidents stated that they would not work with institutions that were boycotting Israeli academics. The ad said, "Boycott Israeli Universities? Boycott Ours, Too."[20] Later the number of signatories rose to over 450. Over twenty Canadian universities came out against the boycott as well.

Another organization that advocates for the Jewish people and Israel, particularly on university campuses in North America, is the Louis D. Brandeis Center for Human Rights Under Law. Following in the first Jewish Supreme Court justice's legacy, this center says about its mission and values that it "will provide the research resources, public policy education, and legal advocacy needed to fight this battle within the broader context of the pursuit of universal principles of justice."[21] Some of the Center's publications include a *Best Practices Guide for Combating Anti-Semitism and Anti-Israelism* and *Anti-Semitism and the Campus Left*. It also created law-student chapters at select American law schools.[22]

Israel Academia Monitor (IAM) monitors Israeli academics, exposing Israeli academics at Israeli universities who abuse their positions by condemning Israeli actions or defaming their own universities. IAM states that it "publicizes the actions of these individuals through their website and the advocate measures [sic] that will harm Israel in general and their universities in particular by using unbalanced prejudiced arguments that fail to live up to the scholarship standards expected of the universities they represent."[23]

Fighting Bias in Schoolbooks

IMPACT-SE, the Institute for Monitoring Peace and Cultural Tolerance in School Education, is an Israeli organization that "endeavors to present a clear picture of how different countries instruct and educate their youth with regard to different religions, societies, cultures, democratic values and the 'other.'"[24]

Their work primarily focuses on counteracting and publicizing fallacious information about Israel published in Middle Eastern textbooks. For example, IMPACT-SE publicized that a Palestinian textbook teaches students that Hitler was a role model.[25]

The Institute for Curriculum Services is a small American initiative that promotes accuracy on Jews, Judaism, and Israel in American primary and secondary schools. To do this, they focus on textbooks and teachers. Their website says: "ICS is dedicated to promoting accurate instructional material and instruction on Jews, Judaism, and Israel for American K-12 students. Its work impacts the millions of public and private school students who learn about Jews, Judaism, and Israel in social studies classes each year."[26]

Legal Action

The Israel Law Center (Shurat HaDin) is a grassroots organization that initiates legal actions on behalf of Israel and others. It was established in 2003. Shurat HaDin says that it combats hatred toward Israel by exposing and financially weakening global terrorists, many of whom are intent on destroying Israel. It sees itself as an Israeli-based civil rights organization and legal-aid fund that tries to fight terror.

The organization assists in the "War on Terror" by pursuing legal action against terror organizations and representing the victims of terror on a global scale. In addition, they also pursue legal action against banks and other organizations that may be assisting terror groups financially. Shurat HaDin also works to educate the public about terror funding through educational speaker series, publications, and missions that it sponsors.

Part of Shurat HaDin's mission statement reads:

> We tend to think of the fight against terrorism as a burden that falls mainly on the shoulders of government—our military, diplomatic, homeland security, and law-enforcement agencies. Yet there is one area where private citizens can play

> a leading role: In stopping the flow of funds to terror organizations. Beginning in the 1990s, Western countries, and especially the United States, passed laws making it possible for victims of terror to sue the regimes that sponsor terror, banks that transfer funds to terror groups, front organizations that pretend to serve charitable causes, and even the terrorists themselves. For the first time, terror victims and their families have a chance to fight back through the courts.

The organization claims that it has attained over $1 billion in judgments against terrorist organizations and state sponsors, the freezing of $600 million in terror assets, and $120 million in recoveries on behalf of victims or their families.[27]

Exposing Christian Hate-Mongering

In several other important areas of the anti-Israeli propaganda war, no organizations are active systematically. CAMERA has activities in the fight against Christian hate-mongers and anti-Israeli boycotters. Its analyst Dexter van Zile is an expert in this field. While his expertise mainly concerns the United States, he has also published on anti-Israelism in the World Council of Churches and the Sabeel organization.[28]

An expert in the field at the Simon Wiesenthal Center, Rabbi Yitzchok Adlerstein, also exposes Christian anti-Semitism mainly in the United States.[29]

NGO Monitor's expert Yitzhak Santis has also published analyses of various Christian Israel-hate NGOs, including several Catholic ones.[30]

In view of the major role of Christians in hate propaganda against Israel, this is one of the areas where the absence of a more systematic pro-Israeli monitoring body is heavily felt. Other areas where this is the case are trade-union anti-Israeli incitement and the systematic monitoring of high schools, a domain where the anti-Semites and Israel-haters of the future may be educated.

CHAPTER TWENTY-ONE

How to Combat Demonization of Israel

THE ANTI-ISRAELI PROPAGANDA WAR HAS been waged for decades already. Its intensity has greatly increased in the new century. Demonization events and incidents are now reported by the Israel media almost daily. One is continuously reminded of this war as well as of the frequent shortcomings of Israel's reactions. Yet there is no Israeli organizational structure that is capable of overseeing the battlefield, let alone one that combats incitement abroad as well as anti-Semitism in a systematic way. This is despite the fact that the war of a million cuts has been raging for so long.

Such an overview of the battlefield would involve understanding who Israel's most dangerous hate-mongering enemies are, what their various modes of activity are, how their operations interrelate, what impact they have, and so on. Such an agency would also assess and develop the best ways of combating the aggressors and guiding Israel's allies on how they can help fight the enemy.

No other country is confronted with a propaganda onslaught of such magnitude. One occasionally hears that the situation of the United States during the Vietnam War was somewhat similar. This is a misleading comparison. The most extreme opponents of the United States aimed to get it out of Vietnam, not to destroy it. Ultimately the Americans withdrew from Vietnam and left the South Vietnamese to their fate. With the disbandment of the Soviet Union, the biggest force of the anti-American propaganda war collapsed.

There is no similar "solution" for Israel. Many of Israel's enemies want "Israel out of Israel." Some want to do this by genocide. Others prefer a "one-state solution," combined with flooding the country with Palestinian refugees and their huge number of non-refugee offspring. It is thus essential to establish an Israeli organization for fighting the global propaganda war as quickly as possible.

Over the course of past centuries, entities that were attacked always developed fitting, often innovative tools to respond to the attacks. They usually analyzed the level, nature, and mindset of the attackers and the methods they used. Over time, new defensive and offensive methods were developed and became more sophisticated.

Structures in Battle

That is how armies developed over the centuries to fight military wars more effectively. Israel's army, the IDF, has become a relatively efficient organization if compared to other armies. Its development was a gradual process, employing trial-and-error approaches that led to improvements. Similarly over the decades, intelligence services evolved to fight terrorism and enemy intelligence. Israel's military and nonmilitary intelligence services—the IDF intelligence branch, the Mossad, and the Shin Bet—are considered among the best in the world.

Israel is also a major target of cyberattacks. There are increasing indications that the vulnerability of the global internet system is so vast that risks are huge. Israel has established a cyberwar unit and aims to become a world leader in this area as well.[1]

In January 2014, Netanyahu announced that a new cyberpark would be built in Beersheba called Cyber-Spark. He said it would be one of the world's most important places in the cybersecurity field. Furthermore, it was announced that the National Cyber Bureau and the Chief Scientist's Office have budgeted eighty million shekels over two years to support Israeli companies in the field.[2]

How a Structure Develops

Once one is heavily involved in a certain field, many more questions emerge for which answers have to be found. By analyzing those and finding solutions, the knowledge and experience in a field increases. This is also clearly the case in the development of Israel's cyberwarfare capabilities. It can serve as an example for the methodological future of the Israeli "contra-propaganda structure."

Israeli Colonel Sharon Afek published a text on the future of cyberwarfare and law that policymakers should make use of. He says that the challenges in this field lead to "a conceptual revolution." Afek notes among other things the need to redefine which actions are "offensive" and which are "defensive." Another question concerns which objects constitute "military targets" under law and which do not. He also observes that cyberwarfare means the difference between military and civilian operators may become blurred. Afek concludes that Israel must be involved and up-to-date in international-law developments concerning cyberwarfare and must also seek to influence these.[3]

Once a nation's leaders are aware of the importance of cyberwarfare and strongly support it, that also cross-fertilizes its industrial operations in the field. The major Israeli military contractor Israel Aerospace Industries (IAI) said that in 2013 it had expanded its activities in cyberdefense and started to work on solutions for clients in Israel and abroad.

Esti Peshin, director of IAI's cybersection, says that Israeli defense industries have to take the lead role so that Israel becomes independent in the field. She points out that cyberwarfare and intelligence activities are intermeshed. Peshin hints that while initially one focuses on defensive measures, ultimately offensive capabilities may also be developed. She also remarks that according to some experts, cyberwarfare may take a leading role in overall warfare.[4]

Diplomats and the Propaganda War

The above gives some conceptual guidance for an Israeli agency to fight the propaganda war. The incitement against Israel concerning alleged "atrocities" is only one of its many aspects. The current propaganda war is very different in nature from past propaganda wars, where nations were the main instigators.

Nowadays propaganda attacks against Israel by foreign governments—mainly Muslim ones, but also others—are only part of the total offensive. Many others come from a wide range of disparate sources. This fragmentation is part of the postmodern character of the anti-Israeli assaults.

One often hears that fighting the propaganda war is the task of the Israeli Foreign Ministry. This is a misjudgment of both the nature of the propaganda war and the aptitudes of diplomats. Professionals in this field must be able to maintain as good relations as possible with others, even if they are hostile. This requires dealing expertly with foreign governments and individuals without causing bad feelings. It often entails not mentioning the full truth or circumventing discussions on problematic issues. People who have these abilities are not very suitable to fight a propaganda war.

More recently, another area of the diplomats' role has developed: public diplomacy. This involves communicating with the public abroad so as to influence them to view the country the diplomats represent more favorably. A variety of tools have been developed for this purpose. One often hears that Israel should be more effective in its public diplomacy. That is true because many people abroad are uninformed but do not have a structured, hostile attitude toward Israel. Fighting the propaganda war, however, is a very different issue. There one does not mainly deal with the poorly informed but, rather, with one's enemies.

The Proposed Structure

The fact that nowhere else does a structure for fighting a propaganda war exist such as the one proposed here is not relevant. No other country in the world is exposed to a global propaganda onslaught as huge as the one against Israel. Israel has often had to develop tools and instruments of battle before anyone else, however unfortunate this may be.

Such an anti-propaganda-war agency would have to involve three major pursuits: research, monitoring, and "operations." The research branch would cover a number of areas. In far greater detail than what has been done in this book, it would have to investigate how the unprecedented total anti-Israeli propaganda war works. This includes analyzing the key motifs of demonization, where major attacks originate, investigating the main perpetrator categories in detail, the interaction between various perpetrator categories, how hatred is transmitted, and so on. Thereafter it would start investigating major enemy bodies. For instance, it would create profiles of leading anti-Israeli media, identifying the main hate promoters in these and their methods.

In other words, for Israel to expose and fight its multiple enemies, it would have to know much more about them than it presently does.In recent years several studies have delved into the methodology of specific aspects of the global propaganda war. Several people have occasionally made methodological observations. The anti-Israeli defamation and hate system is far from having been explored in its totality, however. For the research function, developing understanding about the structured and unstructured anti-Israeli incitement and how it mutates should be an ongoing project.

There is another activity that is not in itself part of the propaganda war yet must be dealt with. Medium and long-term societal and global developments have to be followed so as to discuss possible future impacts on Israel and the Jews. This would gradually enable the design of remedies before potential problems become acute. For instance, if this body had been in existence for some decades already, it would have had a far better understanding of the impact of globalization on Israel and the Jewish people than any current Israeli organization has. It would also have much better understood the nature of the battle for hearts and minds abroad.

Monitoring

A second branch of the proposed agency would have to monitor developments in the main areas of anti-Israelism and anti-Semitism. The overall situation has deteriorated to such an extent that new incidents of incitement and aggression against Israel and Jews are being reported on an almost daily basis.

Such monitoring should be done by specialists in various ways. One group would follow specific countries. Had there already been such a structure in place, the Norwegian hate-Israel movements and individual demonizers under the Norwegian Labour Party-dominated governments—which were in power from 2005 until 2013—would have been fought far more effectively. They would have had a much more difficult time bashing Israel if they had had to confront systematic counteractions. Israel has a number of friends in Norway who could have helped much better if there had been a powerful Israeli agency to advise them or consult with.

Another monitoring group would follow specific worldwide originators of hate. The work of specialists in areas such as media, Muslim countries, Muslims in the Western world, Christians, NGOs, trade unions, the extreme left, the fascist and neo-Nazi right, Socialist and Social Democratic parties, the lawfare operators, academics, schools and so on would afford Israel an overview of anti-Israeli and anti-Semitic activities within these global arenas.

A third monitoring group would follow specific types of incidents such as boycotts, divestments, sanctions, false accusations, applications of double standards, false moral equivalence, scapegoating, and other fallacies.

A major instrument for the monitoring section would be a "database of enemies" to be established. As soon as a new action of one of these organizations or persons would emerge, counteractions could be considered on the basis of the files on his past, including many of the data on his previous hateful actions. The initial database could be built from existing media reports and other publications.

The research and monitoring branches would initially have to make a major effort to integrate and assimilate know-how from the various organizations, grassroots and others, which are presently involved in the combat against anti-Israeli propaganda and anti-Semitism. Studies should also be undertaken of best practices applied by these organizations so as to avoid reinventing the wheel.

Operations and Activism

Activism is a delicate subject for a state-controlled body. Yet intelligence services of many countries are activist bodies under the aegis of the government. The operational branch of the new structure would have to develop increasingly effective methods to fight the anti-Israeli propaganda as well as anti-Semitism. It would have to assess which activities it undertakes itself and which should be left for others, such as other government services, nongovernmental bodies in Israel and abroad, or even some individuals.

One example of how Israeli government services and other organizations collaborated is the action taken before and during the Durban II Conference, which was held in Geneva in 2009. Because of the NGO Forum's hate characterization of Israel at Durban I in 2001, Israel, the United States, and seven other nations boycotted the 2009 Durban Review Conference.[5]

The Israeli Foreign Ministry together with many NGOs and other organizations had devised a campaign for that conference. The result was that the anti-Israeli racists in the antiracist NGO camp—which had been so successful during Durban I—remained at the margins of the conference. However, this battle only concerned one anti-Israeli hate activity, which was limited in time. The 2014 UNHRC commission that will investigate Operation Protective Edge, along with its biased chairman, should be exposed from the outset. The proposed structure would have to deal with all major ones.

To some extent, each major hate case should be studied specifically. This is a time-consuming yet necessary activity to develop effective actions against Israel's enemies.

Funding of the Fight Against Propaganda

There are no figures available on how much annual funding would be required for effectively fighting against the global propaganda war. Guesstimates deriving from some informal conversations with experts reached $200-$250 million per year. For lack of any professional assessment, one has to use this figure as the best estimate available.

Major monies should have been spent already for decades, starting at the latest with the 1982 Lebanon war. Israel is thus by now short of investment in the propaganda field, by several billion dollars.

Not all the funds to combat the delegitimization of Israel in a structured way should necessarily be provided by the Israeli government, even though the majority has to be made available by it. For instance, all the research and monitoring expenses could be carried by the government. As far as activism is concerned, part of the funding could come from private sources whose activities should then not be associated with the government.

A Few Basic Concepts

In the propaganda war, Israel has a structural advantage over its enemies. The ideological and actual criminality of leading political and other bodies in Palestinian society is so major that one only has to shine the spotlight on them to provide counterweight to the anti-Israeli incitement campaigns even before the proposed Israeli contra-propaganda structure is established and operational. There is no need to exaggerate; the Palestinian reality is bad enough.

Palestinian hate campaigns and ideological criminality should also be put in the context of the many atrocities and huge criminality in large parts of the Arab and Muslim world. With the expansion of the Islamic State movement this has reached new extremes. Major criminal phenomena are not limited to the Middle East but also go beyond it, such as in Afghanistan, Pakistan, and several African countries. In some of the latter, the extreme cruelty of the violence of other religious and ethnic groups seems to be in similar categories.

The propaganda campaigns by the Palestinians and other enemies of Israel include accusations about alleged Israeli "atrocities." Some of the crimes attributed to Israel are invented; others pale next to the criminal acts in segments of the Muslim world and elsewhere. Only by ongoing publicizing of the Palestinian, Arab, and Muslim atrocities, crimes against humanity, human rights violations, and so on can one gradually rebuild a more realistic picture of Israel's activities. The main target, however, should be the Palestinians.

Maximum exposure should be given to the widespread anti-Israeli incitement in Palestinian Authority government-controlled media, schools, sports activities, and so on. The PA's glorification of murderers of civilians should be highlighted. It should be stressed that the Palestinian Islamo-Nazi movement Hamas became the largest Palestinian party in the only Palestinian parliamentary elections ever held. Polls in 2014 after the Protective Edge campaign indicated that Gaza-based Hamas leader Ismail Haniyeh would be elected president of the Palestinian Authority if running against Mahmoud Abbas.[6]

The Palestinian Media Watch website provides much information on Palestinian criminality. The major hypocrisy of several leaders of the European Union, many of its member countries, and others in the West can also be exposed indirectly in this way.

Israel's leaders should, indeed, pause to wonder how they have let the Palestinians and their allies succeed in presenting the Palestinian criminals as radically different from the many villains in other Arab countries.

Several broad strategic principles for better conducting the battle against the propaganda war are outlined below. As noted previously, however, each major campaign or case of anti-Israeli incitement merits specific analysis.

No More Free Anti-Israeli Lunches

The first strategic principle is that there should be no more free anti-Israeli lunches for its enemies. Many countries, organizations, and individuals do not hesitate to attack Israel because they know that its reaction will often be weak or even nonexistent. This leads to a situation where the hate-mongerer against Israel believes he has little to lose. Israel has given frequent free anti-Israeli "lunches" to the European Union and many others. The weak Israeli reactions to the hate-mongering of Turkish President Erdogan are an extreme example.

Israel's ambassadors are regularly called in to be reprimanded by foreign ministers of European countries. Any such attacks on Israel should be answered by calling in ambassadors of these nations in Israel. It should be mentioned regularly in such situations that the combined incitement has led to a widespread criminal view of Israel in Europe. As pointed out in earlier chapters, this in turn indicates the criminal mindset of many Europeans. Another recurring issue is that the European countries and others do not meet their commitments under the UN Genocide Convention. This has been pointed out by former Canadian Justice Minister Irwin Cotler.[7]

At the same time, one can only wonder why Israel rarely attacks the term "occupied territories" with full force. There are many legal experts who contest this term and use "disputed territories" instead. There are also leading legal experts who support Israel's rights under international law to build and expand communities in these territories. The European Union's refusal to enter into a debate on this issue is an indication of the highly political and abusive nature of its battle against the settlements.

The often weak Israeli reactions to extreme Palestinian statements have led to a situation where in many circles the Palestinians' image greatly differs from that of Arab countries. Palestinians are often seen mainly as victims. This is at a time when the criminal ideology of the largest Palestinian faction, Hamas, includes incitement to genocide. The Palestinian Authority, Mahmoud Abbas himself, and other leaders practice the glorification of murderers. Many Westerners look away from this. This selective blindness and silence should be made more difficult for them. There are many who attack Israel and ignore Hamas's exterminatory agenda. These hate propagators should be exposed as indirect allies of a Palestinian Islamo-Nazi movement.

Offense Is the Best Defense

Related to the previous strategic principle is a second one: offense is the best defense. This approach is often applied in military, business, and political strategies. In the military field, for instance, it was applied in the 1973 Yom Kippur War when Israel was attacked by Egypt and Syria. After a few days of defense, the Israeli army crossed the Suez Canal and moved into Egypt.

In election campaigns in many countries, much of the publicity of parties and candidates involves attacking one's opponents in addition to presenting one's own plans. This is done because negative advertising has often been shown to be most effective.

Going on offense, rather than being on the defensive, is so important in the propaganda war because no one, however knowledgeable, can have all the information and answers available for the many claims—false or true—against Israel.

An interesting example of the application of this strategic principle concerns Russia and the Netherlands. Although Dutch governments and various other bodies in the country often condemn the behavior of others, Dutch postwar history is marked by extreme moral failures. Some of them concern the large-scale murders and war crimes by the Dutch military in what is now Indonesia.

The Russian Example

In 2013 during a visit to the Netherlands, Russia's President Vladimir Putin used the principle of "offense is the best defense" to deal with his hosts' criticism. Dutch Prime Minister Mark Rutte spoke with him on human rights and the status of sexual minorities in Russia. Putin not only reacted defensively by falsely stating that sexual minorities are not discriminated against in Russia; he then went on the attack by saying that the Netherlands has a pedophile club whereas Russia does not. Putin added that there is a Christian party in the Netherlands that forbids women to become parliamentarians, while all Russian parties are allowed to have female candidates.[8]

In 2014, the Russians went one step further. Their Foreign Ministry published a report on human rights in the European Union. The report included much criticism of the Netherlands. One aspect of it was that foreigners who stay in the Netherlands are continuously discriminated against. The report also mentioned the Russian Aleksandr Dolmatov, who in 2013 committed suicide in a detention center in Rotterdam. Dutch investigations revealed major failures in procedures concerning immigration and asylum.

The Russian report also expressed concern about the lack of protection against pedophiles in the Netherlands. It mentioned the Dutch pedophile organization Martijn, which has since been outlawed, and how a scandal involving a former senior bureaucrat accused of child abuse was whitewashed.[9]

The Ukrainian 2014 revolution and the Russian reactions to it have led to new frictions between Russia on the one hand and the European Union and the United States on the other. Here truth is taking a back seat to propaganda.

Israel cannot afford to use the same direct approach against European criticism as a major power like Russia. Yet it can develop the "offense is the best defense" principle in a far more sophisticated way.

Words Without Backup

One cannot conduct the propaganda war in an incidental way. At the 2014 UN General Assembly, Netanyahu said:

> Weeks before, some of these same countries, the same countries that now support confronting ISIS, opposed Israel for confronting Hamas. They evidently don't understand that ISIS and Hamas are branches of the same poisonous tree. ISIS and Hamas share a fanatical creed, which they both seek to impose well beyond the territory under their control.

Without an Israeli propaganda infrastructure that repeats this comparison and the one between Hamas with other genocidal Muslim movements regularly, such statements have little force.[10]

The same is true for many other statements by Netanyahu. For instance, after the U.S. State Department criticized Israel in October 2014 about building in East Jerusalem, Netanyahu said that it was such criticism, and not the building itself, that harmed the chances for peace with the Palestinians. In his words: "I have heard a claim that our construction in Jewish neighborhoods in Jerusalem makes peace more distant. It is the criticism which is making peace more distant. These words are detached from reality." He added that this criticism "foster[s] false statements among the Palestinians. When Abu Mazen [Palestinian Authority President Mahmoud Abbas] incites to murder Jews in Jerusalem, the international community is silent, and when we build in Jerusalem they are up in arms. I do not accept this double standard."[11]

Once again, Netanyahu was right, but Israel is without an apparatus to make this heard worldwide. That will enable the State Department to continue condemning Israel for building in Jerusalem and the territories while ignoring huge crimes occurring in many of the world's countries. Many more examples can be given that illustrate Israel's problems in this area.

The "Arab Spring" Killings

The falsely labeled "Arab Spring" has greatly increased the opportunity for Israel to go on offense. The present or recent mass murders and atrocities against various groupings in Libya, Syria, and Iraq provide almost unlimited material. To this can be added other Muslim countries where atrocities are common but murders are committed in lower numbers, such as Pakistan, Afghanistan, Somalia, Yemen, Sudan, Algeria, Tunisia, Egypt, and Lebanon.

One may add that a selection of these brutal crimes is probably a good indication of what invading Arab countries and their Palestinian allies would have done to Jewish citizens of Israel had they been successful in Israel's 1948 War of Independence or later battles. The fact that this may be politically incorrect in European eyes does not lessen its truth. To prove the point, one only needs to collect announcements of genocidal intentions from prominent Arabs before and during that war in 1948, as well as testimony from Israeli witnesses of the war on what they heard from the Arab side.

Exposing the Orwellian anti-Israelis and the lies and fallacies they use should be an ongoing endeavor. On campuses this can, for instance, be partly done by using mutations of the famous maxims from Orwell's book *1984*: "War is peace, freedom is slavery, ignorance is strength." The new version concerning foreign universities, as well as a number of teachers mainly in the humanities departments in some Israeli universities, could read: "Propaganda is advancing knowledge, indoctrination is higher education, incitement promotes scholarship."

Sunlight Is the Best Disinfectant

A third related principle is what one may call "sunlight is the best disinfectant." One aspect of it is continuous exposure, without comment, of negative developments in the Palestinian, Arab, and Muslim world. The same goes for certain groups of anti-Israeli inciters in the Western world.

One small example concerns a side issue to the murders by Norwegian criminal Anders Breivik in 2011. Because of the huge worldwide attention that these killings garnered, it slowly became known that there was extreme anti-Israeli incitement on the island of Utoya where Breivik killed most of his victims. A major activity of this camp of the Labour Party youth organization, AUF, was the demonization of Israel.

An example of a different type of exposure comes from the blog *Norway, Israel and the Jews*. This website in English has provided access to information concerning Jews and Israel in Norway for more than five years. Even though part of the website is commentary, much of it just offers facts. Hence it has also become an archive for the hatred, bias, double standards, and other incitement emanating from Norwegian politicians, trade unions, media, academics, church leaders, NGOs, and others in civil society.[12]

This can, for instance, be illustrated by the anti-Israeli boycott campaign at the NTNU university in Trondheim in 2009. There is probably no better source available than this blog on how the boycott campaign started, how its promoters operated, the rector's supporting role for the inciters, multiple reactions from the international community including Jewish organizations, and the campaign against the boycott by Scholars for Peace in the Middle East.

For some time a similar blog modeled on the Norwegian one, *Sweden, Israel and the Jews*, was updated regularly.[13] However, it could not be maintained due to lack of funding. The establishment of similar blogs for a number of other countries would make much more material accessible in English and thus facilitate exposure of anti-Israeli inciters there.

Stop Being Verbal Vegetarians

One should never understate the criminal behavior of one's enemies. Yet when Israel fights back in the propaganda war, it often does so with one hand tied behind its back. Various Israeli political parties and politicians have not only remained silent but have also shown empathy for Palestinian incitement and certain other crimes.

In the past some have suggested that Jordan—the former Eastern Palestine when the British Mandate was created—is the first Palestinian state. Israeli governments have at best usually been very reluctant to promote this claim, however true.

Yet, had a policy been pursued for decades by now of calling Jordan the first Palestinian state, the Jordanians would have understood that it was useless to fight against the truth. That would have made it possible to turn the so-called "peace process" into a negotiation about a second (Palestinian Authority-ruled) Palestinian state and a third (Hamas-ruled) Palestinian state.

This Israeli approach of fighting propaganda with one hand tied behind its back might be called "verbal vegetarianism." It fits in with a major, millennia-old Jewish masochistic current of self-accusation. One of the most far-reaching examples in this century was the unjustified Israeli apology for the supposed killing of Muhammad al-Dura at the beginning of the Second Intifada. It took thirteen years before Israel declared that it had not killed al-Dura.[14]

Expose a Few, Teach Many a Lesson

Israel is a small country, attacked by many. There is no way one can fight all of the attackers simultaneously. This is also unnecessary in view of the fact that many people are cowards. If Israel were to succeed in destroying the reputation of a few journalists, media outlets, politicians, NGOs, church leaders, and academics, many others would think twice before engaging in hate-mongering against it.

The strategic principle is thus: "expose a few, teach many a lesson." One should, however, choose the ones to target carefully. They should preferably be reasonably well known. Even more important is to be convinced before embarking on the attack that the chances of winning the battle are very high. Any defeat would be counterproductive.

All of the principles proposed so far interlink and lead to a larger strategy of fighting the propaganda battle. The emphasis should be on offense but without neglecting defense.

Use Resources Efficiently

As Israel is a small country and the Jewish people are relatively few in number, resources such as time and money have to be used very efficiently. This means, among other things, that court cases should be minimized and used only if there are no other ways to achieve one's goals.

For instance, if one has contact with a parliamentarian, time is much better spent convincing him or her to pose an embarrassing question to an anti-Israeli minister than in writing a letter to the editor of a paper that often will not be published.

In line with this maxim is another principle, that of finding "out-of-the-box solutions." One small example occurred in July 2006: when more than a thousand American professors signed a petition condemning Israel's alleged aggression in Lebanon and Gaza, somebody added the signature "Mr. H. Nasrallah, Joseph Goebbels Chair in Communications at Duke University." With one signature he succeeded in ridiculing the action of all the others.[15]

Another example occurred when in 2013 a Swedish Jewish woman, Annika Hernroth-Rothstein, filed for asylum in her own country.[16] In this way she drew attention to the mounting anti-Israeli incitement and multifaceted anti-Semitism in Sweden. She received much international publicity for her relatively small effort, which was a classic example of how to spotlight the behavior of the many hypocrites in Swedish society and among its leaders.

CAMERA has frequently exposed *The New York Times*' bias against Israel. In January 2014, it applied an innovative approach. It put a three-story billboard on a building facing *The Times*' headquarters. The text read: "Would a great newspaper slant the news against Israel? *The New York Times* does." The text went on to say: "Misrepresenting facts, omitting key information, skewing headlines and photos." Under this it said: "Stop the bias. CAMERA."[17]

Another very successful example is the Latma weekly satirical show, created by a number of journalists. It reached major international renown.[18] Yet another example of an out-of-the-box approach is this author's *Bad News from the Netherlands* blog.[19] On it, only negative news items about the Netherlands are posted. The blog states this up-front and notes that this is a reaction to the many Dutch papers and journalists who frequently apply double standards and distort information about Israel. It also points out that contrary to many incorrect details in the articles these Dutch journalists have written, the facts mentioned on the blog are true. To back up the items posted, the blog provides links to Dutch news sources. Furthermore, it points out that the Dutch media do not tell their readers that they present a distorted picture of Israel, whereas the blog stresses that with the method it uses, it misrepresents Dutch reality by not giving any positive news.

This blog plays an additional role. As there are now thousands of items in its archive, it can also serve as a repository of information that can be retrieved for articles, debates, and so on.[20] The establishment of similar blogs about other countries can provide a resource for exposing their misconduct whenever they criticize Israel. This, however, requires a certain degree of sophistication. A recent example of a similar blog is the section on "Ugly Europe" at the *Tundra Tabloids* blog.[21]

It is known from the business world that one can train people to develop out-of-the-box-solutions via "lateral thinking."[22] Such activity should be promoted by the proposed contra-propaganda structure.

The principle that one should try to use one's resources, both financial and temporal, as efficiently as possible has many other aspects. Cases should be brought before courts only if there is no alternative, as trials are both expensive and time-consuming. The situation gets even worse if such a case is lost. This happened when UK activist Ronnie Fraser brought a case against the British University and College Union. The judge decided against him.[23]

Mobilizing Allies

Partly because of the small number of Israelis and Jews, it is crucial to mobilize allies, the more so as the number of enemies is so huge. A typical example of such a successful mobilization was the defeat of the anti-Israeli boycott supporters at NTNU in Norway. Many Jewish organizations were mobilized in this cause. They in turn succeeded to gain the support of non-Jewish bodies such as the Association of American University Professors and the Russell Group of twenty leading British universities. Although little is known about this, the American ambassador had also apparently intervened with the Norwegian government. The defeat of the proboycotters at NTNU dissuaded people at other Norwegian universities, in particular Trömso University, from initiating similar boycott actions.[24]

Several examples can be found in reactions to American academia. After the 2013 boycott of Israeli academia by the American Studies Association, many universities condemned it.[25] Numerous congressmen came out against the boycott[26] and several universities pulled out of the association.[27] The American Association of University Professors called the boycott resolution a setback for academic freedom.[28]

In January 2014, the New York State Assembly passed a law introduced by its speaker, Sheldon Silver, that bans state funding to colleges that fund groups that boycott countries that host higher-education institutions chartered by the Board of Regents of the University of the State of New York.

Silver had made it clear that he was aiming at the American Studies Association's boycott of Israel and its academic institutions. The result of the bill is that institutions that pay dues to an organization like the ASA or subsidize travel to its conferences would lose state funding.[29]

One major area where Israel should try to find allies is among Palestinian Christians abroad. The exposure of the discrimination and crimes of the Palestinian Authority and Hamas against Christians can best be done by other Palestinian Christians.

Cashing In when One Wins

Yet another important principle for fighting the propaganda war is that Israel and its allies should make the most out of successful actions. This is yet another facet of maximizing the results when one scores a win against one's enemies. It also fits in with the earlier-mentioned principle that many people, including Israel's adversaries, are cowards. Therefore it is important that they realize that there are risks involved in promoting anti-Israeli incitement.

This is probably the only major aspect where the pro-Israeli activists failed in their activities against the NTNU. Little publicity was given to the defeat of the boycotters. Since then various Norwegians, including the previous ambassador to Israel, have been falsely claiming that the Norwegian government and major media specifically opposed the proposed Trondheim boycott from its beginning.[30] The truth is that they came out against it only several weeks after the issue had garnered international attention.

Integrated Attacks

Israel's enemies try to delegitimize Israel by using multiple approaches and techniques. Similarly, once one has defined an anti-Semitic target to be hit, it should be attacked in all ways possible, provided they are within the law.

Major actions in the struggle against the propaganda war are often undertaken ad hoc. One example mentioned previously is the successful effort led by the Israeli Foreign Ministry before and during the Durban II conference in the spring of 2009. The weakness of such an approach became evident, however, when Israel was caught off guard by the publication of the caricatural Goldstone Report. Similarly, Israel barely reacted after the publication of the Kairos Document. Thus an insignificant grouping of Palestinian Christians had a widespread international hate impact. Once again this demonstrated how one cannot be prepared for events if one has no strategic infrastructure to cope with emerging problems caused by anti-Israeli propaganda.

Only when Israel has such an organizational structure for fighting the propaganda war, providing detailed understanding of how the enemy operates, can it start training its officials and supporters to be more effective in the battle against delegitimization.

It will not suffice to continue to improvise reactions to propaganda attacks if one poorly understands the system of delegitimization of Israel and lacks a continuous monitoring mechanism of how it develops. As long as the battle against Israel's delegitimization is not fought with similar strategic concepts to those used on the military and intelligence battlefield, it is doomed to relative failure.

There are so many relevant and important aspects of battling against the propaganda war that, with the current limited resources, one can only formulate a few suggestions. The following are some examples of issues to be considered.

Education

Education about anti-Semitism and its dangers is gradually making its way into the school systems of some Western countries. Education about anti-Israelism in these countries is, however, nonexistent. It is not even widely known that, in those countries where statistics are available, the percentages of people holding demonic views about Israel are shockingly high.

In Jewish circles, some efforts are made to explain how anti-Israelism functions. This has hardly ever been done, however, in a systematic way. Curricula on this subject should be developed as much as possible. How to fight against anti-Israelism should also be taught and promoted.

Before one can even expect that any Western governments will start instituting education against anti-Israelism, this subject should be brought up in the public discourse. This can be done, for instance, in foreign parliamentary debates or through parliamentary questions. This occurred in the Netherlands in January 2014. The Christian parliamentarian Elbert Dijkgraaf raised the issue. Deputy Prime Minister Lodewijk Asscher replied that the facts were "worrisome" and "unacceptable."[31] He did not, however, indicate any measures he intended to take.

Thereupon, in February, Rabbi Abraham Cooper of the Simon Wiesenthal Center sent a letter to Asscher. He asked the Dutch government to investigate the anti-Israelism in the country in view of the finding of the University of Bielefeld that 39 percent of the Dutch adult population think Israel is conducting a war of extermination against the Palestinians. He wrote:

> An important first step should be a government-ordered study to trace how such an utterly false and insidious image of Israel was created. Those who conceive and promote an unjustified extreme criminal view of others should be exposed and held accountable in the court of Public Opinion. We know too well from the 1930s in Germany what can happen when the delegitimization and demonization of a people goes unchallenged.
>
> In our time, in such a climate in the Netherlands, it is no surprise that there are calls for boycotts against the Jewish State. A study by an independent highly professional firm as proposed would focus on how this climate was created and what can be done to remedy this unacceptable situation.[32]

Rabbi Cooper offered his organization's help in defining the terms of the study.[33] A few weeks later he sent rather similar letters to European Parliament Chairman Martin Schulz and German President Joachim Gauck.

After Rabbi Cooper's letter to Asscher, Dijkgraaf posed parliamentary questions to two Dutch ministers. They included:

> Do you acknowledge that a demonized picture of Israel offers a dangerous substrate for anti-Semitic incidents? What consequences do you connect to your own statements that the research findings of the Bielefeld University about the image of Europeans concerning Israel are "unacceptable and very worrisome?" And do you intend to have investigated what the reasons are for the worrisome creation of Israel's image in the Netherlands? If not, why not? If yes, do you intend to define, together with the Simon Wiesenthal Center, the parameters for the research as Rabbi Abraham Cooper has offered in his letter?[34]

Asscher replied to Cooper in the same month, addressing mainly anti-Semitism issues and largely evading the issue of anti-Israelism. In March Rabbi Cooper sent a second letter to Asscher on this subject, addressing the anti-Israelism issue. He asked for another meeting with the minister. Nine months later he had not yet received a reply.[35]

Training

There are many organizations and a sizable number of individuals who are willing to defend Israel. Little is done by the Israeli government to improve their professionalism. Yet there are other, even more urgent matters. It is necessary that all Israeli diplomats are trained to understand and explain fundamental issues concerning the hate-mongering against Israel. This includes why much of the anti-Israelism is essentially identical to classic forms of anti-Semitism, and why expressing opinions on the Palestinian-Israeli conflict without mentioning the genocidal agenda of Hamas constitutes indirect support of an Islamo-Nazi movement.

In a similar vein, Israeli diplomats should be taught how to analyze anti-Israeli lectures and articles. They should understand how to discern false arguments and how to expose them. Only thereafter can they respond effectively to lies promoted about Israel and also to the fallacies, which are much more difficult to understand. They should be trained to deal more professionally with issues such as the application of double standards against Israel, false moral equivalence, scapegoating, sentimental appeals, and so on. They should also be made familiar with the strategic principles outlined earlier.

Similar crucial information should be widely disseminated among pro-Israeli grassroots organizations, students visiting Israel from abroad, and many others.

The Battle of Semantics

An issue that is hardly ever considered in the political battle is how to deal systematically with distortions of semantics. One aspect of this should be the regular exposure of what "peace" means for many Palestinian leaders, namely, an intermediary stage for the destruction of Israel. Much information on this can be found on the website of Palestinian Media Watch.

Yet another issue among many is the use of the term "occupied territories." Foreign diplomats in Israel should be exposed when they use it publicly. This term has permeated international discourse to such an extent that the correct phrase, "disputed territories," is barely ever mentioned.

Foreign diplomats in Israel should also be reprimanded when they speak about 1967 "borders" instead of "armistice lines." When speaking about Jordan, frequent Israeli mention that it is the "former East Palestine" will draw attention to where its origins are.

Other approaches must also be found to clarify how semantics are used as a tool of bias and incitement against Israel. This is a huge and mainly unexplored field that requires major attention. In this vein, Israel's official representatives should be told to use the phrase "a second Palestinian state" concerning the establishment of such an entity in the West Bank and Gaza in the future.

The Battle for the Public Square

Enemies of Israel and anti-Semites have succeeded to remove parts of the Israeli and Jewish presence from the public square in Europe. Violence and intimidation have played an important role in this. Every time a Jew who was used to wearing his skullcap in the public domain removes it out of fear, the anti-Semites have scored another victory. The same goes for Israeli tourists abroad who are advised to hide their identity.

Intimidation takes many forms. Some of it results from lethal attacks by Palestinians and their allies. As mentioned, the murders by Mohammed Merah had a major impact on international Jewish communities. So did the Brussels Jewish Museum murders of May 2014. Other examples occur when pro-Israeli demonstrators are beaten up or aggressed in other ways.

In view of these efforts to eliminate the Jewish and Israeli presence from the public domain, it is very important that pro-Israeli public demonstrations are also held. One country where this happened early in this century is Italy, thanks to the initiatives of a few courageous people. In 2002, Giuliano Ferrara, editor of the conservative daily *Il Foglio*, took the initiative to organize a demonstration called "Israel Day."

Ferrara explained:

> In those days it was not easy to organize a pro-Israel demonstration, but we decided we had to do it. This event was a great success, gaining the support of personalities from both the Right and the Left . . . Romano Prodi, then-president of the European Commission, expressed his empathy. Among backers on the Right was Deputy Prime Minister Gianfranco Fini, leader of the Alleanza Nazionale party.

In 2005, Ferrara organized another demonstration in favor of Israel. He said:

> I felt it a political, cultural, and civil duty to organize a protest against Ahmadinejad's call for genocide. I wanted this demonstration to have a simple goal: to proclaim that we uphold Israel's right to exist and object to a head of state who denies this. An estimated 15,000-20,000 people took part in the demonstration, among them Cabinet Minister Roberto Calderoli who said he represented both the government and his Lega Nord party.
>
> The demonstration was a great political success: it went beyond a gathering of many people who were determined to affirm their principles. Among those

> who marched or supported the demonstration, almost the entire Italian political spectrum was represented, from the Center-Right to the Center-Left. The Rifondazione Communist party was the only one with a parliamentary faction that did not participate. Like other forces of the extreme Left, their prejudice is to support the national struggle of the Palestinians, and their ideology tends toward anti-Zionism.
>
> We succeeded in holding the demonstration one week after Ahmadinejad's initial anti-Semitic and anti-Zionist declarations. Our support went far beyond political parties. *Corriere della Sera*, Italy's largest daily came out in favor of the demonstration along with many other papers. *Repubblica*, the second largest daily treated the rally benevolently, which was the maximum one could expect from them. The communist daily *Il Manifesto* opposed the demonstration, but some of its journalists marched nevertheless. Numerous associations also came out in support and so did various other bodies of Italian civil society, from the Catholic sector and elsewhere. Many intellectuals and public personalities also expressed their backing.[36]

In 2012, then-parliamentarian Fiamma Nirenstein organized another pro-Israeli demonstration in front of the Chamber of Deputies in Rome. Nirenstein's "speaking marathon" featured over fifty pro-Israeli speakers, and a total of 1,500 Israel supporters attended the event. Stressing the importance of the event, Nirenstein said, "I believe that for the sake of peace we need to restore the truth about the ongoing conflict. We need to neutralize the denigratory language used day by day to criminalize Israel and to delegitimize its right to defend its own citizens under attack."[37]

Reactions to Changes in Government

Whenever an important change in foreign governments takes place, assessments have to be made on how it will affect anti-Israelism and classic anti-Semitism. Sometimes this change is somewhat for the better, such as the one in Norway in 2013. The Labour-dominated left-wing government, of which several ministers were part-time anti-Semites and anti-Israeli inciters, was defeated. It was replaced by a government of the Conservative Party (Høyre) and the Progress Party. Several of the new government's ministers had previously belonged to the parliamentary Friends of Israel.

Already in the first few months, it became clear that a minor pro-Israeli change in government policy had taken place. One indication was that after an invitation from King Harald V in May 2014, then-Israeli President Shimon Peres visited Norway. However, this does not affect large parts of Norwegian civil society where the incitement continues. This involves the powerful trade unions, many media, various church leaders, NGOs, academics, and so on. One of Israel's diplomatic aims should thus be supporting the cessation of Norwegian government funding of hate NGOs that promote incitement against Israel.

Yet another issue that should be raised with the Norwegian government concerns a government-financed study's finding that 38 percent of the Norwegian population thinks Israel is behaving toward the Palestinians like the Nazis behaved toward the Jews. Israel would be justified in demanding that the Norwegian government investigate how this extreme and evil mindset was created in Norwegian society, which bodies and structures were responsible for it, and how the situation can be remedied.[38]

On the other hand, in the Netherlands the current coalition of the liberal party VVD and the Labour Party falls far short regarding Israel of the previous coalition of the VVD and the Christian Democrats supported from the outside by the Freedom Party. Before the new coalition came into power, there should have been a detailed assessment of how to deal with the Labour Party's anti-Israeli incitement.

Governments

It should be part of Israeli policy to encourage various governments to investigate anti-Semitism and anti-Israelism. Major studies have been done on anti-Semitism and to a lesser extent anti-Israelism by parliamentary committees or at the request of parliament in the UK,[39] Canada,[40] Germany,[41] and Italy.[42]

Europe

Discriminatory political attitudes and incitement against Israel out of Europe have become an increasingly worrisome problem over many years. It is manifested both at the level of the European Union and of several of its member countries.

European motivations for this are numerous. They believe it serves them well politically in their relations with Arab countries and with Muslim populations in their home countries. Another reason is the empathy of many on the left for the Palestinians, while ignoring the huge ideological and other types of criminality in Palestinian society, and the even greater extent of such criminality in several Muslim countries. A third motivation is that blackening Israel enables Europeans to somewhat whitewash their countries' guilt over the massive criminal conduct during the Holocaust.

Successive Israeli governments have almost consistently reacted weakly to the insults and lies coming out of the political system and civil societies of Europe, including some foreign diplomats in Israel. The reasons for this are not clear. A major one seems to be the tradeoff for good relations in other fields, in particular the economic one. To a much lesser extent, this may be true for research, cultural, sport, and other European-Israeli relations.

One hears Israeli diplomats in Europe say off the record that Israel should not come out too strongly against anti-Semitism in Europe. A typical case concerns Hungary with its political support for Israel and good economic relations. Obviously, this is never phrased explicitly.

Israel has also let the Europeans get their way with the claim that according to international law, the settlements are unequivocally "illegal." This stance has clearly led to incessant European condemnations of settlement expansion. It would have been far more useful if Israel had mobilized the numerous legal experts in Israel and abroad who believe that many parts of international law have a very weak legal basis, as well as those who maintain that under international law, the settlements are indeed legal.

The result of the widespread and ongoing European incitement against Israel is a situation where at least 150 million out of 400 million adult citizens in the European Union hold criminal views about Israel, believing that it is conducting a war of extermination against the Palestinians, or behaves toward them like the Nazis behaved toward the Jews.[43]

Thus, not only is there a huge number of Europeans with a criminal mindset toward Israel, but this reality further facilitates European pressure on Israel. One small example occurred when at the beginning of 2014 the new EU ambassador to Israel, Lars Faaborg-Andersen, warned that European-Israeli relations could deteriorate if no peace was reached.

He used diplomatic phrasing to say that if there was an expansion of settlements, "I am afraid that what will transpire is a situation where Israel will find itself increasingly isolated." He added that "this isolation would likely come not from decisions made at a governmental level but rather by a myriad of private economic actions, such as divestment by pension funds and consumers who will not buy Israeli products."[44]

Yet what Faaborg-Andersen omitted to mention was the contribution the EU had made to the criminal mindset of so many Europeans toward Israel via its frequent, discriminatory condemnations of Israel.

An Israeli policy that neglects structural medium-term risks resulting from its demonization in exchange for short-term benefits is extremely dangerous. An overall and in-depth assessment of how to confront Europe on its incitement and the criminal mindset of many of its citizens must be made. There are many handicaps here, however. One significant one is the small number of Israeli specialists on European politics as compared to the many experts on Middle Eastern issues and American relations. Hence only a few cases of the incitement against Israel and what is behind it are exposed in Israeli and international media. After many years of Israeli neglect of this matter, much more attention should be given to it in the future.

Media

Freedom of speech and "the right of media to know" have been turned into absolute values. Such "absolutism" has led to much abuse against Israel. Israel and the Jews, as in so many other cases, have become a sensor for a great variety of manipulations. As Israel has suffered from biased media attacks for many years that have caused great damage to its image, this issue requires special attention.

Foreign journalists operating in Israel fall into two broad categories: honest journalists and pro-Arab propagandists who falsely claim to be journalists. If both categories have similar rights to Israeli press cards and to attend government briefings, there is no reason why the propagandists should change their approaches.

This became clear once again after the passing of former Prime Minister Ariel Sharon. Several media abroad republished the lie that his visit to the Temple Mount in 2000 triggered the Second Intifada. One wonders why these people are allowed to hold onto their Israeli press cards. Journalists who write about "1967 borders" instead of "armistice lines" should be reprimanded for spreading false information. Only a systematic and determined approach to this problem will yield results.

If an Israeli government structure to fight propaganda were in existence, it would study major media. It would expose them in as many ways as possible on each distortion. As the funds that should be made available for this purpose would far exceed those of organizations such as CAMERA and HonestReporting, such activity could become very embarrassing for some foreign media. In addition, the Israeli government could punish hate-Israel manipulative journalists by taking away their press cards.

The Business Sector

Economic boycotts against Israel have a lengthy history. Normally, the business sector of a country is one where reactions to negative developments occur faster than elsewhere in society because of this sector's competitiveness. In view of the many commercial interests involved, one would have expected Israeli business associations to have developed a structure that battles these actions in a sophisticated way after facing decades of boycotts.

Rather little progress has been seen here, however. On the contrary, in the midst of the American-initiated "peace process" at the beginning of 2014, a group of Israeli businessmen told Prime Minister Netanyahu that "the world is running out of patience and the threat of sanctions is rising. We must reach an agreement with the Palestinians."[45]

To make matters worse, these business leaders not only proclaimed this in Israel but announced their intention to promote these issues at the World Economic Forum in Davos, for which they were departing. They were thus weakening their own side in negotiations. This is even more severe because any senior business leader has experience in negotiations and knows what such undermining means.

This attitude also sheds further light on the damage resulting from the absence of a central contra-propaganda structure. Had it been in existence for many years already, it would certainly have developed working relationships with Israeli business-sector associations, making such actions by senior figures without internal opposition much less likely.

Legal Issues

As aforementioned, Dershowitz was quoted as saying that international law is "a construct in the mind of a bunch of left wing academics."[46] Legal attacks on Israel have intensified so greatly that this should be a priority sector for government funding in the fight against the propaganda war. Legal attacks, and political assaults masked as legal, occur frequently. Presenting settlements as "illegal" and calling the disputed territories "occupied" are just some of the aspects. It should be evaluated whether showing that parts of international law are utopian or unworkable constructs is worthwhile. Its multiple distortions in the propaganda war against Israel should be exposed. The same is true for the distorters themselves.

Cotler has pointed out that many legal and other remedies exist to combat Iran. State parties to the UN Genocide Convention should file complaints against Iran—which is also party to the convention—before the International Court of Justice. Member states should request that the UN Security Council pass a resolution condemning Iran's incitement to genocide and refer the matter to the International Criminal Court, which can indict Khamenei, Ahmadinejad, and their collaborators, as it has done with Sudanese President Omar al-Bashir.[47]

The UN Genocide Convention is a typical example of an accepted international law that is not subsequently upheld by its signatories. The same goes for some legislation concerning anti-Semitism in various countries.

Rabbi Andrew Baker, personal representative of the OSCE chairman-in-office on combating anti-Semitism and director of International Jewish Affairs of the American Jewish Committee, argued before the Canadian Parliamentary Coalition to Combat Anti-Semitism that legislation to punish hate speech can be ineffective or even harmful:

> From what I've observed, my sense is that legislation often does not work. It may exist but it is not uniformly or frequently imposed. In some cases where court examinations have been brought, the length of time between bringing a case and reaching some settlement can often be months or even years. Penalties, when penalties are applied, may be so limited as to really not be a deterrent. And I think in some countries, the mere fact that you have a legal process has allowed political leaders to be quiet, whether by choice or whether by law, to be able to say this is now a matter for the prosecutor, a matter for the courts, and they won't speak. I think we need to do more to determine the best ways of dealing with this hate speech.[48]

Daniel Bodnar, chairman of the Hungarian TEV organization for monitoring anti-Semitism in the country, says, "In Hungary, current laws against anti-Semitic incitement are among the best in Europe. The problem is that the authorities do not apply them. Even worse is that the former Constitutional Court ruled that only in cases of direct and clear danger is there a transgression of incitement laws."[49]

There is a huge pool of law experts willing to help defend Israel. For example, more than one thousand jurists signed a letter in a short period of time that stressed several basic points of false use of legal semantics and other issues of legal bias by the European Union.[50] This pool of potential supporters has, however, barely been tapped.

Academics

The boycott, divestment, and sanctions (BDS) approach in the academic world already started in 2002. In this field, the main burden of the Israeli fight against propaganda should not rest on the government alone. Israeli universities must play a major role here, though they have largely failed to do so far.

There are a multitude of ways to fight boycotts and other anti-Israeli actions. Some of them were demonstrated after the 2013 boycott decision by the American Studies Association. There are also many other ways to deal with anti-Israeli inciters in the academic domain. Sometimes one can obtain ideas from what happens in other countries. In Germany, various politicians lost their jobs because researchers found cases of plagiarism in their doctoral theses.[51]

No academic would like to have someone checking his or her publications systematically for plagiarism, false quotations, and distorted footnotes. One would only have to uncover a few academics in this way and expose them to their universities and colleagues to make the academic Israel-haters aware that also in academia, there are no free anti-Semitic lunches for inciters.

Exposing such academics would also be beneficial to academia. Universities should appreciate those who prove that some staff members are plagiarizers or extremely negligent in presenting their sources. Yet, as far as boycotts are concerned, Jewish and Israeli sources often seem to provide most of the public information. It should be assessed whether this publicity is not counterproductive.

It is far more difficult to fight the reputation of an institution than of an individual. Attacking the UNHRC as an exceptionally biased caricature of human rights is totally justified. Yet in the political reality it may have little impact. Attacking biased anti-Israelis appointed by the council to express supposedly impartial judgments is far easier than attacking the UNHRC as a whole, and could lead to positive results if done professionally.

The same is true as far as attacking *The New York Times* or the BBC is concerned. Exposing the extreme bias of individual journalists is far simpler and can be ultimately successful. Fighting the biased Human Rights Watch NGO has had mixed success. Yet its senior military analyst Marc Garlasco resigned after he had been exposed as a collector of Nazi memorabilia.

Jewish and Israeli Anti-Semites

Jewish and Israeli anti-Semites may not be numerous, but they are often used by proponents of Israel's delegitimization who regard Jewish and Israeli anti-Semites as lending legitimacy to their own causes.

This group of enemies of Israel is one of the most difficult to deal with, as freedom-of-speech issues often come into play. Yet a limited number of these people cause a disproportionate number of problems. This means that however complicated it may be, methods to diminish the damage have to be sought.

A different category is Jewish masochists, a group that varies from mild to severe sufferers of this aberration. In Israel one finds them even at the highest levels of society including the government table. They call for unjustified concessions to the Palestinians. Several of them do so out of fear of what the world will do to Israel if no peace agreement is reached.

Countering Propaganda Visits to Palestinian Territories

One of the most effective methods of Palestinian propaganda is the brainwashing of foreign visitors to the Palestinian territories. Various organizations in the Western world, while diverting their gaze from the genocidal elements in Palestinian society, regularly bring groups to the territories.

They then stress the Israeli restrictions on the Palestinian population, resulting in much publicity abroad about how the Palestinians are oppressed. One element that gets much attention is the checkpoints. These inciters remain silent about the murderous Palestinian attacks that caused these checkpoints in the first place. Instead, imitation "Israeli" checkpoints have emerged in various places in the Western world. They are a regularly recurring tool in the propaganda war against Israel.

During 2012's Israel Apartheid Week, a number of universities across the world erected mock checkpoints on campus. At the London School of Economics, such a checkpoint was positioned outside a campus building. The university's Arab protesters stopped and harassed Jewish students, asking them for identification.[52]

At McGill University in Montreal, a similar mock checkpoint was created that year in addition to a "mock apartheid wall."[53] One Jewish student identified by Apartheid Week organizers as involved in pro-Israeli activism on campus recalled being verbally hectored to enter the mock checkpoint.

At Harvard University, in addition to a mock separation barrier, 2012 Apartheid Week activities also included mock "eviction notices" posted on walls across the campus stating "Your suite is scheduled for demolition."[54]

A mock separation barrier was also erected outside of the Church of St. James in downtown London at the end of 2013. More problematic, this wall was not part of any Apartheid Week activities. Instead it was the initiative of Anglican clergyman Stephen Sizer, who has devoted much of his career to challenging Jewish claims to the Holy Land.[55]

This problem is complex. Israeli embassies abroad and pro-Israeli organizations should be taught to build up networks of people who react to these claims. Such allegations cannot be fought with one hand tied behind one's back. One has to expose the many murderous acts of the Palestinians that led to the restrictions, and sometimes go so far as correctly accusing some of the pro-Palestinian activists as allies of those who glorify murder. How this should be done to avoid legal problems as much as possible has to be considered in each country.

Although trade union anti-Israelism is similar to academic anti-Semitism, much less is known about it. To fight it the Israeli government must collaborate with the Histadrut.

Sentimental Appeals

In irrational environments sentimental appeals often have a good chance to convince one's audience. The Palestinians have understood that far better than Israelis. Sentimental appeals well fit the Palestinian promotion of the image that they are victims of Israel. It is far more accurate to say that they could have had a second Palestinian state, in addition to Jordan, if the Arab countries had not refused it after the UN General Assembly partition resolution in 1947. Nor have the Palestinians made anything like ongoing peaceful efforts to get one since.

One of the best-known sentimental appeals is Palestinian refugees showing the key of the apartment they or their ancestors left or had to leave in the 1948 war. Another sentimental appeal is advanced by some of their Western allies who claim that Israelis should have empathy for the Palestinians. That the Palestinians are weaker than Israel justifies such a claim in their eyes even if the largest Palestinian party, Hamas, promotes genocide of the Jews while the Palestinian Authority glorifies murderers of Jewish civilians.

The reactions to the Protective Edge campaign have once again proved the power of sentimental appeals. Hamas has used human shields, positioned its rocket launchers next to schools, and so on. Many media outlets, however, focused on children killed by Israelis as a result of the Hamas policy. Often that policy was not even mentioned.

Israel is paying greatly for its lack of understanding of sentimental appeals and their power. Nor has Israel's leadership understood that attempts to answer sentimental appeals with rational ones are often doomed to failure. This is particularly so in light of the earlier-mentioned huge number of Europeans with extreme irrational views of the Palestinian-Israeli conflict. Israel will thus have to develop adequate answers to sentimental appeals.

Avoiding Stereotyping

Fighting a propaganda war is usually based on exaggerating the crimes of one's enemies. Those committed by many leading and other Palestinians and in many other Arab and Muslim societies are so major that one only has to publicize them as they are. There is a crucial need to start exposing much more explicitly the huge hate-mongering against Jews and Israel coming out of parts of the Muslim world, and in particular the Palestinian leadership of both Hamas and Fatah. This may, however, easily lead to stereotyping.

There are many vile Islamic religious leaders and other hate-mongers. They promote jihad, issue *fatwa*s to justify violence including suicide bombings, and may incite to genocide. Iranian Supreme Leader Ayatollah Ali Khamenei can be defined as an icon of genocidal Israel-hatred.

Despite all this, Israel and its allies should not fall into the trap of generalization and stereotyping when they take the necessary measures in the propaganda war against extreme incitement from large parts of the Muslim world. They should not go further than saying that these phenomena are typical of parts of the Muslim world, without blaming Islam in its totality or all Muslims. Such generalized blaming is what a number of racist political movements in Europe frequently engage in.

At the same time, one should also expose a number of popular falsehoods. One is that there is "only one Islam." A religion is what its followers make of it at a given time. As contemporary Muslims interpret their religion in rather diverse ways, there is no one Islam. A second falsehood is that the Muslim world consists of a certain number of radicals who are called Islamists and a far larger number of "moderates." A far more correct description is: there is a wide, almost continuous spectrum of Muslim attitudes, with the radical Islamists at one extreme and the moderates at the other.

The Muslims—like the others—who marched in the anti-Israeli demonstrations in the summer of 2014 are indirect supporters of Islamo-Nazis. They are not moderates and should not be considered as such. Muslims who deny the Holocaust are not moderates. Muslims who take the Koran literally and think that Jews are apes and pigs are not moderates; nor are those who think that Jews are inferior beings.

Mahmoud Abbas and the other Palestinian Authority leaders who glorify the murderers of Israeli civilians are not moderate Muslims either. There are also indifferent Muslims who do not care. We do not know how many true moderates there are at the other end of the Muslim spectrum. It may well be that the number of such genuine Muslim moderates is not larger than that of the Islamo-Nazis.

Encouraging Individual Activists

In the past, several courageous individuals have undertaken pro-Israeli activities. To mention two examples from the academic world, Ronnie Fraser in the UK has been a pioneer in fighting—often alone—hate campaigns against Israel in academic trade unions.[56] In the United States, Tammi Rossman-Benjamin has been in the forefront of fighting many cases of anti-Semitism and anti-Israelism on the University of California campuses.[57]

More recently, British actress Maureen Lipman took the private initiative to start attacking the British Labour Party, which she had supported for five decades. In particular she has written to expose Ed Miliband, the head of the party, a Jew who had led the party in the campaign to recognize a Palestinian state. Lipman wrote of Miliband: "He is a second-generation immigrant Jew, whose father escaped Nazi death camps, and inadvertently or not, he is pandering to the antisemitism masking as anti-Zionism, which is once again sweeping across Europe."[58]

It is important to encourage these people in their fearless endeavors, the more so as they are often isolated and encounter much abuse. While this may seem like a minor issue, it is of great psychological importance. The Israeli government not only totally failed in the al-Dura affair but, even worse, hardly supported those abroad who stepped up courageously to expose the falsification of this story.

Even before the proposed Israeli contra-propaganda structure is established, more systematic attention to the issues outlined here can already provide some results. Finally, a central role in all of these battles will have to be played by teams of psychologists, public relations experts, and lawyers. Their expertise will be necessary to make the Israeli actions far more effective.

The above are only a few examples among many in the propaganda war where major Israeli focus and systematic approaches are long overdue. What could not be provided here is a systematic overview of approaches on all major issues. This should be one of the tasks of the proposed new structure.

Conclusion

THE CONCLUSION OF A STRATEGIC document should be short. The propaganda battles against Israel have developed over the past decades into a major war. The battles have also become far more sophisticated. Israel, however, has not properly organized its defenses, which still have a largely incidental character. This has greatly facilitated the task of its enemies.

Arab propaganda has succeeded to turn the Palestinian-Israeli conflict, in many places, into the foremost geopolitical issue. This is convenient for the Arab and Muslim world as it draws attention away from the enormous criminality occurring daily in parts of their world. One only has to remember the roughly 1.5 million deaths in the Iraq-Iran War in the 1980s. To that may be added the hundreds of thousands of deaths in Syria and Iraq and the millions of refugees from that conflict. In addition, there are huge problems concerning Muslims in Yemen, Sudan, Somalia, Afghanistan, Iran, Pakistan, Libya, Nigeria, Mali, and many other countries. It is evident, then, that the problems in the Muslim world and the threats emanating from them to the rest of the world are the main geopolitical issues. Yet many Westerners have fallen for the false centrality of the Palestinian-Israeli conflict.

Let us assume that a miracle happens and there is a sudden viable peace between Israel and the Palestinians. Will the United States and its allies drop one bomb less on ISIS? Will there be fewer refugees from the Syrian civil war?

Will fewer Iraqis die as a result of suicide bombers and other attacks? Will ISIS or the pro-Iraqi-government Shiite tribes behead one less person? And, as far as geopolitics is concerned, will Boko Haram kidnap one less person? Will one less person die in Eastern Ukraine?[1]

While it is difficult to make forecasts, some developments seem probable. The fragmentation that characterizes contemporary Western societies will increase. This will happen in a world that is likely to grow more chaotic. That, in turn, will make analysis of processes such as the delegitimization of Israel and the Jews even more complex. In this postmodern environment the war of a million cuts against Israel will continue to flourish. The collaboration between hate-mongers is also likely to increase. The same is true for the war's sophistication. Even if a peace settlement with the Palestinians is reached in the future, there will be many Muslims and others who will continue to incite against Israel.

At a conference on delegitimization held by the Jewish People Policy Institute, the summary included:

> Clearly we face a global order, agenda and logic that differ from what we have known. We live in a global, multi-polar world with asymmetric wars and a human rights discourse that champions identification with those perceived as being weak and having their rights suppressed. This is a world challenged and frightened by radical Islam, a world with strong voices fomenting radicalism, post-modernism and post-nationalism that question, among other things, the right of existence of the ethno-religious nation-state; a world of non-state actors developing new networks and formats for generating and disseminating information. In this kind of world, Israel, the Jews and the link between the two may well find themselves on "the wrong side of history."[2]

There is a certain fatalism in this forecast, which is not necessarily justified. Israel could have done much to fight the propaganda war in the past decades. It can also in the near future greatly improve its performance, provided it approaches this war in a strategic and structured way.

The Muslim World

Every forecast about the world's future has to take into account developments in the Arab and Muslim world, large parts of which are highly unstable. Even if they were to stabilize, criminal ideology in significant sectors of Muslim societies is so major that it is unlikely to disappear. A lengthy confrontation of parts of the Muslim world with Western democracies seems unavoidable. Extreme elements of the criminal segments in many Muslim societies will continue to aim for genocide against Israel through a second Holocaust or otherwise.

There is not only doubt as to whether peace is possible between the Palestinians and Israel. In the Palestinian camp, there are major forces that see peace as an intermediary step to Israel's total destruction. A peace agreement may well lead to a temporary decline in hate-mongering and incitement from the Palestinian side and some of its allies. However, while the probability for peace is already limited, even if it *were* to occur it would be a very fragile one.

It is commonly understood in Israel that even in the case of peace a strong army must be maintained. Yet it is far from understood that the propaganda war against Israel will continue and that whatever happens, the fight against the propaganda will also have to continue. Since the 1993 Oslo Agreements euphoric, short-sighted, and irresponsible Israelis have hampered Israel's propaganda battles. A recent typical example was when hundreds of Israelis encouraged the British Labour Party to put forward a motion in the British Parliament to recognize a Palestinian state.

Europe

In Europe today, an anti-Israeli infrastructure of criminal thought is widespread. Whoever thinks unjustifiedly that others are extreme criminals has a criminal mindset himself. Even though they are not the majority opinion, these criminal beliefs have deeply permeated the continent's mainstream. The statistics may vary substantially from one poll to another in the future. They can and should not be whitewashed. It is the Israeli government's duty to confront the EU leadership and that of individual countries with these findings and demand that they act against rampant anti-Israelism.

The European discrimination and criminalization of Israel has developed to such an extent that attitudes toward Israel have become an instrument to calibrate the state of overall decay and degeneration of large segments of European societies. The same has been the case in the past with respect to Jews. In the current century, this anti-Semitism is also repeating itself.

Europeans will not actively pursue a second Holocaust against Israel. If forces in the Muslim world succeed to carry it out, besides those who would be shocked a segment of Europeans may rejoice, many would be indifferent, and a large number of the anti-Israeli elites would deny that they contributed to the preparation of the genocide with their double standards against the Jewish state. That would be untrue.

The Israeli Side

Israel is paying a heavy price for its incompetent performance in the propaganda war. This became ever clearer after the 2014 Protective Edge campaign. That price will increase further unless it devotes sufficient intellectual, human, and financial resources to understanding the nature of this war and fighting it in a structural way. An in-depth study of this issue is a first step toward gradually developing adequate tools to counter the attacks competently.

The current delegitimization of Israel is a partially opaque phenomenon. In order to fight it, one first has to understand how the delegitimization process works. This also requires understanding what demonization means, how it overlaps with anti-Semitism, what themes the delegitimizers use, what methods they apply, how they transmit their messages, and who the delegitimizers of Israel actually are.

Successive Israeli governments have fallen very short in taking the necessary measures to fight against the propaganda threats. A key issue in any system that fights against its enemies is improving its weakest link. In Israel's case, it is not the military, the intelligence, the cyberwar units, or the country's social structure. The weakest link is the Israeli authorities' continuing incompetence and carelessness in the global propaganda war.

The main remedies have been set out in the previous pages. There is no substitute for the establishment of a single contra-propaganda structure, able to oversee the entire battlefield, analyze it, design how to fight, and develop actions against multiple enemies. Continuity and perseverance are essential.

There are no shortcuts. Without understanding the nature and content of the delegitimization process in detail, the fight against it will be far less effective than it could be. It will remain, as it is today, a partly losing battle, a partial waste of human and financial resources, combined with neglecting problems and underfunding of the battle. Only after the delegitimization process is better understood will one be able to discuss how to fight it far more efficiently. That will also require a gradual change in the mentality of the Israeli political leadership and of the people who are supposed to oversee the fight against delegitimization.

How Do Israel's Enemies Operate?

The first step that should be taken toward fighting the demonization of Israel and the Jews more effectively is to understand how their enemies operate. This book exposes their actions in a number of areas.

Several authors have published books on topics such as Muslim anti-Semitism and left-wing anti-Semitism. This author has covered additional topics in his earlier books: *Academics against Israel and the Jews*,[3] *Behind the Humanitarian Mask: The Nordic Countries, Israel and the Jews*,[4] *The Abuse of Holocaust Memory: Distortions and Responses*,[5] and *Demonizing Israel and the Jews*.[6]

Many more studies on other topics concerning Israel's demonization and delegitimization are necessary to obtain a broader picture of this huge, global hate-Israel movement. Some subjects for which overview books would be most helpful include the media and anti-Israelism, Christian denominations and demonization, as well as the role of many Muslim immigrants in the Western world in threatening Israel and making life in Europe uncomfortable for Jews.

What Could Israel Do?

If Israel had an integrated structure to fight against delegitimization, it would operate in many regards similarly to intelligence services. It would also have researched the incitement in all countries of relevance, and would have published an overview of the delegitimization of Israel in the Muslim world as well as studies on hate-mongering in many countries. It would occasionally have published case studies on individual issues of larger interest, for instance, the anti-Semitism in the antiracist camp, the United Nations Human Rights Council, the Goldstone Report, the Kairos Document, and so on. It would have trained its diplomats much better to meet challenges while abroad.

A second Holocaust seems possible in two ways. The one most often discussed is the possibility that Iran or a fanatic Muslim grouping will succeed to launch a nuclear bomb at Israel. A second possibility is that the pressure on Israel, from both its enemies and others who falsely claim to be its friends, will be so major that it will have to withdraw to indefensible borders.

The delegitimization process with its million cuts will have an additional consequence. Except for those committing the actual murders, few will feel responsible for what has happened. Not the many enemies who can claim that their individual contribution to the million cuts was insignificant, not the false friends who will say that they did not attack Israel, nor the many bystanders who looked away from the clear genocidal intentions proclaimed in parts of the Muslim world. At the same time, Israel will be accused of being responsible for its own fate because it turned the Palestinians—in reality a crime-permeated populace—into victims. All these lies together may flourish in an increasingly opaque society.

None of this has to happen. There is no reason to be fatalistic unless the present Israeli incompetence in the propaganda war endures. It is not too late to turn the tables on Israel's enemies. It requires, however, an effort that is radically different from what is taking place at present.

There is a postscript to the book as well. This text deals with the perpetrators and phenomena related to the partial delegitimization of Israel. But reading it can also instruct many others. As is so often the case, what happens to the Jews and nowadays Israel is a first indication of what is to come to many other nations. The distorted realities of contemporary Islam, the media, academia, NGOs, parts of liberal Protestantism, trade unions, social democracy, and so on have and will have an impact on many other countries and individuals. Those who are aware of the current Jewish and Israeli experience can use it as a looking glass to understand and treat problems in their own environments.

Notes

Introduction

1 www.i-p-o.org/racism-ngo-decl.htm.

2 Manfred Gerstenfeld, interview with Rabbi Abraham Cooper, "Antisemitism and Terrorism on the Internet: New Threats," *Post-Holocaust and Anti-Semitism*, 20-A, May 16, 2004; Michael Whine, "Cyberhate, Antisemitism and Counterlegislation," *Post-Holocaust and Anti-Semitism*, 47, August 1, 2006.

3 Manfred Gerstenfeld, "The Twenty-First-Century Total War against Israel and the Jews," *Post-Holocaust and Anti-Semitism*, Part 1, 38, November 1, 2005, Part 2, 39, December 1, 2005.

4 *Report of the British All-Party Parliamentary Inquiry into Antisemitism* (London: Stationery Office Ltd, September 2006), para. 20.

5 Yoni Hirsch and Ilan Gattegno, "Netanyahu announces 'digital Iron Dome' to battle cyberattacks," *Israel Hayom*, October 14, 2012.

6 "Netanyahu: We're building a digital Iron Dome," *The Jerusalem Post*, January 1, 2013.

7 Manfred Gerstenfeld, *The Abuse of Holocaust Memory: Distortions and Responses* (Jerusalem: Jerusalem Center for Public Affairs, 2009), 101-115. Second edition available for free at: http://jcpa.org/book/the-abuse-of-holocaust-memory-distortions-and-responses.

8 library.fes.de/pdf-files/do/07908-20110311.pdf.

9 Manfred Gerstenfeld, "Muslim Antisemitism in Europe," *Journal for the Study of Anti-Semitism* 4, 2 (2013): 195-229.

10 "Discrimination and hate crime against Jews in EU Member States: experiences and perceptions of anti-Semitism," European Union Agency for Fundamental Rights, 2013.

11 Manfred Gerstenfeld, *Europe's Crumbling Myths: The Post-Holocaust Origins of Today's Anti-Semitism* (Jerusalem: Jerusalem Center for Public Affairs, Yad Vashem, World Jewish Congress, 2003). Second edition available for free at: http://jcpa.org/wp-content/uploads/2011/12/Manfred.pdf.

12 "Chapter 3: Views of Religious Groups," Pew Research Global Attitudes Project, Pew Research Center, February 4, 2010.

13 "Chapter 2: How Muslims and Westerners View Each Other," Pew Research Global Attitudes Project, July 21, 2011.

14 Jacob Poushter, "The Turkish people don't look favorably upon the U.S., or any other country, really," Pew Research Center, October 31, 2014.

15 Manfred Gerstenfeld, *Demonizing Israel and the Jews* (New York: RVP Press, 2013).

16 For an overview, see Gerstenfeld, *Europe's Crumbling Myths.*

17 "2012 Top Ten Anti-Semitic/Anti-Israeli Slurs," Simon Wiesenthal Center.

18 "2013 Top Anti-Semitic/Anti-Israel Slurs," Simon Wiesenthal Center.

19 "2014—Top Ten Worst Global Anti-Semitic/Anti-Israel Incidents," Simon Wiesenthal Center, 2014.

20 Tovah Lazaroff, "Steinitz: Abbas is world's number one anti-Semitic leader," *The Jerusalem Post,* January 30, 2014.

21 "Statement by the President on ISIL," The White House, September 10, 2014.

22 https://www.youtube.com/watch?v=IFmCkJ92DRw.

23 "Charlie Hebdo—Statements by President Hollande," Embassy of France in Washington, January 9, 2015.

24 Andrew C. McCarthy, "The Islamic State is Nothing New," *National Review Online,* September 3, 2014.

25 *Haaretz* and Jonathan Lis, "MK Zoabi: Israeli combat pilots are no better than Islamic State beheaders," *Haaretz,* October 19, 2014.

26 David Schenker, "There's a Worrisome Amount of Support in Jordan for the Islamic State," *New Republic,* October 20, 2014.

27 Manfred Gerstenfeld, *Behind the Humanitarian Mask: The Nordic Countries, Is-*

rael and the Jews (Jerusalem: Jerusalem Center for Public Affairs and Friends of Simon Wiesenthal Center for Holocaust Studies, 2008). Second edition available for free at: http://jcpa.org/wp-content/uploads/2011/11/Nordic.pdf.

28 Gro Harlem Brundtland, Nyttårstale, "Typisk norsk å være god," *NRK*, January 1, 1992. (Norwegian)

29 Manfred Gerstenfeld, "NATO's new secretary-general: Problematic not only for Israel," *The Jerusalem Post*, April 6, 2014.

30 Richard Orange, "Norwegian camp guards shocked SS with brutality," *The Local* (Norway), November 6, 2013.

31 Manfred Gerstenfeld, interview with Eirik Veum, "Norwegian Collaborators Persecuted Jews in Holocaust," *Israel National News*, January 21, 2014.

32 Manfred Gerstenfeld, "The Deep Roots of Anti-Semitism in European Society," *Jewish Political Studies Review* 17, 1-2 (Spring 2005): 3-46.

33 Gerstenfeld, *Demonizing.*

34 Nahum Goldman, *Mein Leben, USA, Europa, Israel* (Frankfurt: Ullstein, 1984), 213. (German)

35 Yehuda Yaetz, "Ish HaTzlalim," *Mishpacha*, March 24, 2011. (Hebrew)

36 James Hider, "Binyamin Netanyahu warns of Iranian nuclear threat," *The Times*, February 21, 2011.

37 Robert S. Wistrich, *A Lethal Obsession: Anti-Semitism from Antiquity to the Global Jihad* (New York: Random House, 2010.) For the global character, see Daniel Jonah Goldhagen, *The Devil That Never Dies: The Rise and Threat of Global Anti-Semitism* (New York: Little, Brown, 2013).

chapter one

1 www.merriam-webster.com/dictionary/anti-semitism.

2 Manfred Gerstenfeld, "The Deep Roots of Anti-Semitism in European Society," *Jewish Political Studies Review* 17, 1-2 (Spring 2005): 3-46.

3 Robert Fife, "UN Promotes Systemic Hatred of Jews, MP Says," *National Post*, April 2, 2002.

4 www.jafi.org.il/agenda/2001/english/wk3-22/6.asp.

5 Ibid.

6 Per Ahlmark, *Det ar demokratin, dumbom!* (Stockholm: Timbro, 2004), 307. (Swedish)

7 Natan Sharansky with Ron Dermer, *The Case for Democracy: The Power of Freedom to Overcome Tyranny and Terror* (New York: Public Affairs, 2004), 221-226.

8 Natan Sharansky, "Foreword," *Jewish Political Studies Review* 16, 3-4 (Fall 2004): 5-8.

9 Working definition of anti-Semitism, Coordination Forum for Countering Anti-Semitism (CFCA), http://antisemitism.org.il/eng/Working%20definition%20of%20antisemitism.

10 *Report of the British All-Party Parliamentary Inquiry*, para. 26.

11 Working definition of anti-Semitism, Coordination Forum for Countering Anti-Semitism (CFCA), http://antisemitism.org.il/eng/Working%20definition%20of%20antisemitism.

12 Ibid.

13 Sam Sokol, "Israel Urges EU Human Rights Body to Return 'Anti-Semitism' Definition to Website," *The Jerusalem Post*, December 6, 2013.

14 Special envoy to monitor and combat anti-Semitism, "Defining Anti-Semitism: Fact Sheet," U.S. Department of State, June 8, 2010.

15 Manfred Gerstenfeld, interview with Pieter van der Horst, "The Egyptian Beginning of Anti-Semitism's Long History," *Post-Holocaust and Anti-Semitism*, 62, November 1, 2007.

16 Manfred Gerstenfeld, interview with Pieter van der Horst, "The Origins of Christian Anti-Semitism," *Post-Holocaust and Anti-Semitism*, 81, June 1, 2009.

17 Richard Landes, "What Happens when Jesus Doesn't Come: Jewish and Christian Relations in Apocalyptic Time," *Terrorism and Political Violence*, Vol. 14 (Spring 2002) (London: Frank Cass, 2002).

18 Working definition of anti-Semitism, Coordination Forum for Countering Anti-Semitism (CFCA), http://antisemitism.org.il/eng/Working%20definition%20of%20antisemitism.

19 Joshua Trachtenberg, *The Devil and the Jews* (Cleveland: Meridian, 1961), 159.

20 Gerstenfeld, interview with Van der Horst, "Origins of Christian Anti-Semitism."

21 Hadassa Ben-Itto, *The Lie That Wouldn't Die: The Protocols of the Elders of Zion* (Edgware, UK: Vallentine Mitchell, 2005).

22 Manfred Gerstenfeld, interview with Robert Wistrich, "Anti-Semitism Embedded in British Culture," *Post-Holocaust and Anti-Semitism*, 70, July 1, 2008.

23 J. H. Brinks, "Political Anti-Fascism in the German Democratic Republic," *Jour-*

nal of Contemporary History 32, 2 (1997): 207-217.

24 Erez Uriely, "Jew-Hatred in Contemporary Norwegian Caricatures," *Post-Holocaust and Anti-Semitism*, 50, November 1, 2006.

25 *Report of the British All-Party Parliamentary Inquiry*, para. 96.

26 "ADL Expresses Concern Over Conspiracy Theories About Jews Made by Turkish Politicians and Media in Reference to Mining Accident," Anti-Defamation League, May 22, 2014.

27 *Al-Hayat al-Jadida*, December 28, 1999, reproduced in Joël et Dan Kotek, *Au nom de l'antisionisme: L'image des Juifs et d'Israël dans la caricature depuis la seconde Intifada* (Brussels: Éditions Complexe, 2003), 53. (French)

28 *Al-Thawra* (Syria), March 4, 1993; Arie Stav, *Peace, the Arabian Caricature: A Study in Antisemitic Imagery* (Tel Aviv: Gefen, 1999), 202.

29 Manfred Gerstenfeld, "Ahmadinejad, Iran, and Holocaust Manipulation: Methods, Aims, and Reactions," *Jerusalem Viewpoints*, 551, February 1, 2007.

30 Ibid.

31 Joël Kotek, *Cartoons and Extremism: Israel and the Jews in Arab and Western Media* (Edgware, UK: Vallentine Mitchell, 2009), 87.

32 Reproduced in Uriely, "Jew-Hatred."

33 "The Devil and the Jew" (caricature by Oddmund Mikkelsen, *Hamar Arbeiderblad*, July 12, 2003), reproduced in ibid.

34 "Las viñetas antisemitas de *El País*," *Libertad Digital*, May 20, 2009. (Spanish)

35 Joël et Dan Kotek, *Au Nom de l'Antisionisme*. See also Kotek, *Cartoons and Extremism*.

36 Manfred Gerstenfeld, interview with Richard Landes, "Muslim Conspiracy Theories Affect Jews," in *Demonizing Israel and the Jews* (New York: RVP Press, 2013), 151.

37 Malcolm Hoenlein, personal communication.

38 AP, "Iran Blames U.S., Europe in Cartoon Crisis," *The New York Times*, February 12, 2006.

39 Roee Nahmias, "Syrian Paper Accuses Israel of Having Spread Bird Flu to Kill Arabs," *Ynetnews*, February 9, 2006.

40 "Ahmadinejad Warns West over Shrine Blast," Reuters, February 23, 2006.

41 Tobias Jaecker, *Antisemitische Verschwörungstheorien nach dem 11. September* (Berlin: LIT, 2005).(German)

42 Ibid., 54-55.

43 Ibid., 57.

44 Manfred Gerstenfeld, interview with Joel Kotek, "Major Anti-Semitic Motifs in Arab Cartoons," *Post-Holocaust and Anti-Semitism*, 21, June 1, 2004.

45 Manfred Gerstenfeld, "How to Fight Anti-Israeli Campaigns on Campus," *Post-Holocaust and Anti-Semitism*, 51, December 1, 2006.

46 Jonny Paul, "The Emergence of a Silent Academic Boycott of Israel," *EJPress*, May 28, 2006.

47 Sharon Sadeh, "UK Watchdog Backs Writer Who Won't Read Mail from Jews," *Haaretz*, August 5, 2003.

48 Ori Golan, "Same Word, Same Meaning," *The Jerusalem Post Magazine*, January 17, 2003.

49 Simon Kuper, "Ajax, de joden, Nederland," *Hard Gras* (Amsterdam), March 22, 2000, 141. (Dutch)

50 Oliver Bradley, "Anti-Semitism or Endearment?," *EJPress*, June 26, 2006.

51 Margalith Kleywegt and Max van Weezel, *Het Land van Haat en Nijd* (Amsterdam: Balans, 2006), 226. (Dutch)

52 Jerome Gordon, "Gurfinkiel: France may have joined 'Europe's league of fringe anti-Semitic countries,'" *The Iconoclast*, January 29, 2014.

53 Jean-Christophe Ruffin, "Chantier sur la Lutte contre le Racisme et l'antisémitisme," Ministère de l'interieur, de la sécurité interieure, et des libertés locales, October 30, 2004, 30. (French)

54 Aribert Heyder, Julia Iser, and Peter Schmidt, "Israelkritik oder Antisemitismus? Meinungsbildung zwischen Öffentlichkeit, Medien und Tabus," in Wilhelm Heitmeyer, ed., *Deutsche Zustände* (Frankfurt am Main: Suhrkamp, 2005), 144ff. (German). GMF stands for Gruppenbezogene Menschenfeindlichkeit (Group-Targeted Misanthropy).

55 Wilhelm Heitmeyer, "Texte zu Ergebnissen der Umfrage 2004 des Projektes," Universität Bielefeld, Institut fur interdisziplinare Konflikt- und Gewaltforschung, 2004. (German)

56 Kleywegt and Van Weezel, *Het Land van Haat en Nijd*, 214.

57 Ilan Moss, *Antisemitic Incidents and Discourse in Europe during the Israel-Hezbollah War* (Paris: European Jewish Congress, 2006).

58 Ibid., 9-10.

59 Ibid., 19.

60 Ibid., 20-21.

61 Ibid., 23.

62 Ibid., 33.

63 Ibid., 43.

64 Miranda McGonagall, "Lysbakkens and Willochs Holocaust Memorial speeches not at all well received," *Norway, Israel and the Jews*, November 27, 2012.

65 NTB, "Antisemittiske holdninger skal bekjempes," *Verdens Gang*, January 13, 2009. (Norwegian)

66 Robert S. Wistrich, *From Ambivalence to Betrayal: The Left, the Jews, and Israel* (Lincoln: University of Nebraska Press, 2012), 496.

67 Ibid., 480.

68 Manfred Gerstenfeld, *Behind the Humanitarian Mask* (Jerusalem: Jerusalem Center for Public Affairs and Friends of Simon Wiesenthal Center for Holocaust Studies, 2008), 22-23.

69 Speech on the anniversary of the Balfour Declaration, November 2, 1943, quoted in Matthias Küntzel, "National Socialism and Anti-Semitism in the Arab World," *Jewish Political Studies Review* 17, 1-2 (Spring 2005): 109.

70 *Report of the British All-Party Parliamentary Inquiry*, para. 89.

71 "Norwegian YMCA embraces boycott Israel policy," JTA, March 2, 2014.

72 Yehudit Barsky, "Terrorism Briefing: Islamic Jihad Movement in Palestine," American Jewish Committee, 2002.

73 Haim Malka, "Must Innocents Die? The Islamic Debate over Suicide Attacks," *Middle East Quarterly*, Spring 2003.

74 Jonathan Kay, "Hating Israel Is Part of Campus Culture," *National Post*, September 25, 2002.

75 Ted Honderich, "Is There a Right to Terrorism?," lecture at the University of Leipzig, October 19, 2003.

76 "Vattimo, frasi choc contro Israele 'Comperiamo armi per palestinesi' Comperiamo armi per palestinesi' Comperiamo armi per palestinesi...,'" *Corriere Della Serra*, July 16, 2014. (Italian)

77 "Well-known Italian philosopher: 'I'd like to shoot those bastard Zionists,'" *Haaretz*, July 23, 2014.

78 library.fes.de/pdf-files/do/07908-20110311.pdf.

79 Heyder, Iser, and Schmidt, "Israelkritik oder Antisemitismus?"

80 Heitmeyer, "Texte zu Ergebnissen."

81 Heyder, Iser, and Schmidt, "Israelkritik oder Antisemitismus?"

82 See, e.g., Martin Ulmer, "Current Trends in Germany," lecture presented at a conference on "Anti-Semitism and Anti-Zionism in Western Europe since 2000," SICSA, Jerusalem, *haGalil.com*, December 18, 2002; Susanne Urban, "Anti-Semitism in Germany Today: Its Roots and Tendencies," *Jewish Political Studies Review* 16, 3-4 (Fall 2005): 119-130.

83 "Kritik an Israel nicht deckungsgleich mit antisemitischen Haltungen," *gfs.bern*, March 28, 2007. (German)

84 "Antisemittisme i Norge? Den norske befolkningens holdninger til jøder og andre minoriteter," *HL-senteret*, May 20, 2012, http://www.hlsenteret.no/publikasjoner/antisemittisme-i-norge. (Norwegian)

85 "Zusammenfassung zentraler Ergebnisse," Frederich Ebert Stiftung and Bielefeld University, November 20, 2014, 5. (German)

86 European Commission, "Iraq and Peace in the World," *Eurobarometer Survey*, 151, November 2003, 78.

87 "BBC poll: Germany most popular country in the world," *BBC News Europe*, May 23, 2013.

88 Manfred Gerstenfeld, interview with Mark Elchardus, "Belgian Anti-Semitism," *Israel National News*, May 21, 2013; Manfred Gerstenfeld, interview with Günther Jikeli, "Myths and Truth about Muslim Anti-Semitism in Europe," in *Demonizing Israel and the Jews* (New York: RVP Press, 2013).

89 Renato Mannheimer, "E antisemita quasi un italiano su cinque," *Corriere de la Sera*, November 10, 2003. (Italian)

90 Enzo Campelli, *Figli di un dio locale, Giovani e differenze culturali in Italia* (Milan: FrancoAngeli, 2004), 147. (Italian)

91 "European Poll: 46% Say Jews Are 'Different,'" *Haaretz*, January 26, 2004.

92 Stephen Bates, "One in Seven Britons Say Holocaust Is Exaggerated," *The Guardian*, January 23, 2004.

93 "A Fragile Rebound for EU Image on Eve of European Parliament Elections," Ch. 4, Pew Research Center, May 12, 2014.

94 Joint Committees I (on Constitutional, Presidency of the Council of Ministers and Interior Affairs) and III (on Foreign and European Union Affairs) of the

Italian Parliament, Final Report of the Fact-Finding Inquiry on Anti-Semitism, October 14, 2011.

95 Ibid., 36-38.

96 Ben Quinn, "Almost half of Britons hold antisemitic view, poll suggests," *The Guardian*, January 14, 2015.

97 "Discrimination and hate crime against Jews in EU Member States: experiences and perceptions of anti-Semitism," European Union Agency for Fundamental Rights, 2013, 13.

98 The numbers add up to more than 100%, probably because people have had more than one anti-Semitic experience.

99 Ibid., 25-26.

100 Edward H. Kaplan and Charles A. Small, "Anti-Israel Sentiment Predicts Anti-semitism in Europe," *Journal of Conflict Resolution* 50, 4 (2006): 548-561.

101 Ruffin, "Chantier sur la Lutte contre le Racisme," 30.

102 "Campus Anti-Semitism," Briefing Report by the United States Commission on Civil Rights, Washington, DC, July 2006, 3.

103 Manfred Gerstenfeld, *Europe's Crumbling Myths: The Post-Holocaust Origins of Today's Anti-Semitism* (Jerusalem: Jerusalem Center for Public Affairs, Yad Vashem, World Jewish Congress, 2003).

104 "ADL Survey of Five European Countries Finds One in Five Hold Strong Antisemitic Sentiments; Majority Believes Canard of Jewish Disloyalty," press release, Anti-Defamation League, October 31, 2002, 5.

105 "Attitudes Toward Jews In Ten European Countries," Anti-Defamation League, March 2012.

106 "ADL Survey: Attitudes Toward Jews in 12 European Countries: Country by Country Results," Anti-Defamation League, June 7, 2005.

107 "Attitudes Toward Jews In Ten European Countries," Anti-Defamation League, March 2012.

108 "Attitudes Towards Jews in Argentina," Anti-Defamation League, Delegation of Argentine Jewish Associations, and Gino Germani Research Institute, September 2011.

109 "Attitudes Toward Jews In Ten European Countries," Anti-Defamation League, March 2012, 13-14.

110 "Attitudes Towards Jews in Argentina," Anti-Defamation League, Delegation

of Argentine Jewish Associations, and Gino Germani Research Institute, September 2011.

111 "ADL Poll: Anti-Semitic Attitudes in America Decline 3 Percent," press release, Anti-Defamation League, October 28, 2013.

112 http://global100.adl.org.

113 "Chapter 3: Views of Religious Groups," Pew Research Global Attitudes Project, Pew Research Center, February 4, 2010; "Chapter 2: How Muslims and Westerners View Each Other," Pew Research Global Attitudes Project, July 21, 2011; "Muslim Public Shares Concerns about Extremist Groups," Pew Research Global Attitudes Project, September 10, 2013.

114 JTA, "Poll: 26% of Americans believe Jews killed Jesus," *The Jerusalem Post*, November 1, 2013.

115 library.fes.de/pdf-files/do/07908-20110311.pdf.

116 Yaakov Lappin, "IDF releases Cast Lead casualty numbers," *The Jerusalem Post*, March 26, 2009.

117 "Operation Pillar of Defense," Israel Security Agency.

118 Gunnar Heinsohn and Daniel Pipes, "Arab-Israeli Fatalities Rank 49th," *FrontPage Magazine*, October 8, 2007.

119 Noam Chomsky, "Why America and Israel Are the Greatest Threats to Peace," *Alternet*, September 3, 2012.

120 www.bbc.co.uk/news/world-middle-east-24893808.

121 John Reed, "Israel Quietly Treats Syria War Victims," *Financial Times*, November 12, 2013.

chapter two

1 Manfred Gerstenfeld, *Europe's Crumbling Myths: The Post-Holocaust Origins of Today's Anti-Semitism* (Jerusalem: Jerusalem Center for Public Affairs, Yad Vashem, World Jewish Congress, 2003).

2 Manfred Gerstenfeld, interview with Isaac Lipschits, "The Dutch Government: Discriminating against the Survivors through a So-Called Egalitarian Approach," in *Europe's Crumbling Myths*.

3 Manfred Gerstenfeld, interview with Bjarte Bruland and Irene Levin, "Norway: The Courage of a Small Jewish Community; Holocaust Restitution and Anti-Semitism," *Post-Holocaust and Anti-Semitism*, 10, July 1, 2003.

4 Pieter Lagrou, *The Legacy of Nazi Occupation: Patriotic Memory and National Recovery in Western Europe, 1945-1965* (Cambridge: Cambridge University Press, 2000), 293. As quoted by Johannes Houwink ten Cate in interview with Manfred Gerstenfeld, "Holocaust Awareness Arrived Late in Western Europe," *Israel National News*, January 26, 2014.

5 Ibid., 303. See also Manfred Gerstenfeld, interview with Johannes Houwink ten Cate, "Holocaust Awareness Arrived Late in Western Europe," *Israel National News*, January 26, 2014.

6 Michael R. Marrus and Robert O. Paxton, *Vichy France and the Jews* (New York: Basic Books, 1981).

7 Dick de Mildt, I*n the Name of the People: Perpetrators of Genocide in the Reflection of Their Post-War Prosecution in West Germany: The "Euthanasia" and "Aktion Reinhard" Trial Cases* (The Hague/London/Boston: Martinus Nijhoff, 1996), 18-40.

8 Gerstenfeld, interview with Houwink ten Cate.

9 Manfred Gerstenfeld, interview with Shmuel Trigano, "Contemporary French Anti-Semitism: A Barometer for Gauging Problems in Society," in *Demonizing Israel and the Jews (New York: RVP Press, 2013).*

10 Pierre-André Taguieff, *Rising from the Muck: The New Anti-Semitism in Europe* (Chicago: Ivan R. Dee, 2004). The original French version was published under the title *La Nouvelle judéophobie* (Paris: Fayard/Mille et Une Nuits, 2002).

11 "Discrimination and hate crime against Jews in EU Member States: experiences and perceptions of anti-Semitism," European Union Agency for Fundamental Rights, 2013, 18.

12 Ibid., 38.

13 Ibid., 33.

14 Julie Wiener, "French Jewish leader: It's not so pleasant living there as Jews," *The Jerusalem Post*, May 14, 2014.

15 Manfred Gerstenfeld, "What Should French Jews Do?" *Israel National News*, December 11, 2014.

16 Jonathan Sacks, "The New Anti-Semitism," *Haaretz*, September 8, 2002.

17 Douglas Davis, "Sacks: Nobody Will Ever Forgive the Jews for Holocaust," *The Jerusalem Post*, June 16, 2004.

18 Simon Epstein, "Cyclical Patterns in Anti-Semitism: The Dynamics of Anti-Jew-

ish Violence in Western Countries since the 1950s," *Analysis of Current Trends in Anti-Semitism*, 2 (Jerusalem: Hebrew University, 1999), 1.

19 Murray Wardrop, Chris Irvine, Raf Sanchez, and Amy Willis, "Toulouse Siege as It Happened," *The Telegraph*, March 22, 2012.

20 Eugene Kontorovich, "How the EU directly funds settlements in occupied territory," *The Jerusalem Post*, December 28, 2013.

21 Raphael Ahren, "Former European Leaders Call on EU to Enact Settlement Ban," *The Times of Israel*, September 16, 2013.

22 Manfred Gerstenfeld, interview with Shmuel Trigano, "French Society Views Jews through the Prism of Shoah," *Israel National News*, January 23, 2014.

23 Andrei S. Markovits, "A New (or Perhaps Revived) 'Uninhibitedness' toward Jews in Germany," *Jewish Political Studies Review* 18, 1-2 (Spring 2006): 57-70.

24 Taguieff, *Rising from the Muck*.

25 Ibid.

26 Jacques Givet, *The Anti-Zionist Complex* (Englewood, NJ: SBS, 1982), 39.

27 Manfred Gerstenfeld, interview with Simon Epstein, "Fifty Years of French Intellectual Bias against Israel," *Post-Holocaust and Anti-Semitism*, 4, January 1, 2003.

28 David Zohar, personal communication.

29 Manfred Gerstenfeld, "European mistakes offer Israel important lessons on avoiding social breakdown," *Ynetnews*, August 17, 2011.

30 Frederic Forsyth, *Daily Express*, August 11, 2006.

31 Manfred Gerstenfeld, "Double Standards for Israel," *Journal for the Study of Antisemitism* 4, 2 (2012): 613-638.

32 Tovah Lazaroff, "Danish ambassador, JPost's Caroline Glick exchange verbal blows over EU attitude toward Israel," *The Jerusalem Post*, December 12, 2014.

33 Speech of Frans Timmermans, Tel Aviv University, December 9, 2013.

34 Manfred Gerstenfeld, "Rewriting Germany's Nazi Past: A Society in Moral Decline," *Jerusalem Viewpoints*, 530, May 1, 2005.

35 Andreas Zick, Beate Küpper, and Andreas Hövermann, *Intolerance, Prejudice and Discrimination: A European Report* (Berlin: Friedrich Ebert Stiftung Forum Berlin, 2011).

36 Manfred Gerstenfeld, interview with Nathan Durst, "Europe: From Guilt Feelings to Repackaging Anti-Semitism," in *Europe's Crumbling Myths*, 35.

37 Manfred Gerstenfeld, interview with Jeffrey Gedmin, "Experiencing European

Anti-Americanism and Anti-Israelism," in *Israel and Europe: An Expanding Abyss?* (Jerusalem: Jerusalem Center for Public Affairs, Adenauer Foundation, 2005), 142-158.

38 Manfred Gerstenfeld, interview with Susanne Urban, "Changes in German Holocaust Education," *Israel National News*, June 8, 2012.

39 Ibid.

40 Manfred Gerstenfeld, interview with Daniel Killy, "The Tyranny of Political Correctness," *Israel National News*, July 30, 2013.

41 Manfred Gerstenfeld, interview with Benjamin Weinthal, "Germany Bestows Awards upon Anti-Israel Inciters," in *Demonizing Israel and the Jews*, 122.

42 Ibid., 123.

43 Ibid., 124.

44 Ibid., 123.

45 Benjamin Weinthal, "Study: Main German political party foundations fund anti-Israel activity," *The Jerusalem Post*, October 26, 2013.

46 Wardrop et al., "Toulouse Siege."

47 John Lichfield, "How my hate-filled family spawned Merah the Monster," *The Independent*, November 12, 2012.

48 JTA, "Report: France saw 58% rise in anti-Semitic attacks in 2012," *The Jerusalem Post*, February 20, 2013. For the French text, see "Rapport sur l'Antisémitisme en France," Service de Protection de la Communauté Juive (SPCJ), 2012, http://dl.antisemitisme.org/RAPPORT%202012.pdf.

49 "Discrimination and hate crime against Jews in EU Member States: experiences and perceptions of anti-Semitism," European Union Agency for Fundamental Rights, 2013, 32.

50 Auriéle A., "'Yesterday, a Part of My Love for France Left Me,'" *Tablet*, July 18, 2014.

51 Manfred Gerstenfeld, "Paris Killings Aftermath: Symptoms of French Disease," *Israel National News*, January 15, 2015.

52 Michael Wilner, "Landmark Paris synagogue closes on Shabbat for first time since World War II," *The Jerusalem Post*, January 9, 2015.

53 Karel Berkhout, "Synagoge schrapt viering sabbat na dreiging," *NRC Handelsblad*, June 9, 2010. (Dutch)

54 Mikael Tossavainen, "Arab and Muslim Anti-Semitism in Sweden," in Manfred

Gerstenfeld, *Behind the Humanitarian Mask: The Nordic Countries, Israel and the Jews* (Jerusalem: Jerusalem Center for Public Affairs, 2008), 97.

55 Eirik Eiglad, *The Anti-Jewish Riots in Oslo* (Oslo: Communalism, 2010).

56 Andrew Baker, Adil Akhmetov, and Catherine McGuinness, "Report of the Personal Representatives of the OSCE Chair-in-Office on tolerance and non-discrimination issues [on the country visit to] Norway," June 11-15, 2012, Tolerance and Non-Discrimination Information System, published by OSCE, Vienna, December 14, 2012.

57 NTB, "OSSE:—Norge viser intoleranse mot jøder og muslimer," *NRK*, October 21, 2012. (Norwegian)

58 Per Anders Johansen, "Reagerer sterkt på holdninger til jøder," *Aftenposten*, October 21, 2012. (Norwegian)

59 Jostein Gaarder, "Guds utvalgte folk," *Aftenposten*, August 5, 2006 (Norwegian). In English, see www.wiesenthal.com/site/apps/s/content.asp?c=fwLYKnN8LzH&b=253162&ct=2869779.

60 "-Styggeste jeg har lest," *Aftenposten*, August 5, 2006. (Norwegian)

61 "Otto Jespersen reported for offense against Jews," *Aftenbladet*, November 29, 2008.

62 Nina Berglund, "Comedian burns Bible as cameras roll," *Aftenposten*, March 28, 2006.

63 https://www.youtube.com/watch?v=LyBS6j5WR-c.

64 "Humanitarian aid to Gaza continues," Israel Ministry of Foreign Affairs, August 27, 2014.

65 Cnaan Liphshiz, "In Scandinavia, kipah becomes a symbol of defiance for Malmo's Jews," JTA, September 24, 2012.

66 Cnaan Liphshiz, "In Malmo, record number of hate crimes complaints but no convictions," JTA, January 9, 2013.

67 "Discrimination and hate crime against Jews in EU Member States: experiences and perceptions of anti-Semitism," European Union Agency for Fundamental Rights, 2013, 19.

68 Barak Ravid, "Denmark's largest bank blacklists Israel's Hapoalim over settlement construction," *Haaretz*, February 1, 2014.

69 JTA, "Israeli envoy warns against wearing skullcaps in Copenhagen," *The Times of Israel*, December 13, 2012.

70 Hannes Gamillscheg, "Dänemark: Juden fühlen sich unter Druck," *Die Presse*, January 1, 2013. (German)

71 JTA, "Danish Jewry dwindling due in part to anti-Semitism, community leader says," *The Jerusalem Post*, October 8, 2013.

72 JTA, "Poll: 74% of Denmark's citizens want to outlaw circumcision," *Haaretz*, October 23, 2014.

73 Manfred Gerstenfeld, *Behind the Humanitarian Mask* (Jerusalem: Jerusalem Center for Public Affairs and Friends of Simon Wiesenthal Center for Holocaust Studies, 2008).

74 "Danish Nazis killed 1,400 Jews in WWII: new book," The Local DK, October 15, 2014.

75 Claude Meyer, interview with Jean-Claude Milner, *Actualité Juive Hebdo*, 823, December 11, 2003. (French)

76 Per Ahlmark, "Palme's Legacy 15 Years On," *Project Syndicate*, February 2001.

77 Moses Altsech (Daniel Perdurant, pseud.), "Anti-Semitism in Contemporary Greek Society," *Analysis of Current Trends in Anti-Semitism*, 7 (Jerusalem: Hebrew University, 1995), 10.

78 "Israel-Kritik oder Antisemitismus?" *Neue Zürcher Zeitung*, April 26, 2002. (German)

79 Efraim Karsh, "European Misreading of the Israeli-Palestinian Conflict: Finnish Foreign Minister Tuomioja—A Case Study," *Jerusalem Issue Brief*, 27, July 12, 2005.

80 "Antisemitism Worldwide, 2002-3," Stephen Roth Institute for the Study of Contemporary Anti-Semitism and Racism, Tel Aviv University, 2004.

81 Herb Keinon, "Spain: Anti-Sharon Municipality Sign," *The Jerusalem Post*, November 16, 2004.

82 "Islamic cell is accused of 191 Madrid murders," *Daily Mail*, February 15, 2007.

83 Faisal al Yafai, "Cleric Hits Back at Uniformed Critics," *The Guardian*, July 12, 2004.

84 "Sharon the Nazi" (caricature by Finn Graff, *Dagbladet*, April 2002), reproduced in Erez Uriely, "Jew-Hatred in Contemporary Norwegian Caricatures," *Post-Holocaust and Anti-Semitism*, 50, November 1, 2006.

85 "Olmert the Nazi" (caricature by Finn Graff, *Dagbladet*, July 10, 2006), reproduced in ibid.

86 Jan-Erik Smilden, "Århundrets fangebytte," *Dagbladet*, October 19, 2011. (Norwegian)

87 "St. Olavs Orden til Finn Graff," *Dagbladet*, March 7, 2007. (Norwegian)

88 Haakon Lie, *Slik jeg ser det*, Part 2 (Oslo: Tiden Norsk forlag, 1983), 132 (Norwegian), quoted in Uriely, "Jew-Hatred."

chapter three

1 Gospel of John 8:44.

2 Manfred Gerstenfeld, interview with Pieter van der Horst, "The Origins of Christian Anti-Semitism," *Post-Holocaust and Anti-Semitism*, 81, May 5, 2009.

3 Malcolm Hoenlein, personal communication.

4 Top Ten Anti-Semitic Slurs of 2010, "Anti-Semitism Goes Mainstream," Simon Wiesenthal Center.

5 Introduction by the Chairperson of the Sub-Committee of Inquiry into Anti-Semitism, the Hon. M.P Fiamma Nirenstein, October 14, 2011, http://www.jewishresearch.org/quad/10-11/images/documents/Antisemitismo_introduction%20Nirenstein_EN.pdf.

6 Erez Uriely, "Jew-Hatred in Contemporary Norwegian Caricatures," *Post-Holocaust and Anti-Semitism*, 50, November 1, 2006.

7 Guy Millière, "France: Anti-Semitism Now Mainstream," *Gatestone Institute*, October 30, 2013.

8 Manfred Gerstenfeld, interview with Joel Kotek, "Major Anti-Semitic Motifs in Arab Cartoons," *Post-Holocaust and Anti-Semitism*, 21, June 1, 2004; Joël et Dan Kotek, *Au nom de l'antisionisme: L'image des Juifs et d'Israël dans la caricature depuis la seconde Intifada* (Brussels: Éditions Complexe, 2003), 69. (French)

9 Herb Keinon, "Greece repudiates Theodorakis' anti-Semitism," *The Jerusalem Post*, November 14, 2003.

10 Mitchell Bard, *The Arab Lobby* (New York: HarperCollins, 2010).

11 Manfred Gerstenfeld, interview with Mitchell Bard, "The Powerful Saudi Lobby in the United States," in *Demonizing Israel and the Jews* (New York: RVP Press, 2013), 55.

12 Eric Lipton, Brooke Williams, and Nicholas Confessore, "Foreign Powers Buy Influence at Think Tanks," *The New York Times*, September 6, 2014.

13 "The Palestine Committee of Norway," Palestine Committee of Norway.

14 Joël et Dan Kotek, *Au nom de l'antisionisme*, 71.

15 Jenny Booth, "Offensive words," *The Times Online*, September 23, 2006.

16 Manfred Gerstenfeld, interview with Pieter van der Horst, "The Egyptian Beginning of Anti-Semitism's Long History," *Post-Holocaust and Anti-Semitism*, 62, November 1, 2007.

17 Manfred Gerstenfeld, interview with Meir Litvak, "The Development of Arab Anti-Semitism," *Post-Holocaust and Anti-Semitism*, 5, February 2, 2003.

18 Steve Bell, "Are you drinking what we're drinking? Vote conservative," *The Guardian*, April 7, 2005.

19 *Insiders*, TV program transcript, "Cartoonist follows UK contest," Annabel Crabb takes *Talking Pictures* to London and chats with the *Guardian*'s Steve Bell, Australian Broadcasting Corporation, May 1, 2005.

20 Steve Bell, "Michael Howard and the Tory party," *The Guardian*, October 5, 2005.

21 "Anti-Semitic Series Airs on Arab Television," *ADL archive website*, January 9, 2004.

22 Manfred Gerstenfeld, interview with Richard Landes, "The Muhammad Al-Dura Blood Libel: A Case Analysis," *Post-Holocaust and Anti-Semitism*, 74, November 2, 2008.

23 Ibid.

24 Avi Issacharoff, "Israeli physician acquitted of libel against Mohammed al-Dura's father," *Haaretz*, February 16, 2012.

25 Yonah Jeremy Bob, "Committee finds IDF didn't kill Palestinian al-Dura," *The Jerusalem Post*, May 19, 2013.

26 Times of Israel Staff and AP, "Leading critic of French al-Dura coverage convicted," *The Times of Israel*, June 26, 2013.

27 Gerstenfeld, interview with Landes.

28 Gallup Poll Editorial Staff, "Blame for Sept. 11 Attacks Unclear for Many in Islamic World," Gallup, March 1, 2002.

29 "Pew Global Attitudes Project: Spring 2006 Survey," Pew Research Center, 2006, 40.

30 Gjermund Glesnes, "Sammenligner Gaza med dødsriket Hades," *Verdens Gang*, January 4, 2009. (Norwegian)

31 Mads Gilbert and Erik Fosse, *Øyne i Gaza* (Oslo: Gyldendal, 2009). (Norwegian)

32 Erlend Skevik, "Regjeringen støttet Gaza-legene," *Verdens Gang*, September 18, 2009. (Norwegian)

33 Ibid.

34 "St. Olavs Orden," *Det Norske Kongehus*, November 6, 2012. (Norwegian)

35 NTB, "St. Olavs Orden til Mads Gilbert," *Verdens Gang*, May 6, 2013. (Norwegian)

36 Ida Louise Rostad, "Gilbert får kongens medalje," *Nordlys*, May 6, 2013. (Norwegian)

37 www.politicalcartoon.co.uk/html/exhibition.html.

38 Manfred Gerstenfeld, interview with Zvi Shtauber, "British Attitudes toward Israel and the Jews," in *Israel and Europe: An Expanding Abyss?* (Jerusalem: Jerusalem Center for Public Affairs, Adenauer Foundation, 2005), 188.

39 *Al-Dustur* (Jordan), April 4, 1994; Arie Stav, *Peace, the Arabian Caricature: A Study in Antisemitic Imagery* (Tel Aviv: Gefen, 1999), 146.

40 Gerstenfeld, interview with Kotek.

41 Donald Boström, "Våra söner plundras på sina organ," *Aftonbladet*, August 17, 2009 (Swedish). See also Mikael Tossavainen, "The *Aftonbladet* Organ-Trafficking Accusations against Israel: A Case Study," *Post-Holocaust and Anti-Semitism*, 95, March 1, 2010.

42 Press Association, "MPs compare Gaza to Warsaw ghetto," *The Guardian*, June 19, 2003.

43 Nicholas Watt, "Lib Dem MP: Why I would consider being a suicide bomber," *The Guardian*, January 24, 2004.

44 "Baroness Tonge fired over outburst against Israeli soldiers in Haiti," *The Telegraph*, February 13, 2010.

45 Marcus Dysch, "Police to probe Tonge's Israel Apartheid Week rant," *The Jewish Chronicle Online*, February 29, 2012.

46 Janet Daley, "Jenny Tonge loses the Lib Dem whip for anti-Israel rant—and about time too," *The Telegraph*, February 29, 2012.

47 *Al-Ahram* (Egypt), April 21, 2001; see Joël Kotek, *Cartoons and Extremism: Israel and the Jews in Arab and Western Media* (Edgware, UK: Vallentine Mitchell, 2008), 63.

48 Toliadis, *Ethnos*, April 7, 2002; Kotek, ibid., 129.

49 "Sunday Times apologizes for Netanyahu cartoon," *Ynetnews*, February 3, 2013.

50 Joshua Trachtenberg, *The Devil and the Jews* (Cleveland: Meridian, 1961), 159.

51 Raphael Israeli, *Poison: Modern Manifestations of a Blood Libel* (Lanham, MD: Lexington Books, 2002).

52 "German newspaper shows Netanyahu as Peace Poisoner," JTA, August 8, 2013.
53 Benjamin Weinthal, "German anti-Netanyahu cartoon sparks anti-Semitism row," *The Jerusalem Post*, November 14, 2013.
54 Remark made in broadcast and confirmed in personal communication with this author.
55 Manfred Gerstenfeld, interview with Samar, "Dans Les Coulisses De L'Antisémitisme Musulman Aux Pays-Bas," *Lessakele*, October 23, 2012. (French)
56 "2013 Top Anti-Semitic/Anti-Israel Slurs," Simon Wiesenthal Center, 2013.
57 Manfred Gerstenfeld, "Ahmadinejad, Iran, and Holocaust Manipulation: Methods, Aims, and Reactions," *Jerusalem Viewpoints*, 551, February 1, 2007.
58 Gerstenfeld, interview with Kotek.
59 JTA, "Poll: 26% of Americans believe Jews killed Jesus," *The Jerusalem Post*, November 1, 2013.
60 "ADL Poll: One in Four Americans Believe Jews Were Responsible for the Death of Christ," Anti-Defamation League, February 23, 2004.
61 *Al-Rai* (Jordan), December 26, 1991; Stav, *Peace*, 161.
62 Gerstenfeld, "Ahmadinejad."
63 Giorgio Forattini, *La Stampa* (Italy), April 3, 2002. See Kotek, *Cartoons*.

chapter four

1 Manfred Gerstenfeld, interview with Pieter van der Horst, "The Origins of Christian Anti-Semitism," *Post-Holocaust and Anti-Semitism*, 81, June 1, 2009.
2 Luke 6:29.
3 "SPD-Chef: Gabriel spricht über seinen Nazi-Vater," *Der Spiegel Online*, January 11, 2011. (German)
4 "Israels Palästinenserpolitik: Gabriel erntet Kritik nach Apartheid-Vergleich," *Der Spiegel Online*, March 15, 2012. (German)
5 https://www.jewishvirtuallibrary.org/jsource/biography/Weizsaeker.html. library.fes.de/pdf-files/do/07908-20110311.pdf.
6 Aribert Heyder, Julia Iser, and Peter Schmidt, "Israelkritik oder Antisemitismus? Meinungsbildung zwischen Öffentlichkeit, Medien und Tabus," in Wilhelm Heitmeyer, ed., *Deutsche Zustände* (Frankfurt am Main: Suhrkamp, 2005), 144ff (German).
7 Henry Rousso, *Le dosssier de Lyon III: Le rapport sur le racisme et le négationn-*

isme à l'université Jean-Moulin (Paris: Fayard, 2004). (French)

8 Deborah Lipstadt, *Denying the Holocaust: The Growing Assault on Truth and Memory* (New York: Free Press/Macmillan, 1993).

9 Manfred Gerstenfeld, interview with Deborah Lipstadt, "Denial of the Holocaust and Immoral Equivalence," *Post-Holocaust and Anti-Semitism*, 11, August 1, 2003.

10 www.youtube.com/watch?v=mkizDpl7x_E (part 1) (viewed June 2, 2009); www.youtube.com/watch?v=369WqEJ6ChA (part 2) (viewed June 2, 2009).

11 Manfred Gerstenfeld, interview with Michael Widlanski, "Deceitful Palestinian Statements as Strategic Weapons," *Israel National News*, September 23, 2013.

12 Manfred Gerstenfeld, interview with Nadav Shragai, "Libel: Israel Intends to Destroy the Al-Aksa Mosque," *Israel National News*, October 16, 2013.

13 JTA, "UNESCO sets date for contested Jews in Israel exhibit," *Haaretz*, January 28, 2014.

14 http://www.youtube.com/watch?v=JA9nFQyRTdw (viewed July 14, 2014).

15 Fraser Nelson, "Anger over Dalyell's 'Jewish Cabal' Slur," *The Scotsman*, May 5, 2003.

16 Lahav Harkov, "Erdogan: 'Ayelet Shaked has same mindset as Hitler,'" *The Jerusalem Post*, July 15, 2014.

17 Gulsan Solaker and Jonny Hogg, "Turkish PM Erdogan says Israel 'surpasses Hitler in barbarism,'" Reuters, July 19, 2014.

18 Raphael Ahren, "South Africa's ruling party compares Gaza op to Nazi crimes," *The Times of Israel*, July 10, 2014.

19 "Venezuela condems Israeli 'genocide' and 'extermination,'" Reuters, July 19, 2014.

20 Manfred Gerstenfeld, interview with Robbie Sabel, "On the 'Israel is an Apartheid State' Slander," *Israel National News*, December 2, 2013.

21 Benjamin Pogrund, *Drawing Fire* (London: Rowman & Littlefield, 2014), 152.

22 Lilian Alemagna and Laura Breton, "Valls denonce un 'apartheid territorial, social et ethnique' en France," *Liberation*, January 20, 2015. (French)

23 Nadav Shragai, *The "Al-Aksa is in Danger" Libel: The History of a Lie* (Jerusalem: Jerusalem Center for Public Affairs, 2012).

24 Gerstenfeld, interview with Shragai.

25 Günther Grass, "Was gesagt werden muss," *Suddeutsche.de*, April 10, 2012. (German)

26 Günter Grass, "Quello che deve essere detto," *La Repubblica*, April 4, 2012 (Ital-

ian); Ugo Volli, "Poesia dedicata a Günter Grass"; Andrea Tarquini, "Una poesia contro Israele, l'ultima provocazione di Grass Le sue atomiche una minaccia"; Adriano Prosperi, "Se la storia viene capovolta in un brusio di responsabilità," *Informazione Corretta*, April 4, 2012. (Italian)

27 Günter Grass, "What Must Be Said," *The Guardian*, April 5, 2012.

28 Günter Grass, "Lo que hay que decir," *El País*, April 4, 2012. (Spanish)

29 "Dokumentation: Læs Günter Grass' digt," *Politiken*, April 7, 2012. (Danish)

30 Günter Grass, "Det som må sies," *Aftenposten*, April 8, 2012. (Norwegian)

31 Manfred Gerstenfeld, "Part-Time Anti-Semites," *Israel National News*, April 23, 2012.

32 "Vote sur la "Palestine Fillon: 'Israël menace la paix mondiale,'" *Le Monde Juif*, November 16, 2014. (French)

33 "Passover suicide bombing at Park Hotel in Netanya," Israel Ministry of Foreign Affairs, March 27, 2002.

34 "Backgrounder: A Study in Palestinian Duplicity and Media Indifference," CAMERA, August 1, 2002.

35 Tovah Lazaroff, "Erdan: Israel needs to unite against Palestinian delegitimization," *The Jerusalem Post*, September 29, 2014.

36 "Examination of the names of Palestinians killed in Operation Protective Edge—Part Seven," Meir Amit Intelligence and Terrorist Information Center, December 1, 2014.

37 Ari Yashar, "Ya'alon to Kerry: Don't Threaten Intifada," *Arutz Sheva*, November 8, 2013.

38 Appeal to Poverty/Appeal to money. About.com. Retrieved from http://atheism.about.com/library/FAQs/skepticism/blfaq_fall_poverty.htm.

39 Henry I. Silverman, "How in 2010 Reuters engaged in anti-Israel propaganda," *Journal of Applied Business Research* 27, 6 (November-December 2011).

40 Michael C. Labossiere. Fallacies. Fallacy Tutorial Pro 3.0. The Nizkor Project. Retrieved from www.nizkor.org/features/fallacies.

41 Manfred Gerstenfeld, "The Gaza Flotilla: Facts and Official Reactions," *Post-Holocaust and Anti-Semitism*, 102, September 15, 2010.

42 Manfred Gerstenfeld, "Israel against the forces of sentimental appeal," *The Jerusalem Post*, December 22, 2014.

43 Sreenivasan Jain, "How Hamas Assembles and Fires Rockets," NDTV, August 5, 2014.

44 "Finnish reporter admits Gaza rockets launched from hospital," *The Jerusalem Post*, August 2, 2014.

45 "Reporter in Gaza startled by Hamas rocket whizzing over her head," *The Jerusalem Post*, August 3, 2014.

46 "Rhetorical Fallacies," Undergraduate Writing Center, University of Texas at Austin, 2013.

47 "Gazans Want Marshall Plan, Israel Policy Falls Short," Reuters, July 27, 2010.

48 Silverman, "How in 2010 Reuters engaged in anti-Israel propaganda."

49 *Cambridge Dictionaries Online*, http://dictionary.cambridge.org/dictionary/british/double-standard.

50 Working Definition of anti-Semitism, The Coordination Forum for Countering Anti-Semitism (CFCA), http://antisemitism.org.il/eng/Working%20definition%20of%20antisemitism.

51 Reuters and Matt Spetalnick, "U.S.: Israel can do more to avoid civilian casualties in Gaza," *Haaretz*, July 18, 2014.

52 Reuters, "US, UN, France call on Israel to do more to prevent civilian casualties in Gaza," *The Jerusalem Post*, July 18, 2014.

53 Yonah Jeremy Bob, "ICRC: World holds Israel to legal double standards," *The Jerusalem Post*, December 3, 2014.

54 For a more detailed analysis, see Manfred Gerstenfeld, "Bin Laden versus Yassin," Y*netnews*, March 5, 2011.

55 "U.N. chief Ban hails bin Laden death as 'watershed,'" Reuters, May 2, 2011.

56 "World leaders condemn Yassin assassination," *The Sunday Times*, March 22, 2004.

57 Lisa Bryant, "Europe Welcomes bin Laden's Death," Voice of America, May 2, 2011.

58 "World leaders condemn."

59 Gerstenfeld, "Bin Laden."

60 Thomas L. Friedman, *From Beirut to Jerusalem* (New York: Anchor Books, Doubleday, 1990), 72-73.

61 Ibid.

62 "Examining Human Rights Watch in 2008: Double Standards and Post-Colonial Ideology," NGO Monitor, January 13, 2009.

63 Gert Weisskirchen, "Anmassende Abgeordnete," *Jüedische Allgemeine*, July 8, 2010. (German).

64 Manfred Gerstenfeld, interview with Irwin Cotler, "Discrimination against Is-

rael in the International Arena: Undermining the Cause of Human Rights at the United Nations," in *Europe's Crumbling Myths: The Post-Holocaust Origins of Today's Anti-Semitism* (Jerusalem: Jerusalem Center for Public Affairs, Yad Vashem, World Jewish Congress, 2003), 220.

65 "Israel: Billionaire with settlement links targeted in divestment campaign," www.adnkronos.com/AKI/English/Security/?id=3.0.3758448930.

66 Meir Rosenne, personal communication, cited in Manfred Gerstenfeld, "European Politics: Double Standards toward Israel," *Jewish Political Studies Review* 17, 3-4 (Fall 2005).

67 Manfred Gerstenfeld, *Behind the Humanitarian Mask* (Jerusalem: Jerusalem Center for Public Affairs and Friends of Simon Wiesenthal Center for Holocaust Studies, 2008), 22-23.

68 Moshe Yegar, *Neutral Policy—Theory versus Practice: Swedish-Israeli Relations* (Jerusalem: Israel Council on Foreign Relations, 1993), 126-128.

69 Manfred Gerstenfeld, interview with Uriel Rosenthal, "Nederland, Europa en Israel," *Aleh*, February 2014. (Dutch)

70 Manfred Gerstenfeld, "Double Standards for Israel," *Journal for the Study of Antisemitism* 4, 2 (2012): 613-638.

71 Steven Lukes, *Moral Relativism (Big Ideas)* (London: Profile Books, 2009).

72 Quoted in Michael Shermer and Alex Grobman, *Denying History: Who Says the Holocaust Never Happened and Why Do They Say It?* (Berkeley: University of California Press, 2009), 105.

73 Dr. Yohanan Manor, "The 1975 'Zionism is Racism' Resolution: The Rise, Fall, and Resurgence of a Libel," Jerusalem Center for Public Affairs, May 2, 2010.

74 UN Resolution 3379 (XXX), United Nations, November 1975.

75 Manor, "1975 'Zionism is Racism' Resolution."

76 Joël Kotek, *Cartoons and Extremism: Israel and the Jews in Arab and Western Media* (Edgware, UK: Vallentine Mitchell, 2009), 41.

77 Ibid.

78 Richard Landes, "1948-2008 Part I: The Sad Story of the Nakba," *The Augean Stables*, May 8, 2008.

79 "Erdogan: Zionism is a crime against humanity," *Ynetnews*, February 28, 2013.

80 Selcan Hacaoglu and Nicole Gaouette, "UN Says Erdogan 'Wrong' to Link Zionism With Fascism," *Bloomberg*, March 1, 2013.

81 Elad Benari, "Kerry Says Erdogan's Comments are 'Objectionable,'" *Arutz Sheva*, March 1, 2013.

82 Secretary-General Ban Ki-moon, "Note to correspondents," United Nations, March 1, 2013.

83 Meir Litvak and Esther Webman, *From Empathy to Denial: Arab Responses to the Holocaust* (New York: Columbia University Press, 2009).

84 Akiva Eldar, "Tutu to Haaretz: Arabs paying the price of the Holocaust," *Haaretz*, August 28, 2009.

85 Robert Rozett, "An Open Letter to Archbishop Desmond Tutu," *Haaretz*, September 4, 2009.

86 "Le discours prononcé à Constantine," *Algeria Watch*, December 6, 2007 (French), http://www.algeria-watch.org/fr/article/pol/france/discours_sarkozy_constantine.htm.

87 "Israel to Ashton: Retract Toulouse-Gaza comparison," *The Jerusalem Post*, March 20, 2013.

88 "Debate: MEPs call for an immediate ceasefire in the Israeli-Palestinian conflict," European Parliament, July 17, 2014.

89 "Freezing funds: list of terrorists and terrorist groups," European Union.

90 "Israel's protection and Hamas' exploitation of civilians in Operation Protective Edge," Israel Ministry of Foreign Affairs, July 24, 2014.

91 Manfred Gerstenfeld, "The Gaza Flotilla: Facts and Official Reactions," Jerusalem Center for Public Affairs, September 15, 2010.

92 JTA, "John Kerry Compares Gaza Flotilla and Boston Marathon Bombing Victims," *Forward*, April 23, 2013.

93 Jean Bethke Elshtain, *Just War against Terror: The Burden of American Power in a Violent World* (New York: Basic Books, 2003), ch. 1.

94 Adam Chandler, "The Times, The Guardian Misrepresent Conflict," *Tablet Magazine*, November 16, 2012.

95 David Harris, "Israel and Hamas: Moral Clarity, Moral Fog, Moral Hypocrisy," *The Huffington Post*, November 20, 2012.

96 Herb Keinon, "Danish FM: Ze'evi Murder Same as Targeted Killings," *The Jerusalem Post*, October 19, 2001.

97 Anton La Guardia, "Hamas is added to EU's blacklist of terror," *The Telegraph*, September 12, 2003.

98 "European Council conclusions on external relations (Ukraine and Gaza)," European Council, July 16, 2014.

99 "Israel-Hamas prisoner swap casts harsh light on detention practices of all sides," Amnesty International, October 18, 2011.

100 Alan Dershowitz, "The Anti-Israel Double Standard Watch," *The Huffington Post*, July 14, 2006.

101 Harris, "Israel and Hamas."

102 Emre Peker, "Turkey Labels Israel a 'Terrorist State,'" *The Wall Street Journal*, November 19, 2012.

103 Harris, "Israel and Hamas."

104 "Discours de Nicolas Sarkozy à Alger," *Afrik.com*, December 3, 2007 (French), http://www.afrik.com/article13062.html.

105 Mona Levin, "Kan ikke sammenlignes," *Aftenposten*, August 9, 2011. (Norwegian)

106 Melanie Phillips, "The False Equation of Jew-hatred and Islamophobia," *The Jerusalem Post*, September 5, 2014.

107 Manfred Gerstenfeld, "Dutch Jewish Leaders Sign a Damning Declaration," *Israel National News*, September 4, 2014.

108 Gerstenfeld, interview with Cotler, 220.

109 "OIC Secretary General: Israeli Aggression on the Relief Convoy Heading for Gaza Is a Crime and Blatant Violation of All International Laws Norms and Standards," Organization of Islamic Cooperation, May 31, 2010, www.oic-oci.org/topic_detail.asp?t_id=3833.

110 Mats Tunehag, "Iran's Swedish Protector," *The Wall Street Journal*, July 21, 2010.

111 "Swede Bites Dog," *The Wall Street Journal*, July 7, 2010.

112 "Iranian President at Teheran Conference: 'Very Soon, This Stain of Disgrace [Israel] Will Be Purged from the Center of the Islamic World—and This is Attainable,'" Middle East Media Research Institute (MEMRI) Special Dispatch Series, No. 1013, October 28, 2005.

113 Michael Whine, "Terrorist Incidents against Jewish Communities and Israeli Citizens Abroad, 1968-2010," *Post-Holocaust and Anti-Semitism*, 108, July 1, 2011.

114 Naomi Klein, "Israel: Boycott, Divest, Sanction," *The Nation*, January 26, 2009.

115 Rowena Mason, "Gove says boycott of Israeli goods is sign of 'resurgent anti-semitism,'" *The Guardian*, September 9, 2014.

116 Lazar Berman, "Top US academic association decries Israel Boycott," *The Times of Israel*, December 22, 2013.

chapter five

1 Universal Declaration of Human Rights, United Nations, December 10, 1948, www.un.org/en/documents/udhr/index.shtml.

2 Cairo Declaration of Human Rights in Islam, Organisation of Islamic Cooperation, www.oic-oci.org/english/article/human.htm.

3 Turan Kayaoğlu, "It's Time to Revise The Cairo Declaration of Human Rights in Islam," Brookings Institution, April 23, 2012.

4 "Global Terrorism Index," Institute for Economics and Peace, 2014.

5 Juliana Menasce Horowitz, "Declining Support for bin Laden and Suicide Bombing," Pew Research Global Attitudes Project, September 10, 2009.

6 Ibid.

7 "Muslim Public Shares Concerns about Extremist Groups," Pew Research Global Attitudes Project, September 10, 2013.

8 "Concerns about Islamic Extremism on the Rise in Middle East," Pew Research Global Attitudes Project, July 1, 2014.

9 "Palestinian Public Opinion Poll No -53," Palestinian Center for Policy and Survey Research, September 29, 2014.

10 "Common Concerns About Islamic Extremism: Muslim-Western Tensions Persist," Pew Research Global Attitudes Project, 13, July 2, 2011.

11 Ibid., 4.

12 "Saudi Arabia denies discriminating against Jewish passengers," *Haaretz*, June 26, 2011.

13 "ADL to Delta Airlines: 'Do Not Be A Party' To Discriminatory Policies Against Jews And Israel," Anti-Defamation League, June 24, 2011.

14 Khaled Abu Toameh, "PA affirms death penalty for land sale to Israelis," *The Jerusalem Post*, September 20, 2010.

15 "Jews in Islamic Countries: Iran," https://www.jewishvirtuallibrary.org/jsource/anti-semitism/iranjews.html (viewed July 17, 2014).

16 Kobi Nahshoni, "Iran's Jews: Tolerance or veiled persecution?" *Ynetnews*, March 27, 2013.

17 Manfred Gerstenfeld, "The Mahathir Affair: A Case Study in Mainstream Islamic

Anti-Semitism," *Jerusalem Viewpoints*, 506, November 2, 2003.

18 "Dr Mahathir Opens 10th OIC Summit," *The Star*, October 16, 2003. (This article contains the full text of the speech.)

19 "L'editorial du Monde, Antisemitisme," *Le Monde*, October 19, 2003. (French)

20 Raphael Israeli, *Islamikaze: Manifestations of Islamic Martyrology* (London: Frank Cass, 2003), 303.

21 "Morsi answers amen to imam's prayers for destruction of Jews," JTA, October 22, 2012.

22 Haaretz Service and Barak Ravid, "Swiss leader's offer to meet Ahmadinejad compounds crime with a sin," *Haaretz*, April 19, 2009.

23 "Iran, Indonesia can counter unilateralism: Ahmadinejad," Press TV, November 9, 2012.

24 Maureen Shamee, "Jewish leader outraged by Christian groups' invitation to Ahmadinejad," *European Jewish Press*, September 22, 2008.

25 Helene Cooper, "Ahmadinejad, at Columbia, Parries and Puzzles," *The New York Times*, September 25, 2007.

26 Yehuda Bauer, "Reviewing the Holocaust Anew in Multiple Contexts," *Post-Holocaust and Anti-Semitism*, 80, May 1, 2009.

27 Robert S. Wistrich, *Muslimischer Antisemitismus, Eine aktuelle Gefahr* (Berlin: Edition Critic, 2011), 101. (German)

28 Richard Prasquier, "Oui, l'islamisme radical et le nazisme sont deux idéologies comparables," *Le Monde*, October 17, 2012. (French)

29 Manfred Gerstenfeld, interview with Richard Landes, "How Muslim Conspiracy Theories Affect Jews," *Israel National News*, March 7, 2013.

30 Chloë Lebeau, "Pour Luc Ferry, 'l'islamisme radical est aussi atroce que le nazisme dans les années 30,'" *RTL.fr*, November 4, 2013. (French)

31 Mati Wagner, "European Jewish leader: Islamic extremists are the new Nazis," *The Jerusalem Post*, January 27, 2015

32 "Vlaggen met hakenkruis bij demonstratie," *De Telegraaf*, July 12, 2014. (Dutch)

33 Manfred Gerstenfeld, interview with Matthias Küntzel, "The Continuing Nazi Influence on Arab Attitudes," *Israel National News*, November 10, 2013.

34 Matthias Küntzel, *Djihad und Judenhass* (Freiburg: ça ira-Verlag, 2003), 39. (German)

35 Itamar Marcus and Barbara Crook, "Kill a Jew—Go to Heaven: The Perception

of the Jew in Palestinian Society," *Jewish Political Studies Review* 17, 3-4 (Fall 2005): 127.

36 "PA Mufti encourages killing of Jews," Israel Ministry of Foreign Affairs, January 9, 2012.

37 Sheikh Yunus al-Astal, "Suffering by Fire is Jews' destiny in this world and next" ". . .you will taste the punishment of Scorching Fire," http://www.palwatch.org/main.aspx?fi=584.

38 "Hamas MP Al-Astal: We Must Massacre Jews, Impose Jizya Poll Tax on Them," Al-Aqsa TV, March 6, 2014, http://www.memritv.org/clip/en/4202.htm.

39 Dr. Ismail Radwan, PA TV, March 30, 2007, http://www.palwatch.org/main.aspx?fi=584.

40 Gerstenfeld, interview with Küntzel.

41 Manfred Gerstenfeld, interview with Nadav Shragai, "Libel: Israel Intends to Destroy the Al-Aksa Mosque," *Israel National News*, October 16, 2013.

42 Albert Londres, *Le Juif Errant Est Arrivé* (Paris: Arléa, 1997), 209. (French)

43 Manfred Gerstenfeld, interview with Dr. Daphne Burdman, "Indoctrinating Palestinian Children to Genocidal Hatred: A Psychiatrist's Perspective," in *Demonizing Israel and the Jews* (New York: RVP Press, 2013), 48-49.

44 www.palwatch.org.

45 www.palwatch.org/main.aspx?fi=157&doc_id=9308.

46 Manfred Gerstenfeld, interview with Michael Widlanski, "Deceitful Palestinian Statements as Strategic Weapons," *Israel National News*, September 23, 2013.

chapter six

1 "Discrimination and hate crime against Jews in EU Member States: experiences and perceptions of anti-Semitism," European Union Agency for Fundamental Rights, November 2013.

2 Nicole Vettenburg, Mark Elchardus, and Johan Put, eds., *Jong in Brussel* (Leuven, The Hague: Acco, 2011), 278. (Dutch)

3 Manfred Gerstenfeld, interview with Mark Elchardus, "Belgian anti-Semitism," *Israel National News*, May 21, 2013.

4 Günther Jikeli, *Antisemitismus und Diskriminierungswahrnehmungen junger Muslime in Europa, Ergebnisse einer Studie unter jungen muslimischen Männern* (Essen: Klartext Verlag, 2012). (German)

5 Gemeente Amsterdam, "Eindrapport project 'Tweede Wereldoorlog in Perspectief,'" September 23, 2004, 35. (Dutch)

6 Ibid., 31.

7 Ibid., 31.

8 Ibid., 35.

9 Ibid., 31, 35.

10 Cécilia Gabison, "Les musulmans pratiquants ont plus de préjugés," *Le Figaro*, December 7, 2005. (French)

11 Emmanuel Brenner, *Les territoires perdus de la République: Antisémitisme, racisme et sexisme en milieu scolaire* (Paris: Mille et Une Nuits, 2004). (French)

12 Melanie Phillips, *Londonistan* (New York: Encounter Books, 2006), 114.

13 Ruud Koopmans, "Religious fundamentalism and out-group hostility among Muslims and Christians in Western Europe," Berlin Social Science Center, June 25-27, 2013.

14 Naama Lansky, "Sakana Berura Umijadit," *Israel Hayom*, August 22, 2014. (Hebrew)

15 "Report: Gang of youths taser French Jew at Paris monument," JTA, June 11, 2014.

16 Koopmans, "Religious fundamentalism."

17 "French Muslims see Jews controlling nation's economy, media," JTA, November 16, 2014.

18 Manfred Gerstenfeld, interview with Shimon Samuels, "Anti-Semitism and Jewish Defense at the United Nations World Summit on Sustainable Development, 2002 Johannesburg, South Africa," *Post-Holocaust and Anti-Semitism*, 6, March 2, 2003.

19 Per Ahlmark, *Vänstern och tyranniet: Det galna kvartseeklet* (Stockholm: Timbro, 1994), 85. (Swedish)

20 Mikael Tossavainen, "Arab and Muslim Anti-Semitism in Sweden," *Jewish Political Studies Review* 17, 3-4 (Fall 2005): 130.

21 "New York Cleric's Departure from Mosque Leaves Mystery," *The New York Times*, October 23, 2001.

22 "A Fair Sheik?" *The Wall Street Journal*, October 24, 2001.

23 "De ongrijpbare islamitische school," *NRC Handelsblad*, October 20, 2001. (Dutch)

24 Jon Henley, "Antisemitism on rise across Europe 'in worst times since the Nazis,'"

The Guardian, August 7, 2014.

25 Josephine Mckenna, "Italy expels imam for preaching hatred against Jews," *The Washington Post*, August 5, 2014.

26 "Spanish imam calls for killing Jews," European Jewish Congress, August 29, 2014.

27 "Anti-Semitic imam barred from attending Islamic conference in Belgium," JTA, November 5, 2014.

28 New York Times Service, "Terrorist Abu Nidal Reportedly Found Dead," *The Baltimore Sun*, August 20, 2012.

29 Brett Kline, "Two Sons of France," *The Jerusalem Post*, January 21, 2010.

30 "Trial Begins of French 'Gang of Barbarians' Accused of Killing Young Jew after 24-Day Torture," *Daily Mail*, April 30, 2009.

31 Eirik Eiglad, *The Anti-Jewish Riots in Oslo* (Oslo: Communalism, 2010).

32 Cnaan Liphshiz, "In Scandinavia, kipah becomes a symbol of defiance for Malmo's Jews," JTA, September 24, 2012.

33 "In Malmo, record number of hate crimes complaints but no convictions," JTA, January 9, 2013.

34 "Hitler gefällt mir," *Zeit Online*, June 7, 2007. (German)

35 Benjamin Weinthal, "Neo-Nazis, Islamists declare 'You Jews are beasts' during protest of Israeli operation," *The Jerusalem Post*, July 14, 2014.

36 "Gaza-demonstratie verloopt rustig," *DeStadUtrecht.nl*, August 10, 2014. (Dutch)

37 "Tonen nazivlag bij demo 'schandalig,'" *De Telegraaf*, July 14, 2014. (Dutch)

38 "Emoties over Zeeburg," http://nihs.nl/show-hakehilla/page/2. (Dutch)

39 "Dutch minister suspends official who said Zionists created ISIS," JTA, August 15, 2014.

40 Alexander Bakker, "Omstreden ambtenaar krijgt bijval," *De Telegraaf*, August 17, 2014. (Dutch)

41 Arjen Schreuder, "Zo gek is dat niet, om te denken aan zionistische betrokkenheid bij IS," *NRC Handelsblad*, August 25, 2014. (Dutch)

42 Vettenburg, Elchardus, and Put, *Jong in Brussel.*

43 Manfred Gerstenfeld, "Muslim Anti-Semitism in Europe," *Journal for the Study of Antisemitism* 5, 1 (2013).

chapter seven

1 Manfred Gerstenfeld and Ben Green, "Watching the Pro-Israeli Media Watchers," *Jewish Political Studies Review* 16, 3-4 (Fall 2004): 33-58.

2 "The Mideast Coverage of the Second Intifada in the German Print Media, with Particular Attention to the Image of Israel," Duisburger Institut für Sprach- und Sozialforschung, 2002.

3 Manfred Gerstenfeld, interview with Daniel Killy, "The Tyranny of Political Correctness," *Israel National News*, July 30, 2013.

4 Manfred Gerstenfeld, interview with Hildegard Müller, "Israel and Europe: The Positive and the Negative," in *Israel and Europe: An Expanding Abyss?* (Jerusalem: Jerusalem Center for Public Affairs, Adenauer Foundation, 2005), 40.

5 Eva Maria Kogel, "Demonstranten in Berlin greifen israelisches Paar an," *Die Welt*, July 20, 2014. (German)

6 Ulrich Clauß, "Großteil der Medien berichtet voreingenommen," *Die Welt*, August 22, 2014 (German). For more details, see: Anatol Stefanowitsch, "Schlagzeilen mit Schlagseite," *Jüdische Allgemeine*, July 17, 2014. (German)

7 Seth J. Frantzman, "Terra Incognita: Journalists Vs Jerusalem," *The Jerusalem Post*, December 9, 2014.

8 Manfred Gerstenfeld, interview with Shmuel Trigano, "French Anti-Semitism: A Barometer for Gauging Society's Perverseness," *Post-Holocaust and Anti-Semitism*, 26, November 1, 2004.

9 Clément Weill-Raynal, "L'Agence France Presse: le récit contre les faits," *Observatoire du monde juif*, 2, March 2002. (French)

10 Denis Jeambar and Daniel Leconte, "Guet-apens dans la guerre des images," *Le Figaro*, January 25, 2005. (French)

11 Weill-Raynal, "L'Agence France Presse."

12 *Décryptage*, directed by Jacques Tarnero and Philippe Bensoussan, 2002.

13 Manfred Gerstenfeld, interview with Andrea Levin, "Fighting Distorted Media Coverage of Israel," *Israel National News*, May 12, 2012.

14 "Indicting Israel: New York Times Coverage of the Palestinian-Israeli Conflict," CAMERA, October 15, 2013.

15 Manfred Gerstenfeld, interview with Ricky Hollander and Gilead Ini, "The Anti-Israel Bias of the New York Times," *Israel National News*, July 18, 2014.

16 "PM adviser's letter to 'New York Times,'" *The Jerusalem Post*, December 16, 2011.

17 Manfred Gerstenfeld, interview with Alex Safian, "A Classic Media Distortion," *Israel National News*, May 10, 2014.

18 "Dishonest Reporting 'Award' for 2001," *HonestReporting*, January 7, 2002.

19 Jeff Helmreich, "Journalistic License: Professional Standards in the Print Media's Coverage of Israel," Jerusalem Center for Public Affairs, August 15, 2001.

20 Matti Friedman, "An Insider's Guide to the Most Important Story on Earth," *Tablet*, August 26, 2014.

21 Steven Gutkin, "My Life As An AP Bureau Chief In Israel," *Goa Streets*, September 25, 2014.

22 Matti Friedman, "Ongoing Controversy Around 'The Most Important Story on Earth,'" *Tablet*, September 16, 2014.

23 Matti Friedman, "What the Media Gets Wrong About Israel," *The Atlantic*, November 30, 2014.

24 Ariel Cahana, "How the Murder of a Jewish Baby is Reported Worldwide," *Israel National News*, October 24, 2014.

25 Thomas L. Friedman, *From Beirut to Jerusalem* (New York: Anchor Books, Doubleday, 1990), 72-73.

26 Rory Carroll and Ian Black, "TV Row over Mob Footage 'Betrayal,'" *The Guardian*, October 20, 2000.

27 Servaas van der Laan, "NOS geft toe: censuur hakenkruizen bij anti-Israëlprotest," *Elsevier*, July 15, 2014. (Dutch)

28 Hans Moll, *Hoe de nuance verdween uit een kwaliteitskrant* (Amsterdam: Bert Bakker, 2011). (Dutch)

29 Renske Prevo and Judith van de Hulsbeek, "Vertaler van een onoplosbaar conflict: Joris Luyendijk," *De Journalist*, April 10, 2002. (Dutch)

30 Joris Luyendijk, *Het zijn net mensen—beelden uit het Midden-Oosten* (Amsterdam: Podium, 2006). (Dutch)

31 Ibid., 27-28. (Dutch)

32 *Politiken*, December 14, 2002. (Danish)

33 Arthur Arnheim, "Anti-Semitism after the Holocaust—Also in Denmark," *Jewish Political Studies Review* 15, 3-4 (Fall 2003): 151-159.

34 "Dokumentation: Læs Günter Grass' digt," *Politiken*, April 7, 2012. (Danish)

35 Manfred Gerstenfeld, interview with David Bar-Illan, "The Loaded Dice of the Foreign Media Are There to Stay," in *Israel's New Future: Interviews* (Jerusalem:

Jerusalem Center for Public Affairs, Rubin Mass, 1994), 109-119.

36 Gerstenfeld and Green, "Watching the Pro-Israeli Media Watchers," 33-55.

37 See, for instance, David Bar-Illan, *Eye on the Media* (Jerusalem: Gefen, 1993).

38 Gerstenfeld, interview with Bar-Illan.

39 Manfred Gerstenfeld, interview with Trevor Asserson, "The BBC: Widespread Antipathy Toward Israel," in *Demonizing Israel and the Jews* (New York: RVP Press, 2013), 91-93.

40 Manfred Gerstenfeld, interview with Zvi Shtauber, "British Attitudes toward Israel and the Jews," in *Israel and Europe: An Expanding Abyss?* (Jerusalem: Jerusalem Center for Public Affairs, Adenauer Foundation, 2005), 183-192.

41 Jason Deans, "BBC's Arafat Report Sparks Protest," *The Guardian*, November 5, 2004.

42 Ibid.

43 Letter from Natan Sharansky to Jonathan Baker, head of Foreign News, BBC, March 30, 2004.

44 Raphael Israeli, *Fundamentalist Islam and Israel* (Lanham, MD: JCPA, University Press of America, 1994), 132-159.

45 Conny Mus, interview with Ismail Haniyeh, RTL TV, April 20, 2007. (Dutch)

46 Manfred Gerstenfeld, "Als de Media Moordenaars Goedpraten," *Opinio*, July 20-26, 2007. (Dutch)

47 www.palwatch.org.

48 Arieh Stav, *Peace, the Arabian Caricature: A Study in Antisemitic Imagery* (Tel Aviv: Gefen, 1999), 18.

49 Manfred Gerstenfeld, interview with Joël Kotek, "Major Anti-Semitic Motifs in Arab Cartoons," *Post-Holocaust and Anti-Semitism*, 21, June 1, 2004.

50 Simon Freeman and agencies, "Iranian Paper Launches Holocaust Cartoon Competition," *Times Online*, February 6, 2006.

51 Manfred Gerstenfeld, "Ahmadinejad, Iran, and Holocaust Manipulation: Methods, Aims, and Reactions," *Jerusalem Viewpoints*, 551, February 1, 2007.

52 Ibid.

53 Gerstenfeld, interview with Shtauber.

chapter eight

1 Manfred Gerstenfeld, interview with Meir Litvak, "The Development of Arab

Anti-Semitism," *Post-Holocaust and Anti-Semitism*, 5, February 2, 2003.

2 Ibid.

3 Manfred Gerstenfeld, interview with Hans Jansen, "The Deep Roots of Protestant Anti-Semitism," in *Demonizing Israel and the Jews* (New York: RVP Press, 2013), 144-146.

4 James Parkes, *The Conflict of the Church and the Synagogue* (Cleveland, New York: Meridian Books, 1961), 375-376.

5 Declaration on the Relation of the Church to Non-Christian Religions, *Nostra Aetate*, Proclaimed by His Holiness Pope Paul VI on October 28, 1965.

6 Manfred Gerstenfeld, interview with Robert Wistrich, "Reassessing Pope Pius XII's Attitudes toward the Holocaust," *Post-Holocaust and Anti-Semitism*, 89, November 1, 2009.

7 Manfred Gerstenfeld, interview with Aharon Lopez, "Jewish-Vatican Relations: The Possible Beatification of Pius XII and Other Unresolved Issues," in *Europe's Crumbling Myths* (Jerusalem: Jerusalem Center for Public Affairs, Yad Vashem, World Jewish Congress, 2003), 137-145.

8 Sarah Delaney, "Israelis not happy with synod statement, angry over bishop's remarks," Catholic News Service, October 25, 2010.

9 Ibid.

10 Ibid.

11 Gerstenfeld, interview with Wistrich.

12 Ibid.

13 Arieh Doobov, "The Vatican and the Shoah," in Avi Beker, ed., *The Plunder of Jewish Property during the Holocaust* (Houndmills, UK: Palgrave, 2001), 319-321.

14 "The Society of St. Pius X: Mired in Anti-Semitism," Anti-Defamation League, January 26, 2009.

15 Edwin Black, "Funding Hate, Part IV: Audit of Palestinian Group Suggests Lax Funding Controls," JTA, October 16, 2003.

16 Manfred Gerstenfeld, "Misdadigers, slachtoffers, en de rol van Cordaid," *Opinio*, July 6, 2007. (Dutch)

17 Manfred Gerstenfeld, interview with Yitzhak Santis, "Catholic Aid Societies Promote Hatred of Israel," *Israel National News*, December 20, 2013.

18 Manfred Gerstenfeld, interview with Wim Kortenoeven,"The Anti-Israel Lobby in the Netherlands," *Israel National News*, September 15, 2013.

19 "Easter Pogrom Hatemongering: Effigies, Desecration, Caricature: Greek Antisemitism Epidemic Persists," press release, Simon Wiesenthal Center, April 20, 2004.

20 Michael Freund, "Tackling Assimilation and Anti-Semitism in Salonika," *The Jerusalem Post*, February 8, 2004.

21 Centre Simon Wiesenthal—Europe, "25 Months of Anti-Semitic Invective in Greece: Timeline: March 2002-April 2004," presented at the OSCE Conference on Anti-Semitism, April 28-29, 2004.

22 Manfred Gerstenfeld, interview with Moses Altsech, "Anti-Semitism in Greece: Embedded in Society," *Post-Holocaust and Anti-Semitism*, 23, August 1, 2004 (quoting *To Vima*, March 15, 2001).

23 Press release, Greek Helsinki Monitor, June 27, 2004.

chapter nine

1 References to many anti-Israeli church documents and related Middle East positions can be found in Eugene Korn, *Meeting the Challenge: Church Attitudes toward the Israeli-Palestinian Conflict* (New York: Anti-Defamation League, 2002).

2 Dexter van Zile, "Mainline American Christian 'Peacemakers' against Israel," *Post-Holocaust and Anti-Semitism*, 90, November 15, 2009.

3 Ibid.

4 Dexter van Zile, "Key Mennonite Institutions against Israel," *Post-Holocaust and Anti-Semitism*, 83, August 2, 2009.

5 Manfred Gerstenfeld, interview with Rabbi Yitzchok Adlerstein, "Mainline American Christians against Israel," *Israel National News*, July 8, 2013.

6 Ibid.

7 Ron Kampeas, "Presbyterians push back against church group's anti-Zionist study guide," JTA, February 18, 2014.

8 "Anti-Semitic Rant Passes Without Challenge at Methodist Convention," Snapshots, CAMERA, May 3, 2012.

9 Margaret Brearley, "The Anglican Church, Jews and British Multiculturalism," Posen Papers in Contemporary Anti-Semitism no. 6, Vidal Sassoon International Center for the Study of Anti-Semitism, Hebrew University of Jerusalem, 2006.

10 John Bingham, "Church of England vicar denies backing 'anti-Semitic hate-fest' in Iran," *The Telegraph*, October 6, 2014.

11 Manfred Gerstenfeld, interview with Ira Robinson, "Canada, Too, is Home to Anti-Zionism and Anti-Semitism," *Israel National News*, March 20, 2014.

12 Paul C. Merkley, "Anti-Zionism and the Churches: The Canadian Scene," *Post-Holocaust and Anti-Semitism*, 94, February 1, 2010.

13 Manfred Gerstenfeld, interview with Eugene Korn, "Divestment from Israel, the Liberal Churches, and Jewish Responses: A Strategic Analysis," *Post-Holocaust and Anti-Semitism*, 52, January 1, 2007.

14 Manfred Gerstenfeld, interview with Kenneth Collins, "Ein für Juden und Israel brutales Dokument der Church of Scotland," *Heplev*, June 10, 2013. (German)

15 Tim Wyatt, "Israeli Embassy criticizes Methodist BDS briefing," *Church Times*, May 2, 2014.

16 "Sweden Applied Nazi Race Laws in Wartime, Study Shows," *Haaretz*, April 6, 2006.

17 Manfred Gerstenfeld, interview with Zvi Mazel, "Anti-Israelism and Anti-Semitism in Sweden," in *Behind the Humanitarian Mask* (Jerusalem: Jerusalem Center for Public Affairs and Friends of Simon Wiesenthal Center for Holocaust Studies, 2008), 85-86.

18 Manfred Gerstenfeld, interview with Odd Sverre Hove, "Christian Foes and Friends of Israel in Norway," *Israel National News*, November 22, 2013.

19 "Norwegian YMCA embraces boycott Israel policy," JTA, March 2, 2014.

20 Miranda McGonagall, "Oslo chapter of YMCA/YWCA reject YMCA/YWCA Israel boycott," *Norway, Israel and the Jews*, March 13, 2014.

21 Manfred Gerstenfeld, interview with Tzvi Marx, "Christelijk-Joodse relaties," in Manfred Gerstenfeld, *Het Verval, Joden in een Stuurloos Nederland* (Amsterdam: Van Praag, 2010), 164-173. (Dutch)

22 Eildert Mulder, "Noodkreet Palestijnen aangedikt," *Trouw*, April 20, 2010. (Dutch)

23 Letter from the PKN to the Government of the State of Israel, February 17, 2010.

24 Letter from Rabbi Abraham Cooper and Rabbi Yitzchok Adlerstein of the Simon Wiesenthal Center to Ds. P. Verhoeff and A. J. Plaisier of the PKN, March 3, 2010.

25 Letter from the PKN to the Simon Wiesenthal Center, March 10, 2010.

26 Letter from the Simon Wiesenthal Center to the PKN, March 24, 2010.

27 Open letter from Ds. Geert Cohen Stuart to the Synodan Board of the PKN, April 12, 2010. (Dutch)

28 Manfred Gerstenfeld, interview with Justus Reid Weiner, "Palestinian Crimes against Christian Arabs and Their Manipulation against Israel," *Post-Holocaust and Anti-Semitism*, 72, September 1, 2008.

29 Jonas Kooyman, "PKN over BDS," *NIW*, April 4, 2014. (Dutch)

30 Manfred Gerstenfeld, interview with Dexter van Zile, "The Anti-Israel Policies of the World Council of Churches," in *Demonizing Israel and the Jews* (New York: RVP Press, 2013), 70-72.

31 Manfred Gerstenfeld, interview with Rijk van Dam, "Anti-Israeli Bias in the European Parliament and Other EU Institutions," in *European-Israeli Relations: Between Confusion and Change?* (Jerusalem: Jerusalem Center for Public Affairs, the Adenauer Foundation, 2006), 79-90.

32 Manfred Gerstenfeld, interview with David Parsons, "Christian Friends and Foes of Israel," in *Demonizing Israel and the Jews* (New York: RVP Press, 2013), 67-69.

33 Manfred Gerstenfeld, interview with Jim Fletcher, "The Pro-Palestinian Campaign to Woo US Evangelicals," *Israel National News*, October 28, 2013.

34 Dexter van Zile, "Evangelical Anti-Zionism as an Adaptive Response to Shifts in American Cultural Attitudes," *Jewish Political Studies Review* 25, 1-2 (Spring 2013).

35 Dexter van Zile, "Bethlehem Conference Promotes Submissive Dhimmi Narrative," CAMERA, April 10, 2014.

36 Dexter Van Zile, "Palestinian Christian Abuse of Christian Organizations in the West," in Alan Baker, ed., *Palestinian Manipulation of the International Community* (Jerusalem: JCPA, 2014), 127.

37 Manfred Gerstenfeld, interview with Dexter van Zile, "Sabeel Christian Anti-Zionist Organization Gains Power," *Israel National News*, April 3, 2013.

38 Gerstenfeld, interview with Fletcher.

39 Manfred Gerstenfeld, interview with Hans Jansen, "Protestants and Israel: The Kairos Document Debate," in *Demonizing Israel and the Jews* (New York: RVP Press, 2013), 80-82.

40 Gerstenfeld, interview with Weiner, 2008.

41 Manfred Gerstenfeld, interview with Justus Reid Weiner, "How Christians are Persecuted in the PA," *Israel National News*, September 30, 2014.

42 "Nazareth Priest Tells U.N. in Arabic: 'Israel is only country in Mideast where Christians live in safety,'" UN Watch, September 29, 2014.

43 ICEJ News, "Father Nadaf reportedly fired from Greek Orthodox Church," International Christian Embassy Jerusalem, May 12, 2014.

44 Ariel Ben Solomon, "Son of Greek Orthodox priest who supports IDF enlistment attacked in Nazareth," *The Jerusalem Post*, July 12, 2014.

45 "Jesus misrepresented as 'Muslim Palestinian,'" Palestinian Media Watch.

46 Susannah Heschel, *The Aryan Jesus* (Princeton: Princeton University Press, 2008), 2-4.

chapter ten

1 Tammi Rossman-Benjamin, "Anti-Zionism and the Abuse of Academic Freedom: A Case Study at the University of California, Santa Cruz," *Post-Holocaust and Anti-Semitism*, 77, February 1, 2009.

2 Manfred Gerstenfeld, "2007-2008: Another Year of Global Academic Anti-Semitism and Anti-Israelism," *Post-Holocaust and Anti-Semitism*, 73, October 1, 2008.

3 Manfred Gerstenfeld, "Recent Developments on the Academic Boycott: A Case Study," *Post-Holocaust and Anti-Semitism*, 61, October 1, 2007.

4 Manfred Gerstenfeld, "How to Fight Anti-Israeli Campaigns on Campus," *Post-Holocaust and Anti-Semitism*, 51, December 1, 2006.

5 Ronnie Fraser, "The Academic Boycott of Israel: Why Britain?," *Post-Holocaust and Anti-Semitism*, 36, September 1, 2005.

6 Yves Pallade, "New Anti-Semitism in Contemporary German Academia," *Jewish Political Studies Review* 21, 1-2 (Spring 2009): 33-62.

7 Avi Weinryb, "The University of Toronto: The Institution where Israel Apartheid Week was Born," *Jewish Political Studies Review* 20, 3-4 (Fall 2008): 107-117.

8 Alain Goldschläger, "The Canadian Campus Scene," in Manfred Gerstenfeld, ed., *Academics against Israel and the Jews* (Jerusalem: Jerusalem Center for Public Affairs, 2007).

9 Corinne Berzon, "Anti-Israeli Activity at Concordia University 2000-2003," in Manfred Gerstenfeld, ed., *Academics against Israel and the Jews* (Jerusalem: Jerusalem Center for Public Affairs, 2007).

10 Wolfgang Kraushaar, *Die Bombe im Judischen Gemeindehaus* (Hamburg: Hamburger Edition HIS), 2005, 86-104. (German)

11 Gerd Langguth, "Anti-Israel Extremism in West Germany," in Robert S. Wistrich, ed., *The Left against Zion: Communism, Israel and the Middle East* (London: Val-

lentine Mitchell, 1979), 257.

12 Manfred Gerstenfeld, interview with Robert Wistrich, "Anti-Semitism Embedded in British Culture," *Post-Holocaust and Anti-Semitism*, 70, July 1, 2008.

13 "Protest against Call for European Boycott of Academic and Cultural Ties with Israel," original press release, *The Guardian*, April 6, 2002.

14 Manfred Gerstenfeld, *Academics against Israel and the Jews* (Jerusalem: Jerusalem Center for Public Affairs, 2007).

15 Ibid. The second edition can be read for free at: http://jcpa.org/book/academics-against-israel-and-the-jews.

16 See, e.g., Dennis Zachrisson, *FiB-Kulturfront*, 16, 1988 (Swedish); Claes-Adam Wachtmeister, *Expressen*, September 26, 1990 (Swedish); Sven Öste, *Dagens Nyheter*, September 23, 1990 (Swedish).

17 Per Ahlmark, *Vänstern och tyranniet: Det galna kvartseeklet* (Stockholm: Timbro, 1994), 249. (Swedish)

18 Manfred Gerstenfeld, interview with Angelo Pezzana, "Anti-Israeli Italians Abuse Holocaust Memory," in *Demonizing Israel and the Jews* (New York: RVP Press, 2013), 107-109.

19 Goldschläger, "Canadian Campus Scene," 154.

20 Ibid., 156-157 (source: as documented in the archives of the League for Human Rights of B'nai Brith Canada).

21 Paola Manduca et al., "An open letter for the people in Gaza," *The Lancet*, August 2, 2014.

22 Tori Cheifetz, "Jewish Students 'Held Hostage' in Toronto Hillel," *The Jerusalem Post*, February 15, 2009.

23 Na'ama Carmi, "Middle East Conference Anything but Academic," *Toronto Star*, June 30, 2009.

24 Weinryb, "University of Toronto," 113.

25 Jonathan Kay, "Hating Israel Is Part of Campus Culture," *National Post*, September 25, 2002.

26 See Corinne Berzon, "Anti-Israeli Activity at Concordia University 2000-2003," in Manfred Gerstenfeld, ed., *Academics against Israel and the Jews* (Jerusalem: Jerusalem Center for Public Affairs, 2007), 163-173.

27 Report of the Inquiry Panel. Canadian Parliamentary Coalition to Combat Anti-Semitism, July 7, 2011, 60.

28 Ibid., 61-62.

29 www.akademiskboikott.no/opprop-mainmenu-34/14-oppropet/54.

30 Yael Beck, personal communication.

31 Quoted in Manfred Gerstenfeld, *Antisemittismen I Norge* (Bergen: Norge IDAG, 2010), 142. (Norwegian)

32 Cnaan Lipshiz, "Norway University Rebuffs Motion for Israel Boycott," *Haaretz*, November 13, 2009.

33 Martin Kramer, "Is Zionism Colonialism? The Root Lie," *Post-Holocaust and Anti-Semitism*, 35, August 1, 2005.

34 Martin Kramer, *Ivory Towers on Sand: The Failure of Middle Eastern Studies in America* (Washington, DC: Washington Institute for Near East Policy, 2001).

35 www.martinkramer.org.

36 Yarden Skop, "U.S. academic group votes to boycott Israel," *Haaretz*, December 16, 2013.

37 Yonah Jeremy Bob, "NGO threatens to sue US academic boycott group which boycotts Israel," *The Jerusalem Post*, January 9, 2014.

38 Mary Yu Danico, "Official Statement Regarding the Resolution," Association for Asian American Studies, May 3, 2013.

39 Council of the Native American and Indigenous Studies Association, "Declaration of Support for the Boycott of Israeli Academic Institutions," NAISA, December 15, 2013.

40 "AMCHA Posts List of Anti-Israel Professors," AMCHA Initiative, September 3, 2014.

41 Ofer Aderet, "Pioneer of global peace studies hints at link between Norway massacre and Mossad," *Haaretz*, April 30, 2012.

42 Manfred Gerstenfeld, ed., *Academics against Israel and the Jews* (Jerusalem: Jerusalem Center for Public Affairs, 2007).

chapter eleven

1 "Religious racism shocks officials," June 8, 2011, www.newsinenglish.no/2011/06/08/religious-racisim-shocks-officials.

2 Nicole Vettenburg, Mark Elchardus, and Johan Put, eds., *Jong in Brussel* (Leuven, The Hague: Acco, 2011). (Dutch)

3 Nicole Vettenburg, Mark Elchardus, Johan Put, and Stefaan Pleysier, eds., *Jong in*

Antwerpen en Gent. Bevindingen uit de JOP-monitor Antwerpen-Gent (Leuven, The Hague: Acco, 2013). (Dutch)

4 Benjamin Weiser, "U.S. Cites Evidence of Anti-Semitism in School District," *The New York Times*, January 25, 2014.

5 Manfred Gerstenfeld, interview with Mitchell Bard, "Introducing Israel Studies in U.S. Universities," *Changing Jewish Communities*, 39, December 15, 2008.

6 Gary A. Tobin and Dennis R. Ybarra, *The Trouble with Textbooks: Distorting History and Religion* (Lanham, MD: Lexington Books, 2008).

7 Ibid., 125.

8 Ibid., 126.

9 Ibid., 149.

10 Ibid., 150.

11 Barbara Lefebvre and Ève Bonnivard, *Élèves sous influence* (Paris: Louis Audibert, 2005). (French)

12 Emmanuel Brenner, *Les territoires perdus de la République*, 2nd ed. (Paris: Mille et une nuits, 2004). (French)

13 Lefebvre and Bonnivard, *Élèves sous influence*.

14 Barbara Lefebvre and Shmuel Trigano, *L'image des Juifs dans l'enseignement scolaire* (Paris: Alliance Israélite Universelle, 2006). (French)

15 Ibid., 40.

16 Ibid., 40-41.

17 Walter Janssens and Eddy van Eeckhoven, *Taalknikker 6 Werotaal, Leerboek Taal a* (Brugge: die Keure, 1999), 94. (Dutch)

18 Manfred Gerstenfeld, interview with Jehudi Kinar, "Belgium's Attitude toward Israel and the Jews," *Post-Holocaust and Anti-Semitism*, 111, October 2, 2011.

19 Soeren Kern, "UK: Anti-Semitism Rampant in Muslim Schools, Second Generation More Extreme than Parents," *Hudson-NY*, December 9, 2010.

20 Deidre Berger, "Anti-Semitism in Germany," European Forum on Anti-Semitism, June 16, 2008.

21 Gideon Böss, "Veraltet, verdreht und völlig einseitig," *Die Welt*, September 22, 2011. (German)

22 Manfred Gerstenfeld, interview with Rabbi Tzvi Hersh Weinreb, "The Orthodox Union and Its Challenges," *Changing Jewish Communities*, 23, August 15, 2007.

23 Benjamin Weinthal, "NGOs demand German Shoah group pay victims," *The*

Jerusalem Post, October 4, 2011.

24 Benjamin Weinthal, "Germans use 'anti-Israel' Jews to soothe Holocaust guilt," *The Jerusalem Post*, October 16, 2011.

25 Eli Bondid, "Skole anklaget for antisemittisme i elevutstilling," *Norge Idag*, October 26, 2011. (Norwegian)

26 McGonagall, "Anti-Semitic exhibition that was sponsored by Norwegian Church Aid removed after student protests," *Norway, Israel and the Jews*, October 20, 2011.

27 Manfred Gerstenfeld, interview with Johannes Houwink ten Cate, "Nederlandse Joden in een maatschappij zonder waarden," in Manfred Gerstenfeld, *Het Verval: Joden in een Stuurloos Nederland* (Amsterdam: Van Praag, 2010), 260-261. (Dutch)

28 Centraal Joods Overleg, brief aan de leden van de Tweede Kamer der Staten-Generaal, June 24, 2010. (Dutch)

29 CJO aan Tweede Kamer, "Pak antisemitisme aan," January 27, 2011, www.cidi.nl/Nieuwsberichten/CJO-aan-Tweede-Kamer--Pak-antisemitisme-aan.html?lang=en. (Dutch)

30 Bart Schut, "Nederland in 2014: Joden moeten 'etnisch onderduiken,'" *Jalta*, October 2014. (Dutch)

31 "Jonge joden voelen zich bedreigd en willen weg," *Reformatorisch Dagblad*, November 29, 2014. (Dutch)

32 Sverker Oredsson and Mikael Tossavainen, "Judehat bland muslimer tystas ned," *Dagens Nyheter*, October 20, 2003 (Swedish). English translation at www.freerepublic.com/focus/f-news/1005044/posts.

33 Mikael Tossavainen, "Det förnekade hatet—Antisemitism bland araber och muslimer i Sverige," Svenska Kommittén Mot Antisemitism, Stockholm, 2003, 22. (Swedish)

34 Jackie Jakubowski, "'Judarna kommer att brinna i helvetet,' förklarar en elev. Det fick han lära sig i en Koran-skola," *Judisk Krönika*, 2, 2001 (cited in ibid.). (Swedish)

35 The letter is quoted in Tossavainen, "Det förnekade hatet," 24. The peculiarities in the grammar and orthography reflect the Swedish original.

36 Mikael Tossavainen, "Arab and Muslim Anti-Semitism in Sweden," in Manfred Gerstenfeld, *Behind the Humanitarian Mask: The Nordic Countries, Israel and the*

Jews (Jerusalem: Jerusalem Center for Public Affairs, 2008), 94.

37 "Religious racism shocks officials," June 8, 2011, www.newsinenglish.no/2011/06/08/religious-racisim-shocks-officials; "Oslo municipality report in 2011 showed one third of Jewish pupils are physically threatened or abused," Coordination Forum for Countering Antisemitism, May 14, 2012.

38 Martin Bodd, "Country Reports: Norway," presented at the "Anti-Defamation League Conference on Global Anti-Semitism," 2002, www.adl.org/anti_semitism/as_conference_proceedings.pdf.

39 Manfred Gerstenfeld, interview with Irene Levin, "Norway: The Courage of a Small Jewish Community; Holocaust Restitution and Anti-Semitism," *Post-Holocaust and Anti-Semitism*, 10, July 1, 2003.

40 Katharina Schmidt-Hirschfelder, "So verbreitet ist die Angst," *Judische Allgemeine*, June 10, 2010. (German)

41 www.cidi.nl.

42 Marcel van Engelen and Mijntje Klipp, "Scholen verzwijgen de incidenten," *Het Parool*, November 8, 2003. (Dutch)

43 Ted de Hoog, "Kom maar op, kinderen," *NIW*, November 28, 2003. (Dutch)

44 *Hakehillot Nieuws*, March 17, 2005. (Dutch)

45 Van een verslaggeefster, "Docenten kampen met radicale klas," *Het Parool*, July 1, 2005. (Dutch)

46 Manfred Gerstenfeld, interview with Henri Markens, "Insights into the Situation of the Jews in the Netherlands," *Changing Jewish Communities*, 50, November 2009.

47 "Chaotische taferelen bij avondvierdaagse," *Het Parool*, June 8, 2010. (Dutch)

48 Brenner, *Les territoires perdus*.

49 Georges Bensoussan, "Antisemitism in French Schools: Turmoil of a Republic," *Analysis of Current Trends in Anti-Semitism*, 24 (Jerusalem: Hebrew University, 2004).

50 Ibid.

51 Berger, "Anti-Semitism in Germany."

52 Björn Hengst and Jan Friedmann, "Anti-Semitism at German Schools: Insults Against Jews on the Rise," *Spiegel Online*, August 12, 2006.

53 Ibid.

54 "Student Forced to Wear Anti-Semitic Sign," *Spiegel Online*, October 13, 2006.

55 Hadassa Hirschfeld, "Antisemitische Incidenten in Nederland. Overzicht over het jaar 2003 en de periode 1 januari-5 mei 2004," CIDI, 7. (Dutch)

56 Ibid.

57 Philip Mendes, "Anti-Semitism among Muslim youth: A Sydney teacher's perspective," *Menorah Magazine*, January 13, 2011.

58 "La suspension d'une prof juive d'histoire fait polémique," *Le Figaro*, September 1, 2010. (French)

59 Paul Lémand, "Shoah: Catherine Pederzoli, depose plainte auprès du Procureur de la république," *Terre Promise*, March 1, 2011. (French)

60 Alex Weisler, "As Norway's Jews mourn, concern about muting of pro-Israel voices," JTA, July 26, 2011.

61 "ACOD topman bedreigt Joodse scholen omwille van stappen Israëlische regering," *Joods Actueel*, November 3, 2011. (Dutch)

62 "Terrorist Incidents against Jewish Communities and Israeli Citizens Abroad 1968-2010," Community Security Trust, 2011, 30.

63 Ibid., 32.

64 Ibid., 46.

65 Ibid., 38.

66 Ibid.

67 Ibid., 41.

68 Ibid., 42.

69 Ibid., 62.

70 Ibid., 64-66.

71 Bram Eisenthal, "Quebec Leader Tours Firebombed School," *Jewish Journal*, April 15, 2004.

72 Tu Thanh Ha, "How the Montreal Police nabbed two would-be terrorists," *Globe and Mail*, February 12, 2009.

73 Peter Rakobowchuk, "Jews fear 'orchestrated campaign' of hate after attacks in Montreal," *The Star*, January 17, 2011.

74 Edward Cody, "Mohammed Merah, face of the new terrorism," *The Washington Post*, March 22, 2012.

chapter twelve

1 Abraham Bell, "International Law and Gaza: The Assault on Israel's Right to

Self-Defense," *Jerusalem Issue Briefs*, 9:29, January 28, 2008.

2 Dore Gold, "Did Israel Use 'Disproportionate Force' in Gaza?," *Jerusalem Issue Briefs*, 8:16, December 28, 2008.

3 Yehuda Blum, personal communication.

4 Gil Ronen, "Dershowitz: Ignore International Law," *Israel National News*, December 16, 2013.

5 Manfred Gerstenfeld, interview with Anne Herzberg, "Lawfare: The Abuse of the Law to Harm Israel," *Israel National News*, July 21, 2013.

6 Ibid.

7 Ibid.

8 Manfred Gerstenfeld, interview with Jacques Gauthier, "Israel's Legal Sovereignty in Palestine," *Israel National News*, December 23, 2013.

9 http://brandeiscenter.com/blog/iajlj-seeks-lawyer-signatures-for-european-union-petition/#more-.

10 Ibid.

11 Ibid.

12 Eugene Kontorovich, "How the EU directly funds settlements in occupied territory," *The Jerusalem Post*, September 28, 2013.

13 Ludwig Greven, "Putin verstehen mit Gerhard Schröder," *Zeit Online*, March 9, 2014. (German)

chapter thirteen

1 Dore Gold, *Tower of Babble* (New York: Crown Forum, 2004), 238.

2 Ban Ki-moon, "Cairo, Egypt, 12 October 2014—Secretary General's remarks at the Cairo Conference on Palestine," United Nations, October 12, 2014.

3 Manfred Gerstenfeld, interview with Irwin Cotler, "Discrimination Against Israel in the International Arena: Undermining the Cause of Human Rights at the United Nations," in *Europe's Crumbling Myths: The Post-Holocaust Origins of Today's Anti-Semitism* (Jerusalem: Jerusalem Center for Public Affairs, Yad Vashem, World Jewish Congress, 2003), 217-221.

4 Barak Ravid, "For Second Time, UNRWA Finds Rockets in One of Their Gaza Schools," *Haaretz*, July 24, 2014.

5 Anne Bayefsky, "Perspectives on Anti-Semitism Today," lecture presented at the conference on "Confronting Anti-Semitism: Education for Tolerance and Under-

standing," United Nations Department of Information, New York, June 21, 2004; Anne Bayefsky, "One Small Step," *Opinion Journal*, June 21, 2004.

6 Manfred Gerstenfeld, interview with Anne Bayefsky, "The United Nations: Leading Global Purveyor of Anti-Semitism," *Post-Holocaust and Anti-Semitism*, 31, April 1, 2005.

7 Ibid.

8 Manfred Gerstenfeld, interview with Dore Gold, "Europe's Consistent Anti-Israeli Bias at the United Nations," *Post-Holocaust and Anti-Semitism*, 34, July 1, 2005.

9 Manfred Gerstenfeld, interview with Dore Gold, "Europe's Consistent Anti-Israeli Bias at the United Nations," in *Israel and Europe: An Expanding Abyss* (Jerusalem: Jerusalem Center for Public Affairs, Adenauer Foundation, 2005), 49-66.

10 Ibid.

11 Manfred Gerstenfeld, interview with Shimon Samuels, "Anti-Semitism and Jewish Defense at the United Nations World Summit on Sustainable Development, 2002 Johannesburg, South Africa," *Post-Holocaust and Anti-Semitism*, 6, March 2, 2003.

12 Quoted in Tovah Lazaroff, "UN Human Rights Council Singles Out Israel Again," *The Jerusalem Post*, November 28, 2006.

13 Manfred Gerstenfeld, interview with Hillel Neuer, "The UNHRC's Standing Agenda Against Israel," *Israel National News*, November 5, 2013.

14 Manfred Gerstenfeld, interview with Anne Herzberg, "Gazans Learn From Goldstone Report," *Israel National News*, June 2, 2014.

15 Richard Goldstone, "Reconsidering the Goldstone Report on Israel and war crimes," *The Washington Post*, April 2, 2011.

16 Gerald M. Steinberg and Anne Herzberg, eds., *The Goldstone Report "Reconsidered": A Critical Analysis* (Jerusalem: NGO Monitor, Jerusalem Center for Public Affairs, 2011).

17 Alan Dershowitz, "The Case against the Goldstone Report: A Study in Evidentiary Bias," in Gerald M. Steinberg and Anne Herzberg, eds., *The Goldstone Report "Reconsidered": A Critical Analysis* (Jerusalem: NGO Monitor, Jerusalem Center for Public Affairs, 2011), 99-152.

18 Trevor Norwitz, "Letter to Justice Goldstone," in Gerald M. Steinberg and Anne Herzberg, eds., *The Goldstone Report "Reconsidered": A Critical Analysis* (Jerusa-

lem: NGO Monitor, Jerusalem Center for Public Affairs, 2011), 153-180.

19 Ibid.

20 Gerstenfeld, interview with Herzberg.

21 Ibid.

22 Lee-Ann Goodman, Canadian Press, "William Schabas, head of UN Gaza commission, dismisses anti-Israel charge," *CBC News*, August 11, 2014.

23 "NGO: William Schabas must recuse himself from UN Gaza inquiry," UN Watch, August 11, 2014.

24 Kenneth Bandler, "UNRWA: Time to start planning for resettlement," *Miami Herald*, October 20, 2010.

25 Maya Shwayder, "Prosor publicly blasts UNRWA," *The Jerusalem Post*, May 20, 2014.

26 Ari Yashar, "US Congressmen to Kerry: Justify US Aid to UNRWA," *Israel National News*, November 26, 2011.

27 "Factsheet: UNESCO and Israel," UN Watch, January 17, 2014.

28 "Unesco to go ahead with disputed Jewish exhibition," Reuters, January 27, 2014.

29 "UNESCO Corrects: Hamas Man Not a Journalist," CAMERA, November 16, 2014.

30 "UNESCO Director-General Statement regarding Abdullah Murtaja," UNESCO, November 14, 2014.

31 Daniel S. Mariaschin, "No contribution to peace or reconciliation," *The Jerusalem Post*, May 13, 2014.

32 Hillel C. Neuer, "The Struggle against Anti-Israel Bias at the UN Commission on Human Rights," *Post-Holocaust and Anti-Semitism*, 40, January 1, 2006.

33 Manfred Gerstenfeld, interview with Dore Gold, "Europe's Consistent Anti-Israeli Bias at the United Nations," *Post-Holocaust and Anti-Semitism*, 34, July 1, 2005.

34 Gerstenfeld, interview with Samuels.

chapter fourteen

1 Daniel Perdurant, "Anti-Semitism in Contemporary Greek Society," *Analysis of Current Trends in Anti-Semitism*, 7 (Jerusalem: Hebrew University, 1995), 10.

2 "You Can Kill a Jew," Central Jewish Board Information Bulletin, January 1, 1989; *The Washington Post* article was quoted therein.

3 Spiros Payatakis, "City Council Holocaust," *Apoghevmatini*, August 29, 1986. (Greek)

4 Edward Koch, "A Modern Greek Tragedy," *New York Post*, September 11, 1986.

5 Manfred Gerstenfeld, interview with Moses Altsech, "Anti-Semitism in Greece: Embedded in Society," *Post-Holocaust and Anti-Semitism*, 23, August 1, 2004.

6 Manfred Gerstenfeld, interview with Zvi Mazel, "Anti-Israelism and Anti-Semitism in Sweden," in *Behind the Humanitarian Mask* (Jerusalem: Jerusalem Center for Public Affairs and Friends of Simon Wiesenthal Center for Holocaust Studies, 2008), 83.

7 Salomo Berlinger, Stefan Meisels, Torsten Press, and Willy Salomon, "Sweden Can Do Much More for Country's Jewish Community," *Haaretz*, June 10, 2004.

8 Benjamin Weinthal, "Sweden PM's recognition of Palestine violates law, says legislator," *The Jerusalem Post*, October 13, 2014.

9 Isabel Kershner, "Sweden Gives Recognition to Palestinians," *The New York Times*, October 30, 2014.

10 "Swedish Mayor blasts Zionism," *Ynetnews*, January 28, 2010.

11 Mikael Tossavainen, "Mayor of Malmo: Jews to Blame for Antisemitism," *A Blog of Two Cities*, January 29, 2010.

12 Per Gudmundson, "Mona Sahlin, hakkorsen och Hamasflaggorna," *Gudmundson*, January 15, 2009. (Swedish)

13 "Israelska flaggan brändes," *Dagens Nyheter*, January 10, 2009. (Swedish)

14 Per Gudmundson, "Rödflaggat," *Gudmundson*, January 13, 2009. (Swedish)

15 Per Gudmundson, "Swedish Leading Social Democrats in Rally with Hezbollah Flags," *Gudmundson*, January 10, 2009. (Swedish)

16 Erik Svansbo, "Folkbladet uppmärksammar 'bloggkupp,'" *Svansbo*, January 14, 2009. (Swedish)

17 "'Extrema yttringar - tack vare Svansbo,'" *Folkbladet*, January 14, 2009. (Swedish)

18 Per Gudmundson, "Rödflaggat," *Gudmundson*, January 13, 2009. (Swedish)

19 Ole Berthelsen and Ole Peder Giæver, "Støre ønsker Hamas velkommen," *Nettavisen*, April 18, 2006. (Norwegian)

20 Abigail Klein Leichman, "Oslo Grants Visa to Hamas Lawmaker," *The Jerusalem Post*, May 16, 2006.

21 Sissel Henriksen, "Slakter Sveriges," *Klassekampen*, May 19, 2006. (Norwegian)

22 "Suicide bomber kills nine in Tel Aviv," *NBC News*, April 17, 2006.

23 Ashraf al-Khadra and Ole Peder Giæver, "Fordømmer ikke selvmords-angrepet," *Nettavisen*, April 18, 2006. (Norwegian)

24 Berthelsen and Giæver, "Støre ønsker Hamas velkommen."

25 Ole Peder Giæver, "Hamas-parlamentarikeren Yahya Al-Abadsa, som denne uken er på besøk i Norge, tror ikke det brygger til borgerkrig i de palestinske områdene," *Nettavisen*, June 13, 2006. (Norwegian)

26 "UD-representanter møtte Hamas-minister," *Aftenposten*, May 13, 2006. (Norwegian)

27 Harald S. Klungtveit and Morten Øverbye, "Israel avlyser alle avtaler med norsk statssekretær," *Dagbladet*, March 20, 2007. (Norwegian)

28 "Norwegian minister meets Hamas PM," *BBC News*, March 19, 2007.

29 Ibid.

30 "Norway-Hamas Link Angers Israel," *BBC News*, March 20, 2007.

31 Pål T. Jørgensen and Espen Eide, "Støre har hatt hemmelige samtaler med Hamas," *TV2*, January 27, 2011. (Norwegian)

32 Ibid.

33 Jonas Gahr Støre, "Why we must talk," *New York Review of Books*, April 7, 2011.

34 Ibid.

35 Jørgensen and Eide, "Støre har hatt hemmelige samtaler med Hamas."

36 "Israel Must Withdraw Its Troops from Gaza," Ministry of Foreign Affairs, Norway, January 3, 2009.

37 Stephen Pollard, "Gaza Is Not Too Crowded," *The Spectator*, April 24, 2008.

38 "Antisemitism Worldwide 2004," Stephen Roth Institute for the Study of Contemporary Anti-Semitism and Racism, Tel Aviv University, 2005.

39 Efraim Karsh, "European Misreading of the Israeli-Palestinian Conflict: Finnish Foreign Minister Tuomioja—A Case Study," *Jerusalem Issue Brief*, 27, July 12, 2005.

40 John Prescott, "Israel's bombardment of Gaza is a war crime—and it must end," *The Mirror*, July 26, 2014.

41 Verkiezingsprogramma Tweede-Kamer verkiezingen 2010, "Iedereen telt mee. De kracht van Nederland," Partij van de Arbeid, 2010. (Dutch)

42 www.thereligionofpeace.com/index.html#Attacks.

43 Manfred Gerstenfeld, *Het Verval, Joden in een Stuurloos Nederland* (Amsterdam: Van Praag, 2010), 164-173. (Dutch)

44 Manfred Gerstenfeld, interview with Jehudi Kinar, "Belgium's Attitudes toward Israel and the Jews," *Post-Holocaust and Anti-Semitism*, 112, November 9, 2011.

45 Walter Pauli, "Israël moet beseffen dat reusachtige historische WOII-krediet stilaan is uitgeput," *Knack*, August 6, 2014. (Dutch)

46 Faisal al Yafai, "Cleric Hits Back at Uniformed Critics," *The Guardian*, July 12, 2004.

47 Fraser Nelson, "Anger over Dalyell's 'Jewish Cabal' Slur," *The Scotsman*, May 5, 2003.

48 Pascal Boniface, "Lettre a un ami israelien," *Le Monde*, August 4, 2001. See also by the same author: "Est il interdit de critiquer Israel?" *Le Monde*, August 31, 2001. (French)

49 "Former French PM Calls Balfour Declaration 'Historic Mistake,'" *Israel National News*, June 20, 2004.

50 "Michel Rocard règle ses comptes avec le socialisme à la francaise," *Le Monde*, October 5, 2005. (French)

51 Jerry Lewis, "Labor's Miliband set to be guest speaker at pro-Palestinian dinner," *The Jerusalem Post*, November 26, 2014.

52 "Rassemblement pro-Gaza: Cazeneuve aurait manifesté s'il n'était pas ministre," *Le Point*, August 15, 2014. (French)

53 www.wiesenthal.com/site/apps/s/content.asp?c>fwLYKnN8LzH&b>2531-62&ct>285288.

chapter fifteen

1 Manfred Gerstenfeld, "Jews against Israel," *Post-Holocaust and Anti-Semitism*, 30, March 1, 2005.

2 Tony Judt, "Israel: The Alternative," *New York Review of Books*, October 23, 2003.

3 Benjamin Balint, "Future Imperfect: Tony Judt Blushes for the Jewish State," in *The Jewish Divide over Israel*, 65-75, as quoted in Rosenfeld (see next endnote).

4 Alvin H. Rosenfeld, *"Progressive" Jewish Thought and the New Anti-Semitism* (New York: American Jewish Committee, 2006).

5 Richard Landes and Benjamin Weinthal, "The Post-Self-Destructivism of Judith Butler," *The Wall Street Journal*, September 9, 2012.

6 Manfred Gerstenfeld, interview with Afshin Ellian, "Het Midden-Oosten, islam en joden," in *Het Verval, Joden in een stuurloos Nederland* (Amsterdam: Van

Praag, 2010), 132. (Dutch)

7 Manfred Gerstenfeld, interview with Leon de Winter, "Het joodse aan mij is dat ik me met Israel identificeer," in *Het Verval, Joden in een stuurloos Nederland* (Amsterdam: Van Praag, 2010), 138. (Dutch)

8 See the item "Paulus de Santa Maria" in *Jüdisches Lexikon*, Vol. 4, 842.

9 Robert S. Wistrich, *From Ambivalence to Betrayal: The Left, the Jews, and Israel* (Lincoln and London: University of Nebraska Press, 2012), 479.

10 Ibid., 488.

11 Ibid., 489.

12 Robert Wistrich, "The Strange Case of Bruno Kreisky," *Encounter*, May 1979.

13 Sander L. Gilman, *Jewish Self-Hatred: Anti-Semitism and the Hidden Language of the Jews* (Baltimore: Johns Hopkins University Press, 1990), 1-2.

14 Kenneth Levin, *The Oslo Syndrome: Delusions of a People under Siege* (Hanover, NH: Smith & Kraus Global, 2005).

15 Manfred Gerstenfeld, interview with Kenneth Levin, "The Psychology of Jews Who Embrace their Enemies," in *Demonizing Israel and the Jews* (New York: RVP Press, 2013), 79-80.

16 Manfred Gerstenfeld, interview with Elhanan Yakira, "The Communalities of Holocaust Deniers and Anti-Zionists," in *Demonizing Israel and the Jews* (New York: RVP Press, 2013), 82.

17 Ibid., 82-84.

18 Norman G. Finkelstein, *The Holocaust Industry: Reflections on the Exploitation of Jewish Suffering* (London: Verso, 2000).

19 Ronald Zweig, "The Holocaust Industry: Reflections on the Exploitation of Jewish Suffering," *Journal of Israeli History* 20, 2-3 (Summer/Autumn 2001): 208-216.

20 "More than 350 Survivors and Descendants of Survivors and Victims of the Nazi Genocide Condemn Israel's Assault on Gaza," International Jewish Anti-Zionist Network, August 23, 2014.

21 Alvin H. Rosenfeld, "The True Face Behind a New York Times Ad," *Jewish Daily Forward*, August 28, 2014.

22 "Weinstock's ground-breaker, out in Hebrew," English translation of original interview in Hebrew at http://jewishrefugees.blogspot.co.il/2014/05/weinstocks-ground-breaker-out-in-hebrew.html, original article at: http://www.haaretz.co.il/magazine/.premium-1.2315763.

23 Max Blumenthal, *Goliath: Life and Loathing in Greater Israel* (New York: Nation Books, 2014).

24 Ben Cohen, "German Opposition Party Cancels Event Featuring American Anti-Semite Max Blumenthal," *The Algemeiner*, November 6, 2014.

25 Naomi Dann, "Netanyahu plays the blame game at the UN to avoid responsibility for Israeli human rights violations," Jewish Voice for Peace, September 29, 2014.

26 "Presbyterian Divestment," Jewish Voice for Peace.

27 Jonathan S. Tobin, "Haaretz's 9/11 Truther Gift to Anti-Semites," *Commentary*, October 30, 2014.

chapter sixteen

1 "Spanish Jews decry anti-Semitic tweets after Mac TA win," *The Jerusalem Post*, May 20, 2014.

2 "Euroleague condemns anti-Semitic tweets after Maccabi Tel Aviv win," *The Jerusalem Post*, May 22, 2014.

3 Manfred Gerstenfeld, interview with Abraham Cooper, "Anti-Semitism and Terrorism on the Internet: New Threats," *Post-Holocaust and Anti-Semitism*, 9, June 1, 2003.

4 Manfred Gerstenfeld, interview with Abraham Cooper, "Threats of Anti-Semitism and Terrorism on the Internet," in *Demonizing Israel and the Jews* (New York: RVP Press, 2013), 101-103.

5 "ADL Poll: In 2014 More Israeli Teens Encountered Hate on the Internet," press release, ADL, December 2, 2014.

6 Manfred Gerstenfeld, interview with Andre Oboler, "Anti-Semitism in Social Media Includes Twitter," *Israel National News*, September 8, 2013.

7 "Anti-Semitism chief: bring in ASBOs for internet," *Jewish News*, November 5, 2014.

8 Adam Levick, "Anti-Israelism and Anti-Semitism in Progressive U.S. Blogs/News Websites: Influential and Poorly Monitored," *Post-Holocaust and Anti-Semitism*, 92, January 1, 2010.

9 Adam Levick, "Anti-Semitic Cartoons on Progressive Blogs," *Post-Holocaust and Anti-Semitism*, 101, September 1, 2010.

10 Manfred Gerstenfeld, interview with Ronald Eissens, "Fighting Discrimination

and Anti-Semitism on the Internet," in *Demonizing Israel and the Jews* (New York: RVP Press, 2013), 104-106.

11 Manfred Gerstenfeld, interview with Sammy Eppel, "The Jews of Venezuela," *Israel National News*, May 13, 2013.

12 Manfred Gerstenfeld, interview with Trevor Asserson, "What Went Wrong at the BBC: A Public Monopoly Abusing Its Charter through Bias against Israel," *Jerusalem Viewpoints*, 511, January 15, 2004.

13 Susanne Lysvold, "Får skyte 1286 hval i år," *NRK*, February 7, 2013. (Norwegian)

14 Jo Fidgen, "Whale hunting: 'It is like killing an ox,'" BBC, July 14, 2013.

15 Hilde Mangset Lorentsen, "Klarer ikke skyte nok kystsel," *NRK Nordland*, April 14, 2013. (Norwegian)

16 Ibid.

17 Manfred Gerstenfeld, interview with André Gerrits, "The Development of Anti-Zionism in the Post-War Soviet Union," *Israel National News*, May 28, 2014.

18 Manfred Gerstenfeld and Tamas Berzi, "The Gaza War and the New Outburst of Anti-Semitism," *Post-Holocaust and Anti-Semitism*, 79, April 1, 2009.

19 "SVs program 2005-2009," *Rorg.no*. (retrieved August 1, 2013)

20 "USA Threats after Boycott Support," *Aftenposten*, January 12, 2006.

21 Ole Berthelsen, "Halvorsen: - Beklager," *Nettavisen*, January 6, 2006. (Norwegian)

22 Ingjerd Våge, "Israel-boikott på SV-Kristins tabbetopp," *Vårt Land*, October 25, 2012. (Norwegian)

23 Olav Østrem, "Hauken og duen," *Klassekampen*, April 19, 2008. (Norwegian)

24 Manfred Gerstenfeld, interview with Simon Epstein, "The Vicious Anti-Semitism of French Trotskyites," *Israel National News*, October 7, 2013.

25 Manfred Gerstenfeld, interview with Robert Wistrich, "Anti-Semitism Embedded in British Culture," *Post-Holocaust and Anti-Semitism*, 70, July 1, 2008.

26 Pierre-André Taguieff, *Rising from the Muck: The New Anti-Semitism in Europe* (Chicago: Ivan R. Dee, 2004).

27 Bernard Lewis, "Communism and Islam," *International Affairs* 30, 1 (January 1954): 1-12.

28 Robert Wistrich, *From Ambivalence to Betrayal: The Left, the Jews, and Israel* (Lincoln: University of Nebraska Press, 2012), 564.

29 Ibid., 565.

30 Ibid., 566.

31 Ibid., 570.

32 Ibid. 579.

33 Justin Huggler and Josie Ensor, "Anti-Semitism on the march: Europe braces for violence," *The Telegraph*, July 26, 2014.

34 *Le Nouvel Observateur*, November 8, 2001. (French)

35 www.ngo-monitor.org.

36 Manfred Gerstenfeld, interview with Gerald Steinberg, "Non-Governmental Organizations against Israel," in *Demonizing Israel and the Jews* (New York: RVP Press, 2013), 61-63.

37 Robert L. Bernstein, "Why do human rights groups ignore Palestinians' war of words?," *The Washington Post*, September 27, 2011.

38 Manfred Gerstenfeld, interview with Wim Kortenoeven, "The Anti-Israel Lobby in the Netherlands," *Israel National News*, September 15, 2013.

39 Edwin Black, "Funding Hate, Part IV: Audit of Palestinian Group Suggests Lax Funding Controls," JTA, October 16, 2003.

40 Manfred Gerstenfeld, interview with Shimon Samuels, "Anti-Semitism and Jewish Defense at the United Nations World Summit on Sustainable Development, 2002 Johannesburg, South Africa," *Post-Holocaust and Anti-Semitism*, 6, March 2, 2003.

41 Manfred Gerstenfeld, interview with Shimon Samuels, "The World Social Forum is an Enabler of Anti-Israelism," *Israel National News*, August 13, 2013.

42 "Justice and Human Rights Denied: Five Years of NGO Silence on Shalit," NGO Monitor, October 17, 2011.

43 Alan Baker, "International humanitarian law, ICRC and Israel's status in the Territories," *International Review of the Red Cross* 94, 888 (Winter 2012).

44 Ronnie Fraser, "Trade Union and Other Boycotts of Israel in Great Britain and Ireland," *Post-Holocaust and Anti-Semitism*, 76, December 1, 2008.

45 "Canadian teachers union boycotts Israel," *Ynetnews*, May 29, 2006.

46 "LO-lederen vil ha fredsstyrker til Midtøsten," *Aftenposten*, May 1, 2002. (Norwegian)

47 Manfred Gerstenfeld, "Norway's Annual Israel Hate Day," *The Times of Israel*, June 4, 2013; see also Vegard Velle, "Å kjempe er en måte å overleve på," *Fagbladet*, April 30, 2013. (Norwegian)

48 Conrad Myrland, "Palestinsk taler på Youngstorget tegner fiendebilder og maner til kamp," *Med Israel For Fred*, April 30, 2013. (Norwegian)

49 TUC International Committee meeting, October 4, 1982, TUC archives MSS 292D/901/23. As quoted in Fraser, "Trade Union and Other Boycotts."

50 Fraser, "Trade Union and Other Boycotts."

51 "Canadian teachers union boycotts Israel," *Ynetnews*, May 29, 2006.

52 "South African union joins boycott of Israel," *Ynetnews*, June 8, 2006.

53 Manfred Gerstenfeld, interview with André Gantman, "Belgian Anti-Semitism and Anti-Zionism," in *Demonizing Israel and the Jews* (New York: RVP Press, 2013), 189-192.

54 Raphael Israeli, *Poison: Modern Manifestations of a Blood Libel* (Lanham, MD: Lexington Books, 2002).

55 "Der Vorwurf des Antisemitismus wird auch als Knuppel benutzt," *Stern*, June 18, 2002. (German)

56 "Hohmann vor Parteigericht der CDU," *Die Welt*, April 21, 2004. (German)

57 "2010 Top Ten Anti-Semitic/Anti-Israeli Slurs," Simon Wiesenthal Center.

58 "Willoch på studietur til Arafat," *Aftenposten*, April 28, 2004. (Norwegian)

59 Anders Nordstoga, "Willoch er rasist og viser jødehat," *Aftenposten*, January 15, 2009. (Norwegian)

60 Ibid.

61 Mitchell Bard, *The Arab Lobby* (New York: HarperCollins, 2010).

62 library.fes.de/pdf-files/do/07908-20110311.pdf.

63 See Manfred Gerstenfeld, "Israel and the Jews: A Prism for the Western World?," lecture presented at the conference on "Anti-Judaism, Anti-Semitism, Delegitimizing Israel," Vidal Sassoon Center, May 26, 2014. (Written expanded version forthcoming.)

chapter seventeen

1 http://antisemitism.org.il/article/91532/jew-one-most-common-insults-schools.

2 Dore Gold, "From 'Occupied territories' to 'Disputed territories,'" *Jerusalem Letter/Viewpoints*, 470, January 16, 2002.

3 Manfred Gerstenfeld, interview with Georges-Elia Sarfati, "Language as a Tool against Jews and Israel," *Post-Holocaust and Anti-Semitism*, 17, February 1, 2004.

4 Ibid.

5 Raphael Israeli, *Islamikaze: Manifestations of Islamic Martyrology* (London: Frank Cass, 2003).

6 Susanne Urban, "Anti-Semitism in Germany Today: Its Roots and Tendencies," *Jewish Political Studies Review* 16, 3-4 (Fall 2004): 124.

7 Manfred Gerstenfeld, interview with Shimon Samuels, "Anti-Semitism and Jewish Defense at the United Nations World Summit on Sustainable Development, 2002 Johannesburg, South Africa," *Post-Holocaust and Anti-Semitism*, 6, March 2, 2003.

8 Manfred Gerstenfeld, interview with Gerald Steinberg, "European NGOs against Israel," in *Israel and Europe: An Expanding Abyss?* (Jerusalem: Jerusalem Center for Public Affairs, Adenauer Foundation, 2005), 112.

9 See, e.g., Paul Ceaux, "Manif pro-palestinienne autorisée: les organisateurs critiquent Hollande," *L'Express*, July 22, 2014 (French); Manfred Gerstenfeld, "Dutch Jews Wonder About Their Future," *Israel National News*, August 8, 2014; Reuters and AP, "France vows harsh hand on anti-Semitic violence after Paris riots," *Haaretz*, July 21, 2014.

10 See, e.g., "Valls ne laissera pas "le conflict Israélo-palestinien s'importer en France," *Le Monde*, July 13, 2014 (French); AFP, "Hollande: le conflit israélo-palestinien 'ne peut pas s'importer' en France," *The Times of Israel Français*, July 14, 2014. (French)

11 Manfred Gerstenfeld, "France: Importing conflict from, and exporting problems to the Middle East," *The Jerusalem Post*, January 7, 2015.

12 "Iraq conflict resounds on German streets," *The Local*, August 7, 2014.

13 "Reactions to riots in Hamburg, Celle," *Deutsche Welle*, October 8, 2014.

14 "Kurdish protesters break into European Parliament," BBC, October 7, 2014.

15 Philip Oltermann, "Football fans and neo-Nazis clash with police in Cologne," *The Guardian*, October 27, 2014.

16 Maya Rhodan, "Obama: 'No Sympathy' for Hamas," *Time*, August 6, 2014.

17 Manfred Gerstenfeld, "The sustainability of the conflict," *The Jerusalem Post*, January 13, 2015.

18 Ewen MacAskill, "Barack Obama throws full US support behind Middle East uprisings," *The Guardian*, May 20, 2011.

19 Barack Obama, "Remarks by The President at the Annual Iftar Dinner, July 14, 2014," The White House, July 14, 2014.

20 Kim van Keken, "Dominee blijft, de gemeente wijkt," *de Volkskrant*, May 22, 2006. (Dutch)

21 "Doofpotaffaire ds. Mos," *Nederlands Dagblad*, March 18, 2008. (Dutch)

22 Manfred Gerstenfeld, interview with Jeffrey Gedmin, "Experiencing European Anti-Americanism and Anti-Israelism," in *Israel and Europe: An Expanding Abyss?* (Jerusalem: Jerusalem Center for Public Affairs, Adenauer Foundation, 2005), 142-158.

23 Manfred Gerstenfeld, interview with Carla, "Jewish and Cautious in Amsterdam," *Israel National News*, February 24, 2014.

24 "Hague Muslim protest features menacing calls about Jews," JTA, July 7, 2014.

25 Manfred Gerstenfeld, interview with Deborah Lipstadt, "Denial of the Holocaust and Immoral Equivalence," *Post-Holocaust and Anti-Semitism*, 11, August 1, 2003.

26 Manfred Gerstenfeld, "Holocaust Inversion: The Portraying of Israel and Jews as Nazis," *Post-Holocaust and Anti-Semitism*, 55, April 1, 2007.

27 Manfred Gerstenfeld, "The Multiple Distortions of Holocaust Memory," *Jewish Political Studies Review* 19, 3-4 (Fall 2007): 35-57.

28 Manfred Gerstenfeld, *The Abuse of Holocaust Memory: Distortions and Responses* (Jerusalem: Jerusalem Center for Public Affairs, 2009).

29 Manfred Gerstenfeld, interview with Robert Wistrich, "Anti-Semitism Embedded in British Culture," *Post-Holocaust and Anti-Semitism*, 70, July 1, 2008.

30 "25 Months of Anti-Semitic Invective in Greece: March 2002-April 2004," report compiled in cooperation with the Greek Helsinki Monitor, Simon Wiesenthal Center, April 2004.

31 Manfred Gerstenfeld, interview with Moses Altsech, "Anti-Semitism in Greece: Embedded in Society," *Post-Holocaust and Anti-Semitism*, 23, August 1, 2004.

32 David Hardaker, "Israeli Ambassador attacks Swedish artwork," *The World Today*, January 19, 2004.

33 "Wiesenthal Center: By Floating a Pig Balloon Stamped With Star of David at His Concert, Roger Waters Has Moved to the Front of the Line of Anti-Semites," Simon Wiesenthal Center, July 24, 2013.

34 "Pink Floyd's Roger Waters slams Scarlett Johansson, Neil Young for Israel Ties," *The Jerusalem Post*, February 2, 2014.

35 Hugh Schofield, "Dieudonné: The bizarre journey of a controversial comic," *BBC News*, December 31, 2013.

36 "Quenelle salute performed in front of Toulouse Jewish school," JTA, December 30, 2013.

37 Schofield, "Dieudonné."

38 Abraham Bell, "International Law and Gaza: The Assault on Israel's Right to Self-Defense," *Jerusalem Issue Briefs*, 9:29, January 28, 2008.

39 Dore Gold, "Did Israel Use 'Disproportionate Force' in Gaza?," *Jerusalem Issue Briefs*, 8:16, December 28, 2008.

40 "Legal Consequences of the Construction of a Wall in the Occupied Palestinian Territory," International Court of Justice, July 9, 2004.

41 Alan Baker, "The Settlements Issue: Distorting the Geneva Convention and the Oslo Accords," Jerusalem Center for Public Affairs, May 4, 2012.

42 "Anti-Semitism: Attack on Rabbi in Berlin Draws Outrage," *Spiegel Online International*, August 30, 2012.

43 Rachel Hirshfeld, "German Rabbinical College Warns Against Wearing Kippot in Public," *Israel National News*, September 2, 2012.

44 Eli Shvidler, "Report: Jewish man in critical condition after assaulted by Neo-Nazis in Ukraine," *Haaretz*, April 9, 2012.

45 Cnaan Lipshiz, "Swedish mayor fighting sale of anti-Israel T-shirts is attacked," JTA, April 12, 2013.

chapter eighteen

1 "Discrimination and hate crime against Jews in EU Member States: experiences and perceptions of anti-Semitism," European Union Agency for Fundamental Rights, 2013.

2 Sam Sokol, "European Jewish Congress: Amid rising anti-Semitism, Jewish life in Europe unsustainable," *The Jerusalem Post*, April 27, 2014.

3 "Chairman of Keren Hayesod in France, Richard Prasquier, sounds the alarm about anti-Semitism and anti-Israeli hostility," Keren Hayesod, March 27, 2014.

4 Quoted in Raphael Ahren, "Jewish life in Europe 'dying a slow death'?," *The Times of Israel*, July 8, 2013.

5 Nathan Guttman, "U.S. Anti-Semitism Chief Warns Future of Europe Jewry in Danger," *Jewish Daily Forward*, November 14, 2014.

6 Scott Sayare, "Suspect Held in Jewish Museum Killings," *The New York Times*, June 1, 2014.

7 Kevin Rawlinson, "Jewish museum shooting suspect 'is Islamic State torturer,'" *The Guardian*, September 6, 2014.

8 Adam Thomson, "Anti-Semitic attacks rise in France as Gaza conflict stirs tensions," *Financial Times*, August 15, 2014.

9 Adam Withnall, "Israel-Gaza conflict: Frankfurt police agree to let anti-Israel protesters use their megaphone 'to help calm down crowds,'" *The Independent*, July 13, 2014.

10 "Vandals target Jewish school in Denmark," JTA, August 22, 2014.

11 "Windows smashed at Belfast synagogue on Somerton Road," BBC, July 22, 2014.

12 "Rabbi, congregant attacked in Malmo days after synagogue vandalized," JTA, August 4, 2014.

13 "Belgian doctor refuses to treat Jewish woman, citing Gaza conflict," JTA, July 31, 2014.

14 "Iceland's one-man BDS campaign," *Haaretz*, July 16, 2014.

15 Kashmira Gander, "Far-right Hungarian mayor, Mihaly Zoltan Orosz, filmed hanging effigy of Benjamin Netanyahu in protest against Gaza war," *The Independent*, August 4, 2014.

16 Jen Gerson, "Pro-Gaza protests worldwide tainted by anti-Semitism; Calgary organizer to apologize for violence," *National Post*, July 21, 2014.

17 Joanne Hill, "Anti-Israel, anti-Semitic incidents rising in Canada," *Jewish Tribune*, July 29, 2014.

18 Kisa Mlela Santiago, "Bus ride was terror trip of anti-Semitic threats, say Jewish students in Australia," CNN, August 8, 2014.

19 Hugo Rifkind, "Suddenly it feels uncomfortable to be a Jew," *The Times*, August 12, 2014.

20 "BBC chief: Anti-Semitism makes me question Jews' future in UK," *The Times of Israel*, December 21, 2014.

21 Jon Henley, "Antisemitism on rise across Europe 'in worst times since the Nazis,'" *The Guardian*, August 7, 2014.

22 "Joodse gezinnen willen weg uit Nederland," *EenVandaag*, August 1, 2014. (Dutch)

23 Annet Röst, "Nieuw-Mokum in Israel," *NIW*, December 19, 2014. (Dutch)

24 David Serphos, "'De overheid vertrouw ik niet meer in de strijd tegen Jodenhaat,'" *de Volkskrant*, August 29, 2014. (Dutch)

25 Jon Henley, "Antisemitism on rise across Europe 'in worst times since the Nazis,'" *The Guardian*, August 7, 2014.

26 "Warum gibt es keine Welle der Sympathie mit uns Juden?," *RP Online*, July 31, 2014 (German). See also: Zlatan Alihodzic, "Ihre Zeilen haben uns bewegt," *Jüdische Allgemeine*, August 7, 2014. (German)

27 "Knobloch rät deutschen Juden, nicht erkennbar zu sein," *Zeit Online*, July 29, 2014. (German)

28 Philipp Peyman Engel, "Jüdische Gemeinde verlässt Rat der Religionen," *Jüdische Allgemeine*, August 4, 2014. (German)

29 Frank-Walter Steinmeier, "Gemeinsame Sache," *Jüdische Allgemeine*, July 31, 2014.

30 "Angela Merkel: Fighting anti-Semitism is German duty," BBC, September 14, 2014.

31 Sam Sokol, "European Jewish Congress: Amid rising anti-Semitism, Jewish life in Europe unsustainable," *The Jerusalem Post*, April 27, 2014.

32 Alison Smale, "Samantha Power, U.S. Ambassador, Issues Warning on Anti-Semitism in Europe," *The New York Times*, November 13, 2014.

33 Fillip Piatov, "Kann man sich mit Kippa noch auf die Straße trauen?," *Die Welt*, July 20, 2014. (German)

34 Miriam Hollstein, ""Eine Bankrotterklärung von Polizei und Politik," *Die Welt*, July 22, 2014. (German)

35 Ofer Aderet, "German Jewish leader tells Haaretz: Anti-Semitism mounting in my country," *Haaretz*, September 30, 2012.

36 Natan Sharansky, "European idea will die here and survive in Israel," *Jewish Chronicle*, July 24, 2014.

37 Kirsten Grieshaber, "Germany, France, Italy Condemn Anti-Semitic Demos," AP, July 22, 2014.

38 "Gaza conflict: France criticises 'anti-Semitic' riot," BBC, July 21, 2014.

39 Manfred Gerstenfeld, interview with Shmuel Trigano, "French anti-Semitism: A Barometer for Gauging Society's Perverseness," *Post-Holocaust and Anti-Semitism*, 26, November 1, 2004.

40 "Norske barn tør ikke stå fram som jøder," *Dagen* (Norwegian) (retrieved July 31, 2013.)

41 Ibid.

42 Manfred Gerstenfeld, interview with Carla, "Jewish and Cautious in Amsterdam," *Israel National News*, February 24, 2014.

43 "Discrimination and hate crime against Jews in EU Member States: experiences and perceptions of anti-Semitism," European Union Agency for Fundamental Rights, 2013, 36.

44 Ibid.

45 Philip Carmel, "Proposals on yarmulkes, Yom Kippur given mixed reaction by French Jews," JTA, December 14, 2003.

46 Yossi Lempkowicz, "After release of ADL survey, Jewish leader urges each EU member county to set up special body to deal with anti-Semitism," *European Jewish Press*, May 15, 2014.

47 Manfred Gerstenfeld, interview with Henri Markens, "Insights into the Situation of the Jews in the Netherlands," *Changing Jewish Communities*, 50, November 15, 2009.

48 Motti Wolf, personal communication, published in Manfred Gerstenfeld, "Muslim-Jewish Interaction in the Netherlands," *Changing Jewish Communities*, 26, November 15, 2007.

49 Manfred Gerstenfeld, interview with Chaim Nisan, "The Anti-Semitic Experiences of a Religious Jew in the Netherlands," *Tundra Tabloids*, September 25, 2013.

50 "Discrimination and hate crime against Jews in EU Member States: experiences and perceptions of anti-Semitism," European Union Agency for Fundamental Rights, 2013, 33.

51 Ibid., 34.

52 Ibid., 35.

53 Manfred Gerstenfeld, "Anti-Semitism and Anti-Israelism in Western Schools," *Post-Holocaust and Anti-Semitism*, 112, November 1, 2011.

54 "Hakekors, flaskekasting og drapstrusler," *Dagbladet*, March 20, 2012. (Norwegian)

55 Brief van het CJO aan de leden van de Tweede Kamer der Staten-Generaal, June 24, 2010. (Dutch)

56 Revital Blumenfeld, "European Jewish communities ramp up security following Toulouse attack," *Haaretz*, March 21, 2012.

57 AP, "Security up at NY Jewish Sites after France Attack," *ABC News*, March 20, 2012.

58 Rifat Bali, "Present-Day Anti-Semitism in Turkey," *Post-Holocaust and Anti-Semitism*, 84, August 16, 2009.

59 Manfred Gerstenfeld, *The Autumn 2005 Riots in France: Their Possible Impact on Israel and the Jews* (Jerusalem: Jerusalem Center for Public Affairs, 2006).

60 Manfred Gerstenfeld, interview with Shmuel Trigano, "French Anti-Semitism: A Barometer for Gauging Society's Perverseness," P*ost-Holocaust and Anti-Semitism*, 26, November 1, 2004.

61 Ari L. Goldman, "Meanwhile: The Jewish Ghosts of Salonika," *International Herald Tribune*, May 6, 2004.

62 Liam Hoare, "Rising Number of French Jews Making Aliyah," *Tablet*, December 30, 2012.

63 "Founder of French anti-Semitism watchdog moving to Israel," JTA, January 5, 2014.

64 "Les idées du Front national s'imposent dans l'opinion," *Le Monde*, December 14, 2005. (French)

65 Victor S. Schonfeld, "Circumcision—defending the indefensible," *The Jerusalem Post*, January 22, 2014.

66 "Wiesenthal Center Denounces Scandinavian Medical Groups Seeking Ban on Jewish Ritual Circumcision," Simon Wiesenthal Center, January 27, 2014.

67 "Discrimination and hate crime against Jews in EU Member States: experiences and perceptions of anti-Semitism," European Union Agency for Fundamental Rights, 2013.

68 Ibid., 37.

69 Manfred Gerstenfeld, *Het Verval, Joden in een Stuurloos Nederland* (Amsterdam: Van Praag, 2010), 109. (Dutch)

70 Bloeme Evers-Emden, "Burgemeester Cohen moet stelling nemen," *NIW*, May 30, 2003. (Dutch)

71 Manfred Gerstenfeld, interview with Bloeme Evers-Emden, "Ik raad mijn kinderen aan Nederland te verlaten," in Manfred Gerstenfeld, *Het Verval, Joden in een Stuurloos Nederland* (Amsterdam: Van Praag, 2010), 241-248. (Dutch)

72 Manfred Gerstenfeld, "Rabbijn wast antisemitisme zo wit mogelijk," *De Dagelijkse Standaard*, October 4, 2013. (Dutch)

73 "Discrimination and hate crime against Jews in EU Member States: experiences and perceptions of anti-Semitism," European Union Agency for Fundamental Rights, 2013, 35.

74 "Cops wounded, dozens arrested at Paris anti-Israel rally," JTA, July 19, 2014.

75 Roy Yerushalmi, "Turkish Jews urged to apologize for 'Israeli killing of Muslims,'" *Ynetnews*, July 17, 2014.

chapter nineteen

1 Anholt Nation Brands Index Special Report, "Israel's International Image," Q3 Report 2006.

2 "Country Index 2014-2015," Future Brand, 2014.

3 Manfred Gerstenfeld, interview with Irwin Cotler, "Discrimination against Israel in the International Arena: Undermining the Cause of Human Rights at the United Nations," in *Europe's Crumbling Myths: The Post-Holocaust Origins of Today's Anti-Semitism* (Jerusalem: Jerusalem Center for Public Affairs, Yad Vashem, World Jewish Congress, 2003), 221.

4 Manfred Gerstenfeld, interview with Gustavo Perednik, "Argentian, Jews, and Israel," *Israel National News*, January 15, 2013.

5 Jonathan Lis, Avi Issacharoff, Amos Harel, and Barak Ravid, "Sources: Israel not expected to respond harshly to India, Georgia attacks," *Haaretz*, February 14, 2012.

6 Reuters and Israel Hayom Staff, "Timeline: Attacks on Jewish and Israeli targets abroad," *Israel Hayom*, July 19, 2012.

7 Lawrence Joffe, "Shlomo Argov," *The Guardian*, February 25, 2003.

8 Justus Reid Weiner, "Diplomatic Immunity? Terror Attacks Against Israeli Embassies and Diplomatic Representatives Abroad," World Jewish Congress, September 16, 2012.

9 Reuters, "Timeline: Attacks on Jewish targets, Israelis abroad," *The Jerusalem Post*, July 19, 2012.

10 "Israel's Wars & Operations: The Entebbe Rescue Operation," Jewish Virtual Library.

11 James Bennet, "In Kenya, 3 Suicide Bombers Attack Hotel Owned by Israelis; Missiles Fired at Passenger Jet," *The New York Times*, November 28, 2002.

12 Benjamin Weinthal, "Bulgaria names Hezbollah suspects behind bombing of Israeli bus in Burgas," *The Jerusalem Post*, July 25, 2013.

13 "An Updated List of Israelis Abroad," *Israel Football*, February 1, 2012.

14 Mark Misérus, "Hoofdsponsor eist excuses van Vitesse om Dan Mori," *de Volkskrant*, January 10, 2014. (Dutch)

15 Mark Hodgkinson, "Israel's Shahar Peer promised visa for Dubai event by United Arab Emirates," *The Telegraph*, January 5, 2010.

16 DPA, "Israeli tennis star Shahar Peer faces Gaza protest while playing in New Zealand," *Haaretz*, January 8, 2009.

17 Benjamin Weinthal, "Germany marks 40 years since Munich massacre," *The Jerusalem Post*, September 6, 2012.

18 "Israeli team flees to changing room in Turkey," *The Jerusalem Post*, January 6, 2009.

19 "Far-Right Fears: German-Israeli Football Match Cancelled," *Spiegel Online International*, July 9, 2013.

20 "Maccabi Haifa's friendly with Lille stopped early after pro-Palestinian protesters storm the pitch and attack the players," *Daily Mail*, July 23, 2014.

21 Sarah Leah Lawent, "Skinheads Attack Israeli Soccer Team in Poland," *Israel National News*, July 26, 2014.

22 Stefan Laurin, "Nazis beschimpfen in Dortmund Gäste aus Israel," *Die Welt*, July 25, 2014. (German)

23 Jonny Paul, "Irish teachers union adopts full boycott of Israel," *The Jerusalem Post*, April 8, 2013.

24 Andy Beckett, "It's water on stone—in the end the stone wears out," *The Guardian*, December 12, 2002.

25 Corrections and Clarifications column, *The Guardian*, December 19, 2002.

26 Manfred Gerstenfeld, interview with Steven Baum, "A Journal on Anti-Semitism Born out of Adversity," in *Demonizing Israel and the Jews* (New York: RVP Press, 2013), 64-66.

27 Douglas Davis, "Fears Voiced that Academic Boycott of Israel Could Endanger Lives," *The Jerusalem Post*, December 15, 2002.

28 David Meghnagi, personal communication.

29 Jonny Paul, "The Emergence of a Silent Academic Boycott of Israel," *EJPress*, May 28, 2006.

30 Yaniv Halily, "AHAVA closes London store over threats," *Ynetnews*, September 22, 2011.

31 Rachel Hirshfeld, "Norwegian Retail Chain Boycotts Ahava Cosmetics," *Israel National News*, April 2, 2012.

32 Ari Yasher, "United Church of Canada Launches BDS Campaign," *Israel National News*, April 12, 2013.

33 Debra Kamin, "Rihanna and other artists who play Israel feel the pressure," *Variety*, October 16, 2013.

34 Dafna Maor, "In Israel, the Pixies' roar is as touching as a lullaby," *Haaretz*, June 18, 2014.

35 Or Barnea, "Protestors storm Israeli pianist's recital," *Ynetnews*, March 15, 2013.

36 Anshel Pfeffer, "Protesters disrupt Israel's Batsheva dance troupe at Edinburgh festival, but the show goes on," *Haaretz*, August 31, 2012.

37 Jackie Kemp, "Batsheva dance group: my deep shame at this bigoted festival protest," *The Guardian*, September 2, 2012.

38 "Second Israeli-funded Edinburgh Festival Fringe show cancelled," BBC, August 4, 2014.

39 Ben Hartman, "Israeli musician cancels Istanbul concert," *The Jerusalem Post*, June 12, 2011.

40 Maayana Miskin, "Jewish Dancers Attacked in Germany," *Israel National News*, June 25, 2010.

41 Haskell Nussbaum, "Brand Israel turned Canada into a PR battlefield," *The Jerusalem Post*, June 10, 2009.

42 Manfred Gerstenfeld, interview with Irit Kohn, "The Suit against Sharon in Belgium: A Case Analysis," in *European-Israeli Relations: Between Confusion and Change?* (Jerusalem: Jerusalem Center for Public Affairs, Adenauer Foundation, 2006), 211-218.

43 Ibid.

44 Vikram Harman, "Terror police feared gun battle with Israeli general," *The Guardian*, February 19, 2008.

45 Ian Black and Ian Cobain, "British court issued Gaza arrest warrant for former Israeli minister Tzipi Livni," *The Guardian*, December 14, 2009.

46 Martin Bright, "UK arrest scare for top Israeli," *Jewish Chronicle*, July 7, 2011.

47 Danna Harman, "Arrest warning prompts retired Israeli general to cut short London visit," *Haaretz*, July 6, 2011.

48 Barak Ravid, "Deputy PM Meridor cancels London visit following lawsuit threat," *Haaretz*, November 1, 2010.

49 Herb Keinon, "Karmi Gilon forced to leave Denmark before film screening," *The Jerusalem Post*, January 11, 2014.

50 "Building a Political Firewall against the Assault on Israel's Legitimacy: London

as a Case Study," Reut Institute, November 2010.

51 Peter Foster, "Academia Split over Boycott of Israel," *Daily Telegraph*, May 16, 2002.

52 Caroline Davies, "Tricycle Theatre does U-turn and lifts ban on Jewish film festival," *The Guardian*, August 15, 2014.

53 Helen Pidd, "George Galloway interviewed by police over Bradford 'Israel-free zone' speech," *The Guardian*, August 19, 2014.

chapter twenty

1 http://www.worldjewishcongress.org, http://www.eurojewcong.org, http://www.bnaibrith.org, http://www.adl.org, http://www.ajc.org, http://www.wiesenthal.com/site/pp.asp?c=lsKWLbPJLnF&b=6212365#.Uvorr2KSyKA.

2 http://www.standwithus.com/academicboycott.

3 I. L. Kenen, *Israel's Defense Line* (Buffalo: Prometheus Books, 1981), 320.

4 Manfred Gerstenfeld and Ben Green, "Watching the Pro-Israeli Media Watchers," *Jewish Political Studies Review* 16, 3-4 (Fall 2004): 33-58.

5 David Bar-Illan, *Eye on the Media* (Jerusalem: Jerusalem Post, 1993).

6 www.tomgrossmedia.com.

7 Tzvi Fleischer, "Israel in the Australian Media," *Jewish Political Studies Review* 3, 4 (Fall 2005): 133-146.

8 Gerstenfeld and Green, "Watching the Pro-Israeli Media Watchers."

9 "L'AFP, agence indépendante ou gouvernementale?," *Observatoire du Monde Juif*, 2, March 2002. (French)

10 Sergio I. Minerbi, *Mentir Avec Les Images* (Brussels: Louis Musin, 1985). (French)

11 Henry H. Weinberg, *The Myth of the Jew in France 1967-1982* (Oakville, ON: Mosaic Press, 1987).

12 Ibid.

13 "About NGO Monitor," NGO Monitor, 2011.

14 http://www.ngo-monitor.org.

15 Ibid., http://www.ngo-monitor.org/index.php.

16 Itamar Marcus and Nan Jacques Zilberdik, "PA TV teaches children all Israel is 'Palestine,'" Palestinian Media Watch, January 5, 2014.

17 "PA Depicts a World without Israel," Palestinian Media Watch.

18 "About SPME," Scholars for Peace in the Middle East, 2010, 2011.

19 Edward S. Beck, "Scholars for Peace in the Middle East (SPME): Fighting Anti-

Israelism and Anti-Semitism on the University Campuses Worldwide," in Manfred Gerstenfeld, ed., *Academics against Israel and the Jews* (Jerusalem: Jerusalem Center for Public Affairs, 2007), 137.

20 Manfred Gerstenfeld, ed., *Academics against Israel and the Jews* (Jerusalem: Jerusalem Center for Public Affairs, 2007), 61.

21 "Mission and Values," Louis D. Brandeis Center for Human Rights Under Law.

22 "Brandeis Center Announces Formation of Law Student Chapters," Louis D. Brandeis Center for Human Rights Under Law, October 31, 2013.

23 "Board and Mission Statement," Israel Academia Monitor.

24 "IMPACT-SE's Mission Statement," IMPACT-SE, the Institute for Monitoring Peace and Cultural Tolerance in School Education.

25 "Impact-SE's Articles and Papers," IMPACT-SE, the Institute for Monitoring Peace and Cultural Tolerance in School Education.

26 "About ICS," Institute for Curriculum Services, 2012.

27 http://www.israellawcenter.org.

28 Dexter van Zile, "Updating the Ancient Infrastructure of Christian Contempt: Sabeel," *Jewish Political Studies Review* 23, 1-2 (Spring 2011); Dexter van Zile, "Broadcasting a Lethal Narrative: The World Council of Churches and Israel," *Post-Holocaust and Anti-Semitism*, 109, August 1, 2011.

29 Manfred Gerstenfeld, interview with Rabbi Yitzchok Adlerstein, "Mainline American Christians Against Israel," *Israel National News*, July 8, 2013.

30 Manfred Gerstenfeld, interview with Yitzhak Santis, "Catholic Aid Societies Promote Hatred of Israel," *Israel National News*, December 20, 2013.

chapter twenty-one

1 Yaakov Lappin, "IAI joins the cyberwarfare race," *The Jerusalem Post*, January 17, 2014.

2 Niv Elis, "Netanyahu declares Beersheba cybersecurity hub," *The Jerusalem Post*, January 28, 2014.

3 Yonah Jeremy Bob, "Cyberwarfare: A game-changing issue in the next war," *The Jerusalem Post*, January 31, 2014.

4 Lappin, "IAI joins the cyberwarfare race."

5 Elad Benari, "Italy Stands by Israel, Boycotts Durban III," *Israel National News*, July 23, 2011.

6 Yasser Okbi, "Hamas's Haniyeh would trounce Abbas if elections held today, Palestinian poll says," *The Jerusalem Post*, September 3, 2014.

7 Manfred Gerstenfeld, interview with Irwin Cotler, "Existing Tools to Deal with Iran's Crimes," in Manfred Gerstenfeld, *Demonizing Israel and the Jews* (New York: RVP Press, 2013), 49-54.

8 "Poetin: Nederland heeft pedofielenclub, Rusland niet," *de Volkskrant*, April 8, 2013. (Dutch)

9 "Russische kritiek op mensenrechten Nederland," *de Volkskrant*, January 15, 2014. (Dutch)

10 "PM Netanyahu's Speech at the United Nations General Assembly," Prime Minister's Office, September 29, 2014.

11 "Netanyahu rejects U.S. criticism of Israel's eastern Jerusalem housing plans," JTA, October 28, 2014.

12 www.israelwhat.com.

13 http://swedenisrael.blogspot.co.il.

14 Harriet Sherwood, "Israeli inquiry says film of Muhammad al-Dura's death in Gaza was staged," *The Guardian*, May 20, 2013.

15 Jacob Laksin, "Petition for Genocide," *FrontPage Magazine*, July 28, 2006.

16 Spencer Ho and Lazar Berman, "Swedish Jew files for asylum in her own country," *The Times of Israel*, November 19, 2013.

17 Andrea Levin, "CAMERA Billboard Campaign Calls out New York Times Bias Against Israel," January 27, 2014, www.camera.org.

18 http://www.latma.co.il/Elatmatv.aspx.

19 http://badnewsfromthenetherlands.blogspot.co.il.

20 Manfred Gerstenfeld, "One simple example of how to fight Israel's delegitimization," *The Jerusalem Post*, September 3, 2014.

21 http://tundratabloids.com/ugly-europe.

22 http://edwdebono.com/lateral.htm.

23 Jenni Frazer, "Pro-Israel activist's case against UCU fails," *Jewish Chronicle*, March 28, 2013.

24 Cnaan Liphshiz, "Norwegian official: Schools considering Israel boycott," *Haaretz*, November 8, 2009.

25 "55 U.S. universities condemn ASA boycott of Israel," JTA, December 30, 2013.

26 Lori Lowenthal Marcus, "Congressional Letter: Academic Boycott of Israel is

'Thinly Veiled Bigotry,'" *Jewish Press*, January 10, 2014.

27 "More U.S. universities withdraw from ASA over academic boycott of Israel," JTA, December 24, 2013.

28 AAUP Statement on ASA Vote to Endorse Academic Boycott of Israel, www.aaup.org/sites/default/files/AAUPStatementASAVote_0.pdf.

29 "N.Y. State bill ends funding to schools linked to boycott groups," JTA, January 27, 2014.

30 Jakken B. Lian, "Right of Reply: Norway is not anti-Semitic," *The Jerusalem Post*, December 12, 2009.

31 Plenaire verslagen Tweede Kamer, "Noodklok om Jodenhaat," January 16, 2014. (Dutch)

32 Letter from Rabbi Abraham Cooper to Deputy Prime Minister Lodewijk Asscher, February 6, 2014, http://tundratabloids.com/2014/02/tt-exclusive-swcs-rabbi-abraham-cooper-writes-sharp-letter-to-dutch-prime-minister-over-antisemitism.html.

33 Ibid.

34 Written Questions of Parliamentarian Dijkgraaf (SGP) to the Ministers of Social Affairs and Employment and Security and Justice, March 11, 2013. (Dutch)

35 KGS, "Dutch Deputy Pm Asscher Still Hasn't Responded To Swc's Rabbi Cooper's 13th Of March Correspondence Concerning Anti-Semitism In The Netherlands . . ," *Tundra Tabloids*, July 29, 2014.

36 Manfred Gerstenfeld, interview with Giuliano Ferrara, "Marching for Israel against Ahmadinejad," in *European-Israeli Relations: Between Confusion and Change?* (Jerusalem: Jerusalem Center for Public Affairs, Adenauer Foundation, 2006), 204-210.

37 Benjamin Weinthal, "Italians hold speech rally for Israel," *The Jerusalem Post*, November 23, 2012.

38 "Antisemittisme i Norge? Den norske befolkningens holdninger til joder og andre minoriteter," Center for Studies of the Holocaust and Religious Minorities, May 30, 2012, www.hlsenteret.no/publikasjoner/antisemittismei-norge. (Norwegian)

39 *Report of the British All-Party Parliamentary Inquiry into Antisemitism* (London: Stationery Office Ltd, September 2006).

40 Report of the Inquiry Panel, Canadian Parliamentary Coalition to Combat Anti-

Semitism, July 7, 2011, www.jewishvirtuallibrary.org/jsource/anti-semitism/canadareport2011.pdf.

41 Antisemitismus in Deutschland, Bundesministerium des Innern, August 2011, www.bmi.bund.de/SharedDocs/Downloads/DE/Themen/Politik_Gesellschaft/EXpertenkreis_Antisemmitismus/bericht.pdf?__blob=publicationFile. (German)

42 Joint Committees I (on Constitutional, Presidency of the Council of Ministers and Interior Affairs) and III (on Foreign and European Union Affairs) [of the Italian Parliament], Final Report of the Fact-Finding Inquiry on Anti-Semitism, October 14, 2011.

43 library.fes.de/pdf-files/do/07908-20110311.pdf.

44 Herb Keinon, "EU envoy denies European bias toward Palestinians," *The Jerusalem Post*, January 23, 2014.

45 Ari Yashar, "Israeli Business Leaders in Davos Forum Press for 'Peace,'" *Israel National News*, January 20, 2014.

46 Gil Ronen, "Dershowitz: Ignore International Law," *Israel National News*, December 16, 2013.

47 Gerstenfeld, interview with Cotler, 49-51.

48 Report of the Inquiry Panel, Canadian Parliamentary Coalition to Combat Anti-Semitism, July 7, 2011, 70-71.

49 Manfred Gerstenfeld, interview with Daniel Bodnar, "Hungary: Holocaust Denial, Incitement and Intimidation," *Israel National News*, January 14, 2014.

50 Manfred Gerstenfeld, interview with Alan Baker, "The Dirty Legal Hands of the European Union," *Israel National News*, October 23, 2013.

51 Charly Wilder and Andrew Bowen, "The World From Berlin: 'The Chancellor Will Have To Reshuffle Her Cabinet,'" *Spiegel Online International*, February 6, 2013.

52 Rachel Hirshfeld, "'Apartheid' Week: Mock Check Points and Water Balloons," *Israel National News*, February 22, 2012.

53 Barbara Kay, "Barbara Kay shares her 'feelings' about Israel Apartheid Week," *National Post*, March 13, 2012.

54 Yitzhak Benhorin, "Eviction notices in Harvard promote 'Israel apartheid week,'" *Ynetnews*, March 7, 2013.

55 Denis MacEoin, "Response to Anti-Israel Event at London's St. James Church,"

Gatestone Institute, January 8, 2014.

56 Ronnie Fraser, "The Academic Boycott of Israel: Why Britain?," in Manfred Gerstenfeld, ed., *Academics against Israel and the Jews* (Jerusalem: Jerusalem Center for Public Affairs, 2007), 198-213.

57 Leila Beckwith, Tammi Rossman-Benjamin, and Ilan Benjamin, "Faculty Efforts to Combat Anti-Semitism and Anti-Israeli Bias at the University of California-Santa Cruz," in Manfred Gerstenfeld, ed., *Academics against Israel and the Jews* (Jerusalem: Jerusalem Center for Public Affairs, 2007), 122-133.

58 Maureen Lipman, "Maureen Lipman: Why is Ed Miliband Pandering to Anti-Semitism Masking as Anti-Zionism," *The Algemeiner*, November 26, 2014.

conclusion

1 Manfred Gerstenfeld and Jamie Berk, "The greatest lie about geopolitics," *The Jerusalem Post*, December 13, 2014.

2 Michael Herzog, "Delegitimization: Attitudes Toward Israel and the Jewish People," Jewish People Policy Institute, 2010.

3 Manfred Gerstenfeld, ed., *Academics against Israel and the Jews* (Jerusalem: Jerusalem Center for Public Affairs, 2007).

4 Manfred Gerstenfeld, *Behind the Humanitarian Mask: The Nordic Countries, Israel and the Jews* (Jerusalem: Jerusalem Center for Public Affairs and Friends of Simon Wiesenthal Center for Holocaust Studies, 2008).

5 Manfred Gerstenfeld, *The Abuse of Holocaust Memory: Distortions and Responses* (Jerusalem: Jerusalem Center for Public Affairs, 2009).

6 Manfred Gerstenfeld, *Demonizing Israel and the Jews* (New York: RVP Press, 2013).

Other Books by Manfred Gerstenfeld

Revaluing Italy, with Lorenzo Necci (Italian), 1992

Environment and Confusion: An Introduction to a Messy Subject, 1993

Israel's New Future—Interviews, 1994

The State as a Business: Do-It-Yourself Political Forecasting (Italian), 1994

Judaism, Environmentalism and the Environment, 1998

The Environment in the Jewish Tradition: A Sustainable World (Hebrew), 2002

Europe's Crumbling Myths: The Post-Holocaust Origins of Today's Anti-Semitism (Foreword by Emil L. Fackenheim), 2003

American Jewry's Challenge: Conversations Confronting the Twenty-First Century (Foreword by Jonathan Sarna), 2004

Israel and Europe: An Expanding Abyss?, 2005

European-Israeli Relations: Between Confusion and Change?, 2006

The Abuse of Holocaust Memory: Distortions and Responses (Foreword by Abraham H. Foxman), 2009

Anti-Semitism in Norway (Foreword by Finn Jarle Saele) (Norwegian), 2010

American Jewry's Comfort Level: Present and Future, with Steven Bayme (Foreword by David A. Harris), 2010

The Decay: Jews in a Rudderless Netherlands (Dutch), 2010

Judging the Netherlands: The Renewed Holocaust Restitution Process, 1997-2000 (Foreword by Stuart E. Eizenstat), 2011

Demonizing Israel and the Jews (Foreword by Rabbi Marvin Hier), 2013

Books Edited

The New Clothes of European Anti-Semitism, with Shmuel Trigano (French), 2004

Academics against Israel and the Jews (Foreword by Natan Sharansky), 2007

Israel at the Polls 2006, with Shmuel Sandler and Jonathan Rynhold, 2008

Behind the Humanitarian Mask: The Nordic Countries, Israel and the Jews (Foreword by Gert Weisskirchen), 2008

Israel at the Polls 2009, with Shmuel Sandler and Hillel Frisch, 2011

Postwar Jewish Displacement and Rebirth 1945-1967, with Francoise S. Ouzan, 2014

Monographs

The Autumn 2005 Riots in France: Their Possible Impact on Israel and the Jews, 2006

The Norwegian Government: Anti-Semitism and Anti-Israel Policies (2005-2013), with Orna Orvell, 2014

Index

B

C

D

E

F

G

H

K

L

M

N

O

P

T

U

V

W

Y

Z

CPSIA information can be obtained
at www.ICGtesting.com
Printed in the USA
FSOW04n1305201117
41454FS